Re-Founding the World

Jean-Claude Guillebaud

Re-Founding the World

—

A Western Testament

Translated by W. Donald Wilson

Algora Publishing
New York

Algora Publishing, New York
© 2001 by Algora Publishing
All rights reserved. Published 2001.
Printed in the United States of America
ISBN: 1-892941-55-4
Editors@algora.com

Originally published as *Refondation du monde*© *Editions Seuil, 1999.*

Library of Congress Cataloging-in-Publication Data: 00-012988

Guillebaud, Jean Claude.
  [Refondation du monde. English]
  Re-founding the world : a western testament / by Jean-Claude
Guillebaud ; translated by W. Donald Wilson.

  ISBN 1-892941-55-4
  1. Political science—Philosophy. 2. Civilization—Philosophy. 3.
Civilization, Modern. I. Title.
  JA71 .G78 2001
  320'.01—dc21
                              00-012988

Front Cover: "Basilica," Paestum. C. 550 B.C.

Algora Publishing
wishes to express appreciation
to the French Ministry of Culture
for its support
of this work through the
Centre National du livre

New York
www.algora.com

BY THE SAME AUTHOR

In English Translation:
The Tyranny of Pleasure, Algora Publishing, 1999

In French:
Les Jours terribles d'Israël
Seuil, "L'Histoire Immédiate" Series, 1974

Les Confettis de l'Empire
Seuil, "L'Histoire Immédiate" Series, 1976

Les Années orphelines
Seuil, "Intervention" Series, 1978

Un voyage vers l'Asie
Seuil, 1979, and "Point Actuels" Series, No. 37

Un voyage en Océanie
Seuil, 1980, and "Points Actuels" Series, No. 49

L'Ancienne comédie
(Novel) Seuil, 1984

Le Voyage à Keren
(Novel), Arléa, 1988 (Roger Nimier Prize)

L'Accent du pays
Seuil, 1990

Cabu en Amérique
(with Cabu and Laurent Joffrin)
Seuil, "L'Histoire Immédiate" Series, 1990

Sauve qui peut à l'Est
(with Cabu)
Seuil, "L'Histoire Immédiate" Series, 1991

Le Rendez-vous d'Irkoutsk
Arléa, 1991

La Colline des Anges
(with Raymond Depardon)
Seuil, 1993 (Astrolabe Prize)

La Route des Croisades
Arléa, 1993 and Seuil, "Points" Series, 1995

La Trahison des Lumières,
Seuil, 1995, (Jean-Jacques Rousseau Prize), and "Points" Series, 1996

Écoutez voir!
Arléa, 1996

La Porte des Larmes
(with Raymond Depardon)
Seuil, 1996

La Traversée du monde
Arléa, 1998

La Tyrannie du Plaisir
Seuil, 1998 (Renaudot Non-Fiction Prize), and "Points" Series, 1999

CONTENTS

Table of Contents

"I would like to help my fellow-men become accustomed to the idea that reflective thought can be an open activity. As such, it has nothing to hide, nothing to fear. It is a fact that the results of thinking are strangely accompanied by competition and rivalry. No one is able to completely dissociate what he thinks from the real authority its expression will have. And this authority is acquired in the course of games whose traditional, rather arbitrary rules, require the person expressing himself to give the impression his thinking is a flawless, definitive operation. This is a very excusable kind of play-acting, but it reduces thinking to a posturing that no longer has very much to do with a genuine process, which is necessarily painful and open, always in need of assistance, and never of admiration."

Georges Bataille

"RE-FOUNDING", DID YOU SAY?

> *"Humanity is spurred on by its need to create a foundation for living".*
>
> Pierre Legendre

In the Biblical *Book of Psalms*, the first psalm speaks of the "company of the scornful": a society of ridicule and mockery, conniving in what the psalm also characterizes as "the council of the wicked"[1]. Both of these expressions seem to me perfectly consonant with the spirit of our times. They provide rather a good definition of the clever, chattering modern world, which thinks it knows everything and sneers at the idea of re-founding our civilization. It is true that each one of us, in our own way, is a paid-up member of this company of the scornful. The corrosive mockery raining down on us provides us with a habitual alibi — or strategy. As for spontaneous laughter, it works as a kind of exorcism, and also plays a part in the strategy of denial and avoidance that has become second nature to us. Whatever we may say, we have become timid like an old man. Citizens of the modern world, we have come to detest questions that are too direct. On important matters, we prefer to argue about procedure, however Byzantine the discussion may be. Instinctively, we put problems of method ahead of those that are fundamentally more urgent. Where the latter are concerned, oddly, we behave as if certain things *can be taken for granted*, or, at worst, as if thinking about them can be put off until later. In other words, a fashionable offhandedness, an ontological denial, is imposed on us all, like an obligation. Nowadays, no one is prepared to risk facing the essential questions head-on. It almost seems to have become a question of good manners.

I would like to take the risk of breaking that rule. I want to examine some fundamental questions, unflinchingly. But what does this involve? There is a manifestly false ring to the things that we hear repeated nowadays in every conceivable tone, in what emerges from everyday discourse, in what can be discerned behind the "global ideology"[2] (the economist Jean-Paul Fitoussi's expression). In all our calculated celebrations and performances, in our acceptance of relativism, in our adulation of the unaffiliated individual, a hard-to-define tone sets off an alarm in our heads. Is this really what the future will be like? Do we have to resign ourselves to the death of holistic thinking, to the volatile rule of "democracy of opinion", to the pressures of the all-embracing market or of techno-science, to the way rigid law is replacing collective beliefs, to a final fading away of utopianism and hope for a better future? Behind this bric-a-brac we can sense that there are new kinds of domination, that inequality is creeping back, that an entire conception of humanity is breaking down. But, this time, we are defenseless against such perils. We have no idea how to confront them. We find it difficult even to analyze them. The ground is crumbling beneath our feet. Seldom, it seems, have we had a more pressing need to find solid ground.

A new foundation, in other words.

But we have to be clear about our intentions. We always have to beware of possible misconceptions, and try to identify them before we set out, just as a navigator has to familiarize himself with the reefs before leaving port. Where the project underlying this book is concerned, I can foresee at least five.

Do We Have to Talk About "Morality"?

The first misconception obviously concerns what is usually called morality, or values — sober expressions that have become part of the vocabulary of our times, *ad nauseam*. What we have to do, we are told again and again, is rediscover a moral code, or the meaning of things. From time to time, between exercises in ridiculous abandon, we are called upon to participate in some dull practice of restraint or virtuous moderation that is supposed to help us avoid total chaos. I don't much like this refrain, nor the unacknowledged nostalgia and vague remorse it betrays. There is every reason to mistrust the word 'morality', or 'ethics' (with its claim to greater neutrality). Both concepts are accompanied by some sort of intent to control — as if it were just a matter of paying more heed to some command from on high, which we are supposed to relearn how to obey. No, that's not the way we see things at all. Speaking of "morality" to today's men and women means condemning yourself to never being understood; it actually increases the perplexity it was supposed to dispel. And it also means distorting the meaning of the words. Re-laying a foundation doesn't mean issuing a *decree*; the attempt to redefine what Émile Durkheim called "collective representations" doesn't mean moralizing — quite the contrary, in fact!

This is for a simple reason. No one — except perhaps a tyrant, or a political commissar — can bring something back to life once it has lost its vitality. No one, from without, will ever be able to impose a specific way of living together on the emancipated individuals in a free society, other than very temporarily and by use of force. Any attempt to impose morality is a contradiction in terms — even when it is no more than convenient rhetoric. Perhaps it was E. M. Cioran who best expressed the futility of moral sermonizing: "It is vulgar," he wrote in 1949, "to propound dogmas in times of exhaustion".[3]

Similarly, the recurrent debate about values or the "search for meaning" seems quite pointless to me, at least in the form it usually takes. It suggests the idea of a purely convenient choice we can make as the whim strikes us. It's almost as though we were being offered a range of *possibilities* — of ethical "special offers" — among which we only have to choose, as if we were pushing our shopping-cart along the aisles of some supermarket. Now then, what values shall we pick for tomorrow? Or, maybe, what kind of dressing will go best with our lives?

But never mind its comic side, we're perfectly aware that there's a fair bit of deceit implied in the metaphor, unconscious or not. In reality, neither morality nor values can be mere ingredients added to the rest, mere trimmings to improve or embellish the way we live together. It's infantile to reason as though we could just add a few extra finishing touches once the essentials have been taken care of, or add "meaning" the way a good cook adds salt or pepper to a dish to bring out the flavor.

But that's often how we go about things nowadays. It's become the

comforting ritual, in a modern world that has lost its bearings but is looking for easy reassurance, to turn to long-lost values or to a bankrupt moral
code — except that referring to these prospects of redemption, these
"moralities for tomorrow", these desirable virtues or transcendent values, is
like a travel agency offering package deals to its customers. "Let's just try a
little harder, and we'll get this little bonus on top of everything else. Let's
just first make sure the growth rate is healthy, that stocks are going up,
that we're making good use of the Internet, and then we can think about
'meaning'. Let's have just a few more products on the market, and then
we'll tackle this business of humanism, of civilized frills. . . " In any case,
without waiting that long, some have ready-made solutions to offer on the
"values" market, offering a manual or two for sale and assuring the cus-
tomer that he can restore some meaning to his life. It's an innocent way of
making money, and sometimes it is even pleasant — but God preserve us
from moralizers of that kind, from such ontological charlatans, importu-
nate busybodies, trumpeting their dogmas and their prescriptions on all
sides!

The word "refoundation", which I have borrowed from Pierre Legendre, asks us to take an infinitely more vital — and risky — step. A lawyer
and psychoanalyst, Legendre is primarily interested in question of filiation
and transmission. "The genealogical principle, in the final analysis, simply
means that without a founding discourse, there is no such thing as human
life,"[4] he writes. Without some affiliation with a past history, with no
transmission of an inherited consciousness and language, it is impossible to
imagine being human. What is true for the genealogy of an individual and
his formation clearly applies equally to a collectivity. What we need is not
an *addition* of meaning or of morality — something that can always be postponed, that is always negotiable — but minimal foundations, the loss of
which the modern world secretly mourns, as we know only too well. What
is at issue here is not, then, a matter of sophistication, of social or political
civility. It is the very basis of what holds us together; it is literally what
founds our ability to live together, and to go on doing so, from one generation to the next, in obedience to the Platonic quest of the "immortality project". Writing to his sovereign about the Wars of Religion, Michel de
l'Hospital, Chancellor of France, said, "What's important is not knowing
which is the true religion, but discovering a way for men to live together".

The question is not a moral one in the usual sense of the term but, one might say, in an anthropological sense. This is what Cornélius Castoriadis meant when he wrote of the human types the modern age (sometimes he said "capitalism") has inherited but which, on its own, it would not have been able — and is no longer able — to create: "Incorruptible judges, honest Weberian servants of the State, educators devoted to their calling, workers with a minimum of professional conscience. These types [were] created in earlier historical periods, against a background of values that at the time were universally accepted and indisputable".[5] In other words, the problem is not, as the moralists naïvely believe, to train more and more educators and help them bring the proliferating barbarism under control. The real question is the one Marx once asked: "Who will educate the educators?"[6] In other words, from where is our society to derive the infinitely branching corpus of shared convictions, common principles, consensual beliefs, well-defined plans and inherited loyalties that give it cohesion, or indeed a *raison d'être*, while allowing it to situate each of its members somewhere in the context of a humanizing genealogy? What foundations can support the superstructure of our codes, rules, laws, or disciplines, which are endlessly undermined by an incurable incompleteness, by the moral and spiritual vacuum foreseen by Max Weber?

Repeating almost word for word the remarks of that Athenian agnostic Castoriadis, the (dissident) theologian Maurice Bellet has provided his own formulation of the question that is the very subject of this book. "Don't our societies," he asks, "only hold together because of the 'values' (civic responsibility, a minimal professional conscience, a respect for the founding proscriptions, etc.) that have themselves survived because they activate some residual, or debased, notion of what is 'sacred'? It seems as if we are merely grafted onto 'shards' of a lost humanity, as if our collective existences only rested on some spiritual 'residue', some mother-lode now almost mined out, and which, in any case, there is no longer anything to replenish".[7]

We are certainly far from morality and its latest therapists.

How Can We Avoid Nostalgia?

The second [potential] misconception concerns what I would term the futility of *regrets*. Whoever confronts these founding questions, whoever is not prepared to accept either the current injustice or nihilism, is invariably and continuously tempted by nostalgia. Oh, yes! How great things were back then! How harmonious society was, when it was held together by a single *credo*! "One faith, one law, one king. . . " These are just so many worthy, but utterly useless, tears. . . I intend to show how even people who have good reason to rebel against the established disorder can fall into the trap of wanting to resurrect the past. Most critics of the modern world fall into the same trap, and give us the impression they are *largely inhabited by melancholy*. Behind linguistic artifices and the "progressive" rhetoric we can almost always detect some expression of longing for the past, a more or less overt desire to return to it. But this doesn't make much sense.

Why not? Because thinking can never be free of what has, *for good and all*, come to be. There are certain roads we can never re-travel. And there have been radical changes that, in many respects, have re-dealt the cards. Is the prophet of nostalgia aware how ridiculous it is to go on speaking, quite unconcerned, as if neither contraception, nor information technology, nor biotechnology, nor the nuclear bomb, nor heart transplants, nor the aerospace industry — to cite just a few minor details — had not completely changed our relationship to the world, and our lives? Any attempt to rectify our contemporary state of confusion by resurrecting a long-dead reality is doomed to failure. Any claim that order can be restored to society by reviving institutions now in ruins is an illusion. As we know, it has its followers, and its place in public debate, but it doesn't lead anywhere. Or, if it does lead somewhere, it is to disaster. Apart from that — i.e. from providing some satisfaction for posturing egos — what useful purpose can be served by becoming the grinch of modernity, by indicting the present or tirelessly proclaiming the apocalypse, like some Cassandra of the future?

Attempts to bring back the past have never produced anything of lasting value in Western history. We need only think of a famous but abortive attempt made in the fourth century. In 362, the Emperor Julian (called "the Apostate"), having broken with Christianity at a time when the ancient pagan order was falling apart and was in its twilight, attempted to restore the old order through authoritarian means, by struggling determinedly against Christian subversion (viewed at the time as anarchical ferment). He saw the Christians, "who boasted of being innovators", as driving the Empire into decadence, and playing into the hands of the barbarians laying siege to the Roman marches. By means of pamphlets (*Against the*

Galileans) and imperial decrees, Julian set about reviving the old cults, the practice of sacrifice, and the ancient "virtues" — all to no avail. The experiment lasted no more than two years. The time was past, and the process of "disenchantment" was complete. Later, there would be many similar attempts...

Today, the "disenchantments" are even more radical, to say the very least. Indeed, we have already gone through a thousand imperceptible revolutions, each opening up unimaginable perspectives. For the past two or three decades the course of events has moved even faster than thought itself. As the new century dawns, we find ourselves living in a reality that is still, in the strict meaning of the term, *unthinkable*. This enormous break with the past cannot be compared, in its extent, with anything experienced previously, not even with the earlier major upheavals brought about by the printing press, the steam engine, or the Copernican revolution. Nostalgia, however moving and respectable it may be, is a poor counselor.

The same remark, applied here to the rather trivial domain of day-to-day politics and of political chatter, is valid on other levels too. Critical thinking, it seems to me, has often been infected by the temptation to bewail the past. Let me cite just one example: the strange renewal of interest in the ideas of Carl Schmitt (1888-1985), the important German constitutionalist and philosopher of law who has been much re-translated, re-published, and again discussed in Europe over the past decade. It would indeed be a great mistake to underestimate Schmitt's work because, like Martin Heidegger, he supported Nazism. The philosopher Jacob Taubes, who died in 1987, marvelously expresses the dilemma we have to confront when we are dealing with any major body of work that, like Schmitt's, has ended in complicity with evil. Taubes writes, "Even though I am a practicing Jew, I would like to express my respect for Carl Schmitt, a mind that had indeed aged, but was still sharp in the evening of his life. Indeed, I was one of those he termed 'enemies'".[8]

Now, Schmitt's entire works, which are those of a champion of willpower and of "decisionism", are pregnant with the notion of a threatening chaos and an unremitting determination to resist it tooth and nail — a chaos that could only be staved off by a State, endowed with renewed legitimacy by some theological filiation and capable, as Rousseau said, of "imitating the irreversible decrees of the Divinity".[9] Schmitt's work is nostalgic, in the fullest sense of the word. In his fear of the (obvious) weaknesses of liberal democracy, Schmitt saw himself as the great *hinderer*, determined to stand in the way of catastrophe, and to do so by restoring its theological form to a State reduced to ruins by the Weberian "disenchantment of the world".[10] I find it significant that he has recently been so precipitously rediscovered by the extreme right, by certain theorists of the State, and even by a section of the radical left, all at the same time. In fact, justifiably alarmed by the passive defeatism of the current sub-culture, a considerable part of contemporary thinking is once again feeling the temptation of nostalgia, and is endangered by it.

When all is said and done, any questioning of modernity runs the risk of becoming associated in some way with one or other of the great counter-revolutionary traditions, whether that of Louis de Bonald, Joseph de Maistre, Donoso Cortès, German romanticism, or the Comptian current that inspired Maurras in France. These affinities are not always conscious or recognized, but they weaken the criticisms, if they don't render them downright ineffective. Many investigations into the contemporary lack of meaning (including those of Castoriadis, Ellul and the Frankfurt School) have lost their appeal today, and have sometimes been written off because of a real or supposed, but clearly incapacitating, link with the counter-revolutionary tradition. This pitfall ultimately provides the dominant ideology with automatic justification. So, nostalgia never makes a dent in the latter, while providing great pleasure for the "company of scorners".

There is worse. Under the imitative effect of rivalry, two types of thinking, each as unsound as the other, are in perpetual conflict. One arises from a puerile (or strategic) adherence to whatever doctrine is in fashion, while the other dismisses all of contemporary reality out of hand. One proclaims the postmodern bliss of the individual consumer, while the other prophesies the demise of a disenchanted world. And the two of them always go hand in hand, each predominating in turn. The Canadian philosopher Charles Taylor, a professor at McGill University in Montreal, points out how unproductive this twin-like rivalry is. "I find myself dissatisfied with the views on [modernity] that are now current. Some are upbeat, and see us as having climbed to a higher plateau; others show a picture of decline, of loss, of forgetfulness. Neither sort seems right, to me; both ignore massively important features of our situation".[11]

Saying a definitive "no" to any expression of regret for the past is therefore a way to avoid this kind of pitfall. And anyway, why conceal the fact that the simple pleasure of existing, a certain inner disposition, has a part in this *refusal to refuse*? I think we have to discover critical approaches that are considerably less earnest, and even — why not? — lighthearted. In any case, we have to think "ahead", with a clear-sighted openness to what is to come, yet without being prepared to merely submit, to just give in. Without any ill-conceived complaining, we must attempt to identify the barbarisms that have been prophesied, and learn to combat them more steadfastly than ever. We have to claim our right to investigate them thoroughly, and our incontrovertible entitlement to *subvert* them. "We must learn to discern the unrealized opportunities lying dormant in the folds of the present," writes André Gorz. "We must be determined to grasp these opportunities, to take control of change. We have to be brave enough to break with this moribund society, which can never be re-born. We must have enough courage to embark on an Exodus".[12]

In this perspective, I think it is appropriate to speak of "re-founding". The term means just what it says. Re-founding doesn't mean restoring the old foundation; and the difference is significant. As some American writers of the so-called 'communitarian' school have written, there can be no question of reviving any tradition at all unless we reinvent it.

Isn't The Law Enough?

The definition of the third misconception comes, again, from Charles Taylor. It arises from a complicit silence, from a willing and even fearful, reluctance to examine things more closely. What useful purpose can be served by asking what our convictions are founded on, since there is already agreement on the subject? Why undertake a critical investigation of modern values, now that they have not only become universal, but — in theory at least — are sanctioned by the law? For some people, it would be quite enough to resist the new barbarians by relying on the major charters and declarations, by referring to the American and French Declarations of Human Rights, and the Universal Declaration of 1948, which have become the expression of a worldwide moral code that only some exotic tyrannies or a few surviving benighted regimes still fail to respect.

"These charters," writes Paul Valadier, "are nothing but a translation into legal terms of *the* essential moral principle, or of the moral *law* as such, which was made admirably explicit by Kant: namely, that the dignity of all men must be absolutely respected, or that no man may ever be treated merely as a means, but always as an end. This principle provides the moral reference we have been looking for, one that is not arbitrarily imposed on our societies, but the exacting value of which they themselves can recognize, and with which they have freely declared their intention to comply".[13]

For people holding such optimistic beliefs, any attempt to re-lay the foundations has become pointless. On an ontological level, History has indeed come to an end — at least as far as ideas are concerned. It has even been suggested that we have progressed beyond the age of metaphysics. The problem has become purely legal and geopolitical. The task that still awaits us is, indeed, daunting, but it has been infinitely simplified. How can we put the "rights of man", as they have been formulated, into effect everywhere on the globe? How can we, step by step, build up international institutions — including judicial and penal institutions — capable of breathing life into this universally recognized moral code? This, we are told, is what we must do. On the other hand, it is not only pointless but also inappropriate to question the source, the history, the foundation, and the substance of these rights. Any ontological inquiry that revealed the Western "sources" of modernity would deal a blow to modern pluralism. Such is the majority point of view.

These pluralist good intentions nurture and provide a justification for a certain silence on the part of philosophers and social scientists, one that Charles Taylor is certainly right to call "unhealthy": "There is," he writes, "a great deal of motivated suppression of moral ontology among our contemporaries, in part because the pluralist nature of modern society makes it easier to live that way. . . "[14] Actually, this straightforward "rights-of-man" way of thinking, this international reliance on the law, with its readiness to dispense with re-laying foundations or investigating the past — which amounts to discarding memory — provides very little sustenance, it seems to me (just as I find those who are satisfied with it lacking in prudence). I do so because in the first place the existence of the charters in question only represents a "paper" consensus — if not a superficial one — that the Western powers are sometimes the first to reject and betray, and to do so *democratically*. Actually, the global antagonism between different conceptions of the good is still stronger, and no closer to a resolution, than people think. It is even the new violence of this antagonism — as much within our own societies as elsewhere — which makes us return, automatically, to the founding questions. No genuine debate can take place, no struggle can be carried on for the sake of a "universal moral code", if we are prepared to dispense with a return to the sources, out of a kind of civility. What exactly do we believe in? Where did these convictions come from? Are they really convictions? Why, and in what way, are they seriously threatened today? Surely no one will dare to claim that these questions are irrelevant.

And then, how can we forget that the law is never more than a formalization of principles, beliefs and representations that alone give it legitimacy? This is the case even when it is a matter of reinventing what used to be called "natural law". The law, in other words, is at the same time a determining factor, and very unstable. Whoever made it can always unmake it. What is more, History has shown us how the law, in isolation from everything else, could be made to serve several different masters in turn. There was even a Nazi or Stalinist "law" that was perfectly consistent with its own foundations. Today, so many things are coming together to warn us: the rights of man, democracy, the written rules, all the foremost values of modernity and of the Enlightenment, really have been weakened, been left hanging in a void, and, in effect, powerless in the face of a new inegalitarian hardness and a covert questioning of the universalist inheritance.

But that is probably not what is most important. This optimistic faith in the law is also egregiously unreflective. It seems to have neglected a truth that has been confirmed many times over, and that can be expressed in just a few words: whoever relies on the law, and on the law alone, as a basis for social cohesion, opens the way to a proliferation of the law. It is a fact that our societies, having lost their bearings, are tending to fill their inner void by an increasingly petty, obsessive recourse to prescriptive laws, and in particular to criminal law, which a natural trend has placed at the heart of what once was called private space. Lawyers are among the first to express their uneasiness at this "criminalization" of society[15] — a repressive trend that, in its irresistible and desperate advance, attempts to compensate for our lack of bearings by enacting increasingly specific and insidious rules and regulations.

Roman law, which Maurice Merleau-Ponty called, very nicely, the "prose of the world"[16], and of which we are the direct heirs, did indeed embody a kind of universality. But still, from one end of the Empire to the other, it was based on a cosmology, an interpretation of the world, or even a cult, which provided it with a firm foundation. The law, in isolation, has no ability to found a civilization, any more than the judge can become the unwilling miracle-worker of the modern world whom we ask to define for us the border between Good and Evil — a line that is so imprecise that one becomes worn out in the attempt to define its minutest twists and turns.

Indeed, every passing day provides us with the proof of this relative impotence. It is brought to our attention whenever a judge, finding himself confronted by offenders who have never been accustomed to the notion of prohibition in even the most basic way, admits the inanity of the law. Yes, indeed, who is to educate the educators? Tomorrow, in a really fragmented and completely "pluralist" society, will parents be satisfied to merely hand on to their children a vague familiarity with the penal code?

Can We Still Take It All In?

The fourth potential misconception — but it would be better to call it a challenge — results from our own helplessness before the ever more intimidating complexity of human knowledge. "Reality is vast," Edgar Morin once exclaimed, "far surpassing the scope of our intelligence".[17] Who could deny this "vastness"? Is it possible not to recognize our abysmal ignorance? For a long time now, indeed, the possibility of encyclopedic knowledge — the defining ambition of Enlightenment man — has been out of reach. Today, such a notion would make a high-school student laugh, a student who will have chosen a career direction and an area of specialization by the end of childhood. Every passing year, month, or week, sees new branches added to the infinitely ramifying tree of knowledge and disciplines,

We have entered an age of atomized and labyrinthine knowledge. We can only lay claim to competence in partial, local, limited domains. We feel our way forward, towards a horizon of multiple affiliations, plural identities, modest reason, fractal logic, and complex networks. Whether in the "hard" or the "soft" sciences, each of the traditional disciplines has been fragmented into a thousand autonomous domains, each far too preoccupied by the complexity of its own territory to think about communicating with the outside — or even with its close neighbors. In spite of the usual calls for "interdisciplinarity" so often heard at learned conferences, there are no longer anything but fragmented forms of knowledge, each one closed in on itself. Scrupulous respect for this compartmentalization has even become a guarantee of seriousness for any scientific researcher worthy of the name. University corporatism is not entirely wrong to have become sensitive on this matter, even if it is taken to comical excess at times: "Given your specialty, this specific question is outside your area of competence, etc.". Of course, there is — also — a power-play going on here.

So we see economists devoting their entire professional lives to a tiny area of econometrics, doctors who can mend some specific organ but who are embarrassingly incapable of seeing the patient as a whole, sociologists who know everything about unionism in one region of France, historians with a passionate interest in the 18th-century flour wars, physicists who have an excellent knowledge of quarks or protons, impressive computer scientists, but all of them restricted to a particular niche within their discipline. In short, we are gradually becoming accustomed to that archetypal public figure, the Nobel prizewinner lionized by the media, who is at once extremely knowledgeable and extremely ignorant.

Only fifteen years ago Marcel Gauchet underlined the inevitability of this compartmentalization of knowledge — the price that had to be paid for its advancement. "The discrediting of attempts to orient reality in the name of the small, the plural, or the marginal," he wrote, "has been accompanied by an increase in the number of specializations and a bureaucratic fragmentation of knowledge".[18] However, this fragmentation, as undeniable as it is necessary, carries with it a kind of barbarism, or progressive dehumanization, that we find it difficult to accept. Can we resign ourselves to this strange and perverse symmetry that has come to prevail in the public arena, with, on the one hand, the resoundingly superficial generalizations of the media, and on the other the fragmented competencies of the various scientific disciplines; on the one hand, the encyclopedic babble of "la pensée du flux" (the "philosophy of flux"), and on the other a rigorous but incomprehensible erudition? We are, it seems, condemned to either idiotic chatter or microscopic knowledge. Between these two extremes, there seems to be little firm ground. But isn't it precisely this in-between region that we live in, and in which what we used to call a civilization "functions"?

As a necessary precaution and legitimate way to arrange things, this fragmentation of knowledge therefore has repercussions that are not always positive. It lends support to the "discourse of the void", i.e. to those who — for fundamental reasons — reject any attempt at synthesis. In doing so, it lends legitimacy to this contemporary reincarnation of nihilism, to the undeclared renunciation of thought itself and of the civic responsibility that thought allows, as well as to the unreflective withdrawal — not to say desertion — that is all too ready to tolerate the new forms of domination or iniquity. We hear the same refrain all around us. How can I act, or even think, when real knowledge is beyond my reach? And how can I choose sides, when I am so ignorant?

But it so happens that this new inaccessibility of the "global" is often used as an excuse for a simple lack of culture, particularly among the active elite, the public or private decision-makers, and all who occupy positions of public responsibility. It is obviously disrespectful to mention the relative ignorance of our elites. It is breaking a taboo, pointing out a scandal, and endangering the minimal degree of confidence required in representative democracy. It could even be used to justify populist aberrations, with accusations of universal ignorance taking over from those of universal corruption. But even so, the question must be raised — even if the European political fauna is still not doing badly compared with the rest of the world. Paul Thibaud, the former editor of the French review *Esprit*, put the question this way: "We might ask ourselves," he wrote, "whether the isolation of our elites doesn't encourage their lack of curiosity and of culture. The surveys carried out by the Ministry of Culture show that, over the past few decades, the correlation between higher education and reading books has been seriously diminished. Isn't the managerial stratum, the group that thinks 'correctly', more and more composed of educated people who no longer read?"[19]

So let's be careful not to use this new complexity of knowledge as an excuse for dominant stupidity. And let's understand that the challenge must be taken up, prudently but with determination. More than ever, there is an urgent need for perspective, for bringing about a new coherence, and for far-sightedness, even if encyclopedic knowledge is out of reach. "In this, as always," writes Maurice Bellet, "the only real misfortune would be presumption. But anything is allowed, as long as we have the humility to travel whatever path we can, with all the clear-sightedness we can muster, in order to maintain our humanity, keeping ourselves open to any suggestion that will lead us further".[20]

In infringing the taboo, venturing onto ground where I've no guarantee of safety or of academic legitimacy, it's not my intention to pass myself off as a scholar, nor as someone of dazzling erudition. It will be enough for me to act as a messenger between those who do have knowledge. No doubt the old dream that once motivated Condorcet, Diderot, or D'Alembert has become unrealizable — the dream of holding the basic intelligibility of the world in one's hand, of putting together the fragments of the shattered mirror in which we never tire of seeking the image of our humanity. But even so, I don't think it's completely hopeless to attempt to create a dialogue, however imperfect or incomplete, between the various branches of knowledge. Edgar Morin provided a good justification for refusing to be constrained by atomization, and by the system, in 1982. "It's in a dialogue with the unbelievable and the unsayable, in the play of light and dark, that thought takes place," he wrote. "Thought, like life, can only thrive at the temperature at which it burns up. It dies as soon as it confines itself to the system it constructs, in a non-biodegradable idea."[21]

To anyone liable to accept the new compartmentalization of knowledge too easily, to those who feel no concern at this elitist fragmentation of science, let us recall just how far Hegel's idealism went, two centuries ago. In a text dating from 1797, inspired by Schelling and Hölderlin,[22] Hegel maintained that the duty of the scholar consisted not only in communicating his knowledge, but *in making it attractive, and even poetic*, since only poetry, he added, was capable of educating Humanity. So the task of a thinker consisted in giving his ideas esthetic — in other words mythological — appeal. What is needed, therefore, added Hegel, is a "mythology of reason", so that "those who are enlightened and those who are not may one day join hands".

Nowadays, we don't expect that much.

How Can We Avoid Squabbling?

The final misconception, one always to be feared, arises from our spontaneous instinct for dissension, from competition between concepts, and the disagreement which is always jealously maintained as soon as the question of origins comes up. The past is always, as we know, the object of a struggle for appropriation. Its reinterpretation and sporadic reintroduction into the present revive noisy quarrels like those so common at the end of the 20th century. From the anniversary of Clovis to that of World War I, by way of the ninth centenary of the First Crusade (1096), Christ's crucifixion, the wars in the Vendée, or the French Revolution, there are many examples of the way people have become agitated whenever the "founding" past was summoned to bear witness before the present.

It is obviously the same story — and even more so — when we try to recall the birth of the modern West. Here indeed is an inheritance the interpretation of which still creates dissension among its heirs. What then, in our make-up, and in the basis of our present-day view of the world, are the respective roles of Greek thought, of Judaism, and of Christianity? Just asking the question is enough to provoke disagreements over identity (or of boundaries) from which I would rather keep my distance. I understand perfectly what is going on: it is, almost always, a matter of legitimizing some sense of belonging — or some prejudice. For some people, forgetting certain legacies, obliterating certain traces, or minimizing the founding role of a certain tradition is not a problem. Some become infuriated by the Jewish element in the make-up of every Westerner, while others refuse to recognize the indelibly Christian component of our conception of the world. Still others — as we know only too well — would prefer to invoke our Nordic or Indo-European roots, even if it means rejecting the universalism of reason we have inherited from the Greeks. In short, when we turn up any one of these stones we discover numerous petty wars — wars that have become a lot "hotter" since a desperate search for identity has become the pressing issue of the time, a bitter consequence of our sense of loss.

I personally reject such a confrontational approach. It arises from an ancient dualism, and is basically the symptom of a rather absurd hypersensitivity. In reality, our modernity is rooted in a marvelous *convergence*. We have inherited what Maurice Bellet calls an "extraordinary interweaving", the result of a combination of influences, subtle interactions, and recognizable emergences. But what characterizes us above all is that we are the *critical* (and certainly not sanctimonious) *heirs* of our own history. The philosopher Éric Weil provides a nice description of our special relationship with the triple legacy from which our foundations derive. "Europe," he writes, "erected as it is at the crossroads of Greek wisdom, Biblical propheticism, and New Testament utopianism, is a tradition never satisfied with its own tradition". It is, in other terms, a ceaseless questioning.[23]

It would be hard to phrase it better: questioning is always better than squabbling.

PART I

FAREWELL TO THE TWENTIETH CENTURY

"It takes time for a wounded continent to recover from such a century!"

Brian Beedham[1]

CHAPTER 1

AFTER THE SHIPWRECK: TAKING STOCK

*"How have we managed to empty the sea? Who gave us the
sponge to erase the whole horizon?"*

Nietzsche

"Crazed by massacres and dazed by inventions", as Jürgen Habermas
wrote, we leave the 20th century counting our dead — by the millions, by
the ten and hundred millions: the dead of Les Éparges, Kolyma, and
Ravensbrück, of Guernica and Katyn, the anonymous victims of Hiroshima, of Phnom Penh, Madagascar, Shanghai, Izieu, and so many other
places, who have returned one by one in recent years to revive our memories. Night and fog, crimes against humanity, innumerable, "civilized" acts
of barbarism. Commemorating them in Black Books and courtroom repen-
tances, we have set out doggedly, all through the 1990s, to enumerate all
the crimes, lies, and follies of a century that the poet Osip Mandelstam
characterized as "despotic". Have there been many centuries as bloody, and
in which there was such a dearth of reason, as the 20th? Has there ever
been, in all of history, such a sense of waste, such an overwhelming nausea,
such a "secret shame"[1], to use Vladimir Jankélévich's expression?

No thinking about our contemporary state of confusion, no examination of the nihilism that afflicts our age, would mean anything at all if this
dreadful balance sheet weren't taken into account first. Imbued with an
unparalleled historic puzzlement, and driven by an incurable skepticism — not to say an immense metaphysical "hangover" — we have tried
to bid the 20th century adieu. But the process has been more painful than

we imagined. Marked by anniversaries or legal events, the 1990s began to look like one long group psychoanalysis session, which in itself was revealing. Whatever we do, we go on and on drawing lessons from of our recent past. We Westerners will never be done with sorting through the debris, identifying and naming all the disasters that seem to blend together according to a logic that has become familiar — as if the passage of time finally let us see the whole road we have traveled, as if the increasing distance allowed us to better reconstruct the successive phases of the devastation, and to estimate its true extent.

No, it is not by accident, nor even because of our need for commemoration — or our concern for justice — that we have expended so much effort on this strange convening of the century's memory, just as it is ending. It is because we have to, because we are obeying a legitimate imperative: no future can be imagined unless we unburden ourselves of such a past.

For the dead, even in their hundreds of millions, were not the only victims of the 20th century. Far from it. Besides the flesh and the blood, *major ideas* (the loss of which still hurts) were also swept away. From one episode to another, from massacre to massacre, from folly to folly, the principles, beliefs, and hopes that had given shape to the way we experienced history from the Enlightenment on, and indeed for much longer, have been progressively "disabled" (to borrow a computing term). Their disappearance — or, what is worse, their compliance with evil — has left a whole series of vacuums, has pointed to the likelihood of failure, and revealed dead ends, condemning us ultimately to a kind of moral exhaustion, and made us retreat into an attitude of suspicion — if not into the facile nihilism that in the end prefers to take refuge in forgetting.

In fact, there has been a definite period of disenchantment corresponding to each of these tragedies of war or of ideology (of the right or the left). Every episode of this history has been followed by a specific decline in confidence, a disillusioned renunciation of historical optimism, a collapse of our vision of the future. Unconsciously, blinded by the present, we moved on from one mental breakdown to the next. As the heirs of disaster, we find ourselves deprived today of what Hans Jonas has called the "hope principle".[2] Any attempt to re-found our world, any thinking about the new century, first requires a clearer awareness of the century just ended. Our ultimate confusion "closely resembles that of the lover who, once his passionate romance has come to an end, believes he has discovered the 'truth' about his beloved. Realizing that she is not the kind of person he had thought, he says he was taken in by love, as if he had swallowed a magic potion and been in a hypnotic state".[3]

We should first try to understand this hypnotic state. Let us avoid round figures, for they are deceptive. The 20th century, as a historical reality, lasted no more than 75 years. It began with a revolver shot and it ended with the clang of a pickax. The pistol shot was fired on April 28, 1914, at Sarajevo, by a nineteen-year-old Serbian student named Prinzip who assassinated Archduke Franz Ferdinand, the heir apparent to the Austro-Hungarian Empire. As we know, it sparked the First World War, which would engulf the old world. As for the pickax, it was used on November 8, 1989, to demolish the graffiti-inscribed concrete of the Berlin wall, whose destruction symbolized the collapse of the Communist idea. Seventy-five years. . . From that point on it seemed very much as if the premature end of this "useless century" had enabled us to understand better how it evolved, as if today we could recreate the twists and turns of this lengthy aberration with new insight.

This is no doubt what explains the bitter re-reading of history we have embarked on during the past decade. The events in themselves were not so important as the assurances, the shared beliefs, and the founding values, which were caught up in the tumult and consumed in the conflagration.

1914-1918: The Infernal Matrix

Obviously, pride of place must go the Great War. This apocalyptic event, of which only a few perspicacious contemporaries had any understanding, was a portent of the "entombment" of Europe, as the young philosopher Gershom Sholem wrote in his personal diary on August 1, 1916.[4] This somber prophecy echoed another, expressed two years earlier by Pope Benedict XV, who had predicted as early as 1914 that a "European suicide" would follow that same war. And, indeed, was it not the infernal matrix that gave birth to everything else — the initial cataclysm, of which the others were mere aftershocks, in the seismological sense? Between the upbeat departures for the front in August 1914 and the hideous body counts of November 1918, something had indeed taken place, and we are still trying to assess its gravity today. Between the almost joyful warlike spirit of the mobilization for the "war to end wars" (or the "just" war) and the unexpected way the war became mired in bloodshed — the "technical surprise", as Raymond Aron called it — a mysterious threshold was crossed, and a certain idea of the world was destroyed forever. The "technical surprise" (for instance, the Hotchkiss machine gun and the unexpected effectiveness of the German heavy artillery) transformed this mass offensive, still very much in the style of the 19th century, into an unimaginable but very modern slaughter.

An infernal matrix? The most obvious consequences of 1914-1918 are well known, and listing them is sufficient to make the point. The war made nationalist rhetoric and patriotic propaganda — all that kind of "brainwashing"[5] — ineffective. It decimated the strength and the active classes of several nations, including France. Culminating in the humiliating Treaty of Versailles, it foolishly fuelled the motivation and resentment from which Hitlerism would spring fifteen years later in Germany. In France, the disillusionment of the socialist workers and peasants, whose internationalism felt betrayed by the nationalistic "United Front", helped bring about a split in the French left at the Congress of Tours, in December 1920, and the choice of Bolshevism by a portion of it. After all, weren't capitalism and the "arms-dealers" to blame for the disaster? And, finally, we mustn't forget the obtuse pacifism, the weak-kneed betrayal by the intellectuals, heralding the "Munich mentality", without which neither Franco nor Hitler could have enjoyed such success. More broadly, the war sounded the death-knell of Europe as a great power, and the imminent dismantling of its colonial empires.

But the cataclysm's shockwaves were probably even longer lasting in the realm of ideas, and that is what interests us here. Apart from the new doubts cast on democracy, it was historical reason, Hegel's elevation of history, and confidence in the idea of progress, that were undermined by the butchery. "In affirming the preeminence of the march of humanity over human beings of flesh and blood, the idea of progress restored to history, and to human life on earth, the great metaphysical division of being between a lesser reality and a true reality. And suddenly an event occurred that made this abstract division concrete and revealed it in the cruelest way. . . .The notion of historical reason met its end on the battlefield".[6] Thus the universalist and optimistic humanism of the 19th century was engulfed by the war. A Better Future, Science, the Republic — these words written with a capital letter would emerge devalued from the great slaughter that was the result of nationalistic rivalry.

More significant still is the fact that the humiliating mud and stench of the battlefield, the pounding of high explosives that reduced the trembling individual, crouching in his own filth and bodily fluids, to no more than an abattoir animal, discredited holism itself — i.e. the priority of the "we" over the "me", of the group over the individual — for it was this priority alone that had made possible such a voracious consumption of men by the Minotaur of war. The individual, a being of flesh and dreams, suddenly became expendable: 600,000 young men were sacrificed to no good purpose in Artois, the Vosges and Champagne, in the offensives of 1915 alone! This was enough to break a fundamental bond. Never again would appeals to self-abnegation or solidarity, calls for sacrifice or invocations of the national honor, have the same effect. The unwavering comradeship of the trenches was no more than the inverted image — a seditious, and sometimes anarchist one — of the disastrous "we" of the general staffs. Later, France might be covered with monuments and veterans honored for the next half-century, and Victory celebrated piously, and there could even be the wild parties of the 1920s — the *années folles* — but the relationship between France and its individual citizens would never again be the same.

After 1914-1918, a lingering mistrust, a certain sense of meaninglessness, would continue to grow and spread, penetrating the inner reaches of the collective unconscious, undermining and profoundly unsettling the basic postulates of democratic reason — or of reason pure and simple. We could give a thousand examples of this insecurity. The birth of the Dada movement, founded in February 1916 in the Cabaret Voltaire in Zurich, was one of them, with its subsequent well-known history. Initiated by a group of artists, including the Romanians Marcel Janco and Tristan Tzara, the Frenchman Hans Arp and the German Hugo Ball, the Dada movement proclaimed its rejection of all culture, and refused the very notion of an established order. Quickly gaining new adherents in Germany, New York and Paris (Marcel Duchamp, Francis Picabia, Man Ray, etc.), the movement had its own review, *Die Freie Strasse*, by 1916. Its editors denounced blind patriotism and warmongering, exalted individual liberty, and claimed their objective was the destruction of the old world. It would no doubt be unfair to see the Dada movement as nothing more than a sign of the times. But it was that too, and one of the earliest. Surrealism, the universal suspicion of the Pataphysicians, and Louis-Ferdinand Céline's prophecies of "ultimate putrefaction" — to mention but a few — would be its distant descendants.

Everywhere in Europe, other upheavals and manifestations of instability, all consequences of the Great War, grew more or less out of the same distrust. For instance, Jacob Taubes describes how, in Germany, the moral and theological framework of Protestantism was reduced to ruins. "It is interesting," he writes, "to see how German theology reacted to the experience of the First World War. The great teachers who at the time were looked up to as veritable gods, Martin Rade and Adolf von Harnack, lost all their influence, and the whole thing collapsed like a house of cards (I am thinking here of an unsigned letter from Rade to Karl Barth). It became clear that they were no more than servants of the Prussian State. So, the unity of Protestant culture was shattered in the trenches."[7] This theological ruin, it should be said in passing, partly explains the later blindness of some of the German Protestant churches in their dealings with Nazism during the 1930s.

After the Great War, all of Europe was plunged into a state of radical political doubt, from which it is not at all certain it has ever reemerged. The Twenties and Thirties, let us remember, were marked by a rigorous critique of bourgeois and academic values, the abandonment of which was all the more far-reaching in that it had already begun before the Great War. It would later provide a fertile soil for the two great totalitarian ideologies. Nor should we forget all those "ups and downs of the great, and even megalomaniac, movements aiming to invert and re-found all values, which have fallen on fertile ground in European thought from Nietzsche to Junger and Heidegger; we have forgotten their adulation of warlike virtues, their assault on spiritual values, and the call for world war that preceded and facilitated it".[8]

But it would be a mistake to think that only Europe was affected by such a decay of rational thought. The collapse of the democratic myth, for example, inspired a number of writings and reflections, including many by American political philosophers. The willful demolition of the democratic ideal would continue to flourish until the end of the 1930s, reaching a kind of culmination and climax in 1942 with *Capitalism, Socialism, and Democracy* by Joseph Schumpeter. The contest between two models (those of James Bryce and of Walter Lippmann) was at the center of a debate among American political scientists on the eve of the Second World War. Political scientist Francis G. Wilson attested to this in 1939, when he admitted, "For almost a generation, we have been actively engaged in the destruction of the democratic 'myth'".

So, mingled with the cold mud of the former battlefields, scattered across the immense, pockmarked landscapes of the Argonne, of Verdun, and of the Marne, there also lies the invisible debris of former hopes. Yes, an infernal matrix indeed! And even worse was to come.

The Cunning Of Leninist Reason

The Communist adventure itself must be considered one of the radical developments generated by the Great War. It claimed to be a messianic redemption from, and a daring inversion of it — one front in place of another, one class replacing another, working-class internationalism taking precedence over social chauvinism, a radiant future in place of voracious greed. Alain Finkielkraut has shown how, after it was discredited by the wartime slaughter, the Hegelian consecration of history derived new life and energy from the Russian revolution. "History collapsed in 1914, only to give historicism an unprecedented power of seduction, illusion, and destruction in 1917. The image of the Good's painful birth obscured the sense of disaster".[10] It was above all by appropriating the Hegelian notion of the "cunning of reason" that Leninism would triumph. This cunning of reason is a justification of evil and crime in the name of ultimate objectives; it is the assurance that history marches irresistibly onwards, with, if necessary, violence as its marvelous midwife; it is an agnostic appropriation of the Judeo-Christian concept of "salvation", which it transforms into the "course of history". For Hegel, everything contributes to the irresistible forward march of history, and this was its "cunning": everything plays a part in its advance — even evil, from which good automatically results. The new century would put into practice what the previous one had invented. "It was in the 19th century," remarks François Furet, "that history replaced God in exercising total power over human destiny, but it was in the 20th that we witnessed the political madness born of this substitution".[11]

The Communist adventure was also an attempt to restore dignity to the collective "we" which had been brought into disrepute by the "bourgeois" war. It meant restoring an unsullied, aggressive innocence to the collective dimension. Throughout the 20th century, Communism would be, among other things, a reaction on behalf of holism, the erection of a rampart against the corrosive individualism that originated in the 18th — liberal individualism, which early in the 19th century it was already feared would undermine society by diminishing civic responsibility and fragmenting the body of the nation. Leninism was of course not the only embodiment of the revival of this "we". The socialism of Jean Jaurès pursued a similar objective by different means. Soon, it was hoped, the "private" would give way to the "public". "In the tradition extending from Saint-Simon to Durkheim, modern socialism appears above all as an effort to restore the unity of society after the traumatic birth of the modern economy and the spread of individualist principles".[12]

A new consecration of history and the predominance of the "we" over the "me" were indeed the two major ideas into which Leninism breathed new life and made part of its objectives — which, in other words, led to a new and even bloodier disaster. But Communism is based on another value, a value it would bring into disrepute: the value of genuine equality, the aspiration to social justice which had been constantly frustrated by the "formal" equality of bourgeois legalism, and which could only be really achieved, it insisted, by class struggle. Such would even be the main motivating force behind this particular variety of totalitarianism — the justification for the purges, campaigns of terror and mass murders it would carry out in cold blood. François Furet has described how the desire for equality would be gradually heightened by exploiting a smoldering hatred of the bourgeoisie, of the rich and the upwardly mobile, which had been inherited from 19th-century working-class culture (and justified by the vicious inegalitarianism of the industrial revolution!). With Lenin, the rich became not merely participants in a bitter social conflict but an enemy that had to be — literally — destroyed. The class enemy would be seen as having such a fundamentally different nature that the idea of "class" would soon become equivalent to that of "race" in the cleansing struggle. The systematic liquidation of the Russian *kulaks* or the Ukrainian *muzhiks*, the massacres carried out during the Chinese cultural revolution, the massive "purges" in communist Kampuchea (Cambodia) had their roots in a desire for equality that took a murderous turn. Thus, the two forms of totalitarianism, even though their proclaimed objectives were different, were one in the extent and in the principle of their death-dealing activity. Nazism massacred the Jew and the Gypsy, Leninism the rich and the "bourgeois".

This lethal perversion of the desire for justice had more serious conse-quences than is often realized. After the collapse of Communism in 1989, there was a failure to understand right away that the sinking ship had pulled under with it a vital ingredient of the concern for equality itself — or at least that it had given it a badge of shame. Now the concept of equal-ity became more suspect than ever; it was dismissed and denigrated as a possible source of servitude — *The Road to Serfdom* is after all the title the great liberal economist Friedrich August von Hayek gave his diatribe against the directed economy and the obsession with wealth distribution; the text was written at the end of the 1940s and resurfaced, opportunely, during the 1980s. In the new antagonism between the political right and the socialist left, it is now the latter that has to make the case for equality. Very unjustly, it is forced on the defensive. It is all but blamed for the *gu-lags*. Even though it never allied itself with Soviet Communism, it finds it-self obliged to accept some symbolic guilt because of its support for the principle of social equality. As a result, the whole equilibrium of political debate in Europe has been disrupted — and will remain so for some time — without people realizing it right away.

It is true that even today the consequences of the fall of Commu-nism — that historical "enigma", writes Furet — is far from having been studied as thoroughly as they should. Shortly before his death, Cornélius Castoriadis, wasn't far off the mark when he castigated the French political class (particularly on the left) for its slothful irresponsibility in failing to genuinely come to grips with reflecting on such a "momentous event".

Hitler: Crime And The Will

The other variety of totalitarianism, for its part, cared nothing for equality. Surely everything has been said, and read, about the bottomless abyss Hitler opened up in Western consciousness? Not so. Not until sev-eral decades have gone by will we recover wholly from the shock. Years will pass before the shame disappears. Just as time will be needed to com-pletely elucidate the objective collusion between these two totalitarianism ideologies — the red and the brown — all through the century, setting it aflame, the one bolstering the other, giving one another legitimacy even as they fought, major rivals but secretly (and partially) alike.

The concept of modernity was not only compromised but utterly destroyed by Hitler and the Holocaust — both modernity and culture. Right there in old Europe, with its refinement and learning, on the continent of the Enlightenment and of reasonable reason, in the homeland of Goethe, Beethoven and Kant, it was possible for ancient barbarism to rear its head again! And not only to rear its head but, contrary to Leninism, to openly proclaim its true nature! "Yes," Hitler declared, "we *are* barbarians! We want to be barbarians! It's an honorable title. We are the people who will rejuvenate the world. The world is near its end. Our mission is to lay it waste. . . . My teaching is hard. Weakness has to be knocked out of them. In my *Ordensburgen* a youth will grow up before which the world will shrink back. A violently active, dominating, intrepid, brutal youth — that is what I am after. . . . That is how I'll eradicate the thousands of years of human domestication and obedience. Then I shall have before me the pure and noble natural material. With that I can create the new order!"[13]

They were indeed "barbarians", those who threw themselves into the murderous, earth-shaking Hitlerian stampede to revolt against the spineless inaction of the humanist democracies They wanted to restore the world to the merciless ingenuousness of its origins, obliterate two thousand years of Judeo-Christianity, establish the domination of one race, of one people, by planning the extermination of Jewry and the massacre of a few other nations. It was the extraordinary surfacing of compressed hatred and energy, an incredible outburst of archaic savagery, in the very heart of the continent of memory, like some Paleolithic ferment, spreading fire and death from Norway to the deserts of Tripoli.

This resurrection of the "Beast" in the very homeland of civilization and of modern technology, speculative reason and industrial power, by a tyranny in the service of the instincts, would destroy our confidence in history for many years to come. What we had thought could never be reversed, could be! A civilization, unknowingly, could carry its own negation within itself! Welling up from beneath the thin veneer of our civility, a monstrous, ancient form of evil could slumber for centuries, awaiting its chance! (Something Berthold Brecht would express by denouncing the "fruitful womb"). So, the veneer of thought that covers our primitive animal nature turns out to be pretty thin, twenty centuries on.

The lunacy of Nazism did indeed open up a gaping void, a geological fault line, in the European consciousness. And the cataclysm was all the more frightening in that it seemed to take by surprise a Europe that was either too skeptical, or too fatigued. It had seemed so senseless and shallow! In Germany itself, the Jews, whose modernity had made them model citizens — and who were often war veterans — found it difficult to evaluate this hatred accurately, with its inane rejection of history and its determination to unmask the Jew behind the citizen. The whole thing seemed so absurd that it was some time before even philosophers became alarmed. "During the first third of the 20th century the German philosophers, of Jewish extraction in particular, comprised a complex intellectual 'family', enjoying exceptional influence. It seemed to have integrated so successfully that most of its members felt certain they ran no serious danger in Germany, their homeland for centuries — a Fatherland that many of them had served, with exemplary devotion, during the First World War".[14]

As for the ontological breakdowns provoked by the collision between modernity and the dark star of Nazism, they would continue to be heard, rumbling, echoing, and growling, up to the present day, like the echoes of some long, slow, subterranean detonation. Auschwitz, Birkenau, Dachau, Buchenwald, Treblinka, Kulmhof-Chelmno, Belzec, Sobibor, Majdanek, Mauthausen. . . In this respect, the Second World War lasted not five years, but fifty or more. Once the carefree exuberance of the post-war period had evaporated, the enormous questions raised by the death camps and Jewish consciousness would return, brutally ending our inattentiveness. Neither Europe in general, nor France in particular, would be able to close the books till much later. We only have to think of the moral collusion that only came to light a half-century later, of the betrayals discovered so long after, of the grudgingly admitted instances of pillage, of all the complicities, and of the newly discovered archives. The utter evil of Nazism was like a virus, and the extent of the infection is only being discovered with time.

Above and beyond everything that has been said and written about this vast malfunctioning of European history, one obvious truth is emerging today, namely that the value principally brought into disrepute — and deprived of its legitimacy — by Nazism is the will to act, or historical voluntarism. This impulse, unfettered by any restrictions or considerations (and certainly not moral ones!), was glorified by Nazi propaganda. "Our uprising," the Führer proclaimed, "has nothing to do with *bourgeois* morals.

We are an uprising of the strength of the nation. The strength of its loins, if you like, as well." One of the films made on this theme by the director Leni Riefenstahl is called *Triumph of the Will*. And Hitler insists again: "Only a man involved in action is aware that he is the essence of the Universe. . . Man is mistaken about the role of reason. It is not the seat of any special dignity, but simply one resource among many in the struggle for life. Man has been put on earth to act. Only when he acts is he fulfilling his natural destiny".[15]

The monstrous power of the will exalted by Nazism claimed, in their case, to be free of historical fatalities and determinisms. It would flaunt, for the whole world to see — as it did the torches and braziers of the Nuremberg rally — its freedom to dispose of time, space, men, and destiny, exactly as it saw fit. It was Promethean action in a pure state, a godlike activism, capable of remodeling the world as it desired, if need be swallowing up an entire people in the fog of crime. Drunk on itself and sure of its potency, it believed it was free to choose as it wished — even to reject history itself and arrest its flow. The horizon towards which the Führer directed his troops did not lie somewhere ahead, but in the Western past. The heavy Nazi symbolism celebrated the original German forest, from before the Judeo-Christian era. This lethal vitalism turned to supposedly regenerative pre-European origins, adapting Nietzschean revolt to its own ends.

By making a fetish of the voluntarism of the "Master Race", and by opening up to it each and every possibility, Hitler was doing no less than turning Hegel on his head. If indeed history has a course, then that course could be reversed. A "strong and virile will" could make it possible to swim against the current. And Hitler would indeed undertake to retrace all the ground covered by a history he abhorred and distrusted. The consequences of such a radical inversion of Hegelian thinking did not escape certain contemporaries of Nazism. Just think of Carl Schmitt's remarkable comment, on January 30, 1933, the day on which the little Austrian corporal became Chancellor of Germany. He wrote in his diary: "Today, you could say that Hegel is dead".[16]

After Hitler, no one can speak anymore of voluntarism, or of Promethean ambition, as they used to do. Both ideas have been tainted by the horrors of the gas-ovens.

Colonial Wars And The "Unhappy Consciousness"

The defeat of Germany in 1945 and the victory of law over barbarism restored some energy to historical expectation. But not for long. The Second World War was, undeniably, followed by a renewal of political optimism in Western Europe. The stated requirements of the new social contract, the vigor of reconstruction, and the unprecedented (and fulfilled) promises of the "thirty glorious years" of reconstruction following World War II still bear witness to the fact. And Michel Winock has pointed out how, in addition, the Sartrian idea of commitment drew intellectuals, and philosophy, back into the historical arena during those years.[17] However, this recovery and these new foundations erected on the wartime ruins were short-lived. If Nazi tyranny had been overcome, another tyranny was still alive and well. It even acquired additional seductive power from the decisive role it had played in the victory. Stalingrad and the Red Army, in their struggle against Hitler, had heroically restored the legitimacy of the Communist undertaking. So, in the realm of ideas, the entry of the democracies into the cold war helped bring about a fateful revival of the blind spots, moral complicity and errors of the modern spirit.

As a result, considerable numbers of Western intellectuals allowed themselves to be drawn, for more than a quarter-century, into an attitude of fellow-traveling, or of resilient sympathy, the history of which (nor that of the disillusionments that followed) I do not intend to trace here. Suffice it to say that, in spite of the expressions of remorse, this support or complicity would be seen retrospectively as yet another defeat for the intellect — one that came on top of many others, but which would count for a lot in the eventual disillusionment. Emmanuel Lévinas has summed up very well the painful but angry sense of mourning for Communism that, according to him, underlay the events of May 1968. "The year 1968 embodied the joy of despair; a last farewell to human justice, to happiness and perfection, after the truth emerged that the Communist ideal had degenerated into a totalitarian bureaucracy. In 1968 there remained only scattered groups, and a few patches of individual revolt still seeking surrealist forms of salvation, having lost confidence in any collective movement of humanity, and being no longer convinced that Marxism could survive as the prophetic messenger of history".[18]

This was not the whole story. The Western democracies, as victors in a just war and enthusiastic acolytes of liberty, were to discover that they themselves were infected with violence and cynicism, were betraying the values they proclaimed, and were being categorized, *ipso facto*, among the persecutors. First of all came Hiroshima and Nagasaki, of course, and the lasting shame cast a dark shadow over post-war consciousness. After all, this phenomenal use of contemporary science in the service of death, the "qualitative leap" brought about by such a massacre, the calculated flirtation with nuclear apocalypse, had been carried out not in the name of some tyrannical regime but of civilized democracy. The latter, by such a humiliating betrayal of the principles it proclaimed before the entire world, made itself permanently suspect, and deservedly so. The deadly mushroom cloud of Hiroshima would considerably obscure the outlines of the Good.

And then (above all) there came, on the heels of the defeat of Nazism, the uncomfortable ambiguity of colonial or imperial wars. From Indochina to Algeria, from the Portuguese in Africa to the Americans in Vietnam, from the Indian Empire to Latin America, Western democracy — which had actually become "imperialist" — everywhere attempted to use its armed might and technology against the very people who were throwing the same values of justice and liberty it claimed to champion back in its face. In this whole affair, the legitimate heirs of Western history were no longer truly in the West, but in revolt against the West, wherever oppressed peoples were involved in struggle. The three long decades between 1945 and 1975 were preoccupied with this decisive contradiction. To the intellectuals and the youth of Europe and America, and to democrats everywhere, this fundamental betrayal brought anger and confusion. These were to become the source of a nagging uneasy conscience, of an obsessive remorse, the bitter fruits of which would be leftism, interest in the Third World, and the desperate terrorist acts in Germany and Italy in the 1960s and 1970s.

The economic circumstances of the time also helped to strengthen this sense of iniquity and hypocrisy. Indeed, the post-war period had seen the birth of two new concepts that sum up the new, worldwide injustice, namely "underdevelopment" and the "Third World". These two terms, which were to have a long life, conveyed a truth that can be very easily summarized. While the northern hemisphere (primarily Europe and America) was embarking on a period of unprecedented prosperity (a 400% increase of wealth in 30 years!), the southern hemisphere was becoming bogged down in backwardness and famine. This was the other, and no less troubling, aspect of the contradiction.

In the realm of ideas, the whole post-war period, in the broadest sense, would therefore be over-determined — at least on the political left — by this vague self-disgust affecting the Western democracies. The political commitments of those years, and also a considerable proportion of the dominant culture and sensibility, had their roots in this disillusioned rejection of the universalist ambitions that celebrated liberty and equality — ambitions that Europe and America trampled under foot while claiming to represent them. So it was that in people's minds an essential distress, a new Hegelian "unhappy consciousness" came into being. It was an inability to accept oneself, a self-destructive revulsion, of which Jean-Paul Sartre's famous preface to Frantz Fanon's *The Damned of the Earth* is a typical example. For a fair proportion of the citizens of Europe and of America, the "bastion of liberty" that had defeated Hitler had become, in its turn, morally uninhabitable. Western culture, people thought at the time, had no special legitimacy where the law, justice, and liberty were concerned. A modernity of that kind could hardly lay claim to any kind of special status in history.

Frantz Fanon, an archetypical third world activist, was not the only one to brutally (and excessively) rub Western humanism's nose in its distortions and intrigues. Aimé Césaire, the French Caribbean writer and member of the French Chamber of Deputies, the poet of "negritude", expressed himself in even more violent terms: "It would be interesting," he wrote in the 1950s, "to study, clinically, in detail, the steps taken by Hitler and Hitlerism and to reveal to the very distinguished, very humanistic, very Christian bourgeois of the 20th century that, without his being aware of it, he carries a Hitler within him, that Hitler dwells within him, that Hitler is his demon".[19] The overstatement and violence with which he expresses himself are themselves characteristic of the age. Western thought was afflicted by self-doubt as never before; it doubted its past, and its universalist vocation.

This does a lot to explain the errors and aberrations of the age. I am thinking in particular of the militant differentialism, the debased Levi-Straussism of the 1970s that, in rejecting universal values, saw other world cultures through rose-tinted glasses and endowed them with all kinds of virtues. From China to the Near East, from the Amerindians to the tribes of Black Africa, an excessively positive evaluation of the "other" — even to the extent of excusing his crimes — was in direct proportion to the self-disenchantment in the West. The Chinese, it was said, don't have the same concept of liberty as we do... As if brought about by some cunning stratagem of history, this exaltation of difference, this rejection of universal values, this appreciation of particularism, which had historically been a trait of the old counter-revolutionary culture, was taken over by the extreme left — a state of affairs that would prevail until the end of the 1970s.

It took time, bloodshed, and some horrendous excesses to bring people back to their senses. The Cambodian and Chinese holocausts, the pathetic plight of the Vietnamese boat people and the dreadful massacres in Sub-Saharan Africa combined to demonstrate, little by little, the fallacy of differentialist premises and to push Westerners back in the direction of a kind of more or less reconstructed universalism. The emergence of a "human rights" movement, in the form of organizations like Amnesty International (in the 1960s) or Doctors Without Borders (in the 1970s and 1980s), was an expression of this (cautious and partial) revival of universality in the Western imagination. And, simultaneously, the concept of difference, in its radical form, returned to its original home on the extreme right.[20]

The Triumph Of Suspicion

The word "partial" does indeed seem to me an accurate enough characterization of this thin form of universalism, this "for want of anything better", generous and inadequate at the same time, which is supposed henceforth to represent humanitarian activism and the defense of human rights. At the turn of the century, the historical optimism and *Weltanschauung* (worldview) of Western modernity seems to be in tatters. Indeed, every positive motivation seems to have been expunged from the recesses of the contemporary consciousness; every source of energy seems to have been exhausted, every ambition annihilated. It seems as if intellect itself, after so many betrayals and errors, is considered suspect, and is viewed with a strange distrust. It is admonished, and — in the name of rejecting any all-inclusive attitude — asked to explain itself, so it keeps a low profile. This covert renunciation of the intellect, which often almost becomes full-scale relativism, is anything but innocuous. Alain Finkielkraut was quite right to wonder, in 1982, if Holocaust revisionism had not been allowed to prosper as a consequence of this dangerous questioning of thought.

And indeed, a strange kind of censure is in the air at the turn of the century, always ready to point an accusing finger at any over-enthusiastic support for universality. There's an impatient distrust of any general truth or belief. We are almost told not to act *too* decisively any more, not to give in to monolithic belief. Everybody is encouraged to renounce any genuine convictions, in case they should become fertile soil for some form of totalitarianism, which might work to the detriment of the individual. Alternatively, there is an attempt to reduce any kind of conviction to no more than an inconsequential fad or curious preference, requiring no real commitment. "Freedom of conscience has not been denied," remarks Maurice Bellet, "it has been obliterated. For it has been rendered meaningless. Have whatever 'ideas' you like, believe in God or not, in Jesus or Mohammed, or in nothing at all, be a socialist or a liberal — what difference does it make, at the end of the day?"[21]

* *

*

Of course, it would be a mistake to insist too much on historicizing this crisis of ideas. It would be naïve to attribute it entirely to the "rational" deliriums and tragic events that have soaked the 20th century in blood. Other factors come into play, not the least important of which — as we have seen — is the ever-increasing complexity of reality and knowledge, and, again, the influence of modern epistemology. The distancing from the all-embracing uniqueness of reason, the advent of cultural pluralism, and the need for a peaceful organization of what Max Weber called the "polytheism of values", or "warring gods"[22], all have their roots in the very early 20th century. We could even say that the very same question has in fact been being asked since the Enlightenment. At the end of the 18th century, indeed, "the French bourgeois revolutionaries had an unprecedented experience. For the first time they confronted the full extent of the dilemma of modern liberalism, namely the lack, in political and social matters, of any shared belief in the entire citizenry, since each and every one had become the master of what had become merely his 'opinions'. No revolution, prior to the French Revolution, had had to face this collective spiri-

tual challenge, which was to become the common fate of modern societies".[23]

As for the celebrated "triple suspicion" that played such a part in destroying the sovereign subject and his individual conscience — as these
were perceived by the Enlightenment, it obviously belongs to the nineteenth rather than to the 20th century. All this is obvious. But it doesn't
mean that a fundamental aspect of this ultimate defeat of the intellect is
indeed the — even unrecognized — inheritance of the "despotic" century
whose disastrous annals we have been surveying. Apart from transitory
intellectual fashion, the posturing, and the different schools of thought,
one thing at least is certain: this nihilism is *in addition* the defenseless heir of
a specific history, i.e. of a phenomenon we can situate in time. Thinking of
this, it is sometimes tempting draw a comparison with the "post-traumatic
syndrome" observed in the survivors of a disaster — a condition which is
cause for concern, but which, sooner or later, they just have to put behind
them. In the realm of thought, as we have seen, there has been no lack of
traumatic disasters. . . So it is only by putting this crisis in its contemporary historical context that we can grasp its meaning, and attenuate its impact. Perhaps, like Charles Taylor, we should require it to undertake some
degree of self-examination.

The Grave Of Thought?

The simple act of reviewing the most structured forms of this voluntary abdication of intellect, even in such an outrageously summary fashion,
at least allows us to see it in the context of its time — and to attenuate its
impact.

It was during the 1970s that the concept of "weak" or "thin" ontology
became current. Proposed by the Italian philosopher Gianni Vattimo, this
weak ontology was bent on renouncing those all-encompassing theories
that claimed to decipher the intrinsic nature of things and believed themselves able to unravel the complexity of the real world.[24] It aimed to adopt
a steadfastly critical attitude towards all the "great narratives" of the past,
and the adventurous forms of commitment they founded. This type of
thinking, "which accepts its own limitations, is aware that it is essentially
language, a play of metaphors, the production of narratives that take over
one from another in attempting to give a better description of certain situa-

tions or contexts. It cannot express any necessity or truth, for it basically functions on the level of contingency. [For it], no approach, or narrative, is more true than others by virtue of any qualities of their own. . . There cannot knowingly be any universally applicable positions, i.e. without running the risk of a totalitarian tendency to do violence to the diversity of situations and to the contingency of social relations as linguistic ones".[25]

Besides Gianni Vattimo, one of the most prominent representatives of this trend — very influential in the United States — is Richard Rorty, the theorist of what might be termed a post-metaphysical philosophy.[26] For Rorty, the "positive nihilism" of democracy is preferable to all the other various attempts to "organize the world". This type of democracy, precisely because it has no message to offer, can permit the peaceful coexistence of all kinds of messages; it is fundamentally pluralist, and as such represents the best defense against totalitarianism. For Rorty and his disciples, the modern individual must become accustomed to living in societies where there is no overarching point of view. "Liberal democracy, whatever its foibles and weaknesses, is superior to philosophy, and, in fact, to any philosophical approach, which is necessarily limited and dated. The pragmatic attitude of democracy is somehow superior to any theoretical exercise, however great its virtuosity or subtlety".[27]

There is an obvious connection between this relativist trend and the school of thought influenced by Foucault, who, starting in the late sixties, was predicting the demise of the old style of intellectual. For Foucault, intellectuals had to cease doing what they have done since the 18th century, namely attempt to tie together the inheritance of the Greek sage, the Jewish prophet and the Roman lawmaker in a single discourse. To this kind of omniscient and universalist intellectual, irremediably complicit in the betrayals, perfidies and tyrannies of the world, to this committed "great writer", Foucault contrasted the more modest figure of the "specific intellectual". "The figure who combines the functions and prestige of this new intellectual," he asserted, "is no longer the 'writer of genius', it is the 'total thinker'; no longer someone who single-handedly represents the values of all, taking a stand against the sovereign or an unjust government, whose cry echoes down through the ages; it is he who possesses, together with a few others, whether in the service of the State or against it, powers capable of promoting life, or killing it for good".[28] The advent of the "specific intellectual" was inseparable from the notorious "death of the subject" (the subject — "that recent invention"! — which Foucault also sensed, attributing it to the combined offensives of anthropology, linguistics, and psycho-analysis.

This denunciation of the early kind of intellectual, claiming to speak from a "mastery of truth and justice", would be taken up in a more radical form by the adherents of what would be called the *postmodern*. Its principal representative is Jean-François Lyotard, along with Gilles Deleuze and Jean Baudrillard. In a text that has become famous, published in 1983, *Le Tombeau de l'intellectuel*, Lyotard displayed little concern for nuances. "The intellectual," he wrote, "no longer exists, at least in the sense of a mind identified with a subject endowed with universal value, describing and analyzing a situation or condition from such a viewpoint, and recommending a course of action to bring about its realization".

Basically, this analysis is more devastating than one might imagine at a first sight. For Lyotard's anti-humanism, Enlightenment thought itself has to be discarded, for, he writes, it has become "outdated", as has the concept of the universal at the same time. For him, however, this is not a catastrophe — far from it. "The decline, and perhaps the ruin of the universal idea" he adds, "can free thinking and life from totalizing obsessions". This critique owes a great deal to Nietzsche, in that it rejects any reliance on reason itself. We must accept that the truth has somehow been placed beyond our reach, that it has been undermined by the "simulacrum" to which we are confined by technology, the power of the media, etc. It is as though our relationship to the real world has been literally abolished, and no "legitimizing narrative" will be able to give it shape again. After meaning and truth have been dismantled this way, it is impossible for society to be unified: it can be no more than a collection of disparate and autonomous individuals.[29]

"To simplify in the extreme," Lyotard goes on, "I see incredulity towards meta-narratives as 'postmodern'. This incredulity is no doubt a result of progress in the sciences; but this progress is itself based on such a supposition. Corresponding to the obsolescence of the meta-narrative as a legitimizing device there is a crisis in metaphysical philosophy and in the university institution that used to be dependent on it. The narrative function is losing its functors, its great hero, its great dangers, its great journeys, and its great objective".[30]

In an over-simplified or over-schematic form, the postmodern dogma achieved extraordinary media success in the 1980s and 1990s. It is true that it was well-attuned to the spirit of the time. It provided a theoretic basis for the simultaneously hedonistic and disillusioned, playful and anguished, libertarian and tormented individualism that is the distinctive characteristic of those two decades. It was perfectly in tune with what soon would be called market democracy. Gilles Lipovetsky's analyses ("now we are ruled by the void, but a void lacking any tragedy or apocalypse") exemplify the same sensibility[31] — or fashion.

Let us add that a sizable portion of sociology would fall under the influence of this "postmodern" renunciation of totality. Certain sociologists would take the "liberating" disappearance of unified society as a given, and, following Alain Touraine, attempt to demonstrate the new reorganization, and promise of autonomy, of "social movements". It is time, Touraine has often written, "to uncover the meaning, not only of new ideas, but of practices of all kinds, both individual and collective, which show what are the issues, actors, and conflicts of a new world".[32] This sociological current leaves everything to the sovereignty of a rebellious, dissident individual, who rejects the authority of government, or of any collectivity whatsoever. It views the definitive obliteration of holism as a triumph for freedom, like a kind of unprecedented epiphany of the individual, snatched at last from the restrictive discipline of membership in society. Accepting, ultimately, a certain cultural relativism, it shows very little interest in substance, or in values.

And that is the whole problem.

The new cynics in power

"For a long time now, the key positions in society have been given over to a diffuse cynicism, in executive committees, parliaments, administrative councils, and company management, publishers' reading committees, doctors' surgeries, university faculties, lawyers' offices, and editorial offices. A refined kind of bitterness goes along with it, for these cynics are far from stupid, and from time to time perfectly recognize the Nothingness to which it all leads. Their mental faculties are flexible enough to incorporate an ongoing questioning of their own activity as a way to survive. They know what they are doing, but continue to do it because, in the short term, the constraints imposed by facts and the instinct for survival tell them the same thing: that this is what they have to

---

do.

Cynicism is an enlightened false consciousness. It is the modern version of the unhappy consciousness, which the *Aufklärung* worked on, both with success and to absolutely no effect. This consciousness has learned a lesson from the *Aufklärung*, but has not put it into practice and, no doubt, has been unable to do so. Simultaneously well to do and impoverished, it to longer feels concerned by any ideological criticism: its falseness is already armed with reflexive defenses

The End Of The "Postmoderns"?

The journalistic and fashionable success of this "postmodern" gospel made it, for a time, the main component element of the current discourse, the other face of neoliberalism. Its success reduced the basic critiques aimed at it over two or three decades to relative discretion. So the debate, crucial though it was, had few echoes beyond scholarly journals or specialized circles. And yet the criticisms of postmodernism were as numerous as they were immediate. And today they are re-emerging with significant vigor. The "postmoderns" and their disciples were widely accused not only of failing to confront the new social complexity, but also of remaining silent before the present-day manifestations of injustice, tyranny, and inequality. Contrary to the intellectuals Julian Benda accused of betrayal in 1927, they preferred the easy solution of abstention, blasé evasiveness, and absence of hope, now become a fashionable affectation. In the United States, the main assault on them came from what is called the "communitarian" school, centered on the journal *Telos*: Michael J. Sandel, Alasdaire MacIntyre, Michael Walzer, etc.

In France, criticism came mainly from the political left or extreme left. But we should remember that philosophers like Jacques Rancière were already mocking the proponents of the "death of the subject". "Just look around you," he wrote. "In this matter, the French university world of 1973 is as submissive as Soviet society in 1936. There is noplace where the death of man and the liquidation of the subject are not proclaimed: in the name of Marx or of Freud, of Nietzsche or of Heidegger, of the 'subjectless process', or the 'deconstruction of metaphysics'; there are gurus great and small everywhere, nosing out the 'subject' and ridding science of it with as much zeal as Aunt Betsy in *David Copperfield* chasing the donkeys off her lawn".[33]

The charge of desertion of duty being leveled at intellectuals today is not a new one, and neither is the reproach that postmodernism has ingenuously allowed itself to be used as an alibi for conservatism and all the new forms of exploitation. Jürgen Habermas went further again when he assimilated this more or less estheticizing postmodernism to neoconservatism, even seeing it as a form of intellectual regression. In a 1980 lecture he accused the postmoderns of "confusing the incompletion of modernity with its failure". In opposition to the "deconstructionists" he took up the cudgels to defend reason's emancipating power, and the Enlightenment.[34]

But the strongest critiques — and those to which least attention was paid at the time, unfortunately — probably came from Cornélius Castoriadis. For him, it was hardly worth wasting any time on the subject. "What we have here," he wrote, "is a collection of half-truths perverted into strategies of avoidance. . . .Very agreeably dolled-up in modish verbiage about 'pluralism' and 'respecting differences', it ends up glorifying eclecticism, covering up sterility, and extending the principle that 'anything goes' to everything".[35]

Today, with the renewal of a genuine debate of ideas, ten years after the end of Communism, the star of postmodernism is shining somewhat less brightly. As for the criticisms aimed at it, they are taking on a certain bite. Dominique Lecourt, for example, assails the "joyful nihilism dancing on the ruins of the great conceptual contributions of modernity", and speaks ironically of the postmoderns' "little anarchist-chic refrains for the jet set!" In another register, an essayist like Alain Caillé reproaches contemporary sociologists for having become depoliticized through servile association with the State, with institutions, or joining ministry staffs. For him, sociology is seriously deficient ever since it gave up studying the mechanisms of power, new social norms, or the excessive economic emphasis of a society that has become flagrantly one-dimensional. He explicitly reproaches the intellectuals of today for their resignation rather than their betrayal.[36]

In this way, an entire sector of contemporary nihilism is finally being shown up for what it was, i.e., in addition to everything else: a *fin de siècle* symptom.

CHAPTER 2

HISTORY'S NEW CUNNING

*"It is well recognized that the cunning of Hegelian reason is
greatly indebted to Adam Smith's 'invisible hand'."*
Jean-Pierre Dupuy,
Le Sacrifice et l'envie, Calmann-Lévy, 1992.

Now that we have said farewell to the 20ᵗʰ century and its follies,
now that we have dispelled the grinding despair and mental defeats it has
produced, we can return to our subject. After the collapse of Communism
in 1989, it was time, we were told, to return to the historical path from
which we had strayed — the path of the Enlightenment and of liberty.
Now and again we can still hear this fine optimism tinkling like a tiny bell
amid the surrounding hubbub. Those who are doing the jingling assure us
that the catastrophes, tyrannies, and crimes of the 20ᵗʰ century will turn
out to have been nothing more than a dangerous rut in a road that must
inevitably lead to the liberty and peace promised by the 18ᵗʰ-century philosophers.

Only our intense confusion, they add, still prevents us from witnessing the dawn of this new Renaissance, which is already within our
reach — a Renaissance that will once and for all replace barbarous passion
with Montesquieu's "sweet commerce", that will set the administration of
affairs above the regimentation of mankind, overcome scarcity, and allow
the peaceful guiding hands of reason and science to at last make the emancipated individual the only legitimate beneficiary of History. They add that
there will be no more outmoded attachments and confining group loyalties, no more intolerance nor dogmatism, no more fearful defenses, no more
senseless frontiers: it will be an "open society" where an impartial State

will facilitate social diversity day by day, relegating both beliefs and passions to the intimacy of private life. As for everything else, only the benevolent rule of secular law — soon to be extended to the entire world — will settle conflicts of interest and decide what is or is not permissible.[1]

Such optimism sometimes appears in contemporary discourse. It does make some sense. In many ways, it is a respectable kind of optimism, which at times seems preferable to pretentious negativity. We find a trace of it in the great American liberal enterprise, which aims to extend "market democracy" to the entire planet — "enlargement" — an expansion that Antony Lake, President Clinton's security adviser, defended vigorously in 1993 when he declared that during the Cold War the market democracies throughout the world were under threat, but that this threat had now been *contained*, so that the task had become one of *enlarging* the scope of those market democracies.

According to the proponents of this liberal optimism, we have seen the last of lethal passions — exclusive identities and the temptation of obscurantism — at least in the realm of ideas. When he proclaimed the "end of History" in 1989, Francis Fukuyama was saying the same thing. At the time, he was misunderstood: History had certainly not "ended", for when it came to events there would still be earthshaking incidents and even terrible violence, and there would be for a long time to come. But History had reached its end as meaning, as a project, as eschatology. Theoretically democracy, the open society and the market had carried the day. Now all we needed was a little patience — and good luck.

In any case, the "end of History" had been predicted for more than two centuries, by Hegel in particular. "I saw the Emperor, the world-soul, riding through the streets of the town," he wrote on October 13, 1806, in Jena, as Napoleon and the Grande Armée passed by.[2] For him, the battle of Jena, the rumblings of which he could hear from his study, signified the triumph of the universalist ideas of the French Revolution, with France as its messenger. It is true that *in practice* this victory was still not assured, but philosophically the die was cast. Speaking of the French Revolution, Hegel would call it a "magnificent dawn" that would bring us closer to the "final stage of World History". Seventeen years earlier, Emmanuel Kant had reacted similarly when he heard of the same events. It is even said that the old philosopher, teaching Geography and Cosmology at Koenigsberg (Kaliningrad), in the former East Prussia, had never ventured abroad. But, one famous morning, he went stepping forth resolutely and crossed the bridge over the river Pregolia to meet the mail-coach bearing news from Paris. The Bastille had fallen! It was the end of History.

On several subsequent occasions the idea was revived, and the same "end" was seen. In the 19th century, during the industrial revolution, the liberal economists who defended it enthusiastically tended to interpret this apotheosis of capitalism as the end of "the Gothic Age", to use Sieyès's expression. Indeed Marx would explicitly reproach them with this. For their benefit he would write, in his *Economic and Philosophic Manuscripts* of 1844, "Once there was History, but not any more".

In the 1930s, during a seminar on the phenomenology of mind, the philosopher Alexandre Kojève would refer at length to this already old idea. "The end of human time, or of History, which is to say the definitive abolition of Man properly speaking, or of the free and historical individual, quite simply means the end of Action in the fullest sense — signifying, in practice, an end to war and bloody revolution. And an end to philosophy too. . . . But everything else — art, love, games, etc — could continue indefinitely. In short, everything that makes mankind happy".[3] Maurice Blanchot, too, formulated the same hypothesis in 1969, assuring us that the "universal man" of modernity had become the "master of all the categories of knowledge", rendering him "capable of everything, with an answer for everything".[4]

And yet, today, this conception of the post-Communist world as the end of History — a much less novel idea than it seemed — is no longer appropriate. It is even mocked. No one pays much attention to Fukuyama and his like. Or, let us say, no one dares to, anymore. The "end of History", in short, is over! Not just because there are radical new antagonisms springing up almost everywhere in the world, but because experience is teaching us that the "open society" so dear to Karl Popper[5] has not quite turned out the way admirers of the Enlightenment had hoped. It is torn apart by explosive contradictions, it suffers from vertigo, and is accompanied by a curious apprehension. More mundanely, we have difficulty believing that the voracious expansion of a mercenary mentality within a social vacuum, the primacy of the laws of the market, the apotheosis of quantitative thinking, can really represent the perfection of civilization. In other words, we are unable to consider the advent of the global market and the social atomization it brings as resembling in any way the realization of Enlightenment values.

But our modern world finds it difficult to combat or, indeed, even to identify the insufficiencies that undermine it and the iniquities that make it so harsh. No doubt, resistance is necessary — but resistance to what? And how? We need to take up arms, no doubt, but where is the battle-front?

It's All About Bees

This insidious despair cannot just be caused by a few deficiencies that a simple dose of social-democratic politics would soon set right. It arises from a fundamental contradiction, which the usual discussions of liberalism are unable to account for. People are rediscovering just now that today's triumphant "open society" or "market democracy" is based — and to an extraordinary extent — on a Hegelian stratagem of reason. Let us recall that, for Hegel, the cunning of historical reason (which was also used to justify totalitarianism) consisted in the use of an evil to further a good, to make some historical step forward. Whether it was violence, rivalry between nations, or a thirst for power, everything was secretly collaborating to bring about the ultimate triumph of the *logos*, i.e. of reason on the march. If human beings were unable to understand the History they were living through, they still were carried along, amazingly, by its current.

Evil in the service of a good? Is that not precisely the organizing principle underlying the market? Hegelian in this respect, the market is totally convinced that a cunning subterfuge of economic reason is capable of converting the egoistic self-interest of each for the benefit for all. It believes the prosperity of all can be based on the calculated self-interest of each individual. Such, we are told, is the amazing alchemy of liberalism, one powerful enough to transform lead into gold and greed into altruism. An entire philosophy was once born of this paradox, and everything is pointing us to it once again today. It was the ingenious invention of Bernard Mandeville, an English philosopher of Dutch background, early in the 18th century.

In 1705, Mandeville published a text destined to become famous, *The Fable of the Bees*, subtitled *Private Vices, Publick Benefits*. Initially, it was a satirical poem entitled *The Grumbling Hive: or, Knaves Turn'd Honest*. Mandeville, a freethinker and ardent rationalist, observed that in a beehive the egoistic activities of each individual insect automatically produce a beneficial result, i.e. the very existence and survival of the hive, thanks to the making of honey. It is because each individual bee does whatever it wants that the community prospers. It is the same, he assures us, in human life. The success of the latter can never be brought about by disinterestedness, which is unreliable, or altruism, which is too fickle, or constraint, which is intolerable. On the other hand, no motivation is more powerful than this tangle of intermeshing individual egoisms, providentially organized by the dialectics of demand and supply for the benefit of all. Mandeville stressed that in a dissolute society, human failings can be useful to civil society, and can take the place of moral virtue — in short, that private vices create public good.

In 1776 the Scotsman Adam Smith, the true father of economic liberalism, took up the same idea in his celebrated *Inquiry into the Nature and Causes of the Wealth of Nations* when he wrote that "It is not from the benevolence of the butcher, the brewer or the baker that we expect our dinner, but from their regard to their own interest". Thus there came into existence the metaphor of the "invisible hand", the self-organizing capacity of the free market to which all liberal theorists, from David Hume to John Locke, Benjamin Constant and Milton Friedman subscribe. The invisible hand of the market would become a "hidden God" regulating society for the greater benefit of its members.

While it may have demonstrated unmatched efficiency in producing wealth and establishing prices, the "invisible hand", as soon as it is left to its own devices, runs up against a major contradiction, namely that the attempt to exploit the selfishness of each in the service of all ultimately legitimizes this selfishness. Furthermore, it makes an economic virtue of egoism, and, when all is said and done, a virtue pure and simple. In other words, it relies for a motivating force on an instinct — self-interest — that is in contradiction with the minimal virtues that are nonetheless required to form a basis for any kind of social cohesion. So, the very thing that threatens its survival is at the heart of market democracy. It takes a "vice" as its organizing principle, and in doing so extols a selfishness that it simultaneously has to combat, or at least contain. Unreflectively, it considers this fundamental selfishness of the economic actor more effective, and above all less barbarous, than any other stimulus. A number of contemporary writers still express themselves with this original lack of foresight. "Cynicism," says Jean-François Revel, "is more tolerant than fanaticism, and self-interest more accommodating than belief". In the same line of thinking, the Peruvian writer Mario Vargas Llosa, a former Marxist who has become a fervent apologist for libertinage and ultra-liberalism, never misses an opportunity to sing the praises of selfishness, however demented.[6]

Today, this ambivalence is indeed a major snag for a modernity that, after discrediting alternative models, has tended to make the market not just one, but the *only*, ingredient of social organization. How, then, can we not see what is staring us in the face, the fact that the queasiness affecting us as the new century begins is fed by our sense that somewhere, something odd is going on? Has History ever witnessed a civilization that took "vice" (Mandeville's own word) as its fundamental principle? That is the question. In a total market democracy, the "vice" of greed has to be celebrated for its productiveness and at the same time combated as a social menace. What a schizophrenic program! What an unstable combination of cynicism and moralism that, sooner or later, will end up discrediting language itself. For how can words continue to mean anything if they are obliged to express one thing and its opposite at the same time?

American economists and academics are sometimes the first to denounce this ethical inconsistency, the ultimate consequences of which are close to madness. "In the most rigorous expression of capitalist ethics," writes one of them, "crime is simply another economic activity that happens to have a high price (jail) if one is caught. There is no social obligation to obey the law. Duties and obligations do not exist. Only market transactions exist".[7]

But it is in the long term that this absurdity stands out most clearly. Usually, indeed, a society's level of civilization is embodied in a specific scale of values, in a particular hierarchy of qualities or human types that the society in question sets out to encourage and promote by education. The enlightened scholar will win out over the aggressive brute, the honest judge will be preferred to the felon, the creator will be honored rather than the drug-dealer, etc.. The social order — and, above all, the education it provides — will be based on this hierarchy. But the hegemony of the market results in an implicit, albeit devastating, reevaluation of the virtues and vices that merit social recognition. For the market, the enterprising cretin and the wealthy tycoon are equally positive "role-models". The dreamy poet or the virtuous magistrate, on the other hand, is no more than a colorful loser whom it would be better not to imitate. The whole framework of collective representations is thus turned upside down, and what we might call symbolic road markings no longer seem part of the streetscape. What emerges is total relativism, and, in the literal meaning sense of the word, an *in-significance* which is perfectly characterized by the following quotation:

"In the community regulated only by the laws of demand and supply, but protected from open violence, the persons who become rich are, generally speaking, industrious, resolute, proud, covetous, prompt, methodical, sensible, unimaginative, insensitive, and ignorant. The persons who remain poor are the entirely foolish, the entirely wise, the idle, the reckless, the humble, the thoughtful, the dull, the imaginative, the sensitive, the well-informed, the improvident, the irregularly and impulsively wicked, the clumsy knave, the overt thief, and the entirely merciful, just, and Godly person".[8]

To enable its very dynamism, market society is obliged to base itself on what were once considered anti-values, "vices", and even sins. This is so for envy, which, much more than "need", has become the true stimulus of consumption.[9] Without frenzied consumerist appetites, the modern world of the market is shaken to its foundations, becomes desperate, and hastily mobilizes its publicity experts with their so clever ability to manipulate symbols. The imperative given today's citizen is completely unambiguous: "Thou shalt consume!". The implicit message exalts excess and hedonism. By consuming, by enjoying things, and indeed by wasting as much as possible, I am creating work and rescuing the economy. As for the advertising specialist, whose job it is to artfully fan the flame of envy back to life, he is the new prophet of modernity. How earthshaking!

All the talk of "meaning", of universal morality and of business ethics to which our age has become accustomed, means very little in the face of this untroubled amoral contradiction. How can a society simultaneously promote motivation out of individual "self-interest" and the obligation of "disinterestedness" as the duty of both the public figure and the ordinary citizen?

When The Dead Possess The Living

The objection will surely be made that it is almost three centuries since Mandeville came up with his theory about the productive selfishness of bees, and more than two centuries since Adam Smith identified the "invisible hand". Since then, we might add, the benefits provided by the market far outweigh the barbarism it has generated. This is quite true. In general, it is even what has created Western progress, whereas societies that rejected its logic have been condemned to stagnation and tyranny. It is impossible to dispute this, just as there can be no doubt about the efficiency of the market economy. In this respect, what passes for debate about the comparative advantages of a market or a managed economy has become ridiculous. Is there any debate about whether the earth is round? But to stop at that and use it as an argument to put an end to all discussion, is to forget a fundamental point, which can be expressed very briefly: never, until now, has the market enjoyed unfettered sovereignty over a given society. The problem is this primacy, not the market itself as an economic technique.

"Never," writes André Gorz, "has capitalism succeeded in liberating itself completely from the political".[10] A pure liberal economy has never existed anywhere. The market has always had to contend with contrary modes of thought, with strong beliefs, with collective resistance, with some unifying sacred value, or with rival models. It is because of this competition, and thanks to it, that it was able to improve itself morally, to become civilized — and to endure.[11] It was by combining its own logic with the (very different) logic of democracy that it was able to survive and to overcome its rivals. Our progress is a direct result of this confrontation rather than of any simple causality. In other words, the opponents of the market have, from the outset, paradoxically, been its allies. . . We mustn't forget that it was under pressure from their opponents that many conservative governments introduced the social measures that, by civilizing it, allowed capitalism to survive. "An aristocratic conservative in Germany — Bismarck — invented public old-age pensions and health care in the 1880s. The son of a British duke, Winston Churchill, instigated the first large-scale public unemployment insurance system in 1911. A patrician President, Franklin Roosevelt, designed the social welfare state that saved capitalism after it collapsed in America".[12]

Also, when people talk about Adam Smith or the great liberal theorists they forget that their ideas were based on a vision that at the time envisaged society as a whole, still largely bonded by common beliefs and shared values — especially the religious. In other words, there existed in the 18th century a common stock of beliefs and "virtues" capable of mitigating the objectively destructive nihilism of the market. The "vice" of self-interest was contained, so to speak, by the symbolic framework of a common worldview. Society was "at one" with itself, and the theoreticians of the counter-revolution will never resign themselves to the loss of that unity (which it would be vain to attempt to reconstruct). Adam Smith is also known as the author, in 1759 — seventeen years before his discovery of the "invisible hand" — of a *Theory of the moral sentiments*, whose tone our contemporaries would find excessively moralizing. As for John Locke (1632-1704), the great English theorist of political liberalism and the defender of reason and of tolerance, this did not prevent him from suggesting that atheists should be excluded from full citizenship, since, being unable to ground themselves on firm beliefs, they were incapable of loyalty.[13]

So much has changed since the days of Mandeville or Adam Smith. Our pluralistic, multicultural, and autonomous societies are characterized by an anomie of belief, an atomization, a moral polytheism, which magnify exponentially the corrosive effects of the market (with the possible exception of America, where Bible culture and "constitutional patriotism", to borrow Habermas's celebrated expression, still remain unifying factors). It is true that the most radical defenders of the market society go so far as to reject the very notion of morality or shared beliefs. They justify this hostility by resorting to a utopian vision — indeed to a fiction so rudimentary that it would make any psychoanalyst or anthropologist smile: the vision of an individual completely autonomous in his desires, a particle fallen out of nowhere and capable of creating itself by its choosing its own conceptions of Good and Evil in total personal freedom.[14]

And then, politically, since 1989 our situation has been completely different. For the first time the market has been left without any real rival or competitor. Enjoying primacy by default, deprived of any adversary or alternative, market rationality has been carried along by its own impetus. From pragmatic it has tended to become dogmatic, even at the expense of its own efficiency. Historical accidents have in fact conferred a monopoly position on liberalism — something contrary to its own principles, which are based, as we all know, on the notion of competition. This being the case, Lester Thurow is quite right to wonder: "how can a system that believes it is competition that makes firms (within capitalism) efficient adapt to a changing environment and maintain its efficiency, when capitalism itself has no competitor?".

In any case, for a dozen or so years now the liberal credo has been growing increasingly rigid in its self-infatuation. Imperceptibly, it has been acquiring the characteristics of a "belief", of a dogma, and even of a secular religion. In spite of appearances and despite the protests of its defenders, the market has become something like an idolatrous cult, with all the appropriate attributes: intolerance and complacency, superstition, missionary zeal, preachifying, etc.. For some time now, certain economists (even some from the liberal ranks) have been fearing just such a trend, and denouncing in advance. In the mid-1980s, John Kenneth Galbraith, for example, criticized the theorists of the American "conservative revolution" for their dogmatism, for a "theological quality that rises well above any need for empirical proof".[15] Another economist, Paul A. Samuelson, wrote ironically of this new kind of "religious zealot", whose faith is the market. All these tendencies were obviously aggravated after the fall of Communism. Indeed, it has become a commonplace of political debate to point out how the market has been turned into a virtual religion.[16]

The Great Liberal Transformation

Karl Polanyi argued that the market society could not be faulted for being founded on economic principles — since, in a sense, any society, whatever it is, must be founded on them — but that its real fault was that it was based on self-interest, an organizing principle of economic life which he saw as utterly unnatural (in the empirical sense of "exceptional"). "To separate labor from other activities of life and to subject it to the laws of the market," he went on, "was to annihilate all organic forms of existence and to replace them by a different type of organization, an atomistic and individualistic one.

"Such a scheme of destruction was best served by the application of the principle of freedom of contract. In practice this meant that the non-contractual organizations of kinship, neighborhood, profession and creed were to be liquidated since they claimed the allegiance of the individual and thus restrained his freedom. To represent this principle as one of noninterference, as economic liberals were wont to do, was merely the expression of an ingrained prejudice in favor of a definite kind of interference, namely, such as would destroy non-contractual relations between individuals and prevent their spontaneous re-formation."

Karl Polanyi, *The Great Transformation.*

There is something even more surprising. Having defeated Communism and its "scientific materialism" without striking a single blow, this new dogmatic liberalism has become its zealous heir, and, in a sense, has continued it. The dead has possessed the living. Just as Athens once did with Rome, the defeated has "conquered its savage conqueror". Such is the latest ruse of History.

Some disturbing parallels between capitalism and its communist antagonist had already been noticed in the past. The definition of the modern citizen, as Georges Bernanos had noted in 1946, is based upon "a certain conception of man, common to the English economists of the 18th century as well as to Marx and Lenin".[17] And many others (including Jacques Ellul) have pointed to this unavowed similarity between the two rival systems. Today, however, the aberrant dogmatization of liberalism has reinforced the similarity, making it quite striking. Like Marxism before it, for example, liberalism rejects the primacy of politics over economics. Both ideologies reduce politics to no more than an epiphenomenon, or a form of "populism", if not to nothing at all. . . So an antidemocratic complicity that yesterday's bitter rivalry had disguised emerges in the clear light of day. "The liberal economic utopia of the 18th century and the socialist utopia of the 19th," writes Pierre Rosanvallon today, "paradoxically share the same view of society, based on the ideal of abolishing the political".[18] Leo Strauss expressed the same idea when he wrote that liberalism, the movement to which the modern spirit owes its greater efficiency, is characterized specifically by its denial of the political.[19]

After 1989, the long-standing Marxist suspicion of "bourgeois democracy" has become part of the neoliberal vulgate. "Just when were distancing ourselves from the overly 'economic' way of thinking inherited from Marxism, which abolished the role of the political," comments Olivier Mongin, "the economic discourse of liberalism has paradoxically given new credit to the false idea that the political is no more than an inconvenient superstructure".[20]

A former pupil of Althusser, Jacques Rancière, was even more acerbic in his denunciation of this "passing of the torch" from the Marxists to the liberals, a hand-off that has been carried out, so to speak, on the terrain of political cynicism. "The supposedly reigning liberalism has borrowed the concept of objective necessity from an obsolete Marxism in the form of the constraints and caprices of the global market. Marx's scandalous thesis according to which governments are nothing but the business representatives of international capitalism has today become a truth on which 'liberals' and 'socialists' are in agreement".[21]

Make no mistake about it. This last remark is far from expressing some Althusserian nostalgia. Benjamin R. Barber, one of the most eminent American political scientists, voices the same concern in his alarm at seeing the "totalitarianism of the unrestrained market" attempting to "subordinate politics, society and culture" to the demands of the economy, taken as the absolute reference.[22]

All these remarks are simply based on common sense. But I think they no longer go far enough. In reality, the "cunning of history" which, without any opposition, has substituted a liberal utopia for a communist one (which is to say one kind of faith in economics for another) doesn't stop there. The very concept of revolution has been resurrected in the guise of neoliberalism. Even if it is surprising to see the idea expressed thus, it can hardly be denied. If words mean anything, neoliberalism has today become an essentially revolutionary process. In other words, it has robbed the left of the very substance of its rhetoric, and taken over the old symbolism of progress for its own use. With a completely novel audacity it now represents itself as the only true agent of change, while at the same time it tries to depict its opponents as backward-looking conservatives — and this is all even though there is no more reactionary tendency than ultraliberalism with its temptation to return to the unbridled capitalism of the past.

From One Revolution To Another

This substitution — it is tempting to call it an ideological reincarnation — explains the thoroughly unreal character of contemporary political debate. The deck has been dealt anew in the democratic arena: landmarks have been changed and political divides confused. This lack of intelligibility leads to the most absurd misunderstandings. Politics is in a sorry state when it gets left behind by an idea! The neoliberals, for example, have taken over the internationalist utopia so dear to the heart of the labor movement, simply renaming it "globalization". "Neoliberalism wants to destroy nations — not that it has a specific project to this effect, but simply because its logic tends to undermine the nation as a framework within which social compromises can be achieved".[23] Today, the massive campaign for open borders, the prophetic lyricism of the *global* as against the *local*, and the eloquent fulminations against isolationism, have all switched sides. As for the Hegelian reference to the "direction of History", of which modernity thought it had rid itself, has been revived, in a different guise.

Now it is neoliberalism that presents itself as a benevolent universalist project, combating all kinds of nostalgic longing for identity and nationalism, valiantly resisting chauvinism of any kind. It wouldn't be all that difficult for it to repeat Lenin's celebrated diatribes against "village cretinism". It has armed itself, like its former adversary, with the attributes of worldwide progress and modernity on the march — a march, it insists, we are powerless to resist. Doesn't the prevailing discourse repeat over and over to those who fear new forms of barbarism, domination, or injustice, that we "have no alternative", that "no other policies are possible", and that we are carried along by a powerful, irresistible, but salutary current? Adding, of course, that at the end of this long march we shall find the reward that will make all of today's sacrifices — and budgetary readjustments — worthwhile. No one goes so far as to speak of a "glorious future", but the same promise is proffered. The "direction of History" has really changed — a migration that, let us note, took place without Hegel being aware of it.

But that is still not the whole story. Neoliberalism has also made its own the utopia of a classless society. It never wearies of telling us that the class struggle is now obsolete, abolished by the emergence of a huge, prosperous and a-political middle class, with two minority groups at each end of the scale: the excluded and the rich — two marginal "problems" that will have to be dealt with by steps, and which economists discuss in technical terms. For them, the indefinite growth of the middle class will render even the traditional concept of equality more or less meaningless. It is in any case a concept that has been "transcended", or made into something extremely complex. There is an undeniable benefit to speaking like this: it provides a *de facto* justification for the inequality that is making a comeback in most industrial societies.

This revolutionary neoliberalism has also become the most ardent enemy of the traditions, older moral codes, specific cultures, or "bourgeois" values, which, for it, act as a barrier between the emancipated individual and the free market. By making the latter the regulatory authority par excellence, it is paving the way for the "creative destruction"[24] of all these intermediate structures, ingenuously depicted as surviving relics of the past — including, for example, the family, whose defense was once part of the catechism of the bourgeois right in France. Things aren't so simple today, even if this change of heart by liberalism with respect to "family values" has not yet been really grasped by a European left still captive to its old individualist and anti-family phobias.

The fact that the family is no longer at the heart of right-wing values has already been perceived by a number of socialist militants, clearly on the left politically, but no doubt more perspicacious than their comrades. A British Labour Party M.P. noted in 1998 that, like the old left, modern capitalism is little concerned about the family. What was formerly the common nucleus for the accumulation of capital, as well as the reproductive unit for the workers and consumers required by the same capitalism for more than three centuries, has now become a hindrance, if not actually an obstacle. The family, formerly perceived as the enemy of socialist progress, has become an obstacle to the global capitalism of techno-consumerism and to its ultimate purpose.[25]

More broadly, the very idea of norms, whether social, cultural, moral, traditional, or social, meets with the disapproval of revolutionary neoliberalism. In all areas — including those of ethics or of citizenship — genuine liberals set out to "deregulate" absolutely everything. The market, it is true, requires that demand be completely fluid if consumer preferences are to be as flexible as possible, if fashions and desires are to be continually renewed — even the most inconsistent ones, which competitive supply, properly promoted, will be able to satisfy in real time. So it must strive to eliminate any factors tending to immobilize, stabilize, and even provide reassurance. In this respect, the market exists in perfect symbiosis with the media, which are also driven by volatile curiosity, a thirst for novelty, mental rootlessness, and dissatisfaction. The market needs instability, and a lack of satisfaction. André Gorz, speaking of this frenzied state of mind, is correct to point out that for this kind of logic "any sort of rigidity is an obstacle to be eliminated".[26] But it is the theologian Maurice Bellet who, in a splendid formula which expresses both amusement and trepidation, best expresses this requirement for an inherent "productive instability" of the market. "Peace of mind is ruled out: it would throw a wrench into the engine of growth".[27]

Be that as it may, we are still far from arriving at a proper analysis of the conceptual sleight of hand, the symbolic permutation, which makes neoliberalism the last objectively revolutionary ideology of the 20th century. Yet the true meaning of a number of apparently surprising ideological parallels would become clear in the light of certain facts. One of these is the strange coming together between a part of what was once the European extreme left and a right-wing fringe — a meeting of the minds on the ground of so-called "liberal-libertarian" attitudes. The "case" of Daniel Cohn-Bendit — a former student rebel of May 1968, now a "Green", but loudly praised by Alain Madelin's ultraliberal right — was an anecdotal, but significant, example in the early part of 1999. But this was only logical.

This convergence, now quite noticeable, of libertarian Sixties anarchism and what is considered right-wing neoliberalism is not restricted to European countries. Several American scholars have noted the same para-dox in the contemporary history of the United States. In 1996, for example, Paul Berman argued that, contrary to appearances, the anti-bourgeois causes of the 1960s — the campus protests, etc. — and the Reaganism of the 1980s were actually products of the same individualist reaction. He adds that the two phenomena were not political trends leading in opposite directions, but two stages in a single radical historical tendency.[28]

In a noted article, a university professor from Cambridge (Massachusetts), Mark Lilla, has brilliantly expressed and developed the same idea. He points out that anyone familiar with young Americans knows that they have no difficulty in reconciling these two aspects of their daily existence, for they see no contradiction in simultaneously holding low-end jobs under an unbridled world market — the Reaganite dream, the nightmare of the Left — and spending their weekends immersed in a moral and cultural universe fashioned by the Sixties. He adds that, on the psychological level at least, predictions of a cultural contradiction between the two attitudes have not been fulfilled.[29]

So it is bearing all these subterfuges, pretenses, and ambivalences in mind that we must analyze the unexpected emergence, at the end the 20th century, of a revolutionary — and, in certain respects, totalitarian — logic. It contributes to the uneasy impression that this "useless century" turned full circle in the end, and that we have little by little made our way back to the point from which we started.

A Totalitarian Logic?

But isn't it going a bit too far to call it "totalitarian"? Isn't it overly polemical? A bit ridiculous? Of course it is, if you think of it in terms of freedom. Whatever the criminalizing tendencies of modern democracies, and of the United States in particular,[30] there can be no doubt that this particular form of totalitarianism is not an attack on individual freedom. It even flatters itself on being its most vigilant defender, and that's hard to deny. Market democracy, normally, has no desire to create a police state. This is certainly not an insignificant aspect of it. In this respect at least, certain accusations voiced by the extreme left, or by liberation theologists in the Americas, seem a bit far-fetched, without any real justification. On the other hand, market-based society brings with it other temptations or tendencies that are indeed redolent of a totalitarian mentality. They are even a carbon copy of certain excesses of the "communist illusion", to borrow François Furet's expression.

There is in the first place what might be called the ontological cannibalism of the market. By that, we mean the tendency to reduce the whole complexity of human existence and social life to something quantifiable and measurable, to promote the image of a tragically one-dimensional *homo oeconomicus*, and to make the law of supply and demand into a concept just as tyrannical as that of the class struggle or the dictatorship of the proletariat in communist society. The financier George Soros, who should certainly know what he's talking about, minces no words when he proclaims on this topic that he considers "the threat from the *laissez-faire* side more potent today than the threat from totalitarian ideologies".[31]

In bringing up these points, it is not my intention to rehearse the same old after-dinner speech on the reign of money, the dreadful materialism of the age, or the need to find a "third way" between Sodom and Gomorrah. I am referring to an infinitely more fundamental, serious, and basic, invasion of the mind. Imperceptibly, the market mentality is taking over the entire symbolic landscape, insinuating its way into spaces, cracks and crannies that might have been believed beyond its reach. Some of its conquests are rather comic and a bit extravagant, and the economists who argue for them remind us of Stalin's Zhdanovian scientists, attempting to subordinate science to ideology.[32] Let us give a few examples, among the thousands available.

The first exhibit is the highly respected ravings of a Nobel prizewinner for economics, Gary Becker, who has suggested that the marvelous mechanism of the market can be applied to the way we view love and marriage. "Since marriage is practically always voluntary", he explains, "the theory of preferences can be readily applied, and persons marrying (or their parents) can be assumed to expect to raise their utility level above what it would be were they to remain single", and "since many men and women compete as they seek mates, a *market* in marriages can be presumed to exist".[33] For Becker and people like him, it is entirely possible to extend a cost and benefit analysis to any area of human activity, for it becomes a kind of universal grammar, capable of encompassing all other forms of thought.

Similarly, charity and humanitarian action, to cite a second example, are nowadays managed like a market, bringing together the "needy" and potential donors, viewed as "consumers with a need to give that has to be satisfied".[34] So the commercialization of charitable giving and its treatment in the media are much more than the emergence of a disagreeable trend that Bernard Kouchner once called the "charity business". They correspond to the more radical spread of a totalitarian way of thinking. In a conference paper, a specialist in the field summed up this evolution as follows (adding that he found it most disturbing): "By using a commercial enterprise just as a means (for mailing, etc.), the world of charitable giving has finally become part of the neoclassic economic model, with consumers and producers trying to achieve a balance between supply and demand. . . . And, just as in any market, certain products won't find a buyer, won't fulfill any demand, and, still according to the logic of the model, so much the worse for them: their mistake was not to have some more saleable form of misery, some more fashionable sickness".[35]

A third and even more striking example is the invasion of language itself by what the philosopher Dominique Janicaud has called "technospeak", an impoverished hodge-podge of ill-informed scientism and market terminology. This chopping away at the vocabulary by the market — and by media simplification — is helping to destroy what Maurice Merleau-Ponty termed the "miracle of expressiveness". We are little by little becoming accustomed to this *ersatz* language, this jargon with which the power of the market is progressively replacing real language — which Janicaud has beautifully described as "a language rooted in the secret, mobile depths of bodies, aroused by singular accents and inexpressible expectations, a language complicit with silence, the guardian of secrets, a form of speech which allows its most cherished rituals to accompany a group from birth to death".[36]

We could go on indefinitely giving comparable examples. Their proliferation is part of a single phenomenon: the progressive contamination of social relations by instrumental rationality and, in the final analysis, by the market. The characteristic feature of this contamination is its lack of any limits. The primacy of the "market mechanism" is accompanied by a corresponding contraction of government, of the political, and of classic culture itself. It establishes itself in a subtler, but more effective, manner. "With the market, our mentality changes almost without our realizing it".[37] To borrow Karl Polanyi's expression, the economy is no longer "built into" social relations as it once was; now the latter are "built into" the logic of the market. Society is becoming no more than an appendage to the market. It is not at all extreme, under these circumstances, to view this as a totalitarian development — in the literal meaning of the word.

It is, of course, a benign form of totalitarianism. It is above all more generous and extravagant that any other system in history. This is more or less what Schumpeter pointed out towards the end of his life. The capitalist system, he said, is indeed cruel, unjust, and destructive, but it delivers the goods — so stop complaining, since those goods are what you want! This same argument, put forward in a scarcely less perfunctory manner, is still often used in answer to critiques of liberalism. It is at the same time facile and inadmissible. The disadvantages of capitalism, as Schumpeter was able to describe them (he died in 1950), had very little in common with this irresistible penetration of the market mentality, which has become as domineering as any authoritarian ideology, into all aspects of life. This is so, even if its powers of persuasion use different channels.

This one-dimensional character of the market mentality rests, ultimately, on a kind of basic deception. It pretends to reject all dogma, all collective beliefs, all regimentation of thought, in the name of the freedom of the individual conscience and of a liberating "polytheism of values". Modernity even makes this disillusioned pluralism one of its founding principles. Our liberty is a consequence of confining belief to the private domain. In actual fact, the tyranny of market rationality is quite opposed to this so-called liberty. It imposes, *de facto*, a single, collective, sovereign value-system, which virtually destroys all others. Behind the façade of polytheist or anti-metaphysical discourse lurks a triumphant kind of monotheism, or even iron-fisted fundamentalism. This reveals the basic inadequacy of Max Weber's analyses, though in other ways they are so illuminating. Studying the irresistible erosion of values, their polytheist disintegration in a disenchanted world, Weber hugely underestimated the still intact power of one of them: consumer goods. This is why, as one commentator on Weber's ideas has stressed, his analyses "go no more than half-way, inasmuch as they fail to show that the pluralism of values is largely counteracted by the dominance of the value of valuables, market value, the formative value of human activity".[38]

Yet this particular ruse of History has never been subjected to a real examination, apart from a few premonitory but outdated analyses, whether those formulated by Max Horkheimer and Theodor W. Adorno, starting in 1944,[39] or the work of Claude Lefort, Cornélius Castoriadis, Herbert Marcuse, and some others cited earlier. I would like to suggest that there is an extraordinary disparity, in spite of everything, between the amplitude of the phenomenon and the inadequacy of the studies devoted to it. Marcel Gauchet was certainly not in error when he pointed out this troubling time lag in critical thinking: "We are witnessing a real internalization of the market model — an event with incalculable anthropological consequences of which we are barely becoming aware".[40]

A New Arrogance

This time lag, if one thinks about it, is not all that surprising. Among the things liberalism has borrowed from its former communist adversary is one it would be a mistake to underestimate: the certainty of being right. Like Marxists not so long ago, the proponents of the market are convinced they are not expressing an opinion, but *sure and certain knowledge*. In the name of "economic realism" they expound objective laws of growth, and think they belong to the elite circle of reasonable people. Without realizing it, they are behaving exactly like those who formerly called on "scientific materialism" to silence disagreement. And, like their predecessors, they are quite prepared to accuse anyone who gainsays them of ignorance or irrationality. There is a troubling common thread in this way of proceeding, in their language, attitudes and arguments. These new adherents of economic scientism wouldn't have to change very much in the way they express themselves to make their own the famous formulas for which Jean-Paul Sartre was so often criticized. They could state — and, in fact, they do — that the "market is the ultimate horizon of History", and that "all anti-liberals are dogs".[41] This conviction of possessing the truth makes them use a preaching tone when they rebuke their opponents. For isn't it immoral to persist in error? Isn't it shameful not to join the circle of reasonable people?

This unexpected revival of a theory put forward as scientific truth explains the strange sense of *déjà vu* we get when we look at the attitude prevailing among commentators, economists, and the media. Let's just remember what was once the majority opinion in universities and left-wing intellectual circles from the 1950s to the 1970s. Nor should we forget the merciless disdain heaped on dissenting opinions at the time (Albert Camus wasn't the last to experience this). There were always a thousand and one experts in Marxology to invoke the tables of the law, the accepted interpretations, or the lesson of empiriocriticism or of some commentary or other of Lenin's, to dismiss some naïve skeptic. The power to intimidate was used mercilessly. All that was left was for the gainsayers, their incompetence demonstrated, to slink away with their tails between their legs. Which indeed they did. And let us not forget the innumerable meticulous Kremlinologists who, with no one to challenge them on their turf, went on endlessly chronicling the dazzling success and progress of "real socialism".

In its tone at least, the new liberal creed proceeds in roughly the same manner, and exerts the same intimidating pressures. As in the past, its success rapidly won over the prudent, the calculating, and the lazy. Others took up the cause in all good faith, convinced — just like the "fellow-travelers" of yesteryear — that it was not a question of opinion, but of objective truth. As everyone knows, the economists, for their part, developed an affection for punctilious references to the founding texts, or for the Byzantine debates of the followers of Keynes, Hayek, or List. Studying the great authors and the "leading indicators" of the world economy, they have become our new Kremlinologists, the only difference being that Wall Street has replaced the Kremlin. This general conformity to what is presented as self-evident truth — as if under the influence of an irresistible herd instinct — even affected certain quarters that should have maintained a systematically critical attitude. "Unbridled liberalism reigns in academic and official quarters, as if by default, arising from dissatisfaction and disenchantment".[42] This sheep-like behavior has become an international phenomenon, gaining strength as it spreads. That is how an "IMF", a "UNESCO", and a "Brussels" mentality, each anything but non-conformist, have come into being.

Like their recent predecessors, all these believers in the prevailing vulgate remain immune to the counter-proofs provided by reality, to the demonstrated weaknesses in their analysis, and to the calamitous lack of foresight — one more characteristic they share with their predecessors, whose faith remained unshakeable, whatever the failures of "real socialism". Falsehood is singing a different tune,[43] but the self-assurance and sense of rectitude are again the unchallenged masters! The healthy sense of humor that at least allowed someone like Galbraith to mock those charlatans, the economists, with their pretentiousness and prudence, seems all too scarce a commodity. "The pretension of economics that it is a science is firmly rooted in the need for an escape from blame for the inadequacies and injustices of the system with which the great classical system was concerned. And it continues to serve as the defense for a quiet, non-controversial professional life even today".[44]

All that remains is to wonder about the incredible meekness of a good proportion of intellectuals who have also crowded docilely around the banner of this monotheistic market religion, completely forgetting their responsibility to retain their critical faculties. Is it because of an ignorance of economics and financial matters? Or is it because of an unacknowledged sense of guilt they still feel because of their Marxist indiscretions of the past? Or are they submitting, as they did once before, to something they think embodies the new, the future, and progress? Or has simple group loyalty, or sycophancy, played an inglorious part in their surrender? A left-wing economist, Michel Beaud, reminds us of the traditional seductive attraction power exercises over ideas when he observes that "many intellectuals are fascinated by the power of the system".[45]

It all comes down to personality, of course. In the end, such a breakdown in critical sense reminds us of François Furet's thoughts on the historical enigma of the support that Western intellectuals, almost as one, gave throughout the 20th century to one or the other of the two totalitarian ideologies. Why would it be any different with the third?

Democratic Dispossession

The deplorable futility of political debate is above all a consequence of the general confusion of landmarks. The liberals, eager for deregulation and privatization, preach reform, modernization, and a committed adaptation to all forms of modernity. As for the left, vaguely uneasy about future perils and the new inequalities that are being created,[46] it tends to protect its gains — in other words, to save those things that, for the past century, have helped to civilize capitalism. In short, the right wants to reform and the left wants to maintain the *status quo*; liberalism is "revolutionary" and the left is, perforce, conservative. This symbolic reversal gives rise every day to linguistic confusions that would be comical if they weren't the symptom of a profound impoverishment of democracy. The gap is constantly widening between words and things, between political rhetoric and social reality — not to mention the crossovers between right and left that split up each side into querulous and infinitely proliferating clans.

In general, the present-day political landscape is hesitating between three different possibilities, each as disastrous as the next: all or nothing; nostalgia for the past; the "third way".

The first of these re-sets the trap that any revolutionary process has always laid for democracy. In dealing with the ongoing upheavals, with the ravages of globalization, there is no room for any attitude other than total acceptance or total rejection. Every citizen, except for a few minor details, is asked to choose between, on the one hand, pious acceptance of the "great transformation" that is under way and, on the other, steadfast refusal, which is viewed as a rejection of modernity itself. Like all revolutions, the liberal one radicalizes attitudes by using the same implicit blackmail: you have to choose which side of the barricades you want to be on. The entire political debate, for the past fifteen years, has been influenced by this ideological dualism, leaving very little room for rational reflection. Even our vocabulary shows the effect of this impoverishment. You either go along or you don't, you're "part of it" or "out of it", you extol the market or give in to narrow-minded populism, etc.. As has always been the case, historically, this kind of culpabilizing Manicheanism is intimidating enough to disarm any critical examination and swing majority support — formally at least — behind the ongoing process. So the political spectrum is progressively reduced to a vague, insipid consensus, one that enables any genuine opposition to be marginalized, whether on the extreme right or left. Within the "circle of reason", restricted in such a way, the only questions that will be debated will be ones about management. As for democracy, it will just be quietly dismantled.

The second scenario involves nostalgia, in some shape or form. This is also fairly characteristic of revolutionary periods, which always end up in a confrontation between — or the successive ascendancy of — those who favor a complete break with the past and those who want to return to it. Today, the strongest adversaries of market totalitarianism find it difficult not to give in to this desire to return to the past — which can take various forms.

Made uneasy (as indeed they have every right to be) by the newly acquired global liberty of predatory financial capitalism — a genie let out of its bottle — some French people find it impossible, for instance, to say goodbye to their nation and Republic. They often have excellent reasons for this. Up to the present, indeed, it has always been within the framework of the nation-state (and of it alone) that there has been any possibility of taming the power of the market and setting up a regulatory mechanism to counterbalance it. By freeing itself from the nation-state, and destroying it (at least until some kind of supra national, or European, regulatory mechanism is established — something we won't see tomorrow, of that we can be sure), the market can enjoy the luxury of freedom from any controls. As André Gorz has written, "liberated from State and social control. . . , removed from the world and from concrete reality, capitalism is replacing any criteria of human judgment with the categorical imperative of its own growth, and removing its power from human control".[47] Acute (and justified) awareness that this represents a danger induces patriotic Frenchmen to mistrust any hasty abandonment of sovereignty and advocate a return to the French Republic. The problem, unfortunately, is with this word "return". It brings with it a risk of closing off the future, thus playing into their opponents' hands, and ultimately makes any reflection sterile.

The same reasoning could be applied to the class struggle. By declaring it to be outdated, and even mocking the concept itself, the adulators of the market participate in a sleight of hand that everyone recognizes as (also) ideological. It allows people to simply write off the increase in social suffering, the increasing inequalities, and the innumerable injustices, to which the modern world now gives no more than it absent-minded attention. In other words, the elimination of the entire concept of class struggle is a godsend for our new cynics. It frees them from a concern. This explains how social injustice itself has been made to seem innocuous[48] during the past few years, and how resistance to it has been gradually eroded. This makes it easy to understand the indignation of the new so-called radical left in its steadfast refusal to go along with such a conjuring trick and its efforts to restore a social activism based on the class struggle. Such a reaction is as deserving of respect as it is noble-minded, but, once again, we have a problem with the idea of *returning to the past*. Why? Because radical changes have taken place in social design, in the new ways of organizing work, in collective representation and union activism, rendering the traditional kinds of analyses based on the concept of class warfare pretty much invalid. This sort of nostalgia does express a truth, but it too is a trap, working to the advantage of the very people it is meant to oppose. A neoliberalism which is now extraterritorial, stock-market oriented, rootless, and henceforth lacking any social base ("a power without a society", writes André Gorz), is a much more difficult, much more elusive, opponent to combat than the good old bourgeois, exploitative "class enemy" of former days.

The third scenario, lastly, belongs to a recognized historical tradition — that of the "third way".[49] In times of unrest and civil war, there have always been some people in favor of synthesis; there have always been well-intentioned politicians or intellectuals eager to steer a middle course, to discover a reasonable compromise between the opposing sides. Their attempts have always been worthy of respect, but rarely have they produced any tangible result. Today, a good part of the European left — in the United Kingdom, in particular — has adopted what Anthony Giddens, one of its British theorists — calls the "third way". Accepting globalization with its promises and dangers, the supporters of this option suggest rebuilding the social-democratic movement on new foundations. Their analysis has the merit of being pragmatic and realistic. And yet one is struck by the fragility of its ethical foundations and the inadequacy of its critique of neoliberalism. The proponents of this "third way" are only able to oppose the formidable subversive power of the global market at the dawn of a new century with a few vague concepts and — too often, once again — pious wishes. There is something lightweight about this school of thought. It is true that, historically, almost every "third way", while reassuring in theory, has only paved the way for the triumph of the most powerful.

* *

*

So the problem comes down to whether we can accept that politics — i.e. democracy — should be allowed to disappear,[50] and with it the idea of a common good, of the long term, of a superior form of civilization and of the equality of human beings. If we reject such a prospect, how can we dispense with re-founding our world?

PART II

The Legacy of the West

All classifications are arbitrary. Any division of reality cuts through living tissue, makes unjustified distinctions between things that are interconnected, and, necessarily, simplifies something that deserves more subtle treatment. That is also the case for the six founding values whose importance I want to stress here, and whose extraordinary genealogy I want to recall.

All six of them are indeed tied together by an infinite number of links, reciprocal causalities, and complex interdependencies. They are part of the deepest make-up of the citizens of the modern world that we are; yet each contains all the others in a way it is not always easy to discern. So it is cheating a bit to separate and reduce them to a specific number. Why six? Why not ten, or fifteen? The objection is quite justified. The number we've arrived at, by a process of simplification, is a matter of methodology. Anything simple is false, as Paul Valéry said, but anything complicated is unusable. Whatever the risks, we sometimes have to try to make things a little clearer.

The question, at least, is easy to formulate. What are the fundamental supports, the certitudes, now long internalized, on which our conception of the world rests? What moral archeology has produced Western man, without his always being aware of it? Why do we believe spontaneously in one thing rather than another? Equality, Progress, Universality, Liberty, Democracy, Reason. . . What makes us so attached to these beliefs? Steeped in history, accustomed to the natural omnipresence of these values, we have difficulty understanding that each of them is the result of a long historical maturation. Anyone hoping to resist the disintegration going on at the present time has to turn to this history. Indeed, none of these values has come out of thin air; none of them has come about by chance. Above all, none of them is self-justifying, which means it is possible that *they could not exist* — or, worse, that they could *cease* to do so. That's the nub of the matter, for the barbarism we can imagine is best defined by their absence.

Let me say again that examining an inheritance doesn't mean starting an argument. It's basically of little importance to us whether we are "more" one thing or "less" that, whether we owe most to Aristotle, Paul of Tarsus, Plato, Moses Maimonides, St. Augustine, Averroes (Ibn Ruchd), or Descartes.[1] These are some of the figures that we are connected to, over the passage of time. We Westerners have to question our threefold Greek, Jewish and Christian inheritance — not to mention the contribution of Islam which, for several centuries, not only helped revive Greek reason in medieval Europe but also enriched the latter with its knowledge of mathematics. So, whether we like it or not, we are fundamentally Greek, Jewish and Christian, and all of them at the same time. "Nothing disciplines thinking better than to proceed in this way. We must give free rein to whatever wells up within us, now, when our memory is open to everything, free of all fear and anger".[2]

Is there any need to add that the fact that the Enlightenment moved beyond these origins doesn't justify any disdain or amnesia where these essential foundations (which, as we shall see, are largely religious in nature) are concerned?

The importance of these six values is that much easier to appreciate because each of them is at risk at the present time. So, in dealing with each one, I shall set out to define both its fundamental importance *and* how it is threatened, the riches of its genealogy and the serious consequences that would come with its loss. Each aspect illuminates the other. The threat justifies taking a fresh look at the genealogy and, conversely, the genealogy (even if only roughly sketched in) helps us understand better the cost of departing from it, or destroying it. Barbarism has no better ally than amnesia — or the refusal to remember. Daniel Sibony was quite right to point out that "the origin of hatred is a hatred of origins". Sometimes we have to turn — resolutely — towards those origins. What, then are ours?

Jewish propheticism bequeathed us the conception of *time* on which our idea of progress is based.

To Christianity we owe both the concept of the *individual* and our aspiration to *equality*.

Greece invented *reason*.

The Hellenism of the first centuries A.D. and Paul of Tarsus created a certain image of the *universal*.

Judeo-Christian teaching, finally, as inherited and secularized by the Enlightenment, resulted in a conception of *justice* that made sacrifice obsolete, and with it, revenge.

Each and every one of these inheritances is, indeed, in danger.

And I don't think the danger is imaginary.

Chapter III

The Waning of the Future

> *"Today we have witnessed the disappearance of the horizon that could be discerned behind Communism: a horizon of hope, a promise of deliverance. Time held a promise for us. With the disappearance of Communism, deeply rooted categories of the European mind have been overcome with confusion".*
>
> Emmanuel Lévinas[1]

To remind ourselves of the first danger, we must begin with what is most elementary. The platitudes that permeate an age are never quite as vacuous as one might think. Léon Bloy was quite right to study them. Beneath their rather silly redundancy, there often pulsates a kind of uneasiness. They arise out of a presentiment that may be awkwardly expressed, but one we should take seriously. So let's just listen to the refrain that our age has been repeating every day for the past few years now. We are told again and again that, definitely, we no longer have any great "project" or "ambition". Our modernity, we are assured, lacks any "grand plan"; our societies have "run out of ideals". This chorus often seems to contain a reciprocal recrimination. The public reproaches politicians mired in the everyday details of government with their lack of inspiration and vision. And those who take decisions on our behalf are always asking for just a little more enthusiasm, a little more dynamism, daring or democratic input — whether in relation to the Common Market here in Europe, or to our responsibility as citizens, for example. Basically, each party blames the other for what is lacking in both. Mostly, that's as far as it goes. Everyone just sighs: what an age we live in!

It would be a mistake to make too much fun of these conventional lamentations and this lack of reflection. Each of us, basically, senses that something has gone wrong — dangerously wrong — with our relation to time, to the long term, to the future. It's true that the century that has just ended has cured us of our worship of History, now recognized to be the mother of crimes and ideologies. We are no longer prepared to put up with the demands made on us by some Promethean project which supposedly leads to a radiant future, and which, sooner or later, some political police might try to hammer into us. We mistrust grandiose political adventures and utopias — and with good reason. But still! We don't much care for the strange silence of our times concerning what they have in mind for us. We can't seem to dispel a fundamental interrogation that we haven't always the courage to put in words. We wonder where exactly we are being led by the neo-totalitarianism of market society, and by the proliferation of technology. Just how far can the impoverished (not to say meager) kind of hope held out by current neoliberalism get away with such inadequacy? Is there any point looking for even the semblance of a historical purpose in these all-embracing statistical projections?

"Every day, commentators discuss most earnestly whether the GDP will grow by 2.3% or 2.5% this year, as if our fate depended on it. It's become a veritable mania. Consequently, there's no longer any need to justify growth by the benefits it is supposed to provide for the individual or the collectivity. Or, rather, these benefits seem to be taken for granted".[2] It's enough to stand aside for a second from the daily agitation to understand the inanity of this arithmetical "suspense", which reduces human progress to the recitation of decimal points of growth, interest rates, the memory capacity of microprocessors or the mapping of the human genome. Nevertheless, such is what occupies people's minds — those of politicians and of everyone else. Our salvation is supposed to depend on one of the figures preceded by a decimal point: a 2.7% growth in the GDP will mean our salvation, but 2.3%, disaster. Each of us, even if we seem to accept it in our daily lives, understands the lunacy of this obsession with quantification.

At best it serves to conceal — not very well, once again — a truth of which we are obscurely aware: that the future has slowly faded from sight, that our vision of tomorrow has silently crumbled away.

The Future Ain't What It Used To Be

Nowadays, everything and everybody seem to refer to this fading away, at least implicitly. For instance, some experts see the financialization of the economy as a triumph of the short-term, of speculation, of stock-investment frenzy, which has replaced the industrial project that previously motivated the builders of society. Monetary choices (a balanced budget, high interest rates, stability, etc.) reflect a day-by-day dynamic that presupposes — not always, but often — a downgrading of the more distant future — at least as far as the will to act, civilization, and hope in the future are concerned.

The time-scale of the financial markets, which has come to impose itself on all aspects of economic life, is a caricature of this tyranny of the short term, and of the amnesia that accompanies it. "This pathological distortion of temporal structures that can be seen in the way every horizon has been indiscriminately narrowed down to the immediate present has clearly only been made possible by a very strong capacity for forgetfulness. Concerns about the next five years, after striking panic into the markets, are forgotten in half a day — which is quite natural if you want to be free to give yourself over completely to the anguish about the next seven years that follows close on its heels. So, in the etymological meaning of the term, the market is inconsistent. Instead of the long-term view which, basically, should represent the appropriate time span for political action. . . the market arrives at verdicts only with reference to a fragmented time-scale".[3] It is true that markets, by definition, abhor any suggestion of uncertainty. Politics is one such. Democratic voluntarism, based upon free — and therefore unpredictable — debate, is a conceptual horror as far as the markets are concerned. It represents a risk to be diminished or eliminated.

This "global ideology" — in other words, market ideology — has its own logic, which automatically favors investment income, the preservation of wealth, and instant profits. If any concern for the morrow remains, it is no longer quite the same as before. Now it is the concern of future retirees, to whom, whenever necessary, the vital energy of the present is sacrificed — that is, reduced (in Europe) to mass unemployment and (in the United States) to the precarious existence of the "working poor".[4] In companies, the fastest possible growth of capital (the famous "return on investment") pushes any consideration of social cohesion, any shared purpose, any social concern — in short, all those factors that once moderated the impatience of money — off the map.

Even the great liberal captain of industry Jean Peyrelevade is alarmed by an evolution he nevertheless thinks irresistible. "The productive sector and the workers it employs," he writes, "are governed nowadays by the representatives of the present and future non-working population. So we have to ask ourselves whether economic reality is not already being controlled by retirees in their own interest, and productive work being shaped by people who are no longer part of it, or who are looking forward to leaving it".[5] Concern for the future, most certainly, no longer means the same thing when the future in question is that of soon-to-be retirees. In the United States, the latter have already adopted certain economic behaviors, particularly where savings are concerned, that show a polite indifference towards future generations. "As the population ages, less value is placed on the long term. More of the population is elderly, and they are saving far less, consuming far more than their parents did at the same age. Lower savings rates among the elderly partly reflect the fact that they are less interested in the next generation".[6]

In addition, economic crisis, unemployment, and the return of social inequality have combined to statistically distort the generational projection into the future that, twenty years ago, still drew our societies forward. Young adults coming onto the labor market now are more likely to live in reduced circumstances compared to their parents.[7] Where will they find any reason for enthusiasm? As Paul Krugman has pointed out (in the title of one of his books) we — at least the middle class — have entered an "age of diminishing expectations".[8] It is a decisive change. A sort of magnetic field seems to have been strangely reversed in the succession of the generations, as if some weird shift had taken place thirty years ago. The long-cherished quasi-certitude that today is better than yesterday, and tomorrow will be better than today, no longer has any justification. That conviction is fading, at best, and disappearing. Thus we lose the benefit of social and cultural logics, whose importance is very clear in retrospect.

As an illustration let us cite the principle of (upward) social mobility, which once allowed the development of a genuine cultural tradition: the grandfather, a farmer; the father, a schoolteacher; the son, a doctor. That is what Paul Ricoeur called "narrative identity". "This narrative inscribed social progress in extended time, in an accumulation of prosperity from one generation to the next. The individual thought of himself *only* as one in a line of descendants, and set out to increase the inheritance handed down to him, in a society where technical change was still relatively slow".[9] This confidence in the future, which was diminished after the late 1960s (and declined more rapidly in the 1980s), encouraged effort, while ensuring the cohesiveness of a community that retained its solidarity over time. Not so any more. The future no longer beckons us, and in fact it has become inscrutable. Its image has become blurred, like a fading mirage.

That ability to project into the future allowed people to extend their expectation of progress over a span of several generations. Such a temporal dynamic made for peace, by its very nature. The generations succeeded, rather than confronted, one another. When this natural optimism disappeared, all age groups have been reduced to a merciless day-by-day competition. Hostility between old and young has replaced continuity among the generations. Instead of shared objectives, there is wrangling. "The secularization of life," Alain Ehrenberg writes wisely, "has shrunk our experience of time. The notion of equality has no meaning today except within the brief span of a human life".[10] This erasure of the future has brought with it a new harshness of life in the present. The here and now, with its limited horizons, has become an arena of conflict — a conflict all the more bitter in that there is no visible escape route.

In the United States, economists regularly talk about this breakdown in inter-generational cohesiveness. Two provisions of the social contract implicitly established after the Second World War are being shattered: the one that expected parents to assume responsibility for their children, and the one that, conversely, required society (the taxpayer) to ensure the well-being of the parents. "The elderly systematically vote against education levies when they have a chance. The elderly establish segregated restricted retirement communities for themselves where the young are not allowed to live so that they do not have to pay for schools. . . . More and more parents are not taking care of children, and the taxpayer is going to have to retreat from his promise to take care of the elderly".[11] Old-age pensions are evolving irresistibly towards a system in which *capitalization* replaces the concept of *sharing*, providing further proof of this destruction of inter-generational solidarity and even accelerating it.

So we are beginning to understand, today, that by renouncing this solidarity we are immobilizing a social mechanism whose usefulness went far beyond a simple sharing of income or buying-power. Already in 1900, Freud wondered what kind of future a society could possibly have when it was prepared to abrogate the natural passing on of the torch, from father to son — which is the only way for a society to achieve immortality. Plato himself saw this striving for immortality as the essential motor force of any human society.

But the economy is not the only domain in which this waning of the future as a *project* can be observed. Media time, which governs the so-called democracy of opinion — and also imposes its logic on politics itself — epitomizes this tyranny of the short-term. "Global time," writes Paul Virilio, "is a single present replacing the past and the future, which are linked at a speed limited only by that of light. We have put into effect a cosmological constant — three hundred thousand kilometers per second — representing the time of a history with no history, the time of a planetless planet, of an Earth reduced to the instantaneous and the ubiquitous, and of a time reduced to the present".[12]

When it comes to law, the most alert jurists have become alarmed by the appearance of "virtual time" — a time that is flexible, reversible, and subject to the instability of the present, a virtual time that, in their eyes, is more and more opposed to the "historical time" in which we once lived. But it is apparent that the "time-scale of the economy is not the time-scale of human rights. For there is one characteristic of virtual time that seems stubbornly incompatible with human rights, and that is the way norms have become reversible. This is what makes the employee's position so precarious in comparison with the flexibility enjoyed by the firm, at the risk of leaving management no escape from the impossible choice between a sense of instability that destroys confidence and a stifling absence of risk. But this reversibility negates the very idea of the continuous development of human rights".[13]

We could also mention technological time, which gets a little shorter every day as the world becomes more computerized, and which is sliding *out of our control*. So many decisions, calculations, message transmissions, research projects and exchanges are now executed in cyber-time, so quickly that they can no longer be controlled by human intelligence. A "response time" of nanoseconds mocks the inadequacies of our brain. Everywhere you look, the long-term is being discounted. The future is escaping us, slipping between our fingers, abandoning us like an old dream. We are made hostage to a threatening present — even in its most positive aspects: we must buy, consume, triumph, enjoy, all right now! This is the imperative that drives us on, from dawn to dusk. It torments us shamefully. We are no longer borne along by a vision of the future, but *carried away* by an imposed impatience.

Thus, what had already been a cause for concern to Max Weber and Walter Benjamin has been more than confirmed. "Men are torn schizophrenically between unrestrained activism in the service of values and myriad ways of worshipping material goods. They exist with a truly split state of mind which prevents them from thinking about what they are doing, and from experiencing temporality by questioning themselves about the past and the future".[14]

Historical time has been deconstructed. The future has become an old-fashioned notion.

Is Time Still Going Somewhere?

This disintegration of the future sets off a cascade of consequences. Paradoxically, liberal economists are the first to take alarm. The most immediate of the consequences is one that threatens the system itself. The historical dynamism of capitalism was indeed based on a certain conception of the long term that alone could justify investment and make acceptable the costly development of public infrastructures, and the equally costly expenditures on education. These "unprofitable" (in the short term) expenditures were generally undertaken by the public sector which, as the guarantor of the future, coordinated and even created, generation by generation, the conditions necessary for capitalism to succeed. But now the tyranny of the short term, the demand for instant profits, and widespread privatization are endangering this equilibrium. "In some profound sense, capitalistic values are also at war with capitalism. Capitalism will succeed or fail based on the investments that it makes, yet it preaches a theology of consumption".[15]

For example, speaking of the United States, Lester Thurow shows that public investment in infrastructure has fallen by half — in less then 25 years. The stock of public capital fell from 55 to 40 percent of GDP between 1986 and 1996. This lack of investment is all the more disastrous given that the new technologies — especially in the area of artificial intelligence — require enormous public investments over the very long term. But private labs — apart from those who hold a monopoly — have little interest in projects that do not show a profit in less than seven years. For Thurow the problem is simple: capitalism desperately needs something that its own internal logic does not see as necessary.[16]

Things are not so different in France, even if it lags a bit behind. "To steer the evolution of its economy in a timely way, and hold the course towards social progress," notes the economist Anton Brender, "France needs to hold permanently in its sights the image of the future it is creating with the investments it is making (or failing to make) and the decisions it is taking (or failing to take)".[17] And Brender deplores the backwardness of a Planning Commission whose "very name makes us smile" nowadays. And smile very eloquently.

The inevitable ageing of the population is the root cause of everything else, and what is most significant, in spite of all, is the way Western societies are dealing with that recent phenomenon. Most economic, financial, and political choices today are over-determined by the challenge of an ageing population, by the inversion of the proportion of working and non-working members of society, and by the prevalence of values determined by investment income and "gray power" — factors that are obviously not unrelated to the vanishing future. They have rendered demographic discussions ideologically explosive, so that sometimes an attempt is made to reduce them to a confrontation between an extreme Right that favors a higher birthrate, and a Malthusian Left.[18] In reality, it's not that simple. The downgrading of the future and the fall in the birthrate in all of the developed countries are both cause and effect. Even if other factors (such as individualism, or the standard of living) play a role, a society that loses its ability to project itself into the future also loses its demographic dynamism. Conversely, an ageing society will find it difficult to value a long-term view. It's a vicious circle. The trap is closing.

Without entering into these bitter disputes between demographers, it must be observed that, historically, periods of creativity and inventiveness have generally also been times of demographic growth. Fernand Braudel has traced a few of these rises and falls, an aspect of what he calls the "biological urging in its truest form", which "impelled mankind to reproduce, like every other living creature".[19] Alphonse Dupront too has provided a striking demonstration of the concomitance of the fundamental optimism of the Enlightenment and the demographic dynamism of the age. "France in the second half of the 18th century," he writes in his book on the Enlightenment, "witnessed a conscious biological surge in human reproduction. . . . This was a surge in vital energy — one that had been so long awaited that psychologically it inevitably grew and grew, like a luxuriant growth, or a newfound youth. There was, in this vital upsurge in being, a lyricism and an energy of life, and also a euphoric potency".[20] The Marquis de Mirabeau (father of the Mirabeau of French Revolution fame) was in ecstasy, in 1756, at this rediscovered optimism — an optimism all the more meaningful since the terrible ravages of the Black Plague in Marseilles, in 1709, were still recent memories. The title of his book, which has become well-known, speaks for itself: *L'Ami des hommes, ou traité de la population* (The Friend of Man, or, a Treatise on Population).

Certainly, there are numerous connections between a positive image of the future, faith in human progress, the demographic vitality of a society and its inventiveness. And, on the other hand, there are certainly "systemic" effects of a slackening of this optimism. We will merely remind the reader of the "commemorative syndrome" that affects us on a daily basis, and forcefully! Rarely have we lived with our eyes turned so vigorously towards the past: the anniversary of this, the bicentenary or tercentenary of that, memorial celebrations, posthumous settlings of accounts — all collective reflexes that show our inability to prefer the future over the past, our projects over our memories. Deprived of a future, we go on taking refuge in the consoling familiarity of the past. "Social nature abominates a void," remarks Marcel Gauchet. "Take away faith in the future, and what is left to guide the organization of social life? It is only natural for the past to come back".[21]

So, in the final analysis, the paradox of market and technological rationality (what Max Weber called *Zweckrationalität*) is completely summed up by a strange phenomenon: we make a profusion of individual "advances", particularly of a technical or scientific nature, while at the same time we mourn the demise of Progress in any real sense. This kind of rationality "goes on setting goals for itself, while it is radically lacking in any overall purpose (since it recognizes no 'value' apart from science or technology). How has Western man been forced in this way to desire a lack of meaning because of an excess of meaning? Herein lies the *incalculable*: the enigma of a rationality become an end in itself, and caught in the trap of its own power".[22]

We are right to suspect that this painful confusion in our relationship to the future is endangering something essential, deep within us. Can this threaten an immense period of history — and with it a whole civilization — with obliteration? Or with exhaustion? Emmanuel Lévinas reminds us soberly of this great fundamental expectation, the loss of which we may be helpless to prevent: "We had become accustomed to the idea that time was going somewhere".

Accustomed? Somewhere? And since when?

Remember The Future!

In the mid-1950s, the German philosopher and psychiatrist Karl Jaspers (1883-1969) speculated as to the origin and the rhythm of the history of ideas.[23] A representative of what has been called "Christian existentialism", he tried to identify the great historical turning points in human progress. This is how he defined an extraordinary "pivotal time" around the 7th century B.C., during which the great religious and philosophical traditions appeared: Confucius (551) and Lao Tzu (570) in China, Buddha (566) in India, Zoroaster (c. 650) in Persia, Homer (c. 800), Pythagoras (580) and Plato (428) in Greece, etc. For Jaspers, the *fundamental categories* that still allow us to think today were born at that time.

Of course it was during this same "pivotal time" that the great prophets of Judaism appeared in Palestine: Jeremiah, Isaiah, Jonas, Ezekiel, Daniel, etc.. Jeremiah, one of the most famous, was born around 650 B.C., while Judaism properly speaking came into being after the destruction of the first temple in Jerusalem by Nebuchadnezzar, in 587 B.C. This original form of Judaism indubitably bore the trace of earlier religious influences, mainly from Egypt and Iran (particularly where resurrection and angelology were concerned).[24] But it did nevertheless represent a "leap", a fundamental new departure in the interpretation of reality.

The unprecedented message transmitted by the Jewish prophets was in fundamental contradiction, in at least one respect, with the concept of the world that had heretofore been suggested by polytheist or "pagan" teachings: they had *a new perception of time*. Time, as envisaged by the prophets, was no longer curved, or cyclical. It was no longer subject to an "eternal return", but to expectancy and hope. It rejected both Greek "fate" and the Buddhist "life-cycle". This predominance of the future in the Jewish concept of the world was a consequence (among others) of the destruction of the Temple. Condemned to exile and diaspora, the Jews would no longer center their faith on the Temple, but on the Torah. The primordial question would become that of the future: how is it possible to remain Jewish somewhere other than on one's own "territory"? "The ancient religion of the Hebrews, with its attachment to its land and the Temple, organized around a sacrificial cult in the charge of a priestly caste — a religion quite similar, when all is said and done, to those practiced by the other peoples of the region — gave way to Judaism, i.e. to a de-territorialized and de-centralized religion, embodied in a Book, the only moorings of which would become memory and expectation".[25]

The Talmud, in the tractate *Shabbat* (156a), would express this messianic revolution in a single sentence: "For Israel, there is no Fate". In other words, man is no longer the prisoner of a Fate to which he could only submit, as he had been in Eastern religion and philosophy or Greek tragedy. Now he was in a state of expectancy, on the move, migrating towards the other slope of the world, and *towards the future*. In this, Judaism was the first religion to "await, with radical intensity, the transformation of the world". Shmuel Trigano, from whom I have borrowed those words, is right to add: "Hope is without any doubt the most precious gift Israel has made mankind".[26]

There is more. The power of the prophetic outlook, where hope is concerned, lies in the fact that it is rooted in the preservation of memory. Memory and hope are therefore related consubstantially. The prophetic outlook creates the "rectilinear time" that later would give Judeo-Christianity its conception of time. Again, we must quote Shmuel Trigano: "Consciousness (or quasi-consciousness) of the continuity of an age-old line of descent, plunging its roots into an immemorial and archaic past, reminds mankind of its 'origin', bears witness to the *reshit* ('beginning') of the Creation. This memory renews its 'sense of direction'. If mankind can learn from where it came, then it can discover where it is headed, and rid itself of the dross of cyclical time by which it might otherwise be dragged down. Thus, paradoxically, because it is descended from a line extending so far into the past, the Jewish people lights a flame of hope in History, a flame that illuminates the future and urges on the present to transcend itself".[27]

The fourth Hebrew commandment contains a word — *zachor* — which recalls, in a different way, the central place of expectancy in Judaism. Aside from some differences of opinion about its translation, it appears to mean not only "be mindful", but "be mindful of thy future", or "be mindful of the future" — a splendid formula, that Marc-Alain Ouaknin calls a "commandment to live Messianically, to face the future", adding: "'Choose life', such is the Torah's injunction (Deuteronomy Ch. 30). The *shabbat* is the desire and the possibility of building oneself towards the future, of entering into a dynamics to create the meaning of my life to come".[28]

In certain rabbinical commentaries, some claim to see in the Tetragram itself (YWVH) a combination of letters representing the verb "to be" in the third person singular: he has been, he is, he will be. This gives rise to the formulation of the expectancy God suggested to Moses and the Hebrews: "I will be what I will be" — a formulation that refers to "a specific form of the human experience of time", to adopt Stéphane Mosès's explanation: "On the level of their collective history, memory — i.e. the actualization of the past — seems to merge with hope, i.e. with anticipation of the future".[29]

Viewed in this way, hope is not simply expectancy, but also a desire to change a world it considers *incomplete*. Hope is "constructivist", as contemporary economists might say. The world must not be accepted as it is, because it is unjust, imperfect, or "bad", but rather must be perfected, in other words changed. This is indeed the original "subversion" — to quote the Protestant theologian Jacques Ellul[30] — from which everything else (equality, emancipation, liberty, etc.) would spring. This Messianic exhortation to reject "Fate" not only contradicts Greek beliefs but also, for instance, Buddhist detachment from the world, which has little use for our notions of salvation or of progress. "There is no such thing as despair in Buddhism; there is an absence of hope. You exist in the present and avoid projecting yourself into the future. A refusal to hope is the emptiness of *shunyata*. Emptiness is no cause for despair — on the contrary, it is freedom. An absence of hope brings freedom because you no longer have to be concerned about hoping for something, for you already have it".[31]

St. Paul And The "New Adam"

From an agnostic point of view, Jürgen Habermas showed an interest in this "voluntarist" trait of Judeo-Christianity, in his relatively recent book providing a critique of, and commentary on, Max Weber's classic typology. He inquired above all into its role in the genesis of modernity. For Weber, Judaism, and later Christianity, with their encouragement of an attitude of "world-mastery", have a much greater "potential for rationalization" than the Indian attitude or Buddhist detachment. He therefore proposes a typology of the great cultural traditions of mankind in the form of a table, classifying them on the basis of several binary oppositions: activity vs. passivity, rejection vs. affirmation of the world, mastery of the world vs. flight from it. It emerges, obviously, that Judeo-Christianity combines a rejection of the world, a preference for action, and a will to master reality. In other terms, the modern notions of transforming the world, of "linear time", and the concept of progress, have their principal origins in the religions of salvation.[32]

Greek philosophy, in this respect, is far removed from Judaism, and also from Christianity, although it has exchanged many elements with them. It is initially wisdom and (inactive) contemplation. This wisdom consists in accepting reality, in inhabiting the world with moderation and serenity. "I can only act", Epictetus would say in his famous *Manual*, on "what depends on me".[33] That should be the limit of my concern. The idea of rectilinear time, of a temporal arrow pointing to some kind of salvation or progress and justifying "tilling" the soil of the world in order to improve it, is foreign to him. "Aristotle," for instance, writes Paul Veyne, "believes in the eternity of the world, and, consequently, in the Eternal Return. He doesn't see it as the dealing of perpetually different 'hands' in a kind of cosmic poker game, in which the inevitable return of the same combinations, far from having a reason, merely confirms that there is nothing but random permutation (without any causal pattern). He sees it, more reassuringly, as a cyclical re-emergence of the same realities, which the truth of things allows to return. . . . We moderns no longer believe in cyclical time, but in evolution".[34]

Where linear time is concerned, Christianity would immediately inherit, and carry on, Jewish propheticism. It gave it universal application, spreading it over the entire globe. Later, Islam would adoptit as well: "It is from the well-spring of such a message that Christianity and Islam have derived the spiritual energy to make advances that stood the world on its head, and provided this expectancy with an exceptional sphere of activity".[35] Paul of Tarsus, the Jewish Pharisee converted on the road to Damascus, the Roman citizen steeped in Hellenism, would be the first to reformulate this eschatological faith (which the Greeks considered total rubbish) in the language of the New Testament. Using the Greeks' own words, he contrasted the "folly" of the Cross, as the true wisdom, to the vain teachings of the Gentiles (Corinthians 1:23). In Paul's Epistles, indeed, the focal point is outside this world: it lies ahead! We are *initiating* something beyond the order of things, such as all wisdom tells us to be necessary. The Greeks, on the *agora* of Athens, began to laugh when Paul spoke to them of the incredible New Adam, of a possible new humanity!"[36]

We must free ourselves of our present-day mental schemas if we want to understand what Paul's incredible announcement of a "New Adam" might have meant to the pagans whom he was setting out to evangelize in Asia Minor. It was a stupefying radicalization of the whole way philosophy was traditionally defined by ancient culture, i.e. as a "science of self-transformation". Now it was no longer a matter of transformation, but of a radical break and a rebirth. The individual acquired the possibility of rebirth through baptism, something that certain sober, austere pagans found shocking, foolish, and irresponsible.[37] Such is the core of the New Testament subversion, itself rooted in Jewish prophecy.

The expression "new man" that the Marxist revolutionaries were to reinvent — and bring into disrepute — nineteen centuries later — the "*table rase*" ("clean slate") of the *Internationale*, or Castro's *hombre nuevo*, etc. — was used for the first time (it is tempting to say "invented") by Saint Paul in the Epistle to the Colossians (3:11), which at the same time formulates the principle of equality.[38] "Do not lie to one another, seeing that you have put off the old nature with its practices and have put on the new nature, which is being renewed in knowledge after the image of its creator. Here there cannot be Greek and Jew, circumcised and uncircumcised, barbarian, Scythian, slave, or free man, but Christ is all, and in all." This notion of rebirth through baptism and divine grace would cause Emmanuel Kant to say that Christian conversion was *eternity breaking into time*.[39] It would be impossible to give a better description of the transformation of the cyclical time of paganism by Biblical propheticism, and its decisive orientation towards the pole of salvation, its rectilinear deployment towards a future determined by hope. "The present of the future is expectation," Saint Augustine would say in his *Confessions*.

All throughout the early centuries, through missteps, repetitions, innumerable heresies, persecutions, doctrinal disagreements, and interminable councils, the same subversion would continue on and on. Contrary to the desert fathers' flight from the world, there was an active and committed Christianity that rejected the violence, wars, and inequalities of the Roman Empire. For Saint Augustine, in the 5th century, it was the very principle of the Creation, implying a separation of God and the world — the "minus" that the creation represents — that made a transformation of the world conceivable. God is no longer here on earth, but in the beyond. It becomes possible to reject what "remains" (i.e. the kingdom on earth, the "world according to the flesh") and, above all, to improve it. It is the very imperfection of the world, the distance opened up between the world and God, that justifies the will to change it.[40] The original notion of perfectibility is a response to the imperfection of reality — an ideal that would become, as we know, an essential theme of the 18th-century Enlightenment.

As for the hypothesis of a spiritual rebirth, let us add for interest's sake that some people believe they have found traces of this even in the contemporary psychoanalytic experience. Such is the case of Marie Balmary, who writes: "One of the amazing things about our culture is that, just as the scientists specializing in the soul began to pay attention to symptoms instead of condemning them to silence, they discovered the imprisoned subject knocking from inside the Self, and once again found themselves on the path to a spiritual birth they didn't believe in".[41]

The Paradox Of The Enlightenment

Of course, it would be going too far to portray the philosophy of History and the modern concept of progress as direct consequences of New Testament expectation. All through the centuries, successive imbrications and complex branchings, with returns to pagan antiquity alternating with reaffirmations of priestly dogmatism (the entire story of the West!), were to confuse this line of descent considerably. This does not alter the fact that the distant roots in Judeo-Christianity are evident. "The philosophy of History has always been Christian," wrote the philosopher François Châtelet. "In its modern perspective, it dates from the 5th century. Indeed, the first book on the philosophy of History is Saint Augustine's *City of God*".[42]

Today, many writers insist particularly on the importance of the Exodus story as an inspiration for reform or liberation movements. This is in spite of the fact that some members of such movements claim to reject any kind of theological dimension. *Exodus* is a deliberate wrenching away from injustice; it depicts a departure, hope in action, liberation. The late Canadian critic Northrop Frye calls on numerous examples to demonstrate the durability of biblical references in most of the liberation movements that have appeared throughout Western history — including in those that denounced clerical influences on society, or the way Churches collaborated with temporal powers while continuing to proclaim their fidelity to New Testament teaching. The advocates of present-day liberation theology, which plays an active role in Latin America, are its distant heirs.

In this long journey of the Messianic spirit across the centuries, certain reformulations, particularly in the Middle Ages, were to play a role that has long been underestimated. For example, Charles Taylor, like Henri de Lubac before him,[43] stresses the importance of Joachim da Fiore in propagating what would be called "millenarianism". A 12th-century Italian mystic, former Cistercian and founder of the monastery of Corazzo, da Fiore was the author of a number of texts the influence of which would extend over several centuries, for instance his *The Agreement of the Old and New Testaments* and his *Commentary on the Apocalypse*. Da Fiore predicted that a new age would come, the age of the Holy Spirit, following the first two: the age of the Father (the time of the Old Testament) and the age of the Son. For him, this "new age" would be a superior stage of human life, one that would witness the triumph of spirituality.

In ferment throughout the entire European Middle Ages, and periodically revived by various sects and peasant revolts, this "subversion" would reemerge incessantly. "Millenarian expectations also played a role in the Reformation — in the revolt in Münster in the 1530s, for instance. They came again to the fore among certain of the participants in the English Civil War. The Fifth Monarchy men were defining themselves according to another biblical prophesy, from the Book of Daniel: the reign of God succeeds that of the world empires".[44]

This millenarianism would be the subject of philosophical elaborations or reformulations, particularly in Germany. Traces of it can be found in Schiller or Hölderlin and, of course, in Hegel (who in his youth, at the seminary in Tübingen, began training as a clergyman). For him, however, the triumph of History would not depend on a radical break or a dualistic confrontation between good and evil, nor even by a re-birth: it simply leads to a new, superior age. "Hegel incorporates the whole traditional scenario of Western millenarianism, but in a transposed, philosophical form. There are three ages of world history, the crisis of a heightened conflict at the entry of the new age (fortunately now behind us, in the form of the Revolution and its resulting wars) and the new, higher resolution".[45]

It is true that Hegel was not really an atheist. He devoted his early books to Christianity and his concern for rationality was still substantially permeated with mysticism. In his first two texts, *The Spirit of Christianity and its Destiny* and *The Positivity of the Christian Religion*, he stated that he would content himself with making a negative critique of Christianity. His intention was, he said, to "bring out its vital element". He was even convinced of the accuracy of the Gospel insights. "Not only does Hegel have no doubt about the rationality of the Christian God, it is, in a literal sense, the flesh and blood of the System".[46] Marx himself would admit as much, while asserting that the "rational kernel" had to be extracted from Hegel if he was to be of any assistance in effecting a transformation of social and economic reality.

We still have to recall, however briefly, one of the most embarrassing paradoxes of this history, the one that specifically concerns the Enlightenment. It is widely agreed that one aspect of this extraordinary epiphany in the 18th century, which laid the foundations of modernity, was its vigorous rejection of Christianity. What was being repudiated at the time was the age-old heteronomy that made man the prisoner of dogmas and beliefs handed down from on high. The principle of liberty and autonomy expressed by the Enlightenment philosophers — principles that still guide us — marked the end of the Christian era. Concretely, however, the Church, its priests and prelates, have been identified for two centuries now as the enemy that had to be overthrown — or persecuted. "Écrasons l'infâme!" — "Let us crush the infamous" — was Voltaire's cry.

As for Catholicism, it would remain mired for more than a century in its rejection of these "modern ideas", which, until Leo XIII's (1878-1903) endorsement of republicanism, it considered incompatible with Christian belief. Pius IX's *Syllabus* (1864) and the First Vatican Council (1869-70) were still war-machines aimed at "modernism". Under the circumstances, is it possible to consider the modern idea of progress to be simply a secularized version of Biblical salvation? Isn't there a certain audacity, incongruity — or stupidity — in seeing the Enlightenment as the continuation, or even fulfillment, of Judeo-Christian messianism? I don't think so.

From Salvation To Progress

In the first place, because to see it that way would be to confuse institutional Catholicism with the New Testament message, and revolutionary anticlericalism with a rejection of Christianity itself. It would also mean forgetting that the debate on this question — which is still in progress — began immediately after the French Revolution, whereas the Enlightenment philosophers, who were indeed anticlerical, liked to consider themselves deists or outright Christians, like Turgot, Fénelon, Newton or Malebranche. It is true that the men of the Revolution still shared the conviction that a nation cannot dispense with a common religion as "the mortar holding it together". Jean-Jacques Rousseau thought that "never was a State founded without religion as its base". This explains the revolutionaries' concern to re-found a religion (the worship of the Supreme Being) or, better yet, to initiate the Fête de la Fédération, the anniversary of the fall of the Bastille, by. . . a mass, celebrated by a member of the Constituent Assembly, with three hundred priests assisting! Even after 1785 and the complete break with Catholicism (including that of the constitutional Church), the revolutionaries "remained as convinced as in the first days of the Revolution that a State requires a religion, and that it is not overreaching itself in making a profession of faith: Robespierre introduced a Festival of the Supreme Being, in the course of which he set fire to a figure representing atheism, held to be anti-social".[47]

Clearly, things are not as simple as was claimed by the "religious" (and fanatically secularist) history of the Revolution, which had its hour of glory but was denounced by François Furet and Pierre Chaunu, among others. As for the famous Article 10 of the Declaration of the Rights of Man and of the Citizen, which is at the origin of secular republicanism, it does not call for a rejection of religion but rather for religious liberty, stating that "No one may be persecuted for his opinions, even religious ones". The separation of Church and State itself — and this is the greatest paradox of all — has even been seen as the (unrecognized!) child of New Testament teaching of the early centuries: "Christianity contained the seeds of freedom of conscience. In fact, by refusing (out of fidelity to their faith) to sacrifice to the cult of the Emperor, weren't the early Christians the first martyrs, the first witnesses? Some people at least have no hesitation in suggesting that the idea of the separation of Church and State is a Christian one . . . even if the Churches have taken so many centuries to recognize its inspiration".[48]

Actually, the thesis that the civic and egalitarian ideals of the Revolution were a fulfillment of Judeo-Christian values has often been voiced between 1789 and the present. Pierre Manent finds this thesis convincing, to some extent; he writes, "[it] had the merit of reconciling the 'sages' of the two parties in a shared affection — though of different coloration — for the 'new liberty', i.e. those who thought that the hour had come for humanity to attain its majority, and those who were still attached to the old religion. The former saw Christianity as the earliest expression of human liberty and equality, veiled by grace or trammeled by alienation, while the latter celebrated modern freedom as the final victory of the Gospel".[49]

Let us note, however, that apart from Condorcet, *progress* (in the secular and modern sense of the word) was mostly invoked by Christians like the Abbé Saint-Pierre or Turgot, the prior of the Sorbonne. This is not an insignificant detail. In England, the philosopher Joseph Priestly, who would become its most ardent theoretician, related it explicitly to Divine Providence. Of course, this interpretation of salvation is closer to the Pelagian[50] heresy than it is to orthodox Christianity, but didn't this heresy itself "express a permanent temptation rooted in the heart of Christianity"?[51]

It is hardly necessary to add that if secular involvement in the cause of progress took on an anti-religious guise in France, this was not the case in England or in the United States. There, the so-called theory of exceptionalism quite naturally saw a relationship between Biblical and Enlightenment ideas. The first campaign against slavery, for example, was partly initiated by William Wilberforce's movement for Christian renewal and the Clapham sect, which attempted to revive the "progressive" dynamism of evangelical Christianity.

Charles Taylor, a theoretician of multiculturalism to whom I am indebted for these few examples, seems to have had no question about this. The Enlightenment's Judeo-Christian inheritance is an accepted fact, and modern values are still derived from it to a greater or lesser extent. "But secular humanism," he writes, "also has its roots in Judeo-Christian faith; it arises from a mutation out of a form of that faith. The question can be asked, whether this is more than a matter of historical origin, whether it doesn't also reflect a continuing dependence. . . . My belief, baldly stated here, is that it does".[52]

In writing this, Taylor — like Marcel Gauchet in France — is following the example of Max Weber, who insisted on the religious roots of modernity, and on the "rationalizing potentialities of the transcendent religions". But it would not be quite honest to fail to note that several commentators, of a more secular turn of mind, insist, on the contrary, that modernity was able to flourish only because of a weakening, rather than a radicalization, of the Christian religion. H. R. Trevor-Roper, for example, attributes greater importance to the role played by the humanism of Erasmus.[53] However, I find this ongoing debate of limited interest. It concerns above all the speed and the process by which this transmutation of religious values into secular ones took place. In every case, the historical debt is beyond doubt. The interpretation of the Biblical revelation as a paradoxical process of moving away from the religious dimension (as is Gauchet's central thesis), has in any case much in common with Franz Rosenzweig's analyses; he characterizes monotheism as an anti-religion. "Revelation," he writes, "has only one function, which is to restore the world to its non-religious reality".[54]

An Idea Gone Mad?

So how about Marxism? Let us take two of the best known of Marx's sayings. In his *11th Thesis on Feuerbach*[55] he wrote: "Until now, philosophers have merely interpreted the world in different ways. The important thing is to change it". In the introduction to his doctoral thesis on *Differences in the Philosophy of Nature in Democritus and Epicurus* in 1841 (he was 23 at the time) he asserted: "Prometheus[56] is the first saint, the earliest martyr in the spiritual calendar". Doesn't that say it all? He proclaims the need to change the world at the same time that he celebrates the Promethean ambition to overcome the so-called destiny that condemns humanity to a "fate" decreed by the gods. The worldwide uprising Marx touched off in the 19th century looks very much like the product of a Judeo-Christian eschatology, but one that has been secularized and perverted.

So the paradox is maintained, and rendered more acute.

The ideology that developed at that particular time, one that would soon give birth to one of the two great totalitarian movements of the century, proclaimed itself from the outset to be steadfastly atheist. It denounced priestly oppression with combative rage, and saw religion as the "opium of the people". Dialectical materialism proclaimed its intention to put an end to such "fables" and liberate mankind from superstition. And this is indeed what it set out to do. In Leninist Russia, Christianity would be immediately marginalized and persecuted. Every effort would be made to eradicate it. In 1930, Kalinin, President of the USSR, launched the famous "five Godless years". This project, which was introduced with great fanfare, allowed five years to get rid of God, an archaic illusion viewed as obsolete by scientific socialism. So those five years saw the destruction of churches and convents, the deportation of priests, and the unleashing of a new wave of antireligious propaganda. Subsequently, all throughout its history and everywhere it triumphed, Communism, with murder and persecution as its arsenal, attacked religion in general and Christianity in particular.

But the extraordinary and senseless paradox is that, as far as its *promise* is concerned, the essential communist message was much closer to Judeo-Christianity than to any other philosophical tradition. It could even be said that it was a monstrous offshoot from it — its genetic copy. Even its rhetoric borrowed its slogans from Biblical propheticism: a "promising future", a "glorious tomorrow", etc. Early in the 1930s, one particularly attentive observer of the Soviet revolution, Adolf Hitler, was well aware of this. While paying an ambiguous tribute to Marxism, from which he said he had "learned a lot", and which he allowed had some "accurate and correct insights", Hitler reproached it for *its cousinship with Christianity and its 'Judeo-Talmudic' coloration.* For him, indeed, there was little to choose between Christianity and Judaism. "Forget the subtleties," he cried. "Whether it's the Old Testament or the New, or just Christ's words, as Houston Stewart Chamberlain would have it, it's all one and the same Jewish fraud".[57]

Judeo-Talmudic? Biblical? This inheritance, transmitted via Hegel, is obvious, at least in the Marxist desire to project itself into the future and work for a better world. In 1959 the historian François Fejtö spoke of this substitution in these terms: "In a Christian world in which Christian values seem swallowed up by rather sordid reality, Marx (like the utopians before him) founded a new hope for the future".[58]

Here we must point out a misconception. When its opponents liken Marxism to a secular religion, they generally stress the almost liturgical forms its power assumed: the supremacy of dogma, the scrupulous repression of any departure from orthodoxy, the pomp of its ceremonies, the devotion to its "commissar-priests", proletarian heroes and martyrs, etc.. Such comparisons are justified but anecdotal. They miss what is most important. Marxism sprang from Christianity, not in form but in content. In fact, when people quote the famous saying by Marx calling religion the "opium of the people", they generally forget to include the preceding two sentences, which put it in quite a different light. "Religious misery is at once an expression of real misery and a protest against real misery. Religion is the sighing of a creature at the end of its tether, the soul of a heartless world, just as it is the spirit of a state of things from which spirit is lacking. It is the opium of the people".[59]

Speaking as a philosopher in the 1980s, before the collapse of Communism, François Châtelet pointed out the nature of this relationship between Christianity and Marxism. According to him, Hegel's philosophy of History was explicitly Christian. "The World State, according to Hegel," he wrote, "the State of total transparency in which each can be free or not, as he pleases, is no more or less than the end of time according to the Apocalypse of St. John. It is the same thing". Marx, who developed a science (as opposed to a philosophy) of History, had attempted to break with this Augustinian and Christian tradition but was unable to do so, and Marxism in practice was even less able to do so. "The Marxism of today," Châtelet added, "which continues to promise us a radiant future, continues to work with categories that are quite simply no more than a secularized form of the Christian philosophy of history".[60]

Georges Bernanos simply saw Marxism — which he attacked — as a "Christian idea gone mad". This (heretical) folly consisted in a confusion of the principle of hope with that of necessity, and above all in using crime to further its ends. With the passage of time, it has become by no means absurd to assimilate Marxism to one or other of the innumerable heresies that have punctuated the history of Judeo-Christianity — with the proviso that we remember that some of these were both potent and active over several centuries. I am thinking in particular of Gnosticism and its thousand and one variations (Valentinian, Basilidian, the Perates, Orphites and Cainites, etc.), and its medieval successors, whether the Bulgarian Bogomils or the Albigensians of the south of France. The Gnostics, too, were convinced not only that theirs was the true faith, but also, like the Marxists, that they possessed true knowledge. I am thinking too of the uncompromising Manicheans of the early centuries with whom Saint Augustine did battle, having first been influenced by them in his youth. At the time, it is true, you could have counted several dozen such heresies. In 377, Epiphanius, Bishop of Constantia (Salamis) and author of the treatise *Panarion, or Medicine Chest against all Diseases* (i.e. heresies) listed more than eighty!

As just one Judeo-Christian heresy among others, Marxism only lasted, when all is said and done, for a little less than a century — not very long. Much less, for example, than Persian Manicheanism. For its contemporaries — us — this "brief" century of heresy, with all its crimes, lies and concentration camps, will have been quite enough, indeed, to discredit hope for the future.

Fate Makes A Comeback

These necessarily brief historical reminders help us to understand what is happening today to our attitude to time and to History. In the final analysis, the change turns out to be much more profound than we had thought. As we have seen, it has not been enough for disenchanted modernity to discard the promises of the future in order to exalt those of the present. Not only has it lost its heightened vision of the future, it has gradually renounced any attempt to deliberately influence the direction in which the world is heading. In other words, the progressive dismissal of politics, the replacement of democracy by the "market society", the refusal — or the inability — to give itself a purpose, all correspond, neither more nor less, to a *revival of the idea of Fate*, in the old meaning of the word. We seem quite prepared to let the world just drift along on the current, the way it used to do.

This is not a gratuitous hypothesis.

The British economist of Austrian origin, Friedrich von Hayek (1899-1992), Nobel Prize for Economics in 1974 and the high priest of economic liberalism, called the attempt to influence the course of things intentionally "constructivism" — something that, according to him, should be left for the market to regulate. He never spoke of this "constructivism" without a barb of irony, calling constructivists the kind of people who think they have the mental capacity to organize everything intellectually, contrary to their opponents, the liberals, who are aware that we are involved in a process that is part of a deciding mechanism beyond our control. It is significant that in the same lecture Hayek blamed Hegel for having been incapable of conceiving of an order not deliberately created by the human will.[61] As for John Maynard Keynes (1883-1946), Hayek's old rival from Cambridge days, he was an extreme example of "the kind of man who thinks our intelligence is enough to decide what is good and what is bad."

Hayek's expressions, and the content of his criticisms, paint a negative picture of what was to become economic liberalism's avowed temptation: the renunciation of any kind of voluntarism liable to upset the impeccable mechanism of the market. So the triumvirate of the market, technology, and the media — all three driven by a "runaway" logic — represents the new embodiment of a fatality we are unable to master, and to which we have no choice but to abandon ourselves with complete confidence. "The evolution of our societies under the impact of science and technology," writes the physicist Jean-Marc Lévy-Leblond, "largely escapes our desire to control it, and this will be a key problem for the coming decades".[62] This tendency is sometimes expressed in even more provocatively.

In the United States in the 1990s, several essays or political studies were published dealing explicitly with how a part of our history has gotten "out of control". This rather chilling expression was even the title chosen for a book by Zbigniew Brzezinski.[63] Underlying the imaginary world as it is reshaped by contemporary globalization is the abandonment of politics called for by certain Anglo-Saxon neo-liberals, who call it "opting out". Anthony Giddens, the British proponent of the famous "third way" mentioned above, considers indifference to politics — or the right to such indifference — a benefit of market democracy. Politics should no longer be anything more than mere everyday management.[64]

The subordination of political decision-making to the financial markets is part of the same renunciation. The term "automatic pilot" expresses the concept perfectly. As Lester Thurow points out, capitalism's theoretical answer is that there is almost no need for government or any other form or communal activities[65] — social institutions look after themselves. In France, neo-liberal politicians such as Alain Madelin like, with a real or feigned ingenuousness, to compare the "manual pilot" of politics to the "automatic pilot" of the market, while clearly indicating a preference for the latter. So the new anti-Utopia in the air nowadays is one under which our societies will be guided to an unknown destination by a non-human pilot — one who is supposed to protect humanity from itself, and free us for once and for all from any tiresome preoccupation with History. Some even go so far as to call this new flat, circular concept of time that is gradually replacing the democratic project a "reverse millenarianism". This is the expression used by the essayist and art critic Frederic Jameson. To him, the idea of the future no longer carries with it any notion of genuine innovation or voluntary progress: it is nothing more than a kind of indefinite repetition of the same thing. The only "novelties" accepted and desired are those of a technical or consumerist nature.

New Forms Of "Wisdom"

So we have moved beyond — far beyond — the modest malfunctions of the French Republic, the contraction of government, or the unfortunate "breakdowns in morals" that are usually brought up when we talk about our relationship to the future. Unawares, or almost so, we are threatened by something very different. Perhaps we are in the process, as Marcel Gauchet puts it, of "turning our back on the supreme democratic demand, which is for self-government". The gravity and probable truth of this suggestion give real meaning to the paradoxes assailing contemporary philosophy and ethics. Let me cite three of these, for the record.

First, let's turn to what François Chatelet called "cocktail-party Nietzscheism", i.e. the somewhat inane modern preoccupation with the self that glorifies the present moment, expects instant gratification, and asserts, rather pompously, its rejection of any purpose or belief. We all know a thousand examples of such self-serving litanies. The extraordinary thing about them is that they claim to be "subversive", or "audacious", when they are actually just going along with the times. Their pompous invocations of the eternal return and of cyclical time, their glorifying of pagan vitalism, are perfectly in accord with the neo-liberal ideology that hides behind them. This kind of Nietzscheism is to "revolt against society" what a show of patronage is to dramatic art — just ridiculous posturing, collaboration disguised as resistance, infantile silliness.

I find the new kinds of consoling "wisdom" offered to the public by philosophers that are prominent in the media nowadays a bit more respectable than that, but equally ambiguous. They're all really nothing but a modernized form of Stoicism or Epicureanism. They stress the joy of being alive, and the glory of the passing moment, which they prefer to an idealized future. So they urge each individual to work on being happy with a new moderation and a freely chosen virtue. None of these paths to wisdom deserve to be ridiculed or belittled, as they sometimes are. At least they have the advantage of providing a refuge, a temporary solution, and a way of escaping from a sense of desolation or nihilism. They also arise out of a (positive) reaction against the worrisome acceleration of the modern world's hurry to get nowhere — a paradoxical haste, for it no longer knows where it is going, but is heading there ever faster, like a frenzied, anguished, dehumanizing stampede. A reliance on the various schools of Greek or Eastern "wisdom" provides a legitimate outlet for the need for a pause, for some respite, for the immobility of day-to-day happiness. All the same, it is yet another reaction that seems to me all too much in tune with the times. Basically, it rejects the idea of purpose, and, of course, of hope for the future. Olivier Mongin is quite correct to write of André Comte-Sponville that his kind of "passion for the virtues excludes any hope, a virtue too political and messianic in its motivation. . . . This ethical attitude borrowed from Seneca is a respectable one, but it expresses an inability (or a refusal) to project oneself in time and turn towards the future, thus leaving little room for promise".[66]

The same thing could be said of the recent vogue for Buddhism, which, as is widely recognized, makes further inroads into Western society each year. Very worthy of respect, it constitutes a defense against the fading away of the future and the decline of democratic voluntarism. It enables the present to be tolerated, and expresses an aspiration for detachment, perceived as the ultimate way to completely regain a sense of freedom and inner peace. It is a noble objective, but at the same time a transparent symptom.

These three attitudes have one thing in common: they all lead to the renunciation of any attempt to influence, however slightly, the course of History or the state of the world. This is all well and good, but the cost of such a "sensible" renunciation is quite easy to measure. As the Hebrew Bible puts it, it means agreeing once and for all to leave the world to the realists and the rogues — who are often one and the same.

CHAPTER IV:
INEQUALITY BY DESIGN

"Our hopes for the future condition of the human race can be subsumed under three important headings: the abolition of inequality between nations, the progress of equality within each nation, and, finally, the true perfection of mankind".

Condorcet (*Esquisse d'un tableau historique des progrès de l'esprit humain*).

Immediately after World War II, at a time when a new social contract was being developed in Europe, as in America, based on a redistribution of wealth and on social cohesion, no one could have foreseen that inequality would make such a strong — and speedy! — comeback. At the time, competition with the Communist counter-model, the historical optimism of the early days of the liberation of Europe, and an entire century of accumulated struggles and social advances, all combined to make social injustice seem an anachronism on its way to the dustbin. The so-called fatality of human history was thought to have been forced into retreat, never to return. The aspiration for equality seemed to have been recognized and granted legitimacy by the community of nations, fresh from its triumph over Nazi barbarism. The celebrated Article 25 of the Universal Declaration of Human Rights, adopted in 1948, seemed to provide enough evidence of that fact: "Everyone has the right to a standard of living adequate for the health and well-being of himself and of his family. . .".[1] Economic growth and technological progress, it was thought, would be instrumental in consummating this victory of the democratic spirit. And this remained more or less so during the three long post-war decades, up to the middle of the 1970s. But later, this would all be undone.

Less than fifty years after the end of the war, the extraordinary resurgence of inequality came as an unforeseen phenomenon, and as a historical scandal, in the literal meaning of the term — a scandal that neither the various economic crises, nor the oil shortages, nor the globalization of the economy are enough to explain. For inequality and poverty have indeed reared their heads again among the richest nations. "The great upset in the balance of social forces," exclaimed Castoriadis shortly before his death, "has allowed a return to blind and brutal 'liberalism'. . . . We are witnessing the unbridled triumph of the capitalist imagination in its crudest forms".[2] André Gorz expresses the same conclusion when he writes: "By using temporary workers, capital is setting out to abolish practically all the limits that two centuries of the union movement had managed to impose on exploitation".[3]

The symptom is serious enough for us to attempt to minimize its effects as best we can. In the more or less consensual rhetoric that prevails nowadays, this new inequality is represented as an unfortunate drawback — an undesirable one, certainly, but secondary, and debatable. Moreover, people prefer to speak of it in the plural, referring to "inequalities" instead of "inequality". People convince themselves that these inequalities are the price that has to be paid for the tremendous economic transformation under way and from which, eventually, all will benefit. They are viewed as the temporary and tolerable cost of a reworking of the great neoliberal promise. The sacrifices required by global competition, the need for our economies to adapt to technological change, the new individualist logic — all this is surely enough to justify a few "drawbacks" in the area of social justice. People also manage somehow to convince themselves that these "drawbacks" mainly express a profound change in the notion of equality. This is usually described by somewhat sententious talk of "complexity". We must be realists, we must be modern, we are told over and over again. Things aren't as simple as they used to be. The old quantitative, social-democratic notion of equality has become obsolete as a concept and as an expectation. The term "equity" corresponds much better to reality, etc.. . . . These ideas are sometimes useful, at least in the case of the most rigorous thinkers; for example, the analyses of what he calls "complex equality" by Michael Walzer, one of the editors of the journal *Dissent*.[4] But most often, alas, this reference to complexity is no more than a way to avoid facing the problem.

Militant egalitarianism, obviously discredited by the way Communism used it, is no longer anything more than a sentimental attachment (as exemplified by Arlette Laguiller in France) or a populism better left to an extreme left — more a residue than an entity of any significance. Reasonable people, realists and "decision-makers" adopt a nonchalantly sympathetic attitude when confronted with such idealism. They have their feet more firmly on the ground! At best, when the topics of equality or redistribution of wealth are broached, they will admit some discussion of "social liberalism" — an expression that inevitably recalls the famous "elimination of poverty" so dear to Napoleon III and industrialists' wives in the 19th century.

Most of this rhetoric is obviously unacceptable, if not duplicitous. It beats around the bush and never gets to the heart of the problem. It diverts attention from the real problem to matters that are vague or of secondary importance. In reality, this re-emergence of inequality (in the singular, not plural) is not a mere side effect, nor a minor disadvantage. It is completely deliberate.

It is, by default, the objective of a market society that doesn't have many other objectives. It is taboo to mention it, and people don't discuss it. Beneath the appearance of modernity, it is retrograde. It is presented, at best, as a reasonable prerequisite for adapting to the new demands of the global economy, and under this guise it has gradually won vague, listless acceptance. Assisted by apathy and the herd instinct, the inegalitarian design can take advantage of a strange adaptation, which is based in turn on what we can only see as historical irresponsibility.[5]

Why irresponsibility? Because anyone who is unable to arrive at an accurate perception of the founding importance and historically exceptional character of a value that has been left, as if by an oversight, engraved on the front of town-halls in France, is definitely irresponsible — and foolish. This historically exceptional character of the demand for equality, and the eventful story of how it was won, help to explain why it is so fragile. Nothing is less natural; nothing is more foreign to most historical traditions, than the notion of equality. As a value, equality is all the more vulnerable in that it is splendidly voluntarist, improbable, and at the mercy of the slightest historical countercurrent. Its very newness and fragility are what allow equality to die as soon as people cease to demand it. It can never be taken for granted. The force of gravity pulls us in the opposite direction.

Is that a fragile idea? Is it new?

One Man Like Another

In the 1980s there was a philosophical disagreement on this matter between Léo Strauss, a great proponent of natural law,[6] and Luc Ferry, who at that time was writing about political philosophy. Ferry reproached Strauss with advocating a return to the Ancients and to Greek thought, in the context of his critique of modernity. For Ferry, such a desire to purely and simply reintroduce the mental categories of Antiquity into 20th-century modernity involved some extremely serious political risks. Most of the modern "rights of man" are actually concepts perfectly foreign to the mental universe of the ancient world, whether that of the Greeks or the Romans. In ancient thought, "there is obviously no room for what we nowadays call the 'rights of man'. As conceived by the Greeks — a conception that still survives in Roman law — the law could not be considered a norm of behavior — it was no more than a kind of social medicine, consisting in restoring order and putting everyone back in his proper place when the cosmic order was disturbed".[7]

Even more than the idea of individual autonomy, the desire for equality (in the contemporary sense of the word) was unknown to, or considered scandalous by, ancient philosophy. The idea that prevailed back then was a serenely discriminatory naturalism and elitism. This is an obvious truth that has often been overlooked whenever, in the history of the West, an attempt was made to return to Antiquity. From the Renaissance to the Napoleonic Empire, from 19th-century Nietzscheism to its less abrasive present-day form, various attempts to borrow from the Greco-Roman past have always committed this sin of omission. What was forgotten, each time, was this original inegalitarianism, the most obvious manifestation of which was the division into citizens and slaves, into free men and "barbarians". "If Greek citizens could be stockholders in a limited company called the 'polis', it is because there was productive labor-force, provided by people whom the Greeks, in their great majority, didn't consider human beings".[8]

But the inegalitarianism of the ancient world goes much farther than the emblematic question of slavery. We can read aphorisms or judgments written by Aristotle that are enough to make any man of modernity tremble with indignation — the statement, for instance, that "Feet are the one thing barbarians have in common with human beings". The rejection of the "other", of someone from "outside" the *polis*, or who was subjected to it as a slave, was fundamental to the philosophy of the time. This is why it is not always understood what was actually at stake in the celebrated "dispute" that took place in Valladolid, Spain, on April 16, 1550, in the chapel of the San Gregorio convent, when the question was discussed of whether the "savages" of the New World did or did not have a soul. Bartolomé de Las Casas, Bishop of Chiapas, who hotly argued the Indians' case, was opposed by the Spanish canon and philosopher Ginès de Sepulveda, who denied Indians the status of human beings. Of course Sepulveda mainly based his inegalitarian argument on Aristotle — whom he had not only read but also translated. The origin of the word "barbarian" itself, which is derived from the Greek *barbaros* (a foreigner), is an onomatopoeia imitating the animal-like babble of someone without any language.

This inegalitarianism, which is itself consistent with most of the more ancient philosophical traditions, whether Babylonian, Chinese, or Ancient Egyptian, is an integral part of Greek philosophy. In the education system, for example, the celebrated *paideia*, a term that designates instruction in philosophy, self-control, dominating the passions, and civility — was a deliberately elitist concept: "Only the sons of notables had the wealth and leisure to travel long distances from all over the Greek East to linger in the classrooms of a teacher such as Libanius, at Antioch, or Prohaeresius, at Athens. They emerged from an expensive and intellectually taxing experience with no mean opinion of themselves: they were convinced that the 'square-set soundness of [their] speech and its polished brilliance produced by skill' made them as superior to the uneducated as human beings were superior to mere cattle. The *paideia* was a means of expressing social distance".[9]

The true birth of the concept of equality is inseparable from the advent of monotheism, which quite simply made it *thinkable*. Here is where, once more, we can locate the great ontological transformation. It was in reference to a single God that the *sameness* of the human beings living all over the world could be perceived. Lévinas put this very well when he wrote: "Monotheism is not an arithmetic of the divine. It is the (perhaps supernatural) gift of seeing that one man is like another beneath the diversity of historical traditions carried on by each of them".[10] Where the Christianity of the first centuries is concerned, it is of course customary to quote St. Paul's famous Epistle to the Galatians (3:28), which provides an explicit basis for this egalitarian revolution, so disquieting for Roman functionaries and Athenian philosophers. "There is neither Jew nor Greek, there is neither slave nor free, there is neither male nor female, for you are all one in Christ Jesus". Paul declares the same thing in other Epistles, in slightly different words. For instance: "Here there cannot be Greek and Jew, circumcised and uncircumcised, barbarian, Scythian, slave, free man, but Christ is all, and in all." (Colossians 3:11).

Actually, this idea of the equal value of every human being before a single God runs contrary to the hierarchical conception of a world with meticulously differentiated "natural" categories, which was how pagans conceived it at that time. The affirmation of equality was literally revolutionary. The best way to create awareness of this is surely not to accumulate texts and quotes (from St. Paul to John Chrysostom, from the Gospel to the Torah) as is usually done. Any quotation can usually be contradicted by another, and you end up going in circles. A much more convincing approach is to take the opposite tack, and consider the kind of criticisms aimed at Judeo-Christianity during the first centuries by its most steadfast opponents. This negative image is more eloquent. It is easy to see that many pagan pamphleteers classified egalitarianism as one of the "follies" spread by the people of the Book — follies that had to be denounced, of course.

One of the most widely read and commented on among these militant pagans is called Porphyros of Tyre (*Porphurios* in Greek). A great neo-Platonic philosopher of the third century and a disciple of Plotinus, he wrote — in addition to a text on abstaining from food — several tracts against Christianity, including the celebrated *Against the Christians*. Porphyros, a good Hellene, attacked Christianity for its irrationality and for its scandalous "novelty", but also for what we could call its egalitarian demagoguery, careless of the natural order. A century earlier, another neo-Platonist, Celsus, expressed the same criticisms of the Christians, but also of the Jews, in his *On the true doctrine* — criticisms that Nietzsche would unobtrusively take over.[11] As for Plotinus, he was filled with disdain for the poor and the oppressed — "that stinking morass" — who, he thought, were probably doing penance for some sin committed in an earlier existence. In the same way, the Emperor Julian (331-363), called "the Apostate" after renouncing his Christian beliefs, wrote several texts and pamphlets in which he attacked Christianity. He would even try, during his two-year reign, to eradicate it from the Roman Empire. In his treatise *Against the Galileans*, Julian denounced the barbarian origins of Christianity, a religion he called an "intellectual sickness". He was also alarmed at the egalitarian pretension of this so-called revealed religion: "Julian particularly stresses the danger of this egalitarian doctrine from a social point of view. He also criticizes the apostles, held to be ignorant, and the Christians of his time: monasticism and the cult of the martyrs were particularly repugnant to him".[12]

The hostility towards monasticism that became a leitmotif of such writings is revealing. It was usually inspired by an outraged elitism. What! People were supposed to revere and admire these ignoramuses, who had had no education and had not undergone any kind of *paideia*! How could they be allowed to take the place of the wise, who had earned their rank after lengthy training, and to teach "the truth of Christ"? For the Greek or Roman philosophers — whom we would call intellectuals, today — "the rise to prominence of the Christian monks was a warning signal. It announced wider changes in late Roman culture and society. The notables had based their authority on a monopoly of highly formalized codes of speech [to which the monks were now paying no attention.] They could utter the *gros mots* that broke the spell of *paideia*". Such egalitarianism seemed foolish, and prejudicial to the order of things. "We are dealing with what might be called a Christian populism, that flouted the culture of the governing classes and claimed to have brought, instead, simple words, endowed with divine authority, to the masses of the Empire".[13]

Peter Brown, the great specialist on late Antiquity (from whom I have taken the preceding quotes), insists on the effort required for the modern imagination, steeped as it is in centuries of Christian language, to appreciate the radical novelty of this implausibly egalitarian vision of human beings, erasing all differences, subjecting all to the same universal law. And this vision was all the more shocking in that it was applied to everyday existence, and most ostentatiously so. The liturgy of the first centuries, for example, insisted "scandalously" on the equal respect owing to both the poor and the powerful. When a rich man entered a church, the bishop was under no circumstances supposed to rise to welcome him. On the other hand, if a poor man or a destitute stranger should come in, what the deacon should say was: "Do thou, o bishop, with all thy heart provide a place for them, even if thou hast to sit upon the ground". These rulings, "first written before the Great Persecution, continued to be operative for many centuries in Syria. They provide a glimpse of the workaday moral and social horizons within which most Christians of the age of Constantine were content to live".[14]

Actually, in the initial message things are quite clear, for the New Testament sides with the poor against the rich. The poor are blessed; the rich are damned! Some Jewish prophets said precisely the same thing. Isaiah, for example: "Woe to those who join house to house, who add field to field, until there is no more room". The Judeo-Christianity of the first centuries (particularly in Syria) was characterized by the way it distanced itself from the rich and from wealth. In the Epistle of James or Matthew's Gospel there are references to the "little ones" who were to be given particular respect.

In the writings of certain Fathers of the Church, this eminent — and completely novel — dignity of the poor would be forcefully reaffirmed. This was true of St. Jerome, who proclaimed: "He whom we despise, whose presence we cannot suffer, the mere sight of whom makes us vomit, is like unto us, made absolutely of the same clay as us, composed of the same elements. Whatever he suffers, we also can suffer" (Letter 77, 6). The same can be said of the flamboyant Bishop of Antioch, John Chrysostom (347-407), a passionate orator and ascetic who constantly provoked the wrath of the powerful by giving precedence to the poor and, for instance, by housing a leper colony close to an elegant neighborhood of Antioch.

Concern For The Poor, A Godsend For The Rich

But once we have reminded ourselves of this, it would be inaccurate to describe the Catholicism that followed as a resolute, faithful defender of the destitute. Far from it, indeed! In orthodox Christianity as it gradually developed in the second and third centuries — particularly after the conversion of the Emperor Constantine in 312 — things were already becoming less clear-cut. "The post-Pauline Christianity of the Acts of the Apostles and of the pastoral Epistles is rooted in the Hellenistic and pagan society of the Empire, characterized as much by its social stratification as by its syncretism and personal mobility. The point of view adopted by Christianity was that of the local elites: rich, influential or cultured people are directly or indirectly named, addressed or, in the Acts, held up as examples."[15]

For the adherents of Gospel "subversion" and for later millenarians or modern liberation theologians, *that is when Christianity's betrayal of its initial promise began.* Christianity, on becoming the official religion, lost no time in reaching a compromise with realism, with reasons of State, and in establishing a bond with the temporal powers — with powerful people, in other words — for centuries to come. From the 4th century on, in the Roman Empire, a prosperous, self-assured upper class embraced the Christian order and endowed it with aristocratic distinction. In 5th-century Gaul, this take-over was even more evident. "The landed aristocracy of Gaul (many of whose grandfathers had been pagans) took over the government of the Church. Of all the experiments in leadership that characterized this fluid century, the 'aristocratization' of the Church in Gaul was the most enduring. It placed the cities in the hands of men accustomed to exercising power in the Roman manner".[16]

More serious, the biblical theme of love for the poor was used by certain bishops coming from the ranks of the ruling classes to establish their power in opposition to the Roman authorities. A mystical bond was supposed to unite the bishop to the ragged flock that escorted him, comprising what St. John Chrysostom called "the other City". The needy provided a constituency for these new notables. Demagoguery was only a step away. In contrast to the vow of poverty of the earliest Christian communities, there came into being an Episcopal splendor arrayed with all the magnificence and majesty of imperial power, at the same time proclaiming its love for the poor. Its ostentation was sometimes great enough to provoke denunciation, traces of which have been preserved. "Lithomania" (the "itch to build" in stone and erect large buildings) became a permanent temptation. For example, Theophilus of Alexandria was accused of having squandered money intended for the poor on the construction of grandiose churches. "The complaint that the food of the poor was eaten up by stone, by multicolored marble and gold mosaics of new basilicas, ran all around the Mediterranean in this generation".[17]

The Church — too magnificent, too accommodating, and too rich! The reproach would indeed echo throughout centuries of Christianity. It would constantly be repeated by dissident theologians, independent thinkers, and great religious teachers. It would not be unrelated, as we know, to the schism of the 16th-century Reformation and the birth of Protestantism. And indeed these independent minds had good reason for their wrath. Cases are cited of bishops in 6th-century Merovingian Gaul who were endowed with enormous personal wealth and who presided over the construction of "great gold-encased, bejeweled shrines". One of them, Bishop Bertram of Le Mans, owned private estates totaling some 300,000 hectares (120,000 acres), scattered over all of Gaul.[18]

This compromising of the Gospel message with secular power and riches gave rise to a massive religious dispute that, century after century, would remain a constant in Western history. The latter, as we know, would be punctuated by revolts and tensions, by theological revolt, by reforms and more or less dishonorable renewals of support for the powerful. So, even within Christianity — and starting before the Reformation — the question of equality was debated. It was a virulent debate that would have no end. It was provoked in particular by a fundamental question that would also drive a wedge between the theoreticians of liberalism in the 18th century and that is still relevant at our turn of the century — namely, whether the poverty of some is the result of injustice or, on the contrary, is a merited sanction for a deficiency (laziness, lack of foresight, drunkenness, etc.). And should the wealth of others be condemned as an unjust appropriation, or is it deserved, as the fruit of industry or the reward for a specific talent?

The answers to these two questions, which represent two different conceptions of equality, would periodically inflame Christianity. "In every century," writes Jacques Ellul, "there have been Christians who discovered the simple Biblical truth [concerning equality], whether intellectually, mystically, or socially. They include some great and famous names, for example, Tertullian (at first), Fra Dolcino, Francis of Assisi, Wycliff, Luther (except of course from his dual error of putting power back in the hands of the princes and supporting the massacre of the rebellious peasants), Lamennais, John Bost, Charles de Foucault".[19]

It was particularly in the 11th and 12th centuries, long before the Protestant Reformation of which Ellul is a scion, that a doctrinal about-turn took place where equality was concerned. The very extent of this change of direction shows in a negative way what official Christianity had become during the preceding periods. At the time, significant attention was once more given to the poor, called the *pauperes Christi* (Christ's poor), to whom a dignity was restored that they had largely lost in Merovingian and Carolingian Europe. In the 12th century, when a "white mantle of churches clothed the Christian world", to borrow the famous expression of the chronicler Raoul Glaber in his *Historiarum sui Temporis*, the mendicant orders became more numerous, particularly under the influence of Francis of Assisi. The medieval imagination restored the importance of these *pauperes Dei*, seeing them once more as God's favorites, as those whose prayers would most easily be heard, and who, as such, were welcome at the bedside of the deceased.

"This mystical predilection for poverty is a new fact in the history of Western spirituality. Until the 11th century, indeed, indigence had been considered a punishment rather than a characteristic of the elect. People tended to see it as a punishment for sin and, on the social level, as an affliction as unavoidable as sickness, something almost impossible to rectify. Wealth, on the other hand, was considered a proof of divine favor".[20]

Jacques Ellul, who teaches the history of institutions and is a specialist in the crises of the 14th and 15th centuries, reminds us in the study just quoted that in most of the peasant revolts that preceded the Renaissance ordinary priests marched side by side with their parishioners, and often headed the uprisings. This was unfortunately not the case for the clerical hierarchy which, as a body, long continued to side with those in power and with the wealthy. As a dissident theologian, Ellul criticizes this renunciation of the Gospel message in the harshest terms. "All the Churches showed scrupulous respect for, and often supported, the State authorities, making conformism a major virtue, tolerating social injustice and the exploitation of man by his fellows, explaining to one group that it was God's will that there be masters and servants, and to the other that socioeconomic success was the outward sign of God's blessing!"[21]

In the 17th century, from his bishop's throne, Bossuet (1627-1704) would thunder against this neglect of the poor, something he considered incompatible with the Bible's revelation. Such is the meaning of the famous sermon against the "sinful rich", in which the Bishop of Meaux declares: "He truly understands the mystery of charity who considers the poor to be the first-born of the Church, and who, honoring this rank, believes it his duty to serve them, and who does not hope to share in the blessings of the Gospel except it be through charity and brotherly communion".[22]

The Bourgeois Mentality And Inequality

From the perspective of the Enlightenment and the Revolution, the equality called for by the *philosophes* clearly had its source in the New Testament message, even though they were also taking up arms against the clerical establishment. This attitude is consistent with the logic of History. In this passing on of the torch from Judeo-Christianity to modernity, the capital role played by certain founding thinkers, from Emmanuel Kant to Baruch Spinoza or from Desiderius Erasmus to the Jewish philosopher Moses Mendelssohn, is well recognized. To these prestigious names we must add that of Francis Bacon, an English philosopher of the 16th century, who, to quote Charles Taylor, "still expressed himself in Christian terms".[23] In his *Essays on Politics and Morals*, Bacon (1597-1624) stressed the need for practical benevolence, generosity towards the most destitute, and the role of science in relieving "the condition of mankind".[24]

For the French *philosophes* of the Encyclopedia, equality had become a secularized value and an incontestable ideal, in principle at least. "Our hopes for the future condition of the human race can be summed up under these three important headings: the destruction of inequality between nations, the progress of equality among a single people, and, finally, the real perfection of mankind".

Rather curiously, however, the men of the Enlightenment, while struggling for greater equality among men, found it difficult to renounce the practice of elitism, itself inherited from the feudal and aristocratic past. Contempt for everything vulgar, disdain for the masses and horror of the common people were reflexes that remained stubbornly ingrained in the elites of the 17th and 18th centuries. And even thinkers we admire today expressed themselves in a way the most reactionary of our present-day politicians wouldn't dare to do. Where public opinion is concerned, Condorcet stigmatized "popular opinion, which is still that of the stupidest and most impoverished part". Diderot stated that one should be wary of "the judgment of the ignorant and stupid multitude in matters of reasoning and philosophy, for its voice is that of viciousness, foolishness, inhumanity, madness and prejudice". Pierre Charron expressed himself even more strongly:

"The common people are an untamed beast. Every thought they have is pure vanity; everything they say is false and erroneous; whatever they disapprove of is good; whatever they approve of is bad; whatever they praise is odious; whatever they do and undertake is mere folly".[25]

How fragile is this idea of equality! The 19th century, which was to witness the rise of nationalism, the hardships of the industrial revolution, the restoration of monarchies and empires, and the rigid counter-revolutionary stance of the Catholic Church, offers cruel proof of this. The inegalitarian urgings of the counter-revolution largely gained the upper hand — those that derived, for instance, from the social philosophy of an Edmund Burke in the preceding century. The author of *Reflections on the Revolution in France* did not hesitate to suggest that when we pretend to take pity on the poor, on those who are obliged to work (otherwise, the world could not survive) we are trifling with the human condition.

In the Anglo-Saxon countries, a number of measures intended to bring about a redistribution of wealth, such as the Poor Laws in Britain, were reconsidered and reformed in 1834. The economists or sociologists of the time — from David Ricardo to Robert Malthus, Thomas Huxley or Herbert Spencer — tended to view assistance for the poor, or egalitarianism, as undermining the principle of natural selection. Each of them expressed this in unambiguous terms: we must resign ourselves to the existence of the poor and of poverty, without any attempt to relieve them. The large number of people living in poverty in 18th-century English society made a considerable impression on Robert Malthus, an Anglican clergyman (the "dismal Parson"). In *An Essay on the Principle of Population*, published anonymously in 1798, he favored limiting the birthrate, but, above all, thanked God for sparing the wealthy this excessive number of births.

Herbert Spencer (1820-1903), a great admirer of Darwin, applied the latter's theory of evolution to the social domain and became the true founder of an uncompromising "social Darwinism". For Spencer, merciless competition and the survival of the fittest were concepts as legitimate in economics as in biology. Assistance for the most destitute and egalitarian redistribution of wealth was therefore devoid of any justification. Spencer's work had a lasting influence in the Anglo-Saxon countries, one that at times would go far beyond their author's intentions — as when, for instance, they were used to justify racism and imperialism. The anti-egalitarian visions of Spencer, Malthus, Darwin, Ricardo or Jean-Baptiste

Say were perfectly attuned to the general climate of the industrial revolution and, simultaneously, of colonial expansion.

It was during this period, in any case, that in Europe the Roman Catholic Church gave its most scandalous support to this inegalitarian vision of society and the world, so that it is by no means over-reaching to include in this definition the reframing of the Catholic faith around an "ecclesiasticism based on Papal authority and obedience to Rome". This substantially reactionary ecclesiasticism would lead to what is called "ultramontanism", a system centered on the Vatican, and that held itself up as a total vision of world order, if not an "ideology". It is an understatement to say that this ideology was regressive so far as New Testament values were concerned, as least in the way these were interpreted by St. Francis of Assisi or St. Vincent de Paul. It was completely at odds with "Biblical subversion". For the ultramontanists of the 19th century, "inequality among men was a given of nature reflecting Divine providence, for if they are all equal before God as far as their spiritual destiny is concerned and are all called upon to save their souls, here below, on earth, they are necessarily different one from another, and unequal, because they were put on earth to perform different functions, and functions of unequal importance. . . . To work for individual equality therefore would be to go against God's will".[26]

This acceptance of inequality between men as the result of divine will went together, of course, with an acceptance of hierarchy, obedience, and respect for authority. Society was perceived as an organic whole, something like a living body, with each different part devoted to a specific task.

An entire volume would be required to describe in greater detail the triumphed, in the 19th century, of an inegalitarian mind-set that Michel Foucault would call "l'esprit bourgeois". This "bourgeois mentality" achieved even greater dominance by reinterpreting the Christian tradition in a moralistic and authoritarian direction, with the paradoxical support of the Vatican, which was extremely loath to accept republicanism, democracy, and modernity in general. This swing of the ideological pendulum back to the right, this great political and moral shift, was particularly spectacular in the case of equality. Is inequality not, ontologically, at the very roots of capitalism? Fernand Braudel discussed this idea at length, stressing, for example, the importance of geographical inequalities in the development of the capitalist economy. "After all, Western Europe transferred — while virtually reinventing it — the ancient practice of slavery to the New World, and 'induced' the revival of serfdom in Eastern Europe as a consequence of economic imperatives. This lends weight to Immanuel Wallerstein's assertion that capitalism is a creation of world inequality".[27]

It was against the callousness of this "bourgeois mentality" and virulent anti-egalitarianism that early theoreticians took a stand, from Jean-Charles-Léonard de Sismondi (1773-1842) to Jules Guesde (1845-1922), Karl Marx (1818-1883) and Joseph Proudhon (1869-1865). And let us note that, in denouncing the "scientific" arrogance of the economic discourse of liberal theoreticians in the 19th century, Sismondi formulated some stinging criticisms that could be repeated today in almost identical words. "To our regret," he wrote, "we perceive political economy in England adopting a language that grows more sententious day by day, enveloping itself in calculations more difficult to follow, losing itself in abstractions, and becoming, in a way, an occult science, at the very time when suffering humanity most needs this science to speak the language of the people, to devote itself proportionately to the needs of all, to move closer to common sense, and finally come to grips with reality".

The burden of anti-egalitarianism and the urgent need to resist it would in any case overshadow the entire history of the 20th century. However brief, this reminder allows us to better understand what is happening today: a massive revival and an unforeseen revival of themes, ideas, theories, logic, metaphors and so-called certitudes that are a throwback to the 19th century. "The neoliberalism of the 1990s alone," writes Castoriadis once more, "has been able to push aside the few means of control that 150 years of political, social and ideological struggle had managed to impose on it. The anomic dominance enjoyed by the predatory barons of industry and finance in the United States at the end of the last century offered no more than a pale precedent for that".[28]

Identity vs. Equality

We must first agree on the meaning of our terms. A pernicious ambiguity is at work where equality is concerned, blurring our perception of reality and distorting most political discussion. Our times have indeed become more demanding than others as far as what we might call "identity equality" is concerned. Never have people fought so much, demanded so much, written and debated so much as they have done with respect to this type of equality. For current opinion — and this is indubitably a forward step — a certain kind of age-old inequality has become unacceptable today: the inequality of Black and White, native-born and immigrant, male and female, heterosexual and homosexual, legitimate and illegitimate offspring, the healthy and the handicapped, citizen and illegal immigrant, provincial and Parisian, and so on.

So an invisible revolution has taken place that — for the better — has made some things intolerable that were more or less tolerated only yesterday. This is a radical and probably irreversible transformation. Every day a demand for equality is being voiced, a demand that is happily echoed by received opinion and "political correctness" on both the Left and the Right. There is a fairly general acceptance that we should not ostracize a specific category of men or women, that we can express a new respect by changing our language (saying "visually impaired" for "blind", "person of small stature" for "dwarf", etc.), and it would be absurd to underestimate its impact. Marcel Gauchet is quite right to speak, in this respect, of the spectacular emergence of an "egalitarian individualism, in which equality is understood as likeness of being". For him, this identity-based individualism — by which is meant the right for each and every one to finally express (and live) his or her *difference* — is a function of a certain meaning of equality that is perhaps more far-reaching than the traditional one. "It corresponds," he goes on, "to a new face of equality". It would be absurd to deny or even underestimate the contribution made by this contemporary form of individualism — the possibility granted all to be free of the old hierarchies or categories, of which earlier aspirations to equality failed to take sufficient account. These affirmations of identity are a timely reminder that not everything can be reduced to a narrow and quantifiable socio-economic equality.

So far, so good.

The problem is, however, that this egalitarian intransigence over matters of identity, status, or "difference", is accompanied by an incredible indifference towards economic inequality. The desperate quest for identity equality creates a smokescreen, masking the resurgence of flagrant quantitative injustice. Taking it a step further, we might say that our age is ready to take up arms against the slightest hint of discrimination between a heterosexual and a homosexual, but no longer cares about the inequalities, however serious, between two homosexuals who are at the same time hourly workers, managers, or unemployed, etc.. The new cultural sensitivity is helping to anesthetize the old one. "Political correctness" unintentionally allows other iniquities to grow. All the problems arising in the relationship between the moral and the social Lefts (in Europe as in the United States) follows from this paradox.

Even more troubling is the definite correlation between the explosion of this kind of individualism and the increase in social disparities. This is no mere rhetorical debate. The correlation has been demonstrated by a number of economists belonging to the so-called "regulation" school, whether Robert Boyer, Michel Aglietta or even Jean-Paul Fitoussi. What exactly is going on? It is a rather perverse socio-political process, but one that is easy to understand. Individualist values, which have become all-powerful since the end of the 1960s, are helping to make democracy more and more ungovernable. They brought on the post-war crisis in the Fordist model, accelerated the shrinking of government, devalued the concept of a "common good", and gradually undermined the regulating capacity of the political in the economic and social fields. This global weakening of the political, torn between the corporatism and self-seeking of interest groups, continuously opens the way to the market, free competition, and the law of the strongest.[29]

The primary result of this weakening of the "common good" for the benefit of the individual is thus actually to the detriment of the latter — and harshly so. What an irony of progress, what cunning of History! The individual triumphs, but is less protected; he is exalted more than ever before, but also much more exploited; he is basically freed from cultural discrimination, but at the mercy of market mechanisms. This dysfunction of democratic control produces a result desired by no one. It penalizes the poorest, the least fit, and the least competitive. In this way, an extreme schizophrenia is reversed as the individual loses in social terms what he had demanded and obtained in terms of identity equality. He is more fully recognized in his "difference" but he is exploited much more in his daily life; more readily accepted for who he is, but living a more precarious material existence: who wouldn't see this as a fool's bargain?[30]

The perverse nature of this mechanism has further consequences. Because they are becoming ungovernable, and because social cohesiveness has been undermined by an "every man for himself" attitude, our democracies have feebly capitulated to the external constraints we are told about all the time. We would say, contrary to prevailing opinion, that globalization as an ideology is not the *cause* but a *consequence* of the inegalitarian design.[31] The ritual invocations of the "requirements" of international free trade, the litany about reducing budget deficits and the sacrifices this requires, the obsession with external demands, have all taken the place of the former checks and balances of a social contract which the political is no longer in a position to uphold. Disciplinary imperatives from without are called upon to compensate for the inadequacy of democratic control. In many respects, the result is catastrophic. "Monetary discipline and free trade have made up for the breakdown of political and cultural controls. . . . So, the triumph of inequality has come about, particularly in France, under the cover of a discourse denouncing it."[32]

When The Poor Get Poorer

The triumph of inequality? We have to measure the phenomenon in a global, stupidly quantitative, measurable, mathematical way above all. To do so, it is better to forget the usual arguments — like those consisting in a comparison of the different "models" of capitalism. I am referring here to the everlasting arguments about the respective merits of European and American forms of economic liberalism. It is obvious that the American model — with its spectacular dynamism — is infinitely more successful than its European equivalent where job-creation is concerned. Unemployment has already been reduced in the U.S., while it is still massive in Europe. However, it is no less evident that, as far as the social safety net and help for the impoverished are concerned, the European model is superior.

However, for anyone interested in the general aggravation of inequality, these arguments don't mean a great deal. The fundamental trend is the same on both sides of the Atlantic: inequality is coming back in full force. As for the debate between full employment without social assistance (as in the United States) or massive unemployment with a safety net (as in Europe), it merely serves to illustrate two ways of distributing the same overall inequality. "If we submit to the powerful forms of economic dynamism that are at work today bringing about growing inequality in the rich countries, the only choice left to us is which kind of inequality we want to have".[33]

It's true that this is no innocuous political choice, nor is it without

consequences. One may well consider, for example, that the "European option" (of unemployment) is the more pernicious of the two in terms of social dislocation, of marginalization, and loss of hope. Mass unemployment
is indeed accompanied by disastrous systemic consequences. It spreads a
fatal poison throughout the whole social body; it is transmitted from one
generation to the next; it has created an atmosphere of disillusionment and
violence, etc.. But on the other hand, it is possible to think that the
"American option" of full employment at any cost, and of maximal insecurity, is even more barbarous. It means tolerating a kind of harshness in social relations that Europeans find shocking. It's all a matter of political sensitivity and cultural tradition. One thing is certain, however: that the
groundswell, the massive resurgence of inequality, is the same in both
cases.

To confirm this, we can look at the corroborating descriptions of the
inegalitarian process by two economists, one of them French, the other
American. For Pierre-Nöel Giraud, this development is so far-reaching that
it has to be seen as the culmination of a very large historical cycle that
seems to have begun, approximately, in the 17th century. During this exten-
sive period of time, despite occasional but provisional steps backward, internal inequalities tended to diminish within each country, while inequality between nations — particularly between the northern and southern
hemispheres — was on the increase. Since the 1980s, this major historical
trend has been radically reversed. The differences between certain countries of the former "Third World" and the developed countries are narrow-
ing, while a new inequality is taking shape within the wealthy nations.
There is a metaphor that describes the phenomenon very well: some of the
North has been put into the South, and some of the South into the North.[34]

Lester Thurow uses a different kind of metaphor in speaking of this
rather astounding resurgence of inegalitarian thinking in the countries of
the North. "But suddenly, in 1968, much like a sudden surge in a long im-
mobile glacier, inequality started to rise. Over the next two decades that
surge in inequality spread and intensified so that by the early 1990s, both
between and within groups, inequalities were rapidly rising in every industrial, occupational, educational, demographic (age, sex, race), and geographic group. Among males, the group most sharply affected, earnings
inequalities doubled in two decades. . . . By 1993, America was setting all-
time records with the top quintile of households having 13.4 times as much

income as the bottom quintile. . . . It has never happened before in America".[35]

Faced with such a major phenomenon, the proponents of neo-liberalism reassure (and defend) themselves by stressing that this resurgence of inequality has, in spite of everything, taken place against a backdrop of general prosperity, making the newly widened gap between rich and poor less painful and less iniquitous. Explicitly or not, this argument refers to the celebrated analyses of John Rawls, the great theoretician of social justice and defender of minimal state intervention.[36] For Rawls, indeed, an increase in inequality is morally justified if it results in an improvement in the lot of the poorest. In other words, the greater enrichment of the wealthy is acceptable as long as it is accompanied by a relative enrichment, however minimal, of the poor — something that Rawls thinks is generally the case. Whether in America or in Europe, the argument has been repeated over and over, again and again, during the past twenty years. There was a time, in the 1980s, when it was a conference ritual to cite Rawls on this specific point.

The only problem is that this argument is statistically false, at least where the United States is concerned. There, the widening inequality that began in the 1960s has not only been more drastic than people think, but above all it has taken the form of a devastating impoverishment of the poorest. The exact contrary of Rawls' reassuring scenario has come about. "From 1973 to 1994," writes Thurow, "America's real per capita GDP rose 33 percent, yet real hourly wages fell 14 percent and real weekly wages 19 percent for non-supervisory workers".[37] A projection of these statistics into the future paints an unimaginable picture, theoretically at least. Thurow predicted in 1996 that, if nothing intervened to correct the trend in the U. S., by the turn of the century the real salary of non-management workers would have fallen to the levels of fifty years ago, while at the same time the GNP would have more than doubled.

Several North American economists agree that this phenomenon of the impoverishment of the poorest is unprecedented in all of American history (except, of course, for periods of economic crisis like the 1930s). "Never before", Thurow adds, "has a majority of American workers suffered real-wage reductions while the real per capita GDP was advancing".[38] Of course, such a regression is already no longer restricted to American society. The phenomenon has gradually been extended to the entire developed world, at varying speeds depending on the country. Great Britain, for example, has witnessed a similar impoverishment of the poor. OECD statistics show that between 1979 and 1993 the average income there increased by more than a third, while that of the 10% of the least privileged fell by 17%. More spectacularly still, a government report published in London in March 1999 painted an utterly horrifying picture of the anti-egalitarian trend in the British economy. Between 1977 and 1996, economic inequality increased by a third in Great Britain. The authors of the report point out that such a development is almost without equivalent on the planet, adding that "twelve million people (almost a fifth of the population) live in a condition of relative poverty".[39] This social disaster is all the more significant in that for years a flexible and liberal Great Britain was held up by the majority of commentators as a model of dynamism and efficiency, particularly in France. It would be cruel to ask these people today to read out aloud, before the whole world, the things they were still writing in the early 1990s.

To keep everything in perspective, I should point out that this spectacular growth of inequality in Europe was not restricted to Great Britain. More generally, in all of the OECD countries, the disparity between the 10% of the top earners and the 10% of the least well-paid rose from 7.5 to 1 in 1969 to 11 to 1 in 1992.

These figures certainly make one think. They do indeed show what a distance there is between the content of theoretical debates about social justice and the devastating statistical facts. And in that respect, the contradiction provided by reality is exemplary. In a cruel irony of the calendar, it so happens that John Rawls threw his hat into the great international debate at the very moment when — within no more than two years — his argument would no longer be borne out by the facts. The American edition of his major book, *A Theory of Justice*, dates from 1971. But, as Thurow observes, "In 1973, inflation-corrected real wages began to fall for males. Here again real-wage reductions gradually spread across the workforce until by the early 1990s male real wages were falling for all ages, industries, occupations, and every educational group including those with postgraduate degrees. Average median earnings for males working year-round full time fell 11 percent (from $34,048 to $30,407 in 1993 dollars) between 1973 and 1993 even though the real per capita GDP was rising, 29 percent over the same period of time".[40]

So it seems that, astoundingly, statistics were thumbing their nose at theory, that the massive reality of inequality was making a mockery of our subtle discussions, that the divorce between words and things had been consummated.

Eliminating The Least Fit

Everyone, naturally, is wondering the same thing today: why? How can we explain that such a massive regression into inegalitarianism can have taken place in the very heart of the democratic world, in complex and culturally advanced countries? Why such a disastrous step backwards after a century of social progress and reforms, of continually improved controls? Why such an impoverishment of the poorest, just when the accumulated wealth of the Northern Hemisphere has reached levels never experienced in the history of mankind? Why so much harshness in society, when nothing really makes it necessary?

We cannot give a single technical answer to these simple questions. Economists are right to reject monocausal and mechanistic explanations, which are nothing more than demagoguery. It is obviously absurd to accuse "technological progress", a simplification to blame globalization, false to indict competition from outsiders, misleading to agitate for a "tougher" form of capitalism that would imply (however worthy the cause) even more inequality, and extravagant to say that our societies are no longer wealthy enough to support a welfare state, etc.. These false explanations have just one advantage: each, in its own way, appeals basically to some kind of fatality. They all emphasize some "objective" mechanism or other against which political power can only struggle — valiantly, but in vain. It's a good way to absolve the political power of any responsibility while providing prior justification for the next backward step.

Actually, if these causes combine, add up, and are related to one another, it is because in the final analysis they are all grounded in a preference or initial decision which is political in nature — for otherwise none of them would have the same effect. The re-emergence of inequality is a *choice*, or, in other words, a *design*. It is misleading to suggest that our societies "don't have any other option", or that they are condemned to inequality. Bearing this in mind, let us look at a few examples.

It is no secret that the most flagrant inequalities, the ones that leap out at us, are those that have widened the gap between the average wage earner and the CEO. In the U.S. the ratio was only 1:35 in the 1960s; today it is 1:200, or more. But there was no need for such a widening of the income gap! (It is unwarranted to refer to the "law of the market" in this context, since these levels of remuneration are often decided by a small inner circle, whose decisions are far from open to scrutiny). As some American commentators have observed, what has happened is simply that the capitalists have reopened the class war, and are winning it. It is a political choice, in the full meaning of the word.

In the same way, the stubborn struggle against inflation, the need to give preferential treatment to shareholders, the priority given to Finance, have deliberately lowered incomes — the incomes of those at the bottom of the ladder first, and then those of the middle class. At the same time profits, and the incomes of the upper levels, have soared. So the great waves of lay-offs of the 1980s in the United States (the famous "downsizing") made it possible to reduce already modest salaries, if need be by hiring back workers at lower pay, as "temps", or by out-sourcing. But this again was a choice, and was immediately profitable for some. From this point of view, wages have never been anything but "costs" that had to be reduced to a minimum.

"The use of contingent labor," writes André Gorz, "allows capitalism to re-create, for a growing proportion of the labor force, the social conditions that prevailed early in the 19th century: temporary contract workers, part-timers and other short-term employees are like drudges, intermittently employed according to need, for whom the company has to pay neither health insurance, nor paid vacations, nor severance payments, nor provide proper training".[41]

The opening of economies and the choice of free trade have, perhaps, brought about an improvement in world productivity. But above all, they have provided a disciplinary means to allow inegalitarian backward steps to be imposed on public opinion when, otherwise, they would have been massively rejected. These backward steps have been so radical that some economists don't rule out the possibility that in advanced economies the middle class will purely and simply disappear.[42] None of this has come about without a power-play, or without deliberate decisions being made.

On another level, it is certain that technological change has introduced new forms of inequality or exclusion into the workplace. Daniel

Cohen, using analyses carried out by the American Michael Kremer in 1993, has described, for example, what is called the *"O-ring theory"*, named after a tiny seal whose failure was to blame for the dramatic failed launch of the space-shuttle *Challenger*. What does this mean? Nowadays, in any production process, industrial competition has become so keen that excellence is required *at every stage*. In other words, an efficient company must not only employ the best engineers and technicians, it must also have the best switchboard operators, the best data-entry personnel, and so on. This means that the difference between two levels of qualification, however small, can at present lead to considerable differences in earnings. The best are in demand; the less good are penalized, or even rejected.[43] Inequality explodes and changes.

Thus Daniel Cohen speaks of "an explosion of inequality *within each socio-cultural group*. The phenomenon of inequality is occurring within each age-group, each level of education, and each sector of the economy".

To these transformations of a technological nature are added considerable modifications in the way work is organized, on the level of each company. These modifications basically involve a growing individualization of responsibilities and, consequently, of income. The so-called "management by objectives", which introduces a greater degree of "individual flexibility", is part of the change.[44] It results in new forms of inequality, sometimes called "fractal". But to what does this revolution correspond? To something very simple: the market, with its incisive logic, is now penetrating into the very heart of corporations. There, it is destroying the old practices of mutualization or invisible redistribution. The economist Michel Albert speaks of the new "Nietzchean corporation" to characterize this transformation. But we have to understand that this astonishing intrusion of the law of supply and demand is indeed part of a deliberate overall choice: the choice of a market society, considered to be the best we can conceive of.

It is surely not a coincidence that Herbert Spencer, the theoretician of social Darwinism we referred to earlier, the inventor of the "survival of the fittest", has recently been rediscovered in the United States. Books have been devoted to him,[45] and some of his writings re-published. Once more, he is in tune with the age, as he was in the 19th century.

So year after year the workplace, the treatment of workers, and the daily life of the company undergo a harsh process of constant and some-times horrifying inegalitarianism, and the media mostly remain silent about this development. "The conditions for the existence of a genuine working class are disappearing, while those for a modest wage-earning labor-force are intensified, sharing with employers a conception of work as no more than a certain number of hours, no longer with any intrinsic value but only one that is constantly determined — and reset — by the market. The more powerful and close at hand the market is, the more the ability required is simply whatever makes you better than the next person. . . . We are wit-nessing a real explosion of inequality between people of the same age and the same level of education".[46]

Clearly, all these changes result from a combination of causes, uniting technological necessity, the demands of competition, changes in the means of production or marketing, the pressures of individualism, and a deliber-ate choice whose ideological nature is most often hidden. Now this choice, which claims to be attuned to the famous "pure theory of market econo-mies" (still called the "pure theory of the general equilibrium of perfect competition"), is obviously inspired by an inegalitarian design. In a long, damning article published in 1998, Jean-Paul Fitoussi showed how far this theory, so seductive in other respects, could lead.[47] Citing recent work by a couple of American scholars,[48] he demonstrates that if applied by the letter the aforesaid theory might well simply lead to the physical elimination of the least fit. "Full employment would then be guaranteed . . . for the survi-vors . . . , and equilibrium would continue to be a social optimum".

This was a *reductio ad absurdum* — but a polite one — of the senseless-ness of a pure theory that nevertheless claims to be scientific. But this dem-onstration still raises a fundamental problem for which the neoliberals have no solution. "Does it make any sense," asks Jean-Paul Fitoussi, "to consider 'optimal' an economic system prepared to tolerate the 'definitive exclusion' of part of the population? But this peculiarity of the market economy has been pointed out for a long time now, even if it has only re-cently been formalized".

In other words, the very scientific "pure theory" that is invoked on a daily basis does not formally provide for the simple survival of the poorest! The extreme conclusion of this admirable logic is no less than the physical disappearance of the least fit. How can we state, in less diplomatic terms, that using this sententious recourse to the "universal market" to justify the great inegalitarian design is not only in tune with "pure theory", but also with pure stupidity?

Injustice made banal

Commentators like Michael Walzer, who today reflect on the mechanisms of exclusion, reach conclusions very akin to the — (extremely damning) ones expressed by Jean-Paul Fitoussi. Isn't the social, political, and symbolic exclusion of the weakest the ultimate expression of inegalitarianism? Is "exclusion", in principle, so very different from "extinction"? Is it even thinkable that exclusion can be justified, as some "liberal-libertarians" suggest? Walzer obviously answers in the negative. "The [libertarian] myth of just, or justifiable, exclusion, to be realized in some hypothetical future, remains a myth. It is derived from a narrow conception of the individual, which sees all his or her abilities as being of a single type. The individual is either portrayed as systematically competent and self-determined, albeit with strengths and weaknesses that are identified in various areas, or else as systematically incompetent and passive, which everywhere leads to failure. . . . This radical dichotomy is an ideological fiction".[49]

In the same text, Walzer insists on our collective responsibility in this symbolic murder of the most destitute. "We are all colluding, to a different extent," he writes. What does he mean? Is Walzer just expressing some overly culpabilizing whining? Certainly not! He is, it seems to me, simply getting to the core of the problem, and drawing the ultimate lesson. Nothing would have been possible, and in fact, no "inegalitarian design" of this nature could have been put into effect, if it had not been possible to take advantage of the weak-kneed passivity of public opinion as a whole.

During the past few decades we have become accustomed to this irresistible destruction of equality. The dominant credo has gradually been loaded with references, collective representations, instinctive reactions, and sensitivities that give the inegalitarian design a kind of legitimacy. We have insensibly grown accustomed once again to social injustice, while resigning ourselves to the arrogance of the wealthy, the ostentatious lifestyles and greed of the "heroes" of modernity. "Habitual unemployment," writes Jean-Paul Fitoussi, "leads imperceptibly to the perception that the need to reduce it is not so urgent. . . . Unemployment has thus become just one aspect of the growth of inequality to which we are resigned".[50]

Speaking, at the other end of the social scale, of certain significant phenomena like the return of luxury to the symbolic landscape, one commentator noted in 1998: "Periods of depression not only restore social hierarchies, but, what is more, seem to give them legitimacy. The survivors lose their hang-ups. This is precisely the message given by the advertisements from Galeries Lafayette, the French department store chain, in the 1980s: *"Oser le vison!"* ("Dare to wear mink!"): in other words, "You're wealthy, so why don't you just accept what makes you different. . . The social divide is no longer any reason to feel guilty".[51] Periodically, the leftist press in the U. S. protests against the same kind of complacency as expressed in the pages of the mainline economic press in North America. In February 1998, for instance, the review *Dissent* harshly accused *Forbes, Business Week* and *Fortune* for presenting a sanitized version of capitalism by depicting the very rich and powerful as if they were fairytale characters, or eulogizing the heroism of some Joe Blow who is merely trying to pick up a measly million or two million dollars.[52] The same could certainly be said of the European press.

To paraphrase a famous saying, when we stop to evaluate the extent of the damage, sooner or later, it will be hard to say "But we didn't know".

CHAPTER V:
REASON HOBBLED

"The world contains a good number of 'rationalists' who are a menace to the life of reason."
Maurice Merleau-Ponty, Signes,
Gallimard, 1980.

Of all our inheritances, this is one of the most precious! Of all the promises held out by the Enlightenment, this is the one we should keep constantly in mind, day by day. Reason! Reasonable and modest reason! Faith in the liberating power of human intelligence, and the desire to rid ourselves of the fog of irrationality, of tyrannical superstition — and of the dead weight of belonging, and the innumerable layers laid down by tradition. Nothing is more moving than the history of this patient conquest, whose advances and reverses we can evaluate retrospectively, throughout the West's entire adventure.

The emergence of reason was never a natural, predictable development in human progress, one to which we only needed to give our passive consent. It required effort, determination, and a struggle that was often victorious — but was sometimes unsuccessful. Critical reason was always assailed by the forces it held at bay. It was simultaneously in a state of hope and of crisis, at once the choice of human autonomy and a critical attitude dispelling the myths, rituals, and taboos that were obstacles to it. It was victorious over time, but its triumphs were precarious; it was frail, but obstinate. This inherent fragility, this indefatigable exigency, is what gives meaning to the dread that fills us today as we see reason stumbling all around us, or, worse still, betraying its promises. In saying this I am not only speaking of the thousand and one retreats into "magic thinking", "second-sight", esotericism, or any of the varieties of shamanism that are enjoying renewed popularity these days. Without downplaying the threat, we should indeed take a look beyond these gusts of irrationality blowing throughout the world, whether in religious or secular garb. And to these dangers from without, we must add some equally formidable inner hazards that are threatening scientific thought from the inside.

How could we fail to be alarmed by these aberrations, which are all the more dangerous in that, like neoliberalism, they proceed from a consensual arrogance? From the clear light of critical reason to the harshness of instrumental rationality, from penetrating thought to the mechanistic inflexibility of techno-science,[1] from the liberation of the Enlightenment to the primacy of neo-scientism, we sense that a dizzying gulf has opened up between the promise and its fulfillment. This is the real question; this is certainly the source of the greatest threat. But it still has to be truly identified. How can we do that, unless we briefly remind ourselves of the initial promise?

The Greek Apotheosis

Reason is the Greek contribution to the Western inheritance. And what a contribution! It represents that "universal Hellenistic quality, that apotheosis of the *nomos*", transfusing from century to century all the philosophies that came into contact with it, exerting a profound influence on Jewish and Christian teaching while being enriched by them in turn. "This apotheosis," writes Jacob Taubes, "could be celebrated in a pagan manner, which is to say Greco-Hellenistic, or it could be celebrated in a Roman or Jewish manner."[2]

Jean-Pierre Vernant provides a suggestive account of the emergence of reason in the 6th century B.C. in the cities of Ionia. In that period, a new "school" appeared, inspired by thinkers whom the Greeks themselves called philosophers: Thales, Anaximenes, Anaximander, Solon. . . Before that, of course, a certain form of rationality had been known, in Babylon, in China, and elsewhere, but there was nothing quite like that of the Ionians. It was new; it was different. It would, for example, "enable Western science to advance along paths where others could not follow".[3] To recognize such a radical departure doesn't mean adopting a Eurocentric perspective:

it is just to remind ourselves of an obvious fact. Heidegger, in this respect, was quite right to state: "Philosophy is Greek in its very being; it first took possession of the Greek world, and of it alone, claiming it as the place where it would unfold."[4]

The point is capital, at a juncture when, two and a half thousand years after this new phenomenon, the modern West is hesitating between the global imperialism of "McWorld", and the self-questioning that leads to differentialist ideas and "political correctness". So it is time to reaffirm — with modesty and prudence — that the appearance of Greek reason unquestionably represents a new departure in world history, a new beginning that is still part of our foundations, and that requires our commitment. "The Papuan tribesman is reasonable too, but it is one thing to speak of the Papuan, and another of the Greek. . . In philosophy there is something more precise than a general expression of human disquiet. That 'something' begins to appear in Greek philosophy".[5] Husserl was basically expressing the same thing when he said, pointing to the Greek cities of the 6th century B.C.: "The Europe of the mind has a spiritual birthplace".

Can we, by simplifying in the extreme, define the nature of this rational thought, of this "conditioning" that Heidegger called *Einstellung*? The first changes cited by Vernant may seem small, but they are far from it. Beside the traditional poetic forms, the use of prose first appeared in the 6th century B.C. and gradually took root. In the same way, the written text — a more detached and critical form of expression — replaced oral recitation. The written text liberated the reader from the 'spell-bound' and spellbinding emotion by which the listener to oral poetry was possessed. "A written text," adds Vernant, "is a text that can be re-read, and which, in a way, triggers critical reflection. At the time, a transition was taking place between a form with a narrative purpose and a kind of text making an effort to explain the order of things".[6] From this one far-from-insignificant fact we should retain the thought that Greek reason arises out of what we might call a critical capacity. It is, above all, detachment, questioning, and persistent doubt.

In particular, it was a decisive break with the earlier form of rationality, based on the ideas of subjection, authority, and power (*kratos*). Until then, in fact, in most of the traditional cosmogonies, "rationality" was rooted in the notion of rival forces and divine rivalries, and in an order triumphing under the aegis of a power greater than others. In the etymological meaning of the word, the reason of our ancestors was indeed the reason of the victors. Under this archaic type of rationality, "the reference point was knowing who was master of the world and why his reign would last for ever".[7] It was a tutelary authority, the authority of some god or secular power imposing order on the world.

Greek reason would "reason", if we may use the word thus, in a completely different way. It replaced power by principle. What it sought behind appearances was no longer a god, or a power, but the founding principle which underlay the order of things. This was the dawn of the idea that "the world is ruled by law — *nomos* — and not by Zeus". "To establish such a conception of the world," adds Vernant, "the Greeks had to modify their vocabulary. Instead of the names of traditional divinities, seen as authorities, they had to use the names of sensory qualities, rendered abstract and made into substances by the use of the article: *to thermon* (warmth), *to psychron* (cold), etc.

This miracle of Greek reason introduced something new into the perception of reality — a revolution as radical as the one effected in the perception of time by Jewish propheticism,[8] one that would result in the great philosophical categories, and soon lead to Plato (5th century B.C.). This new way of thinking opened the way not only to what we call science, but also to what the Greeks themselves called "democracy". Why? Because they were able to think of society in the same way as the first Ionian philosophers thought of the universe: by emphasizing universal law, rather than might. This law would prevent any one member of society from holding a monopoly of power, the *kratos*. The civic space would play this role, and ensure the famous balance that characterizes Greek thought.

So we can say that from the outset reason made common cause with liberty, but also with moderation and the ability to criticize. It was at the opposite pole from any dictatorial, or, even worse, dogmatic, way of thinking. The best illustration of this is provided by the complex and subtle relationship the Greeks, as the inventors of reason, maintained with their own myths and religious beliefs. We are indebted to Paul Veyne for the best study of this paradox — a fundamental one for, ultimately, it bears on the relationship between belief and reason.

To believe and to know while preserving the ability to differentiate between several possible levels of knowledge; to learn to doubt while negotiating with one's own doubt; to establish subtle hierarchies and comple-

mentarities in our apprehension of the world — none of this seemed beyond the reach of the Greeks. Veyne cites, for instance, the characteristic
ambivalence of Galen (the great Greek physician of the 2nd century A.D.)
regarding the existence of centaurs. On the one hand, in a great book on
the purpose of different parts of the organism, he rejected any possibility
that composite beings such as centaurs could exist. But elsewhere the same
Galen speaks, without batting an eyelid, of the existence of the centaur
Chiron, the educator of heroes. "If our intention is not to be dogmatic
about the existence of God, or Gods," writes Paul Veyne, "we must restrict
ourselves to observing that the Greeks held their gods to be true, even
though these gods existed for them in a space-time that was secretly different from that inhabited by those who believed in them".[9]

This reminder certainly helps us understand why and how the relations between Greek reason and Judaism and, later, Christianity and, later
again, with Islam, have very little to do with what the amnesiac rationalists
of today like to think of as a head-on collision of reason and religion. There
is perhaps a conflict where time and equality, but certainly not reason, are
concerned.[10] The distinction is significant. St. Paul was quite serious when
he reproached the Greek pagans with being excessively religious.
"Athenians," he declared preaching on the Areopagus in Athens, "I perceive
that in every way you are very religious" (Acts 17:22). It is true that the
Greek polytheism of the period was steeped in ritual and sacrifice. Between Greek rationality and the religions of the Book, the relationship is
much more profound, the enrichment reciprocal, and the interpenetration
constant. A good portion of Jewish thought, for example, became profoundly Hellenized following Alexander the Great's conquests. And Alexandrian Judaism, which did its thinking and reading in Greek, saw no fundamental incompatibility in the relations between Hellenic reason and the
message of the prophets.

This is not the place to recall the decisive part played by thinkers like
Philo of Alexandria or historians like Flavius Josephus — both of them
Jews — as bridges between the Hellenism of the majority and a Jewish
thought that was both resilient and open. The Greek translation of the Old
Testament (the Septuagint) was made, we know, at Alexandria, between
250 and 130 B.C., on the initiative of Ptolemy Philadelphus, King of Egypt.
So it was in Greek that the first Christians read what we now call the Old

Testament. "To demonstrate its deep affinities with the Gentiles (here, the Greeks), Alexandrian Judaism sometimes resorted to a fiction: Plato was portrayed as a disciple of Moses. Christianity adopted this fiction, but this was less difficult for it because, much more decisively than the Synagogue, it had assimilated Plato's teachings. It did so quite spontaneously: its theologians, reared under paganism or at least trained in Greek philosophy, used it to enrich their teachings. The 4th-century fathers of the Church took pride in their Greek culture and their Roman citizenship, with which they could confront the barbarians".[11]

Where the Law is concerned, both Jews and Christians were convinced that the Biblical message was *an extension of the logic of Greek thought itself*. They affirmed that the divine "revelation" provided access to a knowledge identical to that which pagan philosophers pursued through learning. This argument would be used by Philo of Alexandria as well as by St. Paul (Romans 1: 18-31). Even though they were contemporaries, Paul of Tarsus and Philo of Alexandria never met. This didn't prevent them from sharing a common cultural heritage in the form of Hellenism, making them essential witnesses of and actors in the interpenetration of the Biblical tradition and Greek thought. "The Jewish wisdom literature, whether canonic or not (the so-called Wisdom of Solomon, Proverbs, Ecclesiastes, and Sirach or Ecclesiasticus), constitutes one of the major links between Paul and Philo, and Greek thought. In any case, there be no doubt that Christianity, from the moment it addressed the Gentiles, was in a way following in the wake of Alexandrian Judaism".[12]

It is now thought that the three synoptic Gospels were originally written in Greek. In addition, several Christian authors would later play an important part in the transmission of Greek teachings in the West. One of these was Boethius (480-524), the author of a famous work whose title perfectly states its purpose: *The Consolation of Philosophy*. "Theological discourse was not content with a narrow adherence to biblical teaching; it was also concerned with *reason*, with rational coherence, so that it was with the help of the philosophical language of the times — mostly neo-Platonic, but also influenced by Stoicism — that the content of the divine revelation would be developed."[13] In a general way, those Christian authors of the first centuries who came to be called the "apologists" set out to refute their pagan critics by insisting on the convergence between Greek thought and the best aspects of Christianity. This was the case for the most famous among them, Justin Martyr, the author of the famous *Dialogue with Typho*. Justin had no doubt about this: it was from Moses, "the first of the Prophets, more ancient than Greece herself", that Plato had taken, for instance, his doctrine of creation. In this respect, "the Christian apologists borrowed one of the central ideas of Judeo-Alexandrian apologetics".[14]

In the 12th century, the great Jewish thinker Moses Maimonides (1135-1204), who was also a physician at the court of the Kurd Saladin, set out to reconcile Judaism with Aristotelian philosophy. His writings, though attacked by orthodox rabbis, would play a considerable role in the development of Jewish thought.

Much later, during the Italian Renaissance — in the Florence of 1439, to cite just one example — Cosimo de Medici would found a "Platonic Academy" whose artistic and cultural curiosity was intended to revive the sensibility of 3rd-century Hellenic and Jewish Alexandria. An attempt was made to reconcile the Biblical message with the Platonic, and even Egyptian, inheritance, as is shown by the figure of Hermes Trismegistus (Thrice Great), a mythical incarnation of the ibis-headed god Thoth, the master of knowledge and a "contemporary of Moses". "Religious truth became philosophical, and the Bible was read with Platonic spectacles. There was a pre-established harmony between the Jewish revelation and Greek thought, and that is why philosophy is the truth of religion".[15]

This not at all to say that Christian theology was exempt from purely fideist or exclusivist temptations — i.e., which deliberately set faith above reason. St. Anselm, in the 2nd century, maintained that one should not seek God by reason, any more than one should light a candle to look at the sun. For Luther and Calvin, human nature was so corrupt that reason was impotent compared to faith, and so on. But this didn't prevent reason and faith from being seen most often as pertaining to two distinct and complementary orders of truth, as two human faculties that could illuminate one another. Where Judaism is concerned, the Torah insists on the diversity of interpretations and on the unending search for truth. The definition it gives of idolatry is enlightening in this respect: "For the Bible," writes Stéphane Moses, "idols are not the beliefs of others, but any belief, including our own, when it becomes set in its ways, made into a fetish, and removed from the unending process of the quest for meaning".[16]

In Praise Of Critical Reason

In our contemporary polemics, in the peremptory judgments we pronounce on what we call "religious irrationalism", we readily forget this
original mutual attention, this complex, fertile complementary relationship
between Greek rationalism and Biblical belief. To the sensibility of the first
centuries, "criticism was not a threat to faith. On the contrary, the freedom
to be critical (meaning, first and foremost, to be self-critical) derived from
the freedom of faith. That is why the historiography of primitive Christianity should take advantage of this liberty".[17]

The case of Islam is even more revealing. Today, when brutal fundamentalism is tarnishing the inheritance of the Koran and personifying barbarism itself, it may be difficult to remember the part this same Islam
played in the dissemination and success of rational thought in the medieval
West. Arab science, algebra, arithmetic, trigonometry, geometry, etc.,
played a much more important role than is generally recognized. It is even
thought that the learned al-Tusi, among other, had a decisive influence on
Copernicus.[18]

For a long time, until the dawn of the Enlightenment, Averroes personified philosophic thought for European scholars from Paris to Padua. In
book after book, specialists like Alain de Libéra have attempted to do justice to Islam by reminding us how deeply the West is indebted to it where
reason is concerned. "The facts speak for themselves: the Islam of Andalu-
sia transmitted not just the philosophy of the Greeks to the Latins. . . It
was by way of the translations of the Arab scientific corpus (made in
Toledo) that the 'West', in the 1150s, acquired a considerable part of the
knowledge that subsequently allowed the medieval university to come into
being: psychology, the philosophy of the mind, physics, metaphysics, ontology, natural sciences, and optics".[19]

In this message, passed on by Muslim philosophers, Greek reason was
never considered to be a pure, tyrannical rationality. It was also (above
all?) a "subversion of the consensus", to borrow Libéra's apt expression. It
was inseparable from spiritual freedom and from what today is called tolerance. In other terms, it rejected authoritarian unanimism and obedience to
dogma. To exist, "philosophy had to be free, hence diverse, for reasoning
cannot be subject to constraint". As for theology, it damned itself as soon

as it claimed to point to a "single path": "The apologist, whose proclaimed objective was to 'defend religion against its enemies', had only one genuine function, namely to produce 'enemies of religion', just as, in other times, psychiatry would produce the madman, and the policeman the criminal".[20]

This essential emphasis on criticism is the crimson thread we must grasp; it is what we must keep in mind when we discuss the subsequent difficult transition of reason throughout Western history. Those like François Châtelet, Peter Brown and Charles Taylor, who attempt to retrace its path, insist on the radical nature of this requirement — which is all the more precious in that it would constantly be in conflict with disastrous (and frequent) clerical or theological acts of perfidy, whether the Catholic condemnation of a Christian precursor like Copernicus, or the rabbinical actions that led to Spinoza's expulsion from the Synagogue after his *Tractatus Theologico-Politicus* was published anonymously in 1670, or the one that caused Luther use the words "that whore" in referring to dogmatic reason. Reason is not so much in conflict with belief itself as it is with closed-mindedness. Hence, many exemplary struggles of reason against dogmatism took place *within* faith, rather than against it — a circumstance that, in retrospect, makes religious dogmatism all the more deserving of condemnation when it tries to muzzle reason.

This was Galileo's case: here was a good Christian and a respectful son of the Church who was nonetheless condemned, egregiously, by the hierarchy. The same could be said of Montaigne, an apologist for doubt and the freedom to criticize, but whose *Essays* are nevertheless full of explicit homages to the Christian faith.[21] In a completely different way, Rabelais (1494-1553), a great exploder of hypocritical piety and moralistic bigotry, was a no less stalwart defender of the faith. And, at a time when Christianity was riven by fratricidal wars, even the Rabelaisian heroes, steeped in the New Testament, "set out to rehabilitate the Christian in his liberty" and promote the image of "a subject of reason and desire living his faith in his heart". The list could go on *ad infinitum*. Newton, a mathematician of genius, the discoverer of gravity and co-founder of modern science, was both a great mystic and the author of books on theology. On the question of the *cogito* and inwardness, the great Descartes, whom Hegel considered the true founder of modernity, is also the direct heir of St. Augustine. "Descartes is in many ways profoundly Augustinian", Charles Taylor reminds us, and it is even possible to situate his contribution "in the stream of revived Augustinian piety which dominated the late Renaissance on both sides of the confessional divide". This is so even if, unquestionably, "this new conception of inwardness, an inwardness of self-sufficiency, or autonomous powers of ordering by reason, also prepared the ground for modern unbelief".

We could equally well cite Kant and his critical rationalism, of which François Châtelet has written: "Reason has only one theoretical, cognitive use, which is to criticize itself, to be able to set limits for itself".[22] Or we could again mention Hegel, for whom Christianity "played a part in constructing the spirit of humanity" and "paved the way to discovering the infinite of reason, of the mind that knows itself". Hegel's lesson, contrary to simplifying interpretations, is actually that "the theologico-religious was one of the conditions of the possibility of the rational, and contemporary culture is so deeply impregnated with it that it must be possible to rediscover something theological in reason and in the use of reason".[23] As for the deism that became widespread in the 18th century — particularly after John Locke — and that opened the way to the secularism of the Enlightenment, we could say that it was characterized by a rational approach to faith rather than by a rejection of it. "It is a central idea of deism, as it developed, that God speaks to human beings as rational beings, that his objectives fully respect their autonomous reason".[24]

Are all these reminders merely rhetorical? Are they superfluous? Certainly not! They help us understand the precise nature of reasonable reason, and identify more accurately the real promise the scientific mind hoped to contribute. In the 17th and 18th centuries, indeed, science embodied not only speculative values but also liberating ones. Jean-Marc Lévy-Leblond, a steadfast opponent of modern-day dogmatic scientism, points out this intrepidly "militant" aspect of the original scientific spirit: "It was precisely from its youth, its fragility, and even its immaturity, that science inherited this aggressive quality. In their common adolescence, science and democracy did indeed go hand in hand. There can be no 'liberty, equality and fraternity' except that which is wrested from — and must continually be wrested from — the dominant powers".[25]

The scientific spirit was threatened from the outset by a totalizing temptation, resulting from "nature's mathematical enterprise". It therefore had to learn to coexist with a number of counterweights (beliefs, poetry, ethics, moderation) capable of "keeping the specter of totalitarianism at a distance".[26] From this standpoint, the reign of reason is not unlike that of the market: it is only a liberating factor when it recognizes its own inadequacies in advance, and never loses sight of its limitations. By definition, reason is only reasonable when it is modest.

Science and The Enlightenment

In a striking passage, Alphonse Dupront speaks of the extraordinary concomitance of scientific inventions and discoveries in the second half of the 18th century. To him, the Enlightenment was

... like an eruption, which overloaded the chronology and has to be grasped in the raw, in its almost quantitative, and European, dimension. In the same year, 1767, James Watt finished building his steam engine, which he would sell to Wilkinson eight years later, and Joseph Priestley published his *History of Electricity*. We are on the island of England, at the onset of an "industrial revolution". But only four years later, Monge defined analytical geometry, and Lavoisier analyzed the composition of air. 1774 saw Priestley's studies on oxygen and the construction by Herschel of his great telescope, while two years later came Jouffroy d'Abbans' attempts to launch a steamship on the river Doubs. Buffon's *Époques de la nature* dates from 1778; in the same year Lamarck began the publication of his *Flore française*, which was completed in 1795, while Jussieu's *Genera Plantarum* appeared in 1789.

Just a few years later the indefatigable chronology lists the "inventions" that created modern science: in 1781 Herschel discovered the planet Uranus; two years later, in 1783, Lavoisier successfully analyzed the composition of water, and Berthollet that of ammonia in 1785. During these same years the hot-air balloon rose into the sky above Annonay (and later Paris), Blanchard crossed the channel in a balloon, and Mont Blanc was climbed for the first time. The great treatises, which laid the groundwork for new sciences, are also capital inventions: Lagrange's *Mécanique analytique* (1787); Monge's *Traité élémentaire de statistique* (1788); Lavoisier's *Traité de Chimie* (1789), and, in 1792, *De viribus electricitatis*, by the Italian Luigi Galvani. We could also include technological advances in this chronological digest: they were made, and made public, just as thick and fast. The more the century approached its end the more progress seemed to accelerate — or, to be more precise, we might say that the great explosion of discoveries took place in the decades between 1770 and 1790, i.e. shortly before the events of the French Revolution.

Clearly, this intense activity demonstrates an inventive and creative

"potency" of astounding vigor. Rarely has an epidemic been more violent
and explosive, and therefore more necessary.

Alphonse Dupront, *Qu'est-ce que les Lumières? Op. cit.*

The Return Of A Closed World

Is this still the case today? We know very well it is not. In the technological triumphalism that has come to occupy the entire modern landscape
by itself, we can perceive a globalizing intoxication, disdain for whatever is
foreign to it, and a refusal of any limitations: traits that have lost the connection with critical reason. Instrumental rationality, like the market, has
become cannibalistic. Little by little, it is devouring everything opposed to
it. It is setting out to colonize every nook and cranny of the world's intelligence. It is in this perspective that we have to understand Leo Strauss's
remark that modern-day 'totalitarianism' is essentially based on
'ideologies', and, in the final analysis, on a popularized or perverted form of
science.[27] People are coming to depend on this scientific and technical ex-
crescence, and on it alone, to carry the burden of whatever remains of human hopes. After the failure of ideological or religious forms of messianism,
it is called upon to embody the ultimate imaginable or practicable undertaking, the final horizon towards which we can turn our steps. I see at least
three components in the vague uneasiness we feel when confronted with
this demand.

In the first place there is the notion of totality. We are already beginning to perceive this imperious form of totality as an iron cage. In the name
of this form of totality, we are asked to dismiss everything else, so that we
may better imprison ourselves in a one-dimensional and mathematical reality, quite the opposite of the "infinite universe" discussed by Alexandre
Koyré in his book *Du monde clos à l'univers infini* (From the Closed World to
the Infinite Universe) in which he paints the triumph of the Enlightenment
and of reason as a liberating force.[28] Contemporary technology, by rejecting
any spiritual dimension, is reinventing, this time to its own benefit, the
closed-mindedness from which reason was precisely supposed to liberate
us. "The world of scientism is stifling," remarks François Lurçat, reminding
us of how Lévinas and Rosenzweig had attempted to break "the iron bands
of totality, within whose embrace present-day scientism is again confining
us".[29]

It is an irony of history that at the very moment when our age ostensibly rejects any overarching discourse it is asking us to adopt a perception of the world that, when all is said and done, turns out to be even more all-inclusive than anything that went before. The technological system, as Jacques Ellul has observed, is setting itself up as a symbolic system, and justifies itself endlessly by creating its own images. Dominique Janicaud points to the same paradox when he reproaches the technological rationality of today with "hastening the ruin of what it set out to save". And Janicaud, quite rightly, does so in the name of reason itself. "A lucid (still rational) thought," he writes, "can and must proclaim that the total rationalization of life is the most insane undertaking in all of History".[30]

The ethologist Boris Cyrulnik expresses the same concern and denounces the same totalizing intent when he compares — in a more facetious tone — the different definitions of human unhappiness. "The Middle Ages told us that unhappiness here on earth, in this vale of tears, enabled us to hope for bliss somewhere else. The 19th century explained that happiness has to be merited and that the needy deserve their lot, since they have failed to earn redemption. Today, the discourse that bestows legitimacy on our technical exploits would have us believe that unhappiness is a sickness due to a decline in our serotonin levels".[31]

Gabor's Rule

The second cause of our anxiety comes from the uncontrolled nature of the technological process. It is as if the creator was losing control of the thing he has created. Disorienting, hyperactive, all-conquering, techno-science has become an entirely self-generated mechanism, an all-devouring monster that nothing can tame, nor direct. Fragmented, made more complex, and computerized, technological rationality is rapidly moving away from the simple hypothesis that it can be even partially controlled by human reason. It is a pure explosion; we can only stand back and observe. Such is in any case the attitude imposed on us by contemporary "techno-speak" — a degraded, impoverished, and dogmatized form of discursive reason. "Science doesn't think," said Heidegger. It seems that today it is "thinking" less and less.

"It is [even] possible, and no doubt even plausible, that we are entering an age in which science, having turned into techno-science as a result of its practical application, may disappear under the sheer weight of this technology it has transformed, just as a river is sometimes buried beneath the slippage from the banks it has carved out for itself".[32]

Those who reflect on this mechanism that is now autonomous from reason itself are aware of what is sometimes called "Gabor's rule". Formulated in the mid-1960s by the writer Dennis Gabor,[33] it goes as follows. In the logic of technology, "everything that is technologically feasible ought to be realized", whether this is considered morally good, or to be condemned. Technology wins out over knowledge. It is in a position to dictate its reasons, to impose its rhythm, to establish its own ambitions and priorities. "Every concept has been turned into a thing, every idea has been turned into a machine.", says Lévy-Leblond. Technological advances now obey their own logic and are no longer guided by what was traditionally called "knowledge". We might even ask whether, in this context, it is still legitimate to speak of scientific thought or culture. No doubt these notions have become nonsensical without our being aware of it.

Finally, the third ambiguity could be characterized as the political and moral impunity of techno-science, the only ideology of our times never to have been subjected to a real questioning in the realm of values. Researchers like Jean-Marc Lévy-Leblond and Jacques Testard regularly denounce — and rightly so — the strange way that science has managed to emerge unscathed from a century that should have been able to at least moderate its arrogance. It is actually an understatement to point out that, in the past, scientist pretensions have compromised themselves with totalitarian ideologies — with Communism, obviously, but with Nazism too. In addition to Nazi "sentiment" and estheticizing kitsch, there were Hitlerian scientific claims in biology, human reproduction, "scientific racism", etc.. Alain Finkielkraut has shown how, in this way, Hitler enlisted science in his simultaneously crazy and monstrously scientific enterprise.[34] Nazi Germany set out to be more scientific and at the same time more barbarian than England or France. A collective work, published in 1993 gave innumerable concrete examples of this disastrous symbiosis.[35] As a result, it should have become impossible to automatically assimilate rationality to reason or to civilization. But, curiously, this enlisting of rationality in the cause of tyranny, this certitude of being (scientifically) correct — against a background of massacre — has inspired remarkably little retrospective thought, and it has not led to the slightest expression of repentance.

For this reason, it is amusing to see rationalists accuse "religion" of every moral turpitude imaginable, or reproach the Catholic Church with being too tardy in expressing certain regrets.

In this respect, Michel Serres sometimes evokes the moral rupture represented for the democracies themselves by the destruction of Hiroshima and Nagasaki, that apotheosis of scientific and technical achievement. According to him, this acceptance of technological "evil" ushered in a new historical era more than a half-century ago, just as the fall of Troy brought the earliest phase of Greek history to an end. This new moral reality should at least have been thought out and controlled. It invited mankind to question its own power. But no one was prepared to do this, apart from a few exemplary individual cases such as those of several American physicists, including Julius Oppenheimer (1904-1967), the director of the center for nuclear research at Los Alamos, who refused to work on the hydrogen bomb and was accused of collusion with the Communists before being — belatedly — rehabilitated.

This ontological "recklessness" where Hiroshima is concerned was, as a disastrous epilogue to World War II, the major symptom of the self-proclaimed moral impunity of techno-science. "Anguished prudence might have been relieved by the moderating power of reason: a decision to impose a general moratorium and the creation of extremely strict international controls. Instead of trembling at the heat of a hundred thousand suns, this would have been Kantian. But what did we witness? The sacred terror of the first witnesses became one more curiosity in the sequence of news flashes. The horror itself, described in detail by the media, became boring. Then came Bikini: it became a swimsuit".[36]

The same compromise of principles and lack of prescience are at work today. The critical dimension that is nevertheless an essential component of reason has been quietly sidelined. Science is automatically endowed with a positive aura as first cousin to the Good, to progress, to enlightenment, all as a corollary of naïve (or calculating) optimism. But everything should discourage us from presuming any such thing. Indeed, contemporary history shows us that today, as in the past, modern science, deprived of its capacity for self-criticism, is perfectly ready to adapt to the latest forms of fanaticism, tyranny, or totalitarianism. Techno-science, itself incapable of producing human values, is perfectly compatible with a barbarism that rejects them.

Do we need to give examples? In the Muslim world, university Science Departments have been the principal sources of militant fundamentalism, as is well recognized. In Turkey and Morocco, scientists often make up a majority in the most radical fundamentalist movements. In Malaysia, the clandestine organization Jema'ah Islam Malaysia (JIM) first appeared in the science departments of British and American universities. Some of those behind the Palestinian Hamas in the West Bank and Gaza were engineers. Even in Israel, the most intolerant of orthodox Jews (including the assassin of Yitzhak Rabin, on November 4, 1995) are often first-rate computer technicians. As for the Japanese cult Aum Shinri-Kyo, which was responsible for the deadly gas attack in the Tokyo subway on March 20, 1995, it counts a good proportion of highly qualified young scientists among its members. What is more, the sect could boast that in Kamikuishiki, near Mount Fuji, it owned laboratories and factories where the latest cutting-edge technologies were available.[37]

Obviously, all this doesn't mean that scientific thought is essentially evil. The mistake made by visionaries of all kinds is precisely to spread this falsehood in order to justify a return to unvarnished irrationalism. On the other hand, crediting science with an inherent moral superiority — in particular by opposing it to established religion — comes from an equivalent blindness, which is equally to be condemned.

Bouvard And Pécuchet Redivivi

But that is what the current wisdom tells us. Not only does it not require any self-criticism of science, it actually enjoys reviving 19th-century positivist debates! And with what delight! The newspapers, television, books and even serious magazines take a peculiar pleasure in going over the familiar arguments — God vs. Science, Reason vs. Faith, Belief vs. Rationality, and so on. In most cases it amounts to expressing, with a touching but unflagging condescension, the superiority of the scientific approach over all others — whatever these may be.

It is quite true that since the 19th century these tired old debates have been "one of the favorite resorts of Catholic apologetics and of anti-Christian polemics" — a useless debate in principle, but which always rises once more from its own ashes. "On this topic, it is possible to go on arguing indefinitely, listing off the names of 'scientists with belief' — who have never been in short supply — and amassing contentious cases, but nothing will ever dispel the uneasiness we feel at this irrelevant debate".[38]

Jean-Marc Lévy-Leblond is right recall Flaubert's *Bouvard and Pécuchet* in this regard. At least this novel — dated, but eternally valid for all that — enables us to understand that there also exists a purely scientific form of stupidity, even if it is usually repressed or denied. It is the blindness of the man who plows his furrow without paying attention to anything else. In this respect, indeed, the two eternally cogitating asses portrayed by Flaubert seem strangely contemporary. "These bovine blinkers are worn by Bouvard (very appropriately named) and Pécuchet, and even if they never manage to reach the end of their successive furrows, they have all the myopic determination of those who till the soil with more effectual science".[39]

Far be it from me to compare the emblematic figures of Bouvard and Pécuchet to that of an eminent researcher like Claude Allègre, who was appointed French Minister of Education by Lionel Jospin in 1997. Yet in what he has written it is possible to find types of reasoning, simplifications, and even traces of scientific conceit that are not so far removed from the simple-minded positivism ridiculed by Flaubert. The ministerial post held by this researcher become decision-maker gives us a reason to pause for a moment to consider him.

In 1997, Claude Allègre published a book with the somewhat pretentious title, *Dieu face à la science* (God through scientific eyes) (Fayard). This is actually a rather classic, 19th-century type of anticlerical pamphlet, written in a lively style, in which religious dogmatism, the obscurantism of the Church and even of Christianity are denounced with vigor. Reading these pages, one is irresistibly reminded of certain declarations made in the 19th century, such as Émile Vacherot's: "Science: there is the light, the authority, the religion, of the nineteenth century".[40] And yet Claude Allègre's text was perfectly in tune with present-day sensibilities. He was feted in all the media.

The following year, a theologian, noted biblical scholar and Emeritus Professor at the Catholic Institute of Paris, wrote a most erudite little book in reply to Allègre, using an amused (rather than vindictive) tone.[41] Its author pointed out the innumerable blunders, factual errors, malicious or biased interpretations, and historical misreadings, accumulated by Claude Allègre — his discussion of the doctrine of original sin, his erroneous references to the Council of Trent (supposed to have imposed 'papal infallibility"!), or his absurd references to certain modernist theologians he claimed were persecuted, like Duns Scotus, William of Ockham, Nicholas of Oresme, Jean Buridan, etc.. The author suggested that Claude Allègre should actually read the texts and authors he had quoted without having any first-hand knowledge of them. He even went as far as to give specific bibliographical references on the major points.

We must add that this book received hardly any mention, other than in the Catholic press. Claude Allègre's few thousand readers thus remain convinced to this day that they "learned" a lot from him about the "errors" of Christianity. There is of course nothing dramatic about this anecdote. It seems to me that it speaks volumes about the new scientific dogmatism, so self-assured in its intrepid anti-religious rationalizing that it is able to argue from its own ignorance. But this is a paradoxical approach for someone to take who, government minister or not, claims to speak in the name of knowledge.

Actually, the important debate has ceased to be the overblown opposition of science versus other cultural or spiritual attitudes. It is, rather, the confrontation of contemporary scientific thought with its own promises, its own postulates, and its own unfortunate blunders. Scientific thinking has much less need of a strident, narcissistic attitude than of a critical, and even self-critical approach. But the attention-getting (and very media-savvy) "challenge" to God, belief, or religion, fulfils the opposite function. It allows techno-science to dispense with any questioning of itself and of and the ideological vacuousness in which it is imprisoned by its own autistic approach. In other words, it distorts the order of priorities to suit itself.

"If the popular mentality was as religious three and a half centuries ago as it was twenty-five centuries ago, that no longer the case today. If specialists are to have freedom of thought, it is no longer so much the gods they must rid themselves of, but rather the popular mind-set created by the media and by advertising. These do, indeed . . . inoculate us with us a morality, a vision of the world and of humanity — in other words an ideology — to which scientists are not immune".[42]

Scientist Superstition

Superstition? Of course, applied to science in this way the word reveals a polemical intention. The paternity of the idea is usually attributed to the philosopher Jeanne Hersch.[43] But an American scholar, Jacques Barzun, was the first to call science itself a "superstition".[44] Was he going too far? I don't believe so. To see why not, one only needs to think of the barely concealed violence of the new defense of scientism as it emerges from most of the texts. Think, for example, of the famous Heidelberg Appeal, made by several hundred scientists to the heads of state assembled in Rio in June 1992. The purpose of this appeal, which was largely financed by major pharmaceutical laboratories, was to denounce "the emergence of an irrational ideology which is opposed to scientific and industrial progress and impedes economic and social development". Actually, it was an attempt to reject any form of ethical, ecological or political control over technoscience in the name of research and "scientific freedom".

This appeal provoked innumerable reactions and commentaries. It came as a revelation of the ideological rigidity of neo-scientism, ready to denigrate any caution issued to science in the name of prudence, reason, or even common sense. This out-of-hand rejection of any constraint or moratorium on scientific research is the negative corollary of a preconceived notion that is indeed not very far removed from superstition plain and simple. "Science in the world of today is still, to a certain degree, authentic science, but it has become a superstition. Scientific research, which fails to distinguish between true and false science, is developing at a frenetic speed; the people involved in research constitute what is called a psychological mob, in which no-one remains capable of reflecting personally on the consequences of such runaway activity".[45]

A few significant examples, selected with prudence, will suffice.

The first and not the least interesting is that of Jean-Pierre Changeux, former chair of the French National Committee on Ethics. The successful and celebrated author of *L'Homme neuronal*[46] (Neural Man) 1983, Changeux restored to a renewed and self-assured neo-scientism its public, and its dominance of the media. No doubt his hypotheses were in tune with the mood of the moment, but in any case they were very well received. Rejecting the very existence of the "mind" in the traditional sense and reducing the concept of the self to no more than a neural alchemy, he reformulated the old positivist postulate in a new way, basing himself on the incredible advances in biology, adding a barely veiled criticism of religious, spiritual or merely "idealist" traditions.

In a subsequent dialogue with the Protestant philosopher Paul Ricoeur, Jean-Pierre Changeux would express even more clearly what might be called the "hard core" of his convictions. "There is nothing unknowable, only what we don't know".[47] In other words, the fundamental human problems are basically a product of our provisional ignorance, of a lingering haze that science will sooner or later be able to dispel. So, for him, there is no metaphysical angst, or ethical or ontological conviction, that science — and science alone — will not eventually be able to resolve.

This rationalist optimism — or over-confidence — implies consequences the scope of which is poorly recognized. It places all "belief" in question, reducing it to the level of ignorance or passing superstition. In the closed universe of scientism, the very concepts of liberty, choice, idealism, or conviction, are refused any real standing, when all is said and done. They are condemned as obsolescent. The individual is mechanistically reduced to his biological nature, and to his inability to form judgments for himself. Scientific rationality, as a mode of knowledge, is endowed with an authority that discredits all others. It is "totalitarian" in the sense that it refuses any legitimacy to other ways of apprehending reality — intuitive, poetic, metaphysical, mystical, and so on. It literally closes off the horizon of knowledge. Changeux, without saying so directly, is thus discarding a good part of human culture, seen merely as outmoded magical thinking.

There is obviously something rather frightening — and, when all is said and done, a bit silly — in this peremptory reduction of human life to conform with scientific "knowledge" alone — i.e. to something that other scholars have recognized to be as much a "representation" as anything else.[48] We can even ask if this approach is based on science and on "reasonable reason". Many are asking this question. "As soon as science goes beyond its own limits and applies its methods and way of thinking to the realities it bracketed to make it possible for it to exist, it immediately ceases to be science and becomes scientism. . . . Scientism is opposed to science in every respect: while science imposes limits on itself that it does not permit itself to transgress, scientism declares that there are no limits, and wants to have the last word about everything".[49]

It is in this specific respect that the criticisms addressed to it — by Paul Ricoeur among others — seem convincing. They are all the more so in that Changeux erroneously enlists the support of certain philosophers, reinterpreting them to serve his own cause. "For Spinoza, for example, whom Changeux cites frequently, scientific knowledge was only one of the three types of knowledge — the second, which he considered to be transcended by the third, metaphysical knowledge".[50]

Towards A New Darwinism?

Other criticisms of, and debates about, scientist ideology seem to me even more alarming. Charles Taylor, citing the American sociobiologist Edward O. Wilson, shows that the ultimate pretension of contemporary neo-scientists is to provide morality with a biological foundation — which means, in the final analysis, to absorb it. For Wilson, "Human emotional responses and the more general ethical practices based on them have been programmed to a substantial degree by natural selection over thousands of generations".[51]

Such a radically scientist proposition is a throw-back to Nietzsche's famous biologism in the 19th century: "It is essential above all," said Nietzsche "that all the tables of values, all the imperatives that History and ethnographic study speak of, be clarified and explained in terms of their physiological dimension".[52] Taken this far, neurobiology is not just a scientific discipline, but is becoming the kernel of a kind of anthropology — if not ideology — that views man as a mechanism, deprived of his freedom. This proposition has been adopted by Jean-Pierre Changeux, who likes to speak of a "neural predisposition for ethics". This idea was even the topic of a conference held in 1991, the proceedings of which were published.[53] Of course, it would be absurd to evoke, in respect to this anthropology, our sinister memories of the way socio-biology was once enlisted by theorists of racism. But, on the other hand, one thing at least is certain: the moral and political taboo that has been placed on socio-biology for decades is quietly being removed. "For some time now," writes one scholar in 1993, "in interdisciplinary gatherings, I have been encountering sociologists who, despite their instinctive hostility to socio-biology, declare they can no longer tolerate the fundamental taboo placed upon it. This line of argument is indeed on its last legs."[54]

Now, this surreptitious way of restoring legitimacy to socio-biology, which is also a response to the rhetorical excesses of some of the recent ostracism to which it has been subjected, is a sign of the irresistible weakening of two values that once went unquestioned: on the one hand, progressive voluntarism (nurture vs. nature), and on the other the aspiration to equality (the idea that every individual, at birth, is like a blank slate on which he must create his own being). It isn't difficult to understand why and how, on these two points, neo-scientism is perfectly in synch with the intellectual climate of the moment.

Without impugning its intentions, nor absurdly suspecting it of being bent on extermination, one might raise questions about the obvious risks represented by a loss of control, by indifference, or by conceptual laxity. Contemporary biologism and *physicalism* are advancing through a minefield. Physicalism, by the way, is being reinvented today but it is not, in fact, a recent discovery. As early as 1948, a symposium of American scholars approved a statement asserting that, in the final analysis, the phenomena of behavior and of the mind can be described in terms of concepts derived from the mathematical and physical sciences; indeed, they even considered it an article of faith.

Revived later, in particular by James Watson, who was jointly responsible in the 1960s for the discovery of the structure of DNA, this physicalist presupposition led to a somewhat chilling conclusion, namely that there is nothing "special" to distinguish mankind from the rest of the animal world. Watson explains his thesis as follows: "There has always been a tendency to think that something special differentiates man from everything else. This belief has found expression in man's religions"[55] There is no need to add that, for Watson, this "belief" is obsolete today — it is merely old-fashioned humanism.

François Lurçat, to whom I am indebted for the above references, is quite right to remind us that these developments echo almost word for word what was written in the 19th century by Vacher de Lapouge, the ideologist of racism: "All men are related to all other men, and to all living beings. So there are no 'rights of man', no more than there are rights of the three-banded armadillo or the web-fingered gibbon, the carthorse, or beef cattle. Deprived of his status as a special being created in God's image, man has no more rights than any other mammal. The very idea of rights is an invention. Nothing exists but might".[56]

In describing the implicit — and extremely serious — risks that accompany this revival of socio-biology, the same François Lurçat, for instance, reproaches Jean-Pierre Changeux for praising the German biologist Haeckel, (a convinced Darwinist, and patron of the International Society for Racial Hygiene, founded in 1905), in his book *L'Homme neuronal*

(Chapter VIII, p. 342). But Lurçat is certainly not the only one to feel concerned. "Humanist" scholars like Pierre Thuillier, Albert Jacquard, Jean-Marc Lévy-Leblond, Stephen Jay Gould, Richard Lewontin, Isabelle Stengers, Eugène Enriquez, and many others have good reason to fight tooth and nail, in book after book, against the risks of instrumentalizing biology under the cloak of "scientific reason". But it must be acknowledged that their alarm-calls have not met with the attention they deserve. Drowned out by the triumphant, prevailing brouhaha, they are most often perceived and held up as the representatives of a pleasant but minority dissident movement. Like the neoliberalism of which it is an ally, neo-scientism is still, for the time being at least, a dominant ideology.

This is what Pierre Legendre also has discovered, to his dismay. After expressing his alarm at such a perversion of reason ("The notion that science can do anything") he adds: "That Science is a mythical reference is no longer in doubt, for now it sets itself up as the divine guarantor of truth. The quest for an impossible knowledge, so valued by Westerners ever since the early days of Scholasticism — the famous questioning *fides querens intellectum* (meaning literally 'faith in search of what is understood' 'faith seeking for intelligibility') — is considered dead."[57]

The End of a Culture

The question raised is ultimately this: is there still any such thing as scientific culture, in the strict meaning of the term? Most of the dissidents listed above are tempted to respond in the negative. Nothing less resembles a culture, with all that the word implies by way of coherence, openness and responsibility, than techno-science. Taking a deplorable turn, this particular form of rationality has rebuffed reason and become its most immediate enemy. Picking up Max Weber's concern, the philosophers of the Frankfurt school expressed the same thing when they feared that the instrumentalization and mythification of reason would, in the end, lead to its self-destruction. Think of the lines written by Horkheimer and Adorno at the end of the last war: "With the spread of the bourgeois market economy, the dark horizon of myth is illuminated by the sun of calculating reason, under whose chill light the seeds of barbarism are once more springing to life".[58]

For these two German philosophers, as soon as reason sees its status as critical thought evolve into that of assenting reason, as soon as it allows itself to become the servant of an existing order (the order of the market, in this case), its own truth "vanishes into thin air". "In this respect, instrumental rationality brings about, not an apotheosis of thought, not the liberty promised by the *Aufklärung*, but a regression all the more pernicious in that it represents itself (without any justification) as being rationally unassailable".[59] Jürgen Habermas's analyses, though less hard on modernity in general, are based nevertheless on a comparable critique of scientific ideology.[60] As for Cornélius Castoriadis, he never tired of explaining in book after book that this instrumental rationality not only served to legitimize capitalism, but that it was a creation of the latter.

Even if he expresses himself differently, it is from a comparable viewpoint that Jean-Marc Lévy-Leblond questions the entitlement of a modern science — afflicted with amnesia, fragmentation, loss of connection, and subverted by technology — to claim the status of "scientific culture" on which it prides itself. "An activity has meaning," he writes, "only if it first grasps the meaning of time and sees itself as leading from the past to the future. Could this not be taken as a possible definition of culture and as the reason why science is not — or is no longer, and perhaps is not yet — a part of it?"[61]

Incapable of embodying a genuine culture, caring little about the demands of critical or democratic reason, betraying the promises of the Enlightenment, techno-science nevertheless continues to make an unjustified claim to moral and intellectual pre-eminence. In opposition to politics and traditional morality and religious belief, the "techno-scientists" are able, as a result, to claim unrestricted freedom in matters of research. Therein lies the principal contradiction (if not imposture).

One might object that there are "ethics committees" whose official function is to control this frenzied research activity and, if necessary, to disallow certain proposals. But one has to wonder whether the real purpose of these procedures is not to provide an alibi for the headlong stampede, or even to prepare public opinion to accept innovations it would otherwise spontaneously reject. It is furthermore somewhat paradoxical that scientists — and even believers in scientism — play a preponderant part in such committees, rather than philosophers, ethicists, politicians or theologians, who seem to be somewhat intimidated token members. These ethics committees, by "feeding the media discourse on the new technologies, make the collective imagination more compliant, and provide advance justification for the very undertakings they claim to delay or prevent".[62]

In a context of widespread privatization, when the shrinking of government and the undermining of democracy are gaining impetus, the real power of these committees in any case becomes illusory. Nothing can stand permanently in the way of private research pushing its endeavors as far as they can go, however crazy they might be. The law itself, which attempts to the best of its ability to moderate the Promethean activism infecting biology, is seen to be largely powerless. The different texts, directives, guidelines and circulars pile up and multiply — particularly in Europe — to the extent that people can talk about a "biologization of the law". But their effect remains mostly theoretical. "Compared to the globalization of research networks, the powers of international institutions are still ridiculously ineffective", and there is a risk that very soon "economic and commercial arguments will gain the upper hand".[63]

Ultimately, neither ethics, nor morality, nor democratic decision-making will actually be decisive: it is the market, and the market alone. In this way "Gabor's rule" mentioned above, which says that everything technically possible must be realized, and that anything that can be sold will be manufactured, will be proven true. The ultimate "choice" will be made by the law of supply and demand alone. Such is the true picture underlying the problems raised, for example, by biotechnology and human cloning.

One example among many: in October 1998, after the media announced that American biologists had "transplanted" the nucleus of a sterile woman's oocyte into that of a fertile donor — the first step in cloning — Noëlle Lenoir, chair of the European ethical committee, denounced the prevalence of such purely mercenary thinking. "In practice," she wrote, "there are no controls. . . . Industrial lobbies have openly campaigned not to have any of this mentioned in federal legislation, not even in regard to the embryo."[64]

It would be a mistake to see this concern as an example of European caution as opposed to American intrepidness — an argument often used by supporters of techno-science and liberalism. Equally severe criticisms of the abjectly mercenary servility of applied research are made in the United States. Let us single out the book by the American journalist Jeremy Rifkin, in which he describes the way a handful of major multinational companies have made life their own property. "It's likely," Rifkin adds, "that within less than ten years, all one hundred thousand or so genes that comprise the genetic legacy of our species will be patented, making them the exclusive intellectual property of global pharmaceutical, chemical, agribusiness, and biotech companies".[65]

In reality quantitative criteria, the law of the market, a spirit of pure competition between laboratories, the newsworthy technological achieve- ment and the desire for dominance have infected scientific research as a whole. "The criterion of validity is now whether something functions, whether it works! The only thing left is to learn how to 'manage' your effi- ciency as well as possible, to put your management skills to work".[66] So scientific thought is not merely confronted with a "crisis in its founda- tions" (Lurçat): it must now become accustomed to a hobbling of reason itself.

But reason hobbled in such a way is the exact opposite of the superb definition of knowledge proposed by Emmanuel Lévinas: "Knowing be- comes knowing of a fact only if at the same time it is critical, it questions itself, and looks back past its origin".[67] The theologian Gustave Marelet expresses a rather similar kind of critique in providing an illuminating analysis of the concept of conscience and of the "wounded transcendence" that — in the face of all kinds of scientist reductionism — is what distin- guishes mankind from mere living matter.[68]

Set Reason Free!

Maurice Bellet suggests giving the name *écorègne* ("econo-reign") to the imperialism of market rationality, to this profuse and unrestrained ac- tivism that has taken the place of the old human objectives. The term de- scribes the blind, whirlwind expansion of the economy, an expansion ca- pable of striking down, day after day, "the constructions that gave man a certain idea of man".[69] In this respect, techno-science is merely one aspect of "econo-reign". It has evolved in close combination with it. It, and it alone, made the latter possible, supports it and stokes the boilers of the machine.

Thus defined, techno-science no longer appears solely as the rival or enemy of reason: it is, rather, the *prison* of reason. What is most urgent at the moment therefore is not to exalt "reasonable reason" but, more simply, to set it free. Setting reason free means returning it to its original modesty by renewing its ability to listen, and its openness. This is what Edgar

Morin wanted when he pleaded for a "dialogic principle" between reason and belief. Such an approach is much more essential than any physicalist conceit or binary conflicts *à la* Bouvard and Pécuchet. There is more intelligence in an attentive dialogue with other forms of knowledge than in any tired denunciation of philosophical or religious "obscurantism". "Science," writes Lévy-Leblond again, "is creating itself in opposition to itself". It is the neglect of this demand for the sake of a simplifying rationalism that results in the provision of a fertile ground for the esoteric bafflegab, magic cults, and manipulative sects that flourish in the modern world. Neoscientism and illuminism feed off one another, as if they were two aspects of the same intellectual disarray.

Once this has been understood, we should no longer be surprised if some people at the cutting-edge of science, like Francisco Varela or Henri Atlan, admit to a keen interest in the thousands of years of observations of the workings of consciousness by ancient forms of wisdom — in this instance, Buddhist or Hasidic. We may find it revealing that a specialist in information technology and cyberculture like Pierre Lévy simultaneously devotes a significant portion of his work to a reflection on Biblical mysticism or the teachings of the Orient.[70] Nor will it be a surprise to note that the Pope himself, in his encyclical *Fides et ratio*, in October 1998, called for a rehabilitation of reason in order to combat scientism (explicitly mentioned).[71] Nor will it seem any more surprising that "idealistic" preoccupations with consciousness and metaphysics are today enjoying a renaissance in certain international scientific conferences.

CHAPTER VI:
GLOBAL VS. UNIVERSAL

What are we to think when we encounter different cultures that all claim the universal as their private property? Each group wants for itself the illusory privilege of being the chosen people, but there's only one world and humanity can't escape from itself.

Claude Sahel, La Tolérance.
Pour un humanisme hérétique, Point Seuil, 1998.)

For centuries now, the problem of the universal has been haunting Western history. It's a "difficult question". It gives rise to confusion and misunderstanding. It confounds categories, subverts political and religious positions, and periodically provokes fantasies and intolerance. It also encourages simplistic oppositions: the universal vs. the particular; the emancipation of urban life vs. rural idiocy, the aspiration to be alike refusing singularity, world-wide internationalism as a replacement for nationalist chauvinism, the intellectual adventure of the mind vs. naturalist rootedness, global morality vs. pluralism of values, ideas vs. place, creative flexibility vs. entrenched ideas, etc. Behind these quarrelsome oppositions lurks the same question, that of the universal. It can be expressed very briefly: is there a human principle, an essentially superior value, capable of transcending racial, cultural or sexual differences, and of defining our common humanity? Should this value be set above all others? The question is indeed vital.

Early in our era it was already at the heart of the productive encounter between Jews, Christians, Greeks and Romans. For the Romans, the law, their great gift to the Western world, represented a certain notion of the universal — restricted, it is true, to the geographic extent of the Empire, and inseparable from the rank of Roman citizen. Later, the same question of the universal would preoccupy and divide Judaism, torn between "missionary Jehovism" and rabbinical isolationism.[1] In the Enlightenment, it became a permanent bone of contention between the *philosophes* of the Encyclopedia and counter-revolutionary thinkers for whom abstract idealism was a tyrannical concept, and an ideal humanity a disastrous invention. The great totalizing enterprises of the 19th century — liberalism, colonialism, post-Hegelian Marxism — all proclaimed themselves to be universalist, and pitted the march of "progress" against benighted indigenous traditions. This spread of Western universalism did not take place, as we know, without violence or disasters. "Civilizations which were in other respects highly refined, but based on the collective consciousness of the group, tribe, or caste, were swept aside by the advent of Western man. Not because he possessed firearms or horses, but because he had a different mentality, one that gave him the ability to detach himself from the world and then rediscover it through inner activity".[2]

After World War II, in the 1950s, 60s and 70s the positions were reversed within a single generation. It is true that at the time the complicity of the civilizing instinct with imperialism and post-colonial repression had encouraged a section of the political left to adopt a differentialist attitude which, consequently, had changed sides — provisionally.[3] This was a time of guilty conscience in the West, and of the "tears of the white man". Once, as Bardaisan (154-ca. 222), the philosopher of Edessa (modern Urfa, in Turkey), saw it, speaking of the East, the singularity of "countries" was exalted, as compared to the unifying centralism of states or empires.[4] Today, the same problem of the universal has been reformulated around the idea of globalization. Paradoxically, this time around it is done in a more ambiguous and troubling fashion, since current attitudes towards the universal actually reflect two contradictory requirements, one universalist, the other differentialist.

In the economic and political sphere, globalization is represented as an internationalist utopia full of promise, something to which it is difficult not to subscribe, in theory at least. Choosing — or forcing — the opening of economies and societies to the winds of change, abolishing borders, and diminishing regional differences and national sovereignties, it claims its objective is the transformation of the world into a "single country", a total village, where all will be able to enjoy the abundance springing from free trade, the rights of man, and democracy. It is in such terms that the "global ideology" I have referred to several times expresses itself. It opposes the universalist openness of the day after tomorrow — the right to interfere, freedom of movement, and the application of international criminal law — to the regressive, and potentially oppressive, compartmentalizations of the day before yesterday. Compared to residual forms of resistance — whether nationalist, religious, or protectionist — this openness represents the Good of universality against the Evil of particularism and the retreat into difference.

The global village and the prospect of a united world with no individual sovereignties[5] are held up as an alternative to the emotionalism and intolerance of local attachments. Tomorrow, we are assured, it will no longer be acceptable for some national difference or exception to be used to block the worldwide expansion of human rights and the "market society". Hence, any debate on globalization is loaded with prescriptive connotations. The obliteration of borders and the deregulation of world trade are represented as drawing different peoples together, something which could only be rejected out of some kind of tremulous self-centeredness: "The universal is often invoked in this debate," writes Shmuel Trigano, "as a moral imperative opposed to particularism, fundamentalism, and communitarianism."[6]

On the home front, on the other hand, the norms are reversed, almost word for word — the same rhetoric is turned inside out, like the finger of a glove. Now what is exalted is difference, singularity and irreducible identity, as opposed to social conformism or majority norms. When it appeals to social cohesion or the "common good", universalist discourse is now seen in a negative light, suspected of concealing the usual old Western or Judeo-Christian arrogance. This is the accusation repeated by "postmodernists" and "deconstructionists" like Richard Rorty, who in 1996 affirmed at a UNESCO meeting that universalism was nothing but the morality of the wealthy West.[7]

In multicultural democracies, pluralism and diversity of identity are preferred to the old globalizing visions and assimilationist policies. Contemporary sociology sometimes even goes so far as to question the very concept of society as having become meaningless in a context characterized by individualism and multiculturalism.[8] The most important things are differences and tribal variations, with each clinging to its own worldview, and even to its own conception of morality. Any all-encompassing perspective, any suspicion of holism, is rejected with horror. Let's be rid of radical universalism, with any need for shared values!

Within the limits of the law, the "society of individuals", to borrow Norbert Elias's expression,[9] allows each the sovereign affirmation of his or her identity. For the proponents of American "political correctness", for example, the universalist creed has become a somewhat absurd anachronism. It falls under the heading of what is for radical differentialists an "imperialism of assimilation". It suggests above all a form of domination that must be resisted. Only a WASP, with his indifference or condescension towards other cultures, can propose universalism. Someone like that is a threat to the legitimate rights of minorities. Humanist culture itself is suspected of being used as a weapon by an oppressive majority: Beethoven, Mozart, Proust and Faulkner have committed the unpardonable sin of being white, male, dead, and Western. Forgotten African cultures or Maori cosmologies are far preferable. In daily life, the "collective representations" so dear to Émile Durkheim and the social sciences are rejected in the name of uniqueness. Such a worshiping of differences and separate identities is a function of what the sociologist Michel Maffesoli calls "the return of the tribes", which he defines as an archaic survival, a "Dionysian ferment which is set fair to contaminate the entire social body".[10]

It is easy to see — or it should be — that there is a fundamental incompatibility between these two analyses. The concept of universality can't stand for both Good and Evil at the same time. As for the emphasis on identity, it is difficult to reconcile with any kind of appeal to the universal. "The transformation of beliefs into identities," Marcel Gauchet notes, "is the price to be paid when pluralism is taken to such an extreme that any conquering universalist ambition no longer has any meaning, where no form of proselytizing is any longer possible".[11] Strangely, this doesn't prevent both divergent views from being invoked alternately, and often by the same people! So the opposition between universal values and differences finally turns into a contradictory imperative. It is rather like the celebrated "double bind" spoken of by psychiatry (meaning an impossible choice). The most frequently cited example is the absurd urging to "be spontaneous"!

In fact, the ambivalent message regarding universal values more or less comes down to this: renounce distinctive identity, but assert your difference! This angst-producing impossibility lies, it seems to me, at the heart of our present-day confusion, and makes it even more acute. It explains why so many have lost their sense of direction. Such a contradiction calls for careful examination.

A New Kind Of Imagination

Let us first dispose of the problem's purely economic dimension. Globalization, which has been put into effect at an increasingly rapid pace since the beginning of the 1980s, is above all an industrial and — primarily — financial process. Free trade and the unhindered movement of capital are turning the whole planet into a single market. Seen in this light, it is not nearly as recent a phenomenon as people usually think: it is a fundamental aspect of the liberal idea, and has been from the beginning. "Capitalism," remarked Fernand Braudel, "has always been monopolistic, and goods and capital have always circulated simultaneously, for capital and credit have always been the surest way of capturing and controlling a foreign market".[12]

From the Renaissance on, long before Montesquieu's "sweet commerce", the extension of trading links to the entire known world was believed to encourage universal harmony and peace between nations. In the 18th century the Marquis René Louis d'Argenson (1744-1747), the French Secretary of State for Foreign Affairs, was already saying: "All of Europe should be no more than a general common market".[13]

Furthermore, the 19th century would indeed witness a temporary erasure of borders, and globalization of trade. "André Siegfried, born in 1875, was 25 years old when the century was born. Much later, in a world bristling with frontier barriers, he recalled with pleasure how he had once gone around the world with only one piece of identification: his calling card!"[14] From an economic point of view, the process of globalization has today been accelerated and amplified by a technological revolution that is abolishing time and distance. There's no doubt about that. And yet its nature is less radically new than is generally thought.

Be that as it may, this purely economic and financial view of globalization, interpreted as an "external constraint", is no longer adequate. The phenomenon has acquired a completely new dimension. The most significant analyses — particularly those by Jean-Paul Fitoussi, Philippe Engelhard,[15] and Zaki Laïdi — quite rightly insist on its simultaneously cultural and ideological make-up. This is what makes it truly new. Globalization now makes a case for sweeping social change, rendering analogies with its earlier forms obsolete. "Globalization now links all of social reality in a chain of cause and effect, with a starting point supposedly on the global, rather than local, level".[16]

In this respect, the notion of the "global" is accompanied by a slew of cultural references, consumerist aspirations, and symbolic representations, which actually combine to create a new kind of imagination. Found in the majority of people, or at least in the young, this imagination is vaguely based on some notion of universal values, on what Walter Benjamin called "what is alike in the world".[17] The same kind of sensibility spreads by way of thousands of channels, creating a virtual link between the young on every continent. Lifestyles are similar and cultures are enriched by diversity while at the same time they are blended into the same mix from one corner of the globe to another. People consume the same products, wear the same clothes, and ask for the same brand names, etc.. "World music" and "world literature" reinterpret local folklores and memories, while displaying an inexhaustible creativeness in making them universal.

The globalization of the media, in turn, increases the impression of a new planet-wide transparency, with the result that everyone has the sense of being permanently in contact with far-off places and sharing the basic emotions, the same instantaneous sentimentality, with several billion people like themselves, resulting in a progressive homogenization of affects which constitutes the great message of television. The problem is not so much whether this accessibility and proximity are largely illusory. They are experienced as realities, and create reactions in everyday political behavior. Furthermore, they are transforming politics itself from the inside out. To the "democracy of public opinion" there is now added what we might term a "diplomacy of public opinion". For better or for worse, a worldwide, explosive emotionalism has undermined the cynical old *raison d'État* and *Realpolitik* in the way people react to international crises. People are suffering and it is shown on television, so something has to be done.

Such a globalization of opinion is accompanied by both unquestionable progress (the propagation of a world-wide morality) and disastrous perversions (volatile reactions, selectiveness and manipulation of indignation, a sense of urgency with rapid forgetfulness as its corollary, and so on).

The principal ambiguity of this new universalist mentality arises from the fact that — like everything else — it has its roots in an ideology: the ideology of the market. In spite of appearances, therefore, the symbolic reality it offers cannot be reduced to just a moral requirement or a blossoming of "niceness" and "humanity" on the ruins of the old cynicism of the State. It could even be argued that this ethical assertiveness of "human-rights-ism" is often used as a smokescreen — and alibi — for an indefinite extension of market rationality. The devaluing of loyalties, the depreciation of national or social attachments, the discarding of collective identity in favor of a kind of fusional solipsism, all accelerate the disappearance of any reality intervening between the individual and the market. So globalization means above all the globalization of trade, publicity, and commercial vulgarity. We might call this the "Benetton strategy". "There can be little doubt that the consumer mentality, combined with the disappearance of any particular objective, reinforces this desire for direct and rapid access to a product or to knowledge".[18]

Retribalizing The World

It is hardly excessive to suggest that what Western society is doing, with false ingenuousness, is not so much making its own values universal, but its own *nihilism*. Behind a semblance of democratic universality, it is imposing its own most questionable features on others: the cynicism of power, individualist atomization, the thirst for profit, and contempt for the weak. It is doing this in an extremely aggressive manner, taking advantage of the almost total control it enjoys over channels of communication and cultural products. The market considers the latter subject to the rules of industrial competition. These rules are being made into weapons in a strategy for domination. Thus the unquestionably worthy defense of human rights and democracy allows a desire for economic expansion to be disguised as benevolent proselytism. Just as the Christian missionaries' desire to convert the heathen was once used to legitimize colonial conquest, the defense of human rights is used today to clear the way for multinational companies.

As for the debates about globalization, these obviously miss the mark since, generally, those who argue for and against aren't talking about the same thing. The former see themselves as the advocates of a greater freedom, while the others denounce a strategy of conquest. But they both use the same word "globalization" — a concept that it is nonsensical to reduce purely and simply to a form of the universal. Jean Baudrillard is quite right: "Globalization and universality don't go hand in hand, but rather are mutually exclusive. Globalization applies to technology, the market, tourism, and information. Universality is a question of values, human rights, liberty, culture, and democracy. Globalization seems irreversible, but instead the universal is fast disappearing".[19]

Aggressiveness in matters of trade and the ambiguity of the universalist design in any case explain the violent refusal it provokes in reaction to it. Traditional societies are reacting in a more complex manner than is realized against the irresistible power of this commercial imposition of uniformity, They are digging in their heels, it is true, but there is more to it than that. A jealous fascination exists side by side with the suffering of the displaced, while the need to imitate and the attraction of individualism and consumerism coexist more or less — or alternate — with violent rejections and retreats into identity — with, unfortunately, a strong preference for the latter. Thus, globalization automatically provokes its opposite. Universalism — having gone largely astray — is producing an excess of difference, in the worst sense of the word. André Gorz gives a good description of this paradoxical, and exponential, process: "Culturalism, racism, fundamentalism, are the various reactions, charged with resentful aggression, by which the victims of power apparatuses attempt to preserve some ultimate kind of belonging. . . . The price that has to be paid for this sense of security is total submission to the traditions, rites and leaders of the community, a total renunciation of independent existence by the individual".[20]

The "tyranny of communications",[21] i.e. in this instance, the globalization of the media, is merely one aspect of this vast disruption of universal values. But it is typical enough to deserve analysis. Here again, things are not as simple as is generally thought. The world-wide dominance of CNN, the proliferation of appealing networks, the omnipresent — from Dakar to Shanghai — soap operas and "wheels of fortune" — it's impossible to view all this as merely the triumph of inanity over universalist morality. The intrinsic nature of the media plays a part in this distortion of the message.

When people speak these days of the somewhat worn theme of the celebrated "global village" once prophesied by the Canadian scholar Marshall McLuhan, they forget that McLuhan himself foresaw that this shrinking of the world by the media would go hand in hand with its retribalization. For him, "the compressional, implosive nature of the new electric technology is retrogressing Western man back from the open plateaus of literate values and into the heart of tribal darkness, into what Joseph Conrad termed 'the Africa within'".[22] The open society, the visual heir of the phonetic alphabet, he added, no longer has any meaning for the retribalized youth of today. He believed that the closed society, "the product of speech, drum and ear technologies", was in the process of being reborn."

To illustrate his argument, McLuhan even referred to a symptom foreshadowing this regression, namely the way Hitler used radio — and the "emotional eloquence" it made it possible — to broadcast to a "psychological mob".[23] After all, hadn't Hitler "used the radio to retribalize the Germans and rekindle the dark atavistic side of the tribal nature that created European Fascism in the Twenties and Thirties"?

McLuhan may seem to be overstating the case. One might object that the same radio, used by the Allies, served the cause of freedom equally well. General de Gaulle's appeal, broadcast by the BBC on June 18, 1940, is proof of this. And yet! Many present-day reflections on the workings of the audiovisual, with its appeal to the emotions rather than to reason, and many accounts of the power of the media to erode politics and distort democratic debate, are greatly indebted to McLuhan's initial intuitions.

The Specter of America

One misapprehension should be disposed of at this point. It is common, in Europe and elsewhere, to interpret this imposition of uniformity on the world as Americanization. In other words, globalization is seen as merely an imperialistic ploy to expand American hegemony. It is said to be allowing the United States impose its own model of liberalism — that of the market society — on the entire planet. By Americanizing the world, by enabling certain standardized types of behavior to triumph, it is said, we are producing robot-like consumers, eager to share in the "American way of life". Thus we are supposed to be working to further the ends — both ideological and industrial — of the foremost world power.

Such an analysis is at once partly true and mostly false. It is partly true because it is undeniable that the standardization of the nature of consumption and of individual behavior serves American interests above all. Since the collapse of Communism, the dizzy increase in the United States' power and the strengthening of its cultural, political, military, and economic hegemony (with each of these four aspects reinforcing the others) are beyond question. This desire for supremacy has even, as we have seen, been advanced in Washington as a theory by advocates of "enlargement".[24] So the process of globalization does indeed benefit the American economy.

But that is not the whole story — far from it, indeed. The endless arguments on this point between "pro-" and "anti-"Americans appear rather ridiculous once political passion is set aside. Let us first point out that the United States is itself undergoing a deep political crisis, a democratic "dispossession" to which all the phenomena described above — the decline in voter participation, the weakening of the political compared to the media, the crisis in social cohesiveness and the grinding to a halt of the mechanism of integration (the "melting pot"), the decline of Anglo-Saxon culture and even of the English language, the criminalization of society, etc. — are anything but foreign. From this point of view, the United States is in the same boat as the other developed countries. It is confronting the same dangers and struggling with the same contradictions.

We could go a little farther, and make a paradoxical suggestion: if indeed the world is becoming Americanized, America itself is in some danger of becoming "de-Americanized"! In a long, hard-hitting article in *The Atlantic Weekly*, the American political scientist Robert Kaplan didn't mince any words in describing this American crisis. "But when voter turnout decreases to around 50 percent at the same time as the middle class is spending astounding sums in gambling casinos and state lotteries, joining private health clubs, and using large amounts of stimulants and anti-depressants, one can legitimately be concerned about the state of our American society".[25]

As for the — genuine — American culture, it is as much threatened as the others by the mass media of Hollywood or Atlanta. When we automatically see this sub-culture as in some way the essence of America, we are forgetting that North American intellectuals themselves do not take it seriously. Most of these are among those who find it distressing. Disneyworld and *Dallas* alone do not represent all American culture. "For the American intellectual," comments René Girard, who has lived in America for a half-century, "genuine culture comes from Europe, and what is produced in America is often considered a commercial phenomenon which doesn't even deserve the name of culture".[26]

On the topic of globalization, it should be added that the most critical analyses have come from American commentators. It is among the faculty at Princeton, and Berkeley, for instance, that we find the most radical critics of this mindless "McWorld" which is today spreading its cultural vacuousness over the entire globe. They are the first to castigate this caricature of universalism, this obscene picture of Western culture our age offers the other nations of the globe — or imposes on them. For such as these, the important thing is clearly to denounce not the Americanization, but the devastation, of the world.

Benjamin Barber, a professor of Political Science and a radical critic of the global sub-culture (of American origin or not) offers a good analysis. According to Barber, the perversion of universalism by "McWorld", and the reactions of rejection, intolerance or fundamentalism that it provokes (which he calls "Jihad"), make a couple from hell: the two trends go hand-in-hand, reinforcing one another and contributing to the same outcome: the torpedoing of the universalist design. In the age of globalization, he writes, "ideology is transmuted into a kind of videology that works through sound bites and film clips. Videology is fuzzier and less dogmatic than traditional political ideology: it may as a consequence be far more successful in instilling the novel values required for global markets to succeed".[27]

Like his European colleagues, Barber finds disastrous the disguised violence of this kind of "persuasion" which forces people to make an impossible choice: it results in either a copycat submission that disconnects them from their own culture or a revolt in the name of identity that, ultimately, removes them from the modern world. The case he makes against "McWorld"-style globalization is basically an attack on a violent uprooting imposed from without. The Frenchman Marcel Gauchet is saying the same thing when he accuses Westerners of having so much faith in the universal validity of their technology and principles — even when these are warped — that they leave others "no choice but to adopt them en bloc, thus repudiating their entire history and existing culture".[28] But, he adds, in substance, a value coming from elsewhere and represented as universal can only be adopted if this adoption is the result of an internal decision. Quite the opposite is coming about with this tidal wave that is imposing everywhere — and at great speed — the same market rationality, the same individualism, and the same "disenchantment" (*Entzauberung*) discussed by Max Weber.

"This is what gives the various 'fundamentalisms' their meaning, and their roots: they function as substitute social identities, protecting the individual against competitive social relations and preserving his identity against the values, pressures and changing requirements of the surrounding society".[29]

Signs Of The Tribe

For Benjamin Barber, this aggressive confusion of universal values with the calculated self-interest of multinational corporations calls even more for criticism in that it is deliberate and, so to speak, self-sustaining. By this, I mean that it corresponds to a change in the nature of capitalism, which is transformed by global competition. Nowadays, the huge firms that compete for a share of the markets are no longer really selling products, but *signs*. Competition is basically no longer a matter of the quality of the goods on offer — of their durability, their design, their novelty, and so on. In these respects, most are of equal worth, and even identical. Competition is no longer even mainly a question of price, at least as far as the mass market is concerned. Price competition has certainly not disappeared, but it now plays a marginal role. Now, the real trade war on the global front is being fought on the terrain of the image, of the logo, and of symbolic loyalties.

When, early in the 1990s, Nike, the sports shoe manufacturer, or Gucci, the leather-goods producer, opened stores in former iron curtain countries such as Hungary or Poland, they were not counting on the actual quality of their products to make inroads into these new markets. They were basically selling signs, which locally were identified with Western "superiority". By purchasing a brand-name product — costing an arm and a leg — the young Hungarian or Pole was acquiring, above all, a sense of belonging. When it was later shown off to friends and strangers, the function of this symbol would be to signal their imaginary membership of a group, a tribe, a superior category of being. In this way all consumption is transformed into a trade in symbolic identity, and this imaginary value has won out in spades over value in the narrow sense of the word.

Even more grotesque is the fact that in Vietnam, which is still communist but increasingly open to Western consumer goods, tobacco manufacturers came close to bankruptcy because of the mimetic infatuation of the Vietnamese with American cigarettes. In the streets of Ho Chi Minh City or Hanoi, the average consumer needed real courage to buy a packet of Vinh Hoi, Du Lich, Melia or Thang Long cigarettes for twelve *dongs* with the whole world looking on, rather than a packet of Lucky Strikes for a thousand *dongs*. To limit the damage, the local manufacturers had to change the names of their own cigarettes to something with a more Anglo-Saxon resonance. What an ominous symptom of the loss of self! And what a splendid example of the triumph of sign over substance!

So what exactly does this all mean? That the companies competing on the world market are literally obsessed by the manipulation of symbols. They are quite rightly aware that the success or failure of their products depends on it. But this war of symbols is obviously dependent on conditioning through advertising. "Brand-names are ciphers for associations and images carefully cultivated by advertising and marketing".[30] The escalation of advertising budgets over the past few decades shows this increasing erosion from substance to symbol. The figures given by Benjamin Barber are quite incredible. Worldwide expenditures on advertising have grown a third faster than that of the world economy, and three times that of the world population. They increased sevenfold between 1950 and 1990, from $39 billion to $256 billion. Per capita global spending grew from $15 in 1950 to almost $50 by 1995.

But we have to take our analysis a little further. This substitution of sign for substance, this transformation of the playing field of trade competition, has had important consequences. There is today a perfect assimilation of the values the industrialized societies claim to defend with the products they want to sell. In other words, values have become products, and products have become values. The collusion between the advocacy of universal values and commercial marketing has as a result been strengthened to an incredible extent — it almost amounts to a total assimilation. There is no need to point out that in the process values have lost their fundamental legitimacy. For adherents of traditional cultures, it has become quite logical to see globalization, as controlled by the West, as a monstrous manipulation of the claim to universality. This manipulation, as we have seen, implies undermining the reality, not only the world, but also of humanity and its genuine needs. "These necessary goods are condemned to 'die' as use values, for their only remaining value is as commercial exchange values. Human needs themselves are condemned to disappear. They will simply be transformed into market preferences. In this way, everything pertaining to the organic bond between people is destined to be emptied of its corporal reality and projected into the infinite spaces of abstract values".[31]

We can go farther still. With the conquest of markets becoming contingent on the triumphant promotion of symbols of belonging, with commercial competition taking place more and more in the realm of symbols, advertising has been able to draw the conclusions. It has become a matter of stimulating the urge to imitate one thing (wearing Nikes, for instance) rather than another, then holding up an imaginary identity (I belong to the clan of Nike-wearers), and attributing universal appeal to this fantasy (*everyone* dreams of wearing Nikes). Advertising hype, targeted ever more unerringly, adapts its content to the desired objective. It all comes down to selling identity, meaning difference. Tribal loyalty — basically differentialist — has in this way become the central concept of sales propaganda. So globalization's universalist advocacy is turned on its head, or shown to be a sham.

If it was only a question of advertising and trade, we could still see things in relative terms and console ourselves that it is possible to further the universalist cause in other ways. It would be extremely foolish to do so. Indeed, the boundary between the media and advertising, between the concept and the slogan, is becoming more permeable every day. On this specific topic we may again borrow a telling example from Benjamin Barber —MTV, which for him embodies nothing less than "McWorld's noisy soul". Owned by Viacom, itself owned by Sumner Redstone, MTV has been able to make itself into one of the most powerful of world media. It broadcasts music videos (particularly rock), news, and children's programming, from Tokyo to Los Angeles and from Calcutta to Lagos. It was with MTV that "a landmark in the history of media" took place: "the boundary between entertainment and advertising has completely disappeared. . . . On MTV, everything is promoting something or other."[32]

In this way, an unnatural union between discourse and merchandise was consummated. "This media universe exploits all the genres, blending them skillfully, mixing in fictions and creating myths to put some life into consumption, some consumption into meaning, meaning into imagination, imagination into reality, reality into virtuality, and, coming full circle, virtuality into real life, so that the distinction between virtuality and real life is obliterated, and everything is bastardized."[33]

This exemplary apotheosis of "McWorld" coincides with the no less exemplary defeat of the universalist design. The question we have asked, ultimately, should encourage us to reflect on what one Parisian commentator has called "blissful globalization". "So who, then, will defend the public interest, our common good, in this kind of Darwinian universe of predatory companies only too willing to take control of civilization's essential symbolic references?"[34] wonders Benjamin Barber.

Is there any need to remind the reader that MTV has been extensively imitated and that, in the United States as in Europe and Japan, the new powers that be in field of communications are embarking on intense competition to create media empires on a global scale, all subservient to the same predatory cynicism. We have probably not yet seen the true extent of this battle for control of the multimedia, which creates much greater risks than the imposition of uniformity on the world. "The objective of each of these titans of communications is to become the citizen's one and only interlocutor. They want to be able to offer him news, data, leisure and cultural activities, professional services, financial and economic information, and to have him connected by every means of communication possible".[35]

We have come a long way from the grand universalist design we started out with. So let us briefly return to it.

A Return To The Source

In a recent essay, Alain Badiou, a strongly atheist philosopher and still faithful to the memory of the French student revolt in May 1968, speculates about the decisive importance of St. Paul in the creation of universalism. While rejecting the essential aspects of the Christian message ("those fables"), he notes that the fourteen Pauline Epistles (and in particular the famous *Epistle to the Galatians*) contain what is indeed a "founding" statement of universalism.[36] For Paul, the definition of the human being should no longer depend on any particular identity (Jew, Greek, man, woman, etc.), but only on the affirmation of faith in Jesus Christ. Badiou holds that this unlocking of the prison of uniqueness in the name of a higher principle able to transcend all differences corresponds exactly to the demands of modernity. Apart from his faith in the resurrection of Jesus Christ, Paul of Tarsus can, it seems, be viewed as a thinker of our times, if not a former student demonstrator from May 1968!

Of course this odd kind of exegesis, which consists in interpreting an idea by amputating it from it origins, has been the butt of irony: after all, it would just as well enable us to see Nietzsche, the son of a Protestant minister, as an unconscious mystic, Ernest Renan, a former seminarian, as an anguished believer, Émile Combes, the moving force behind secularization in France, and also a former seminarian, as a closet Catholic, or St. Augustine, the theoretician of inwardness, as the distant inventor of psychoanalysis! But once this criticism has been formulated, Badiou's point isn't so far-fetched as it appears. The Epistles of St. Paul do indeed contain "unprecedented" statements about equality as well as universality (which is its corollary), and these would indeed have far-reaching consequences. Paradoxically, what we can blame Badiou for is basing his reflection on the Epistles alone — i.e. on Paul himself — while neglecting the wider historical and philosophical context.

I am thinking, of course, of Judaism and Hellenism, of their interaction and reciprocal influence. I am also thinking of the early disagreements between Jews and Christians that would see Christianity break away from its Hebrew foundations and expand gradually into a Gentile world steeped in Greek philosophy. In each case, the question of universality is involved. It is even crucial. It would be presumptuous to attempt to summarize several centuries of controversies, philosophical debates, persecutions and heresies, and innumerable texts, all in a few paragraphs. Furthermore, today's new fashion for Biblical exegesis, and the erudite reexamination of this productive period, are symptomatic. What was at stake during these early centuries (and even earlier) was to be of the greatest importance for the men and women of today. So we can at least give a few pointers to the period.

In its initial relations with Judaism, the influence of Greek thought was considerable, although it would be a mistake to minimize the specific contribution of the Jewish tradition.[37] Judaism, from just after Alexander the Great's conquests in the Mediterranean region (from 333 to 324 BC), came into contact with a universalist Hellenism which would "open the gates of the universe to Jehovism", to use Jules Issac's expression. Indeed, Alexander, who dreamed of forging the Macedonians, Greeks and Persians into a single race, saw himself as the soldier of the universal. In his eyes, the unity of the human race (*konia*), had to be based on a single language (*koine*) — a spoken version of Greek. "In the Jewish communities of the Diaspora, scarcely more than a generation was required for the ancestral languages, Hebrew or Aramaic, to be abandoned in favor of Greek, the language of the victors, and so deserving of its triumph. From the 3rd century B.C. the Diaspora spoke and wrote Greek".[38]

This dominance of the Greek language was accompanied by that of philosophy's conceptual categories. The Greek translation of the Torah, of the Pentateuch, and later of the Prophets and the canonical texts, was not only a technical undertaking that would result in the creation of the Septuagint (the Bible in Greek translation), for it also meant a stronger hold of Greek ideas on the Judaism of the Diaspora. This monumental translation de-emphasized anything in the Hebrew texts likely to shock an enlightened pagan, and reduced the distinctively Jewish elements of the message, making it more universal. It spiritualized the image of God contained in these texts. In other words, it "transposed specifically Semitic turns of phrase and concepts, using words and concepts borrowed from the Greek schools of philosophy".[39]

This contact — which, as we have seen, is what defines Alexandrian Judaism — led to the triumph — though for only a few centuries — of a universalist trend that struggled against a tendency for an "offended withdrawal" — and would de so for a long time. In 168 B.C., the destruction and pillage of the Temple by the Seleucid king Antiochus IV, who raised a statue of Zeus on the site ("the abomination of abominations", later texts would call it), was to exert a similar influence on Judaism in that it wiped out its misguided "national" character. "Once this Temple was destroyed according to Divine will, Judeo-Alexandrian thought felt much more free to proclaim — this time in the most authentically Jewish line — the advent of a religion of the spirit for all men of good will".[40] Philo of Alexandria, is, as we have said, the most admirable representative of this Judeo-Hellenism, with its explicitly universalist teaching. We could provide any number of quotes to support this, including, for instance, the following, which is extraordinarily close to St. Paul's Epistles, and very modern in its inspiration: "The world is attuned to the law, and the law to the world, and a man subject to the law is by virtue of that fact a citizen of the world".[41]

We can consider the Pharisees of Jerusalem, with whom the first Christians would come into conflict and of whom St. Paul was initially one, to be the direct heirs of this Judeo-Hellenic universalism. This is in any case the theory Isidore Lévy proposes,[42] adding that they had managed to "reconcile Moses and Pythagoras, or, if you prefer, Plato". "The Pharisees, becoming ever more numerous and active as we approach the Christian era, were the Palestinian disciples of the Hellenistic Jews of Alexandria". This fact allows us to know better the tradition of which Paul was really the heir, and the mental categories he assumed at the time of his conversion on the road to Damascus, something of which his Epistles would obviously bear the trace.

Flesh And Spirit

The birth of Christianity and its distancing of itself from Judaism would lead the latter to "repudiate the idea of universalism". As Christian missionaries, influenced by Paul, turned their attention to the pagan world and gradually converted it, Judaism turned inward on itself. It took refuge in rabbinic law, or placed itself under the protection of the Persian Empire: "The Judaism of the Alexandrian variety, with its Hellenistic and universalist spirit, disappeared, and the Talmud became the center around which the spiritual energy of Israel regrouped".[43] This rabbinical and Talmudic retreat became even more pronounced as Christianity took over the Roman Empire.

The universalist teachings of Philo of Alexandria became the butt of criticism, whereas this same Philo (who has today been rediscovered by Jewish intellectuals) might have played a role for Judaism something like the one a Father of the Church played for Catholicism.[44] The Septuagint was abruptly set aside, from the second century on, in favor of the so-called "Bible of Aquila", closer to the original Hebrew. This belated hostility to the Septuagint would even be taken to an extreme. "The Palestinian rabbis declared that the day this translation was created was as disastrous as the day the golden calf was made, and that on that day darkness covered the earth for thirty days".[45] It is true that in the meantime the Christians had made not only the Septuagint their own, but also the works of Philo, and turned them into weapons for use against the Jews.

The early Christians, in any case, held themselves up as the only bearers of the universalist message — as *"Verus Israel!* The new Israel!" Their quarrel with Judaism hinged on this particular point. By establishing a new Israel "according to the spirit" in opposition to the old Israel "according to the flesh", Paul was actually pointing to the primacy of the universal over the particular, i.e. the priority of faith in Christ's resurrection over membership of a group or race. This is precisely the point at which the three inheritances of the Western tradition, the Greek, the Jewish and the Christian, came together. The essential aspect of Paul's message is not so much, as his detractors have maintained, the way it opposed faith to the law, as it did universalism to identity according to the flesh. "At the root of Paul's thinking is the Christological principle: 'For if many died through one man's trespass, much more have the grace of God and the free gift in the grace of that one man Jesus Christ abounded for many' (Romans 5: 15)'. There is no difference between Jews and Greeks: 'For we hold' he says elsewhere, 'that man is justified by faith apart from works of law'" (Romans 3: 28).[46]

From this point of view it is indeed possible to maintain, with Alain Badiou, that Paul played a part in "founding of universalism", but only on condition it is pointed out that this proclamation by St. Paul is inseparable from his faith in the Resurrection and that, furthermore, it did not come out of thin air, so to speak. It was part of a process, of a maturing, in which Hellenism and Judaism played a part. Just like the Jews of Alexandria, the first Christians were not content to merely borrow concepts and "categories" from the Greek world in which they lived. They were steeped in it. What took place was not merely an encounter between Christianity and Hellenism, but a partial Hellenization of Christianity. This would be particularly true in the 3rd century, during what would be seen as the golden age of patristics. Some of the Greek Fathers of the Church would indeed carry on the Judeo-Alexandrine tradition, but from a Christian point of view, and would remain more or less under the influence of Philo's teachings. This was so for the most famous among them, Clement of Alexandria, the author of *The Tutor* and the *Miscellanies*, apologetic texts in which we can detect the influence of Plato and of Stoicism.

It is fair to add that this Hellenistic influence would not always be looked upon very kindly by orthodox theologians, perpetually on the lookout for the slightest hint of heresy. "The heretics [in their eyes] wanted to blend elements borrowed from the philosophy of the age with the true doctrine. Such is the thesis defended by Irenaeus in his *Adversus Haereses*, and systematically applied by Hippolytus in his *Philosophoumena*.[47] But these doctrinal tensions would not stand in the way of a mutual interpenetration of Hellenism and Christianity.

Taken up and renewed in this way, Greek universalism would even assume the character of self-evident truth under the Christian banner. "Indeed, as Christianity extended its conquests, when the Emperor himself was officially Christian and a Christian culture was created, nourished entirely on classical culture, the dividing line introduced in the beginning became fainter: people became — or, more often now, were born — Christians without ceasing to be "Hellenes"."[48] As for the refusal of Judaism "according to the flesh" to join the *Verus Israel* and recognize Jesus as the Messiah, it would, for centuries, as we know, fuel Christian prejudice against Judaism and the "teaching of contempt" to which we shall return later.[49]

The universality of values called for by early Christianity in any case explains the energy with which it spread during the first centuries — an expansion of which neither the extent nor the speed is always fully recognized today. We are of course familiar with the steps by which the European West was converted to Christianity, from Gaul to Ireland and from Spain to the Germanic lands, or even to eastern Africa (Ethiopia was evangelized by the 4th century!). On the other hand, the success of Christian proselytism in an easterly direction — in Mesopotamia, Greece, India, or even China — is less well known. It is true that it was usually carried out by Nestorian missionaries — followers of Nestorius, the former Patriarch of Constantinople, whose teachings were declared to be heretical by the councils of Ephesus (431) and Chalcedon (451). If this expansion deserves a brief mention here, it is because it was motivated by a universalist attitude, and made a considerable effort to conduct an ongoing scholarly dialogue with Greek philosophy.

The most spectacular example is without any doubt the university at Nisibis, created in the 5th century, on the confines of Mesopotamia and Persia. Founded to teach the Christian scriptures, it rapidly welcomed thousands of students from Mesopotamia and elsewhere and became one of the great centers of learning in the Near East. There, innumerable translations were made, and the scholarly confrontation between Greek thought and Christian teaching was systematized. At Nisibis, "elementary logic, whose rules had been laid down by Aristotle, was essential for understanding the exact meaning of crucial passages in the Scriptures. It was also necessary for religious controversy. It was a sternly impartial, 'technocratic' tool, wielded by an elite prepared to enter with zest into religious controversy with its many Christian and non-Christian rivals".[50]

This is just one instance. It helps us to understand how the spread of Christianity, and later of Islam, which continued uninterrupted for several centuries, also meant, indirectly, the spread of Abrahamic and Greek values. The progressive secularization of these universalist values should not allow us to forget their initial source, and how they came into existence. Such is the paradox of this lengthy — perhaps too lengthy — correlation between Judeo-Christianity and Western modernity. It is a paradox the modern mind finds difficult to accept, and more difficult still to come to terms with in full knowledge of the facts. I find the interpretation suggested by Shmuel Trigano enlightening where Judaism is concerned: "Islam and Christianity changed the face of the world by pushing back paganism: in a way they 'civilized' (in Judaic terms), or 'Judaicized', a major portion of the world, something that gave the people of Israel an immense audience and a sphere of activity it would never have acquired otherwise. . . . In other words, both Abrahamic religions contributed to building the universality of Israel and the message of Sinai".[51]

The Deracination Of The Self

We still need to understand why this prodigious expansion of Western universality, soon to be secularized, was accompanied by so much violence, so many crimes, and so much aggressiveness towards different cultures. A lengthy study of history isn't needed to turn up myriad examples of arrogant and destructive universalism. The way things turned out, it seems that the urge to liberate oneself from one's roots, which is the essence of the human spirit of adventure, became destructive once it was made into an absolute. The nagging awareness of the innumerable devastations, the grim accompaniment of progress, leaves the Western world with a burden of historical responsibility that it has to learn to deal with. What is needed is for it to resolve the problem of the universal and the particular in some other way than by the desperate — or hypocritical — "double bind" mentioned above. Neither the destructive aggressiveness of instrumental rationality (a debased form of proselytizing), nor the exalting of difference (an uneasy conscience, leading nowhere), represents an acceptable answer today — even less so when the tragedies they have caused are taken into account! But we still have to find a way to reconcile the universalist heritage and difference.

It is a characteristic of globalization, in the perverted form given it by the market economy, to simultaneously threaten both universal values *and* differences. It destroys its opposite even as it destroys itself. Therefore, both must be rehabilitated and defended together. Such is the problem we have to confront. I don't think there are many more crucial ones. The question is no longer essentially religious. It is, for example, a stumbling block for lawyers attempting to develop a genuine world law, or to extend the minimal morality expressed by the various international charters to the entire planet. Today, indeed, what is commonly called the idea of human rights — even when it is not perverted by market cynicism — provokes the same kind of reaction as missionary Christianity or victorious Islam once did. "The 1948 Declaration of Human Rights has often been accused of expressing the predominance of Western culture".[52] Most conflicts and misunderstandings arise from this ambiguity. We have to advance beyond this point. Hence the need to promote not just the "modest reason" that can help us turn our back on the scientist temptation but also a non-exclusive universalism that leaves room for singularity, without ever ceasing to question it.

I find it revealing that this new harmonization of the particular and the universal is also the mission Shmuel Trigano has assigned to Judaism itself. "It is no more by measuring itself against the past, or against prevailing ideas, that Israel will forge its presence in the world, but rather by basing everything on its power to enlighten, by staking all on the one, by opening up for humanity the path to the universal under the one. Indeed all Humanity is called to a similar reversion".[53]

We must indeed learn to combine these two dimensions of our destiny differently, namely the uniqueness that defines us, and the universality that invites us to transcend the former. Better yet, we need to understand, despite the dogmatism and intolerance of our times, that it is uniqueness itself which makes us receptive to universality — on condition the former not be exclusive, nor imposed by violence, nor restricted. The plenitude of the human condition consists ideally in piecing together these two contradictory imperatives: on the one hand our deep-seated need for roots, and on the other our need to free ourselves from them. Our need to belong is as great as our need for liberty, but this belonging can now be "diverse", to use contemporary language — although this makes it is no less necessary (just as the desire to escape from one's finite condition, and above all to escape from the obtuse barbarism which always sees the other, and other places, as dangers, is equally necessary). "The universal is the local without walls", as the Portuguese writer Miguel Torga so brilliantly put it, in 1954, in a lecture given in Brazil.[54] The most clear-sighted legal-minds express the same paradoxical truth when they discover, by experience, that "it is only through the mediation of a specific culture that each individual can achieve humanity".[55] Let us note that, in another form, this is what Hegel was saying when he differentiated the spirit of peoples (*Volksgeister*) and the World Spirit (*Weltgeist*) — though without treating them as opposites, adding that the former discover their truth and destiny in the latter.

This perpetually sought-after and perpetually unstable balance, this ability to recognize the existence of the other without capitulating to his prejudices, ultimately defines tolerance in the strict meaning of the term. It asserts itself, but without demagoguery or renunciation; it rejects both closed certitude and irresponsible relativism. "Tolerating different opinions un the name of an allegedly permissive morality is often little more than an admission of actual indifference: if all opinions are equal, they are all reduced to being objectively worthless, and in fact there is no norm against which they can be judged".[56] True tolerance doesn't lead to indifference to the truth; accepting the other doesn't mean renouncing one's self; allowing room for difference doesn't stand if the way of a quest for similarities. The philosopher Simone Weil, the author of a famous book on *The Need for Roots* (*L'Enracinement*), died in 1943, long before the term 'globalization' became popular, yet she gave the best conceivable definition of what might be a peaceful form of universalism when she wrote, in substance, that it is our duty to uproot ourselves, but it is always a crime to uproot others.

Chapter VII:
"I" in Search of "We"

"Nowadays we no longer look for emancipating ideas, because
we are already emancipated. That's the whole problem".
Joël Roman, Chronique des idées contemporaines,
Bréal, 1995.

Here we are, liberated individuals, growing dizzy as we reflect on our own victory which is by now so complete that it frees and oppresses us all at once. Every day, deep within ourselves, we recognize how serious our dilemma is: we enjoy complete liberty, combined with a deep perplexity. Modernity has bequeathed both of them to us, so we know they are indissolubly linked. We feel trapped. We would not give up our precious autonomy for anything in the world, but we just can't bear this feeling of emptiness any longer. We hesitate constantly between our consciousness of enjoying a privilege and a vague sense of loss. The privilege is what Kierkegaard called "the ability to choose who we are", the unheard-of ability to create ourselves and live the way we wish. The loss is what D.H. Lawrence defined so depressingly when he called it the "crucifixion of individual solitude" — an indefinable emptiness. "In today's world," wrote Louis Dumont, "individualism is on the one hand all-powerful, but on the other it is continually and irremediably haunted by its contrary".[1] It would be hard to give a better definition of our malaise. So we have become solitaries: autonomous, but angst-ridden. We are at once the lucky beneficiaries of, and uneasy participants in, a history we can neither totally reject nor accept.

Our good fortune is far greater than anything past generations could ever have dreamed of. We have to remind ourselves of this, above all, and never forget it. The new forms of liberty, the conquests, often won after difficult struggles, are genuinely living realities, whose importance cannot be minimized. Whether it is the emancipation of women, the liberty of the citizen relative to those who govern him, or the dignity that is now automatically granted the individual, our inheritance is vast. It is quite understandable for us not to want to trade it away, and that we should even be prepared to defend it — and to do so resolutely — against any kind of nostalgia or tendency to return to the past that might diminish it. In other words, we are prepared to do battle on that front. We don't want to give up anything of what we have won — and rightly so.

And yet, at the same time, we can't conceal the fear, vertigo and confusion we feel when we are confronted with our sense of nothingness. We experience, almost physically, the sense of a surplus, of an excess, of being menaced from the rear. Beside this torment, the arguments between liberals and conservatives, or Democrats and Republicans seem so trivial, the polemics about "revolt" against the social order so insignificant! What social order? The rhetoric and pointless skirmishing in the public arena just seem unbelievable, as if some very ancient battles were still being fought. The contradiction seems so much more profound, so much more serious, in the form in which each and every one of us experiences it.

We must try to plumb these depths, the way we sound out the bed of a river before we venture to travel up it.

Awareness Of The Self

How can we do that, without first remembering how extraordinary the *personal* freedom we enjoy today is, in time as well as in space? In writing this, I am not only speaking of the ideal of liberty (which pertains to the political order), but of the simple *awareness of self*, the way we have taken possession of our selves, and the limitless autonomy we now enjoy. Charles Taylor is quite right to speak ironically of those naturalist philosophies that "tend to think we have a self the way we have a heart or a liver".[2] In fact, the "self", as a primordial value, is a recent invention — even a very recent one. Only a deficiency of memory and thought allow us to see the individual as a banal, everyday reality, remaining oblivious to its amazing historical novelty and to the qualitative leap our election of this value has brought about in our relationship to the world. True, the past has never been devoid of exceptional individuals, of solitary, extraordinary ones, real people of whom literature and history have spoken for centuries. But, on the other hand, what was still impossible then was the individual as a conquest, and as a horizon.

The Greek and Roman worlds, for instance, lacked any conception of the person or the individual. The Latin word *persona* — like the Greek *prosopon* — was the name for a theatrical mask. "Ancient thought saw the *persona* as above all a social function assigned by society to one of its members. The concept was borrowed from the theatre and judicial procedure, not from psychology. People had no consciousness of existing as a person".[3] The great sociologist Norbert Elias also likes to insist that it was impossible for the ancient mind to conceive of an individual devoid of any collective dimension, considered as an isolated person, enjoying priority over the group.[4]

As a historian, Fernand Braudel also speaks of this almost inexistent individual consciousness in the times, not so long past, when humanity was still immersed in what he calls "material life" — by which he meant a communal reality, preoccupied with survival, and making proportionate demands, a ghostly presence we still sometimes sense looking over our shoulder. "Countless inherited acts, accumulated pell-mell and repeated time after time to this very day, become habits that help us live, imprison us, and make decisions on our behalf throughout our lives. These acts are incentives, impulsions, patterns, ways of acting and reacting that sometimes — more frequently than we might suspect — go back to the beginning of mankind's history".[5] We have to understand that, for millennia, the idea of escaping from this necessary solidarity of the group was quite simply unthinkable. The ancient prayer chanted by medieval liturgies never expresses a desire for liberation from the group, but from all kinds of other things: *A peste, fame et bello, libera nos, Domine* ("From plague, famine, war, deliver us, O Lord!").

Better still: today, when we speak of our "inmost thoughts", when we think of our inner being as a place composed of infinite domains, of secret, unexplored nooks and crannies, we don't realize that this localization is not a "universal given", but a historically limited way of interpreting the self that has come to predominate in the modern West; it had a beginning in time and in space, and it could very well have an end, too.[6]

A Western invention? To dispel any doubt that might remain, it should be enough to turn to any of the great non-European teachings — the Chinese, for example. A scholar like François Cheng is of invaluable assistance here. A Chinese philosopher and calligrapher, with an excellent knowledge of our culture (he has translated Jacques Derrida into Mandarin), Cheng is an indefatigable intermediary between the Eastern and Western traditions. He regularly stresses in his writings and interviews that Chinese thought has never explored the notion of the "subject" as a free and independent entity in any depth. It has never really undertaken such an interpretation other than in contact with the West (and even then has done so only rarely).[7] The same could be said — and has been said by Louis Dumont — of Hinduism or Buddhism, for whom individualism and wisdom can only be acquired at the cost of withdrawing from the world.

Smoke And Crystal

But we should first define our terms. The word "liberty" is inadequate as a definition of our prodigious conquest. It refers to just one aspect of the phenomenon, and, for that reason, falsifies most debates about the "society of individuals", to borrow Norbert Elias's expression. The most useful approach is certainly one that combines two classifications. They are separate, but complementary. The first, dear to Louis Dumont, is the opposition between holism and individualism; the second, often used by Marcel Gauchet, instead opposes heteronomy and autonomy. What do these terms mean?

Holism, from the Greek word *holos*, meaning 'whole', is, literally, an epistemological point of view according to which a scientific account is necessarily dependent on the entire field in which it appears. By extension, the word characterizes the priority accorded the group, the whole, the community, rather than one of its "elementary particles", namely the individual. Holistic societies give pride of place to collective values — those of survival, identity, cohesion, or defense — by deliberately limiting the liberty of each member. Basically, the history of the world has been dominated by holism, even if it took a more or less oppressive form depending on circumstances. Jacques Monod gives a good description of this age-old servitude when he wrote: "For hundreds of thousands of years, the fate of a man was one with that of the group he belonged to, with that of his tribe, outside which survival was impossible. As for the tribe, it could only survive and defend itself by preserving its cohesion. Hence the extreme subjective power of the laws that organized and guaranteed this cohesion".[8] Need we add that the same kind of holism is still the rule today in most societies of the southern hemisphere, even if they are beginning to be affected by individualist subversion?

In an extreme form, absolute holism is a characteristic of totalitarianism (in which the *totality* rules). In this respect, the fusional forms of twentieth-century totalitarianism were no more than "diseases of modern society, [resulting] from the attempt, in a society where individualism had deep roots and was predominant, to make it subordinate once more to the primacy of society as a whole".[9] Hitler himself provides a perfect example of this desire for a return to total holism in his declaration to Hermann Rauschning: "The age of individual happiness has passed. Instead, we shall feel a collective happiness".[10]

At the opposite extreme, radical individualism would represent anarchy, in other words the tyranny of disorder. On the one hand, the inflexible order of crystal, on the other the random turbulence of smoke.[11]

Actually, no society has ever been monolithic to such an extent. Most have combined a certain amount of holism with a greater or lesser degree of tolerance for individualism. But it remains true that the dominant value was — universally — holistic, and that this was so until modern times. "Even on the eve of the Declaration of the Rights of Man, the individual was still not recognized, except as an impediment: he had no social existence apart from his place in the circle or network of communities to which he belonged".[12] The entire trend for emancipation, particularly since the Enlightenment, can be seen as a slowly progressing appreciation of individualism, accompanied by a corresponding decline in holism. This liberation should be understood in a broad sense. The modern individual doesn't just become free of his subjection to the State. He has also been freed from a whole range of restrictions placed on him: by his village, his family, culture, community, biological inheritance, etc. He frees himself from such roots, to confront the universal.

As for the opposition between heteronomy and autonomy, it refers to a markedly different aspect of the same question. Heteronomy, from the Greek *heteros*, "the other" and *nomos*, "the law", signifies the fact that the rules governing one's conduct, ones impulses and the principles on which one acts, are derived from a source outside rather than within oneself, autonomously. Until modern times, the law was anchored in — and founded on — some transcendent reality, usually religious in nature. It was laid down from without, or rather from above, by a ruling authority that imposed it on its subjects. This is the meaning of the famous principle, *cujus regio, ejus religio*, which was put into effect, for example, at the conclusion of the Peace of Augsburg, in 1555, following the wars of religion. The religion, chosen by the prince, with its specific prescriptions, naturally applied to the prince's subjects.

But religion, it was thought, was imposed on the sovereign himself, and was supposed to set limits to his omnipotence. Thus it was favorable to the exercise of freedom. Tocqueville defined the paradoxical advantages of a certain amount of religious heteronomy when he noted: "Thus while the law permits Americans to do what they like, religion prevents them from conceiving, and forbids them to commit, anything rash or unjust. Religion, for the Americans, never interferes directly in the government of society, and should therefore be considered the first of their political institution; for if it does not give them a taste for liberty, it singularly facilitates the use of it".[13]

Our democratic societies have definitively rejected all such forms of heteronomy, even residual ones. They aim to give themselves an autonomous foundation, i.e. they aim at self-creation, or self-organization, to quote Cornélius Castorides. Even better, they allow each member the capacity to choose freely — though within the bounds of the law — the person he wants to be, the values to which he adheres, the moral principles he recognizes as legitimate, the beliefs he accepts, etc.. For the modern sensibility, the very hypothesis of a value originating from outside, from on high, or anywhere else, is perceived as prejudicial to personal liberty. We have freed ourselves for once and for all from what John Stuart Mill called the "despotism of custom"

So the modern utopia combines individualism and autonomy; it places the "self" at the center of its design and has to accept its own incompleteness, but now without the assistance of any transcendent reality. This incompleteness is sometimes explained by (erroneously?) transposing Gödel's famous theorem, which originally applied to mathematical logic. It was formulated by the American logician of Austrian origin, Kurt Gödel (1906-1978), whose work changed our conception of mathematics forever.[14] For Gödel, consistent systems cannot be complete, and complete systems cannot be consistent. Transposed into the domain of the social sciences, this means that no collectivity can find its foundations within itself. So it seems that any community, to ensure its own coherence, must turn to a reality outside itself, to some kind of "elsewhere".

But it is precisely this supposed inevitability of heteronomy that our democratic societies reject. They rely on what we might call a self-institution of values, conceived as minimal, of which the legal order seems the best approximation. Total autonomy then, under the exclusive surveillance of civil and criminal laws! Such a polytheism of values, regulated by the law and by the law alone, takes literally the utopia formulated by Eugène Fournier, an independent socialist of around the turn of the last century, who wrote in his *La Crise socialiste* (1908): "We have smashed all traditions and now are more liberated and more destitute than the early American pioneers, who had at least brought their Bible with them. Our schools are godless and our villages priestless. We only have our individual consciences, open to any kind of criticism, to guide us, with only the penal code to hold it in check".[15]

Of course these few brief lexical remarks may appear very simplistic or perfunctory. Nonetheless, they help us understand the extraordinary ontological and historical revolution represented by this victory of the "I" over the "we", and by "here" over "elsewhere". It allows us to put our finger on what is new about a transformation that, after a lengthy history, has led to the creation and complete triumph of that strange invention, the modern individual. And, conversely, it also casts some light on the nature of the various forms of nostalgia that at times assail us.

"Go Into Thyself"

In the collision of cultures[16] resulting today from the spread of modernity throughout the world, individualism is considered the most Western value of all. It is in reaction to it (to its "egoism", its corrosive power and the nihilism it brings with it, etc.) that traditions which feel threatened are in revolt. It is also the thing pointed to when the West is accused of cultural imperialism. This is no accident. More even than progress, equality, reason, or a belief in universality, the primacy of the individual is, for better or for worse, at the very heart of our Judeo-Christian inheritance — it is even tempting to say of our Christianity itself. Neither historians nor theologians are in any doubt on this point. "The individual, defined as a person to be accepted without consideration of his qualities and constituted by a choice independent of his membership of social and ethnic groups, is a Christian invention".[17]

However, Greek thought did have a part to play in this "invention". Christianity was built on foundations laid by Plato. On this specific point,

Nietzsche was quite right to see Christianity as "Platonism for the people". But we still need to see how the transition between the two took place. For Plato, access to a superior life depends on unifying the self and mastering the passions. This ability to attain, inwardly, the realm of the Ideas is not bestowed on us by education. It is an individual capacity peculiar to us, allowing us to see, calmly and lucidly, how we should act. It invites us to be "masters of ourselves", i.e. both reasonable and free.

It is in the name of this triumphant sovereignty, of this inner wisdom, that Plato maintains in most of his dialogues (the *Gorgias*, for example) that it is best to be a just man, even if this comes at the cost of suffering or renunciation. It is always a superior choice to one of outward success earned by an acceptance of injustice. This crucial departure allowed Plato to dismiss the "ethics of honor" and the heroic values that prevailed in most ancient cultures — including Greek culture itself. Prior to Plato, the essential duty, the only virtue imaginable, consisted in the quest for fame and glory in the social domain, or the warrior's *agon*. These attitudes were in conformity with holism, and bowed to fatality in everything else. By preferring a tranquil contemplation of the cosmic order and the soul, Plato turned everything on its head, to the benefit of individualism. He effected a transvaluation of values, to borrow Nietzsche's famous injunction: "Transvalue all values!" For Plato, the superior life is no longer identified with glory won in society or on the battlefield. It is, rather, "when reason — purity, order, moderation, the immutable — governs the desires and limits their tendency to excess, to instability, to caprice, to conflict".[18]

Behind Plato's self-control we can discern an intention to unify the self that represents a first step towards the modern concept of the individual. The "self", envisaged in this way, is able to detach itself from particular communities, affiliations, and societies. It became able to oblige Athenian public opinion, even when unanimously hostile, to recognize the stubborn solitude of its personal freedom, as Socrates did. And this was not all. For Plato, only ignorance can separate us lastingly from love of the Good, since the latter is the supreme form of happiness. If we fail to choose the Good it is because we are still in a state of ignorance. So it becomes the responsibility of each to overcome ignorance. Victory over the passions, desires and prejudices will be the natural result. No painful decisions will be required. Full recognition of the concept of the sovereign individual is not far off.

The next step — a modest but decisive one — would be taken by Christianity, and by Saint Augustine in particular. The notions of choice, faith, and the will, were given new prominence. In the Gospel message and in St. Paul's Epistles the recognition of the individual as a primordial value emerges unambiguously. Indeed, faith, or conversion, is not and cannot be a collective decision. It can only depend on a direct relationship with God. In fact Jesus says so explicitly: "There are many standing at the door, but those who are alone will enter the bridal suite". "Baptism, which is to say the abandonment of idols for the true God, or the decision to place one's life under the Lordship of the Crucified One, implies a personal choice and *a readiness to make decisions by which the individual, in choosing his God, also chooses himself as a person endowed with an individual conscience*".[20] This is the heart of the Biblical injunction.

In other words, the locus of ethical decision has become the individual rather than a communal imperative, social law, or imperial authority. In this resides the radical subversion carried out by early Christianity. It was a break — to some extent — with holism. The priority granted personal conscience freed it from the constraint of social norms and made resistance to them possible. This is precisely what the early Christians would do, defying the Roman *imperium* even at the cost of the famous persecutions. Of course, this emancipation from collective norms and the law was not limitless. The individualism of St. Paul did not completely reject everything that derived from holism. But these restrictions on the "gift of freedom" of which the Scriptures speak were enumerated by St. Paul in a limited way: respect for the freedom of others, voluntary obedience to those in power and the construction of the community. Paul justifies these limits in the Epistle to the Corinthians when he says that "not everything is useful", or "not all things are helpful". In all other matters *liberty became the rule, and law the exception*.

Need we point out that this affirmation of inner freedom implied a distancing from Judaism — not only where the Law in the collective sense was concerned, but also in regard to the notion of impurity, which is not unrelated to the way people conceive of inwardness? For the Jewish tradition, impurity comes from outside, with respect for the *kashrut* (kosher) laws providing protection for the inner self. Abstention from certain foods prevents the impurity from getting in. But according to the New Testament message, as it is expressed for example in St. Mark's Gospel: "There is nothing outside a man which by going into him can defile him; but the things which come out of a man are what defile him. . . . (Thus [Jesus] declared all foods clean)" (Mark 7: 15-19). If there is any impurity, it is in man from the beginning, and it is for him to reject it. But from now on the path to purity will lead from the inner to the outer world.[21]

It was Saint Augustine, a fervent reader of the Neo-platonists and of Plotinus, who truly theorized the primacy of the individual. "The human *ego* was then given a new interpretation, and was seen as the oneness of a substance endowed with conscience and will-power, of a person on whom reason and emotion have been bestowed. The center of the universe is the *self*, the face-to-face with the Creator".[22] It is traditional to add that in writing his *Confessions* — at the same time inventing what we call "autobiography" — Augustine was testing his own individual consciousness and illustrating both its depth and its complex evolution. So did Augustine invent a literary genre? There is no doubt about it. However, the genre in question is just the product of a much more essential "breakthrough": one that promoted both inwardness and the will, the two being interconnected.

Inwardness is a central theme in St. Augustine.[23] He initiated a philosophical and epistemological tradition that has left traces throughout all of Western history. He introduced what was a completely novel doctrine in the 5th century, and pointed to a specific path, "leading from the outer to the inner, and from the inner to the higher".[24] Truth was no longer to be found in the outside world, but within the self. Salvation was not to be found in a wisdom exiled from the world, but in voluntary consent, assisted by grace. Why was grace required? Because, in the Augustinian theory of the two types of love (charity and desire) the will of man, perverted by the Fall, is incapable of choosing the true form of love on its own, without the assistance of grace. Augustine's lengthy dispute with Pelagius and Pelagianism would turn on this point.

Setting aside this question of grace, which is a theological one, it has been said, and rightly so, that it was actually St. Augustine who invented the *cogito* long before Descartes by granting the individual conscience pride of place in the search for truth. A single saying by the Bishop of Hippo suffices to sum up this whole Augustinian meditation on inwardness: *Nolis foras ire, in teipsum redi; in interiore homine habitat veritas* ("Instead of looking without, go into thyself, for truth resides in the human heart").[25] To this we could add a second maxim — this time a definition of human free will: *Ego, non fatum, non fortuna, non diabolus* ("I myself, not fate, nor destiny, nor the devil").

This combination — which is, in fact, ambivalent — of *inwardness* and will seriously crippled (or transcended) the basic Platonic mastery of the self. It was no longer just a matter of recognizing the "sovereign Good", which we could reject through ignorance. With St. Augustine, the problem became one of self-awareness, of personal liberty and, above all, of choice. It was at this point that individuality acquired its modern meaning. "Because of its doctrine of the immortality of the soul and individual judgment, there is no doubt that Christianity contributed to establishing the incalculable value of the individual".[26]

Towards Modern Identity

From Erasmus to Spinoza, from Descartes to Locke or Hobbes, from Montesquieu to Rousseau, from Condorcet to d'Holbach, from Kant to Hegel or Mendelssohn, from Smith to Tocqueville or Fichte, from Schopenhauer to Nietzsche and many others, we can trace the subsequent deepening of this confrontation between the individual and the group, between the aspiration to freedom of conscience and the religious or secular heteronomy that attempts to suppress it. All of Western history, with its advances and retreats, can be interpreted as a slow and irresistible victory of the "I", corresponding to the construction of the modern identity. We should be grateful to Charles Taylor, who has so magnificently traced this development for us. In describing the genesis of individualism, he suggests we distinguish four major stages.

First, the invention of inwardness by Plato and Saint Augustine would be taken up and developed by laymen such as Montaigne, Descartes and Locke. Taylor sees Descartes, for instance, as one of the founders of modern individualism because his theory confronts the individual thinker with his own responsibility, requiring him to construct an order of thought for himself, in the first person singular.[27] The second stage was the Reformation, which would help to affirm the ethical value of "ordinary life", conceived as family life and work. Thirdly, the 18th century would discover, most notably through Rousseau, the "voice of nature" in the human conscience. Rousseau, in this respect, "is the starting point of a transformation in modern culture towards a deeper inwardness and a radical autonomy"[28] — an autonomy which would be demanded in the name of a "civil religion", and in opposition to the ecclesiastical dogmatism that Rousseau condemned, even though he was a believer and considered Christianity a major spiritual and individualist revolution in the history of mankind.

"Whoever dares to say: 'Outside the Church there is no salvation' must be expelled from the State', we can read in *The Social Contract*. Such a dogma is only valid under theocratic government. Under any other kind, it is pernicious".

Kant, in turn, gave Augustinian inwardness a new foundation by rejecting the heteronomy of the moral codes of the past and, of course, by rejecting any need for divine grace. He asserted the (autonomous) capacity of the human spirit to define morality by looking within itself. In this respect, "Kant's theory is really one of the most direct and uncompromising formulations of a modern stance".[29] The final stage was when, during the Industrial Revolution, middle-class mentality and Victorian sensibility imposed a reading of history as moral progress for which all are responsible and from which all benefit.

Two elements were to accompany this gradual victory of individualism over the centuries: a progressive emancipation from religion and the increasing power of economic logic.

The distancing of established religion and the longing for autonomy would be the major contribution — never fully realized — of the Reformation, followed by the Enlightenment and the French Revolution. Protestantism, unquestionably, first radicalized Christian individualism by encouraging a return to New Testament sources, and to a direct relationship with the Divine. It de-clericalized religious faith, making it a personal matter. "Protestantism in its Puritan form (and also certain of its repercussions on pietistic Catholicism) was to give the West new impetus. Individualism taken to an extreme gave rise to a radically secular and economic 'morality': Utilitarianism".[30] But the upheaval initiated by Protestantism was by no means restricted to this.

The Reformation also expressed an obsession with social disorder, as has been shown by Michael Walzer. For Calvinists, not only the unemployed, the poor and the homeless represented threats to the social order, but so too did a licentious and undisciplined nobility. Calvinism therefore advocated a self-disciplined, even ascetic form of individualism in order to reconstruct the social order on the basis of personal responsibility, to be rewarded by earthly success. So, starting with the Reformation, the meaning of religious belief and obedience were also transformed. "The relationship with an entirely different kind of God no longer meant acting through an intermediary; on the contrary, it required an act of faith performed by an autonomous conscience. The pendulum of religious legitimacy swung towards the individual believer, liberating an enormous potential for subversion, the effects of which would be felt far beyond the Reformation itself, and even its political repercussions".[31]

This birth of the bourgeois mentality — permanently afflicted with an inferiority complex towards the nobility — was also accompanied by a new formal critique of the "code of honor" and of aristocratic vainglory (which Plato and the Stoics, and later St. Augustine, had also condemned earlier). The exalting of everyday life, the parsimonious practice of "sweet commerce" and quiet family life were seen as the real characteristics of civilized life. A "new model of citizenship in which the practice of commerce and the acquisition of property played an unprecedented part"[32] replaced an ethics of glory, of extravagance and of conquest (the *libido dominandi*). Traces of this sensibility are to be found in Hobbes as well as in Montesquieu, Pascal, La Rochefoucauld, Molière, and others.

The Enlightenment, and later the French Revolution, were in line with this simultaneously bourgeois and individualist perspective. It was a matter of defining an autonomous society uniting free men, a "modern" society — i.e. one without a past or traditions, and totally open to the future. The progressive disaffection from religion, the increasingly emphatic rejection of heteronomy and transcendence, created a vacuum that would gradually be filled by economic rationality alone, and by a liberal order that "had no collective myths apart from those representing money, or the dynamics of quantity".[33]

From the outset, furthermore, this economic logic directly influenced the emergence of the modern individual, rendering it both possible and necessary. It made it possible because individual autonomy, as we recall, is also a "luxury" that is only permitted by at least a relative victory over scarcity and the fatalities of famine, epidemics, and private wars. It made it necessary because the development of trade and, above all, industry, required new, and more individualistic, types of behavior.

Schumpeter has clearly demonstrated how these "new types of work and behavior became a break with the stable order of earlier times, with the cultural milieu that for centuries had immobilized and protected preceding generations. Their development accompanied the loosening of the ancient bonds linking workers to the village, to the manor, or clan, and often even to the extended family. Individualism came into being because the opportunities to give shape to life that had always been shared by the group became individualized".[34] Schumpeter reminds us that individualism resulted, not only from the secularization of the Christian heritage, but also from the fact that, from the outset, it went hand in hand with industrialization and capitalism, a "flood breaking down all the traditional dams", and which began around the time of the late Middle Ages.

In an unjustly neglected book, Louis Dumont stressed the extent to which individualism, having become the founding value of our modern societies, was an integral aspect of the primacy of economic reality over ethics or politics. It was one of the conditions of the all-encompassing economy.[35]

Empty-Handed?

As for the rest, it is striking to note that the fear that excessive individualism would result in desolation has always been present throughout this long development. Having repudiated the traditional myths and models, the bourgeoisie of the Enlightenment and the French Revolution were obsessed by the fear of being left "empty-handed", to borrow Alphonse Dupront's expression. According to him, the major drama of the French Revolution — a drama whose aftermath we are still experiencing — was "its evident inability to create an image, a mythology, or a conscious definition of society", its obvious failure to provide itself with an "order of spiritual values capable of providing it with a foundation or justification".[36]

Contrary to what is sometimes thought, this vague uneasiness provoked by the triumph of individualism was not only to be found among thinkers of the counter-revolution or the theoreticians of *Sturm und Drang*[37] and of German romanticism (Johann Gottfried Herder, for example). It also occurred in some self-confessed partisans of the Enlightenment. Tocqueville, for instance, expresses the fear that democracy might be weakened by an "excess" of individualism, leading the citizenry to lose interest in the social pact. "In some dark pages of his book *On Democracy in America*, Tocqueville foresaw that one of the principal threats to the new-born democracies would be their inability to protect the liberty of all from the individualism of each".[38]

It is impossible to re-read these pages today without being struck by their prophetic intuition. "I want to imagine," writes Tocqueville, "under what new traits despotism might arise in the world; I see an innumerable mass of men, similar and equal, who restlessly turn in circles seeking after trifling and vulgar pleasures, with which they fill their souls. Each one, existing apart, seems a stranger to the fate of all the others; his children and personal friends for him make up the human race in its entirety".

A similar pessimism can be found in Max Weber, though he is considered the inventor of "methodological individualism" and a resolute opponent of holistic trends. Weber feared that the emergence of a purely pragmatic and rationalist individualism might lead to a kind of moral ice age, where the only relations with others would be commercial. For Weber, "men [therefore] risk being restricted to activities whose means will be based on rational calculation, but whose purposes, if not renewed, will have less and less meaning for them".[39]

This uneasiness is naturally more visible in some modern theoreticians who are more or less nostalgic for holism. They speak of the desocializing power of individualism, and of the risk that each individual, in an atomized society, will be at the mercy of the more powerful. This was true of Auguste Comte, Marx, and Durkheim, to cite only a few instances. For Marx, it was clear. "Let us note above all", he writes, "the fact that 'rights of man' distinct from the 'rights of the citizen' are nothing but the rights of a member of bourgeois society, which is to say of egoistic man, of man isolated from mankind and from the community".[40] In his *Sixth Thesis on Feuerbach* he again stresses this idea: "The essence of the human," he writes, "is not something abstract, inherent in the isolated individual. It is actually social relations taken as a whole".

For Durkheim, the concept of autonomous individual interests is absurd. No society can free itself completely from the "collective representations" on which its cohesion depends, and which contribute to the identity of each member. In other words, it illusory to speak of independent individual thought. Objectively, no such thing exists. It is necessarily social in nature. As for the interests of the individual, these are also strongly social in nature, even if this is not recognized, for they depend on mental categories that have been developed collectively and that it is dangerous to put into question. Durkheim's pessimistic view is all the more interesting in that, at the same time, he considers the old holistic forms of solidarity, the symbols and collective myths of the past, to be dead and gone. So he points gloomily to a new vacuum, with nothing to fill it. "One characteristic of the way we have evolved is that it has destroyed all pre-existing social conditions one by one; they have been given their marching papers one after another, whether by the gradual erosion of time or by violent revolution, but in such a way that nothing has been done to replace them".[41]

Paradoxically, this basic disquiet coexists in Durkheim alongside a voluntarist belief in progress and liberal democracy. Everything points to a permanent conflict in him between pessimism and determination. The way he has assumed this contradiction makes his work all the more engaging. "His passionate defense of liberal values, and his uneasy questioning of their ability to survive, show that he was personally in favor of a culture of the future, a culture of the individualist market — a preference that condemned his theory to complexity and contradiction".[42]

Georg Simmel, an important sociologist, Durkheim's contemporary (and friend), also spoke, in the early years of the 20th century, of "this abstract individualism that goes hand in hand with the money economy". While acknowledging the merit of the modern economy in freeing the individual from the "inter-personal" burden of tradition, he admitted fearing the advent of an age in which monetary intercourse would be the only link between people.[43]

Closer to us, in the 1970s certain American sociologists, like Christopher Lasch and Richard Sennet, have expressed the same kind of uneasiness at the ravages of contemporary individualism.[44]

An Invisible Frontier

Today, as we enter a new century and millennium, it is easy to see that this uneasiness has turned into fear. Greater danger is brought by the triumph of individualism, to a degree neither Tocqueville, Durkheim nor Weber could have anticipated. The very extent to which the "I" has triumphed gives its full meaning to the anxiety it has provoked. We mustn't minimize the extent of this triumph. No past age has ever come close to this reality, this new continent, no less astonishing than the America of the conquistadors or the mythical cities of Cibola, a continent where the individual has been liberated from age-old forms of subjection, freed of the constraints, fatalities and moral codes that dominated his existence ever since he first appeared on earth. No society before ours ever attempted to have individuals live together without any constricting absolutes or dogmas to define a common Good, whether mythological, philosophical or religious in nature. No human group has ever achieved such a coexistence of diverse liberties and disparate beliefs, each a micro-sovereignty on its own. No one had ever been able to enjoy, individually, this providential latitude, this *play*, in the mechanical sense, in which each person's whim is only restricted by the whims of others. Yes, the extent of this triumph is indeed impressive.

The uneasiness it stirs up in us is no less impressive. This time, we seem to have gone beyond the point of no return, beyond which not only does society threaten to disintegrate, but individualism itself backfires on the individual. The massive liberation of the "I" ultimately runs up against a brick wall. If we push its victory to the limit, we will have fallen into the trap: we will have gone beyond the stage of liberation to a state of disaffiliation — of solitude, in other words. And this is as true of the victory of autonomy over heteronomy as of individualism's dismissal of holism.

Marcel Gauchet posits that the last remaining traces of transcendence or heteronomy were probably obliterated some time around 1970, or a little later. At this time in our history the autonomy of society, the citizen and the individual had won a conclusive victory. All connections to the divine, even indirect, were broken, and no one any longer felt "controlled from on high". Paradoxically, this elimination of the religious dimension hastened a corresponding crisis in the secular "transcendence" that had grown up in opposition to it. Without an adversary, secularism as a unifying cause also ran into trouble. Its collapse left us without a voice, but not immune from anguish. And with good reason! "What has been carried away in the flood is the whole notion of the *res publica*. The entire civil edifice we had erected to meet the challenge of metaphysical dependency saw its foundations crumble".[45]

Where individualism is concerned, the ancestral dynamic of emancipation — of "we" against "me" — seems to have been surreptitiously turned on its head. Once centrifugal, it is now centripetal, for now we gaze longingly towards the center of the group. A new kind of suffering is coming into existence. No longer is there really any desire for emancipation, but, instead, fear of exclusion. There is less readiness to fight social restrictions than to prevent the ultimate loosening of the few remaining bonds that unite us. People feel less need for heroic rebellion than for some reassuring sense of belonging. The individualism we desired just a short time ago has today been replaced by an imposed, or "negative" individualism, replete with fear and distrust of others. The new causes taken up by activists — those of the marginalized, the stateless, the homeless, and the unemployed — are a symptom of this reversal. The symbolic meaning of this present-day vocabulary deserves more attention: it points to an extraordinary change. The social struggle is no longer carried out in the name of "freedom", but instead denounces the harshness of exclusion from society, the injustice of exile. It no longer expresses a desire for emancipation, but longing for society.[46] Even when, as is sometimes the case, this longing is expressed through violence.

Sociologists working in the field who are trying to understand the nature of this conflict have been the first to notice this symbolic reversal. "It is striking to see that the suburban riots . . . are anything but a revolt against oppressive authority, anything but the portent of a revolution threatening the economic system. Confrontation is not the last resort in a context of power struggle, but an attempt to be part of that context, to be taken account of, to be listened to, to establish a social connection through conflict, since there is no other way to do this".[47]

Ultimately, individualism itself has come to mean something new. While the chattering classes continue to sing — and even trumpet — its praises, as a lived reality it is no longer what it was: now it is seen as a negative. The gold of freedom has turned to dross. "The amputation of collective reality has helped bring about a loss of confidence in oneself and in others, and the sense of being part of an unstable, erratic, dangerous world, in the grip of invisible and uncontrollable powers. With an individualism that is no longer one of conquest, but rather of loss, the question that obsessed people at the turn of the century has become central again: how can we create and maintain a society?"[48]

If I spoke of the "chattering classes", it was no accident. Indeed it is amusing to see that, in this respect, a profitable form of Nietzscheism has survived in spite of everything — one that is still able to set the tone and occupy itself by excoriating often imaginary tyrannies, combating worn-out clericalism and standing up with false daring to yesterday's "authorities". These people claim to be fighting last night's blaze, when the real threat is today's flood. Is this a paradoxical anachronism? "For a good century now, let us say since the days of anarchistic Nietzscheism, the destruction of idols in general and of morals in particular seemed to be the high road to the emancipation of the individual. We have moved abruptly to a situation where morality has again become central to the self-creation of the individual".[49]

But let's waste no more time on such antics: it's as easy to pick the wrong priorities as the wrong war.

Individualism vs. The Individual

So, at the very moment when he could be celebrating his victory, the individual senses he has been cruelly deceived. If he has lost his chains, he has also been deprived of any role to play, any place, any identity. He is relieved of his obligations, but has also lost any identity, security, or clearly recognizable social function. Lacking any place in the collective memory, freed of any cultural allegiances, he strays through his newfound liberty like a frozen wasteland. The interminable rise in unemployment and the continuously increase of instability have only shown him all the more clearly how painfully he has been cast adrift. "Society has turned out to be incapable of producing individuals to serve it, and of making use of the individuals it produces. Society no longer has enough reality to allow individuals to define themselves by the way they serve it. Instead of serving it, they now have to produce it".[50]

Confronted with the way the "we" has been demolished for the (theoretical) benefit of the "me", the individual seems each day to regret more and more the terrible price he has had to pay. The main reason for his bitterness is the paradox he has discovered: the fact that today's "market democracy" is built on a furious valorization of the individual, but, in reality, shows little respect for the human person. This is the biggest surprise! In the world of work, for instance, the hierarchy of values is reversed. It's no longer the individual who is expected "make himself useful" by fulfilling a productive function; now it is society that generously grants him employment. Work, even when hard, and underpaid, is considered a "privilege". Furthermore, with the new forms of business management as with the sharing out of profits, this very work, in excess supply and therefore of little value, is sacrificed to profit. The wage earner carries very little weight compared to the financial priorities that have subverted the economy.

In the day-to-day organization of production, the paradox is even more obvious. The individualized style of management that is now the rule is rarely to the individual's advantage. The sociologist Robert Castel, a respected expert on matters concerning the workplace, has pointed out the perverse consequences of this individualization of responsibilities within the firm. Made possible by technological advance, but encouraged by the need to maximize profits, this excessive division of labor works to the advantage of some but penalizes the great majority. It makes the weakest extremely vulnerable. As for the new management, which skillfully exploits the mantra of "self-development", it sometimes turns out to be more devious and restrictive than in the past. "Management-speak says: 'Give of yourself, identify with your company.' This is different from the demands made of the Taylorian worker. He was asked to perform a difficult and alienating task, but otherwise was left in peace. Away from the workplace, he was free at last. And perhaps this explains how the working class was able to organize and create its own forms of reaction. Today, if the managerial discourse is applied to the letter, not even this distance remains".[51]

Everything else has moved in the same direction. The disappearance of working-class culture, the disappearance of the firm as a community, the destruction of the union movement, have all helped to free the individual, but left him defenseless against the new ways of thinking and of exercising power, against which he can do very little. This is all the more true because even the most elementary requirements for social cohesion have been sacrificed on the altar of international competitiveness. This was a fool's bargain, and many economists are now asking whether it was necessary. One of them, Anton Brender, has shown the foolishness of a shortsighted calculation that meant sacrificing a society's cohesiveness to the supposed competitiveness of its companies (by accepting massive layoffs or wider inequality, for instance). It was foolish indeed, for people are coming more and more to recognize that the new international competition between international economies is placing an increasing importance precisely on the "intangible differences" represented by education, a national consensus, equality, and civil peace — in other words on everything that contributes to social harmony — a harmony ultimately based on shared values, confidence, political stability, etc..

However, in most Western countries, all these factors have been neglected for the past couple of decades, with an astounding lack of foresight. A fool's bargain, indeed! "The conditions under which competition between nations is carried on have been reversed: sectors and activities that previously seemed to have little to do with international competition [transportation and education, for example] now play a decisive role. But these sectors were the most neglected during the 'business decade', just when the country was rushing to join the global economy".[52]

This intellectual error provides rather a good metaphor. By systematically downgrading the "we" in favor of the "me", we laid ourselves open to the same perverse consequences. If we wanted to paraphrase the economic jargon, we could say the "competitiveness of all" in the quest for happiness also depends on the "invisible goods" that only the "we" is in any position to provide. By "invisible goods" we mean the sense of belonging, of sharing in a collectivity, a social class, a language, a memory, a party, or a common history — all the things the individual has partially lost, and that he loses forever as soon as he is excluded from the great mechanism of the market. "To quote the apt words of one member of a team that deals with the homeless on a daily basis, 'the world around them doesn't talk about them any more'! Let's say their membership has been cancelled, that they've been written off, which adds up to a very different kind of exclusion than mere poverty".[53]

Is there any need to add that this new and vulnerable form of solitude to which we are condemned by total individualism is an additional factor of inequality? It affects the underprivileged much more profoundly than anyone else. For the richest, social cohesion can survive without too much difficulty. "The dissolution of social ties and the process of disaffiliation which is going on in certain sectors of the population are not conducive to maintaining, let alone strengthening, the many bonds that characterize the great families of the well-off aristocracy and the higher bourgeoisie," write the authors of an excellent survey of the wealthy aristocracy and of the middle class.[54]

From One Imperialism To Another

All these desocializing processes explain why people feel today, in a chaotic and sporadic way, a powerful need for society. The new social activists — the army of social or charity workers — are untiring in their efforts to rebuild, bit by bit, a social bond that has completely fallen apart. In the depths of society — and in opposition to the predominant individualist ideology — people are desperately trying to rebuild some kind of "we". Such is the meaning we must ascribe to movements as disparate as Foodbanks, anti-racist organizations, 'Habitat for Humanity', and so on. "The act of creating an association already gives expression to a desire for social belonging, to create a contract between individuals, if only to achieve limited objectives. It's not by chance that the interest in voluntary associations is playing an essential part in this desire to re-create social bonds".[55]

And yet, can we really derive much hope from such a social trend, however big-hearted and diverse it may be? Alain Touraine, for one, is prepared to do so. For him, these social conflicts and forms of political action, which are being, renewed under our eyes "show what are the issues, the actors, and conflicts of the new world".[56] I find such optimism excessive. It neglects the fact that these various movements are generally short-lived, lacking in coordination, and limited in scope. They are more active in exerting social pressures and exploiting the media than in politics properly speaking. As for the activists who run them, by their own admission "they feel like Sisyphus, pushing a rock that always rolls back down the hill because the crisis in society is going from bad to worse".[57]

But there is another ambiguity in this respect, and an infinitely more dangerous one: it affects the desperate search for identity to which these movements bear witness. Two sociologists close to Alain Touraine have shown very clearly how the new vulnerability of the individual has made him more acutely aware of the need for a recognizable identity. And this is even more so because, in the dominant individualist culture, "anyone who isn't a free subject, the master and sovereign of himself" becomes an object of "social disdain". So everyone feels obliged to lay claim to, and affirm, his or her "difference", just to earn a little respect. Even more, "individuals are no longer satisfied with a private identity, and the spread of the individualizing process is now accompanied by the urge to affirm one's identity publicly".[58]

This is precisely the trap. Why so? Because the consoling affirmation of identity, the public proclamation of "difference" in the context of a multicultural society, requires membership of a group, a community, a "tribe", or a category, all of which are all jealous of their collective differences. Such groupings confer communal identities and enable a surrogate sense of belonging. But they do so only at the cost of unqualified loyalty, or even of abject obedience to the values and codes of the group in question. Nothing is more alien to them than unique individuality, or dissidence. In other words, they obliterate the individual by absorbing him. They recreate a new, formidable form of holism in miniature — a holism of identity. It always operates in exactly the same way, whether it is membership of a neighborhood gang or a racial, religious, or sexual minority.

An Italian intellectual has clearly pointed out this paradoxical consequence of multiculturalism, which, while hoisting the banner of difference, creates small-scale forms of conformism that are even more constricting than the old ones. Just as the real worker in the past only gained respectability through membership of a "class", the young Arab immigrant in

France, the feminist or the homosexual of today, only gain recognition on the express condition that they belong to a certain "category", while at the same time they abandon their uniqueness as a person. In the final analysis, while claiming to provide a cure for the solitude of the disaffiliated individual, "the ideologies of difference actually abolish differences" (in this case, individual differences). They recreate, on the scale of a social minority, an imperialism of assimilation that has often been decried".

In this way, a largely rhetorical individualism backfires on the individual, who self-destructs just at the point when he thinks he has won. Such is the "hypocrisy" of a modernity "that, even as it promotes individualism, couldn't care less about the individual".[59]

A Mild Lobotomy

But we can't stop there. Social disintegration and the erosion of identities that accompanies it are only the visible, external aspect of even more deep-seated erosion. We sense very well that the disruptions occurring today go much further than the various forms of emancipation described earlier, which, ideally, liberated the "self" from its old attachments, whether to a village, a family, a social entity, or a nation. Today, disaffiliation is affecting the very core of the "self": filiation, procreation, sexual difference, integrity of the body, etc. We are even witnessing the deconstruction, one by one, of the genetic codes, those essential points of reference by the Promethean efforts of biology. The human person is subject to a new kind of "suspicion" the consequences of which are much more serious than the suspicion cast on it some years ago by psychoanalysis. The deconstruction presently under way is more devastating than the enfeeblement that resulted years ago from Freud's discovery of the "subconscious". Since then, we have been feeling our way towards a horizon of unstable affections, insecure genetic identities, fractal personalities, and complex networks. Yes, alas, the individualist adventure has turned out to be a more risky one than we could ever have imagined! The individual is no longer merely rendered vulnerable and defenseless: his very substance is in question.

The new kinds of angst, as all those who deal with human suffering nowadays come to hear them — psychiatrists, psychoanalysts, and general practitioners — no longer result from unstable social conditions. The vague fear expressed in the confidentiality of the consulting room involves questions of filiation, personal identity, and genealogical inheritance. The contemporary individual senses that an essential part of him — one he finds it difficult to define — may be threatened. What exactly is a human being? The warnings expressed by Pierre Legendre take on their full meaning in this context: "Scientific certitudes are not enough to found our being as human subjects. If they are to be part of the problematic of social ties, they must be recognized, by which we mean given a place, under certain conditions, in the founding discourse, raised to the level of the prescriptive framework of a society, like the ancient or primitive teachings that we so aptly call 'mythological'. In the industrial age, as in any other, we need a *true story*".

But this "history" is slipping more and more between our fingers. No form of entertainment is really able to distract us from our concerns, no chemicals to cure us. Is it by chance that both these things have acquired such importance in our everyday lives? Such a surfeit of distracting "signs" and televised images, such over-consumption of "uppers" and "downers", the troubling fickleness of the modern consciousness: it all betrays a fundamental *lack*. In the worst of cases, we dismiss it and seek refuge in a kind of daze which Boris Cyrulnik quite rightly compares to a mild lobotomy: "Are the people who set out to create a culture of security, meant to dispel our *angst* by offering us endless distractions to combat boredom, really offering us anything but cultural lobotomy? If such a culture existed, we would experience a sequence of instantaneous euphorias and find satisfaction in a state devoid of any meaning, for we would experience nothing but a sequence of presents".[60]

So what are we being tempted to flee, if not our terror of non-being? Everywhere around us, we see signs that the dissolution of the "human subject" is no longer completely inconceivable. From the way medicine has been reduced to no more than a technique (the treatment of organs rather than human beings) to the profound transformations in procreation (anonymous donors, cloning, etc.), from digital abstraction to the triumph of virtual reality, something seems to be dizzyingly crumbling away in the texture of the "self".[61] The triumphant individual begins to fear total dissolution. It is hardly surprising if so many men and women react to this danger of disintegration by indulging in an excess of organized, conscientious narcissism.

All the movements dealing with what is called "personal-growth" and "human potential" that are proliferating in America bear witness to this silent panic. Reviving 19th-century American naturalism or expressivism, they bring together people exclusively concerned with developing themselves, and whose links to others seem more and more tenuous.[62] These men and women wrap themselves in a solipsism that is hardly tribal, but which is widely treated as though it were a medical problem, and have lost any ability to identify with any kind of *political* collectivity. They have, indeed, undergone a voluntary lobotomy. They represent the potentially innumerable clientele for a cult, whichever one is in fashion at the time. These sudden impulses that reveal the utter confusion of the contemporary "self" are all the more pathetic in that they are the prisoners of an imitative conformism which, from the outset, makes any pretension to an "authentic self" ridiculous.

The philosopher Michel Meyer is quite right to speak ironically of these desperate waves of "new age" egocentrism. "Everybody wants what the other person wants because the other wants it, and not because his choice is determined by intrinsic reasons (which are now losing their strength). Man is now 'without qualities', the empty vessel for an exhausting narcissism, which makes each person into the frustrated recorder of his neighbor's actions, small-minded in his arrogant stupidity, totally immersed in the comforts of his existence and the certainty of being "like everyone else" — in short, someone who counts. This is all at the expense of the next man, who behaves the same way when he's the same kind of person".[63]

* *

*

At the end of such a long journey, after such a magnificent conquest of freedom and autonomy, the individual is unquestionably coming up against a truth that can be put quite simply. It is not enough to say that the "I" needs a "we" if it is not to sink into disaffection and solipsistic despair. There is an even stronger dependency. The truth is that the "we" is what makes the "I". The presence of the other by no means "deprives" me of a part of myself, as if it fed off me in some way. Quite to the contrary, this presence is what makes me what I really am. I am made of the other as though from an original matter. From him I receive language, awareness, and identity. It is he who defines me as a person, and makes me into something more than a "living puppet", to use Pierre Legendre's expression. The emancipated individual of Western culture, whether he likes it or not, is engaged in relearning about the other, something individualism has made him forget. If the "I" is today in search of a "we", it is so that it may rediscover itself. That is of course the good news, and the possible commencement of a re-foundation.

In dealing with the excesses of contemporary solipsism, it may be useful to recall the astute foresight exhibited by Raymond Aron, who was nonetheless a proponent of economic liberalism. In his refusal to adopt the radical and ultraliberal views of Hayek, for instance, he was perfectly aware of the limits of individualism. For Aron, if "the need for a private sphere is perhaps an essential aspect of the demand for liberty", it is nevertheless "unacceptable for this single criterion to be applied to all present-day societies". In other words, if we claim the freedom of modern beings that we desire, it is dangerous to renounce the kind of freedom that consisted for the ancients in sharing in political power. We must learn to combine the two, without ever dissociating the "I" from the "we".[64]

The amazing thing is that not only theologians, moralists, poets, philosophers, or lovers, are inviting us to rediscover the other. Today, scientists, somewhat surprisingly, are the first to emphasize the need. "When a child enters the world, it knows that it exists, but it doesn't know what it is. It is only progressively, under the combined effect of the sense of the self as the other sees it, that it discovers it is a human being. The common idea that emerges from work on the ontogeny of the sense of self is that its construction depends on developing a sense of the other".[65]

That's well-said.

CHAPTER VIII:

SACRIFICE AND VENGEANCE RETURN

> *"You have the impression that the old, primitive kinds of fatality, that were pushed aside for a time by the light of the Prophets and the Gospel, are reasserting themselves behind a mask of scientific and technical imperatives."*
> René Girard,
> *Quand ces choses commenceront*, Arléa, 1994.

A strange vocabulary has asserted itself as we enter a new century. Certain words and expressions, heard all around us, are giving new life to some very old symbolic images. People talk of media "lynchings" and of "scapegoats". We are becoming more accustomed all the time to the rumblings of mob psychology, with its demands for someone to be identified as a "guilty party" and "sacrificed" on the altar of the media. No natural disaster can take place, be it a flood, fire, or avalanche, without a unanimous outcry for one or several individuals to be punished — a punishment which we can expect to bring peace, at least in the media.

In different circumstances, we'd find it easier to accept such an instantaneous demonizing of some adversary, some "other" — a rival, or a group of immigrants, seen as a threat to be eliminated. This casting of blame is reminiscent of the single-minded desire for vengeance on the part of a group subject to the herd-like impulses typical of a mob — a sort of behavior that anthropologists recognize instantly. But our need to blame becomes more insatiable every day. To satisfy it, we are prepared, if necessary, to reinvent the figure of the villain, the monster, the "born criminal" who must be destroyed, or the powerful individual who must be dragged down — all 19th-century stereotypes of the criminal of which modern justice had managed to rid itself. But they're back again!

The itch to eliminate, to marginalize, to exclude, can be felt every day.

It indicates a vague fear, a nameless anxiety. It has become so insistent that the need for "punishment" has infected our rules and regulations.[1] Even international politics, now so heavily influenced by the media, contributes to this instinct to demonize which, in matters of justice, is one thing that unites an international community where certitudes are in short supply. A journalist for the *New York Times*, David Bindera, has written of the tyranny of the media's victim-making machine, created by journalists' herd instinct. Speaking of the media's influence on foreign policy, he pointed out that, in its overseas conflicts, America is capable of recognizing only one villain at a time.[2]

We can sense something in common between all these reactions and types of behavior — some hidden logic, some link. It isn't easy to define, but it does awaken an echo deep in the recesses of our collective memory, something repressed, the memory of an ancestral ritual we are reluctant to talk about: the ritual of sacrifice.

The sacrificial procedures or rituals described by the great French anthropologist Marcel Mauss (1872-1950), and also by Freud in *Totem and Taboo* and in *Moses and Monotheism*, are still present in all human cultures,[3] as René Girard has shown. Sacrifice is the real or ritualized slaughter of some "guilty" individual with the purpose of reestablishing the unanimity and stability of the group. It expresses the desire to reject some figure of evil from the community, in the form of one individual.

Of course, the universal morality handed down by Judeo-Christianity, but become secular for the past three centuries, rendered such sacrificial rituals illegitimate. We could even go so far as to say that the progressive abandonment of sacrifice and the gradual, very gradual, replacement of private vengeance by the legal system, are perhaps what best define the emergence of what we call "civilization". Civilization prefers *civility* to sacrifice — a bold choice, as Nietzsche recognized, when he wrote that "the individual was taken so seriously and made into such an absolute value by Christianity that he could no longer be sacrificed. However, the species can only survive thanks to human sacrifice. [But] the pseudo-humanity that calls itself Christianity wants precisely to ordain that no-one be sacrificed".[4]

Is it too much to suggest that the rituals of vengeance and sacrifice are re-emerging today, in a guise that won't deceive us for much longer?

From Justice to Litigation

The field of law, litigation, and justice is the most immediately significant. I won't spend any time here on what judges themselves call the
"criminalization of society", a phenomenon that, though barely noticeable
only a few years ago, has already become a commonplace in political debate. It is one of the perverse effects of contemporary individualism, and,
above all, of the pluralism of values. Thus understood, it can be briefly defined as the predominance of incarceration as the ultimate means of social
control. As beliefs or collective representations that once were internalized
lose their force, punishment is intensified. There can be little doubt that
this corresponds to a sacrificial mechanism. Criminal law, by the very nature of things, replaces weakened social or political ties. The concern is no
longer to include all members of society in a common norm, but first and
foremost to eliminate the threat represented by a potentially culpable individual. Antoine Garapon, a judge and Secretary-General of the Institute of
Higher Studies on Justice, speaks explicitly of this revival of sacrifice with
respect to a specific case, namely the criminalization of political life, a
criminalization that it is all the more emotional and less subject to control
in that it is being carried out under media scrutiny, and is, more than any
other, a mob phenomenon. "We are witnessing a drift into sacrifice," he
claims, "under which the identification of a guilty party — especially if he
is someone without any power — is expected to deliver us from evil".[5]

Criminal law — together with the law of the market — is tending to
become the ultimate mechanism of control in a society that has lost any
strong beliefs and genuinely shared values. In other words, the number of
individuals in prison is inversely proportionate to the strength of shared
beliefs. The weaker the latter, the fuller the prisons. Behind a moral order,
to which a so-called "return" is announced with familiar insistence, there
lies a much more real development: the creation of a justice system which
is the inverted image of, or substitute for, such an order. It is a strange
paradox: the general permissiveness of society automatically results in an
increase in the prison population. As disorder and confusion gain ground, a
kind of judicial totalitarianism, a greater inflexibility of social life resulting
from an obsession with judicial action, replaces the social straitjacket. The
phenomenon is all the more disturbing in that it is accompanied by a progressive undermining of the law, which lacks any genuine foundation in
such a context of "weak ontology".

Psychoanalysts have not taken long to highlight this paradoxical tendency to criminalize, or this proliferation of the justice system, at the same time stressing the dead end to which the phenomenon leads. One writes: "It is useless to hope to provide new bearings by means of legislative action — not that these are uncalled-for, but because the law is itself subject to the same infiltration. The proliferation of legal proceedings we are witnessing today confirms that the symbolic Law lacks the power to continue symbolically regulating what is now often no more than an imaginary exchange, a general, unrestrained skirmishing".[6]

The New Penal Order

The way democratic societies have become criminalized can be seen by the spectacular increase in prison populations and the trend toward more severe sentences. The examples of France and the United States are telling in this respect.

In the United States, according to the statistical department of the prison administration, there were 1,630,940 convicts in 1996, or 615 per 100,000 of the population (seven times the European figure). This percentage does not merely establish a kind of world record; it indicates an unprecedented increase in this same prison population in the course of the past few decades. There were 290,000 in prison in 1960, 494,000 in 1984, and 744,000 in 1985. This represents a 51 times increase in less than forty years. During the same period, the severity of sentences has increased considerably, so that nowadays the words "severe sentence" are often heard. We might add that in 1995 California spent twice as much on its prisons as on its universities, and four times as much per criminal as per student.

In France, the prison population has increased by around 100%. The incarceration rate has risen from 50 per 100,000 of population to 90 today. This new severity can also be seen in the sharp drop in the number of paroles granted: 30% of eligible prisoners were granted parole in 1972, but only 10% in 1992.

However, it is not enough merely to point out this criminalization of society, however significant it may be. The revival of sacrifice in the legal sphere takes subtler and more fundamental forms. It is inherent even in the way the philosophy of law has evolved. The new function of the contemporary fascination with the law is to enclose each individual — infected by what Antoine Garapon calls "timorous individualism" — within a protective shell of "negative rights" that protects him from others but at the same time throws him back into the rather strange enigma and pathos of his private beliefs. The fragile legal peace of modernity is a reaction to the way all beliefs, convictions, and certitudes have been made relative. Confined to the private domain and tolerated on that condition only, their symbolic status has been diminished and their ability to provide order weakened. Belief has become nothing but a kind of idiosyncrasy, an inoffensive eccentricity, an amiable oddity with which to confront an outside world and a neutral, pragmatic State without any remaining beliefs. In addition, everyone has become a rival to everyone else, even in the realm of what used once to be called morality. The only remaining way to arbitrate this rivalry is to invoke the spoken threat or the harm suffered by one of the parties as a way to justify, if need be, the sacrifice — the sacrificial expulsion — of the other.

The way the law has come to emphasize the individual — in other words, no longer stressing the idea of social cohesion, but rather the protection of individuals — results in a proliferation of legislation, an increase in the number of cases, an incursion into private space by the law and by criminal law in particular. "Far from disappearing," notes Irène Théry, "civil law is proliferating, just as people's expectations of the justice system are growing, as is also the tendency to sue".[7] Now it is the law — and the law alone — that is supposed to protect the weak from the strong, the child from the adult, the woman from the man, and, in general, everyone from everyone else. Or, more precisely, we have substituted the ideas of correcting wrongs and ensuring security for that of the punishable offence (for what is an offence in a relativist context?). "A wrong is repaired without any distinction between voluntary and involuntary acts, for nowadays it is the victim who demands compensation, rather than those fictional entities, the State or society".[8]

This obliteration of the common interest, whether termed civic responsibility or citizenship, in the name of the sacred rights of the omnipotent individual is also a 20th-century inheritance and the indirect consequence of recent forms of totalitarianism, whether fascist or communist. These demonstrated that political power, even when exercised legally in the juridical meaning of the term, could behave criminally in the name of the "common good" and they surpassed all imagination in doing so. These disastrous historical demonstrations have resulted, for better or for worse, in the granting of total primacy to the victim. "The ability to have something considered sacred has changed sides: it no longer resides in sovereign authority, nor indeed in power, but only in bringing a legal action".[9]

However, while the defense of the victim is indubitably a moral advance, nothing is a greater menace to justice as a value and as an institution than this relentless reduction of the justice system to a proliferation of cases intended to "right" private wrongs, within the framework of a criminal law that has taken on inordinate dimensions. "Criminal law," adds Antoine Garapon, "is being reconfigured in the context of protecting the victim, and no longer along therapeutic or judicial lines (how to cure the criminal, reform him, save him)".[10] What is even more serious is that this priority accorded the victim's point of view is somehow related to the Nietzchean notion of innocence — a concept that can easily be used to justify extermination. The modern individual is possessed by a desperate need for innocence.[11] He rejects the Judeo-Christian idea according to which he is himself complicit with evil. Evil is now, and can be, only *outside* him, in the other person. So it becomes possible — and tempting — to eradicate it (or him). As Charles Taylor writes, evil, or failure, is identified with an individual or a group. My conscience is clear because I am different from this individual or group, but what can I do? They are an obstacle to the well-being of all, and should be liquidated.[12]

Just as dangerous as the religious fundamentalists' dream of purity, this Nietzschean innocence that refuses to accept the inner nature of evil finally becomes an obsession with purification. No, it's no accident that terms like "lynching" and "exclusion" crop up so often in today's vocabulary. The way we apply the law proceeds, in the final analysis, from a dangerous trend: the privatization of justice, which is to say a revival of vengeance. Pushed to the extreme, the tyranny of egocentric confrontation is a symptom of the break-up of society. Collective life is reduced to the eternal, never-fulfilled quest for personal compensation for harm done — real or imaginary — a harm that people are no longer prepared to simply write off, nor to accept as an inconvenience of life in society. We are no longer prepared to "write off" anything in order to be able to live together.

Describing the rise of this almost "private" individualistic justice, a law professor at the University of Lyons quite rightly comments that "individualist perceptions of interest increase the potential for conflict". "The generalization of contractual relationships induced by the market," he adds, "creates potentially litigious situations on the level of society as a whole. The exchange economy is based on a law it extends to all social relations".[13]

As for social cohesion, it emerges weakened from a war that pits everyone against everyone else; so we see an increase in sacrificial lynchings carried out symbolically in the media. They reveal a strange need to ascribe guilt, and for sacrifice. And as social cohesion is increasingly threatened, ever more sacrifices are required to restore it. The pacifying effect of sacrifice is less and less durable, so that the scapegoating mechanism takes on its own impetus, at the expense of justice, gradually destroying the latter's sovereign, calming equanimity. "The defeat of justice," writes Blandine Kriegel, "is not just an institutional fact, but a cultural phenomenon. It is not merely a political fact, but also a symbolic one. The marginalization of justice goes hand in hand with a weakening of the legitimacy of the idea of justice".[14]

Need we add that sacrificial behavior is tending to replace politics itself? Whether it is a question of foreign or domestic policy, putting the emphasis on punishing the guilty — whether real or imaginary — conveniently does away with a difficult undertaking, namely solving problems to the best of one's ability. A flamboyant crusade against some convenient "personification of evil" makes it possible to avoid the practical decisions which have to be made in the day-to-day management of society, in which perfection is always unattainable, and where one is eternally the butt of criticism. But if "evil" creatures do exist, and deserve to be dealt with, the problems and contradictions that allow them to prosper are no less real. Prosecuting the guilty can also be a cowardly way to avoid real politics, if not indeed an outright abdication of responsibility.

Sacrificing the Weak

The law is only one of the areas where this phenomenon is visible. A comparable trend can be seen in the economic sphere. In writing this, I have in mind our present-day lexicon with its clearly sacrificial connotations. The survival of the fittest, a theory expressed in the 19th century by the Darwinian sociologist Herbert Spencer, implies, conversely, the sacrifice of the less fit.

Productivity, competition, or the reestablishment of a proper balance, we are told, all require sacrifices. Our new age of inequality[15] has no problem coping with the growing numbers of marginalized and neglected people, whom we can without exaggeration compare to sacrificial victims, and who are also liable to attempts to make them responsible for their own exclusion (by invoking, for instance, the excessive cost of labor).

So, beyond these linguistic symptoms, what liberation theology has to say on the subject is not all exaggerated — far from it. Consider in particular the Brazilian, Hugo Assman, who acknowledges that he has borrowed some of his analyses from René Girard. He expresses them in an illuminating way: "The words we are using," he writes, "suggests a possible comparison with the thinking of René Girard, who expresses himself in terms similar to our own. . . . Has the ancient need for scapegoats — i.e. for expiatory victims so that reconciliation may take place — been transformed to such an extent that something which once required the procedure to be carried out openly in public view has been so completely built into the daily reality of commercial relations that it now operates as an ongoing, tacit process that passes practically unnoticed? We are making this provocative suggestion in the hope that, once this metamorphosis of the sacrificial victim as a consequence (among others) of the economic paradigm has been recognized, the necessary protest 'We've had enough sacrifices' may take on a new urgency".[16]

For Assman, as for most liberation theologians, the ideology of the all-embracing market amounts to making economic rationality the handmaiden of the sacrificial process. The false gods of the economy too are hungry for victims. Like the pagan gods, they call for ever more barbarous sacrifices. For Assman, the theoreticians of liberalism — from Adam Smith, on — have ignored the New Testament message by exalting egoistic self-interest over and above love for one's neighbor. This perverse tendency of "hard-core" economic thought, until now concealed behind all kinds of dissembling, is coming back into the open with the merciless trend of the modern economy. Quoting a line from the Brazilian poet Moacyr Felix, "*The verb 'to have' is the death of God*", he calls these false economic gods idolatrous. "To point to what are all too clearly gods, to speak of idolatry in the economic sphere (as in other domains), is to dispel the obvious. It means showing up those gods, so that everyone may finally become aware of their role in the system of oppression".[17]

This oppression, enforced with the help of a new economic kind of idolatry, says Assmann, has only become possible because, in the name of market rationality itself, we have managed to reformulate the meaning of human life. The reduction of the human person to the narrow limits of *homo oeconomicus* is the best example of this. This strange creature, this one-dimensional man (to quote Herbert Marcuse), has apparently no needs apart from those that money and merciless competition enable him to satisfy. "The 'infinite perversions' (of capital, of the market, etc.) are nothing but negative utopias, restricting all hope to what is already 'there'".[18]

Liberation theologians smack of heresy, for with a single voice they denounce the all too frequent support shown by the official Church for this idolatrous logic. They point, in other words, to the historical persistence, ever since Emperor Constantine's conversion, of a sacrificial form of Christianity that is for them a betrayal of New Testament values. When they speak like this they are reviving a theological dispute as complex as it is explosive — one to which I shall return later. Is it a valid objection to say that the revolutionary extremism of this type of theology, and its active sympathy with the extreme left in Latin America, make it irrelevant? Can it be said that this radicalization, as a militant response to economic liberalism, is more appropriate to the inegalitarian societies of Latin America than to the European context?

I cannot believe these objections are enough to invalidate the question raised. The mechanism of sacrifice is well and truly present in liberal economic theory, and "leftist" theologians are not the only ones to point this out. Pierre Dupuy, who teaches at the École polytechnique in Paris and at Stanford, a recognized specialist in American neoliberal thought, has discussed this question in a major piece of research. He demonstrates how Anglo-Saxon utilitarian thought — handed down from Jeremy Bentham and John Stuart Mill — has been used to provide a theoretical basis for sacrificial behavior by giving it a rational foundation. For the Utilitarians, the sacrifice of an individual or several individuals is acceptable as long as it provides a benefit for the greater number. It is indeed on this precise point that adversaries of utilitarianism such as Richard Nozick and John Rawls, or "communitarians" like Michael Sandel, have focused their criticisms.

"Sacrificial utilitarianism," writes Dupuy, "makes the mechanism of victimization (i.e. unanimity recreated against a single victim) transparent, showing it up in the harsh light of rational calculation, a light which is itself intolerable".[19] For Utilitarians, the benefit of the greater number is enough to justify the "loss" suffered by the few who are less able to defend themselves, or less talented. Dupuy shows that, as a result, utilitarian thinking is thus undermined by an ethical contradiction it has never been able to overcome. By accepting the idea of the sacrifice of an excluded third party, it is in breach of the very principles of civilized conscience that it nevertheless claims to respect. "If this other person is my neighbor, how can I consent to sacrificing him; or, again, conversely how can I recognize the features of sameness in the other who is being sacrificed?"[20]

This theoretical quarrel is not just academic. It underlies most of the present discussions about whether or not we should give priority to the pursuit of full employment, the increase in inequality, or the new exclusionary mechanisms that are an integral feature of neoliberalism, etc.. The more or less open acceptance of the elimination of the least fit — their symbolic sacrifice, in other words — is often held up as a rational attitude, since it enables the salvation of the greater number. Is it not justified to lay off masses of workers in order to save the company? Isn't unemployment the price that has to be paid to make the economy more competitive? In fact, behind this seemingly rational clear-sightedness, the neoliberal case consists in accepting sacrifice. In this respect, it is less reasonable than it claims, as John Rawls has tried to point out.[21]

As for the communitarian Michael Sandel, he quite rightly mocks the cynical utilitarianism underlying the present-day acceptance of a sacrificial economy by wondering if it was justified to throw even a single Christian to the lions for the sake of providing considerable pleasure to a large number of Romans.[22]

The Revenge Of The Persecutors

If modernity is regressing imperceptibly to a sacrificial mentality, it would be very foolish to take this trend for no more than a resurgence of violence within the well-policed universe which Norbert Elias has termed a "civilization of morals".[23] Yet it is undeniable that just such a resurgence is taking place, and we must discuss it. There is a direct connection between it and the sacrificial tendency. I'm not just speaking here of the normal delinquency, crime, everyday disputes, or widespread aggressiveness that seems to set people, corporations and groups at one another's throats — an inexhaustible subject for political debate (which is as far as democratic permissiveness goes) this is not just a current preoccupation. I am also thinking of all the forms of incivility, both omnipresent and more difficult to identify, from ordinary vandalism to a coarsening of human relations. We sometimes grow dizzy at this regression of democratic society into a kind of archaic savagery.

This regression actually nullifies the benefits of a long, arduous historical development, which Elias saw as progress towards civilization brought about by a voluntary internalization of rules of behavior. "In a certain sense" writes Elias, with Platonic overtones, "the battlefield has been shifted to within man. That is where he has to grapple with some of the tensions and passions which once took an outward form as struggles in which men confronted one another directly".[24]

From medieval man to courtly nobility, from naked rivalry to the codifying of social relations or the rules of politeness, from private wars and other social conflicts to the monopolization of force by the State and by it alone, our entire history can be read as an attempt to rid ourselves of violence. This attempt has never met with total success and therefore has to be renewed eternally. Indeed, the rules of polite conduct, rituals, and propriety, can always conceal veiled, but nevertheless cruel, forms of violence. (Think, for instance, of Japanese society.) And we mustn't forget the "symbolic violence" in inegalitarian social relationships that Pierre Bourdieu has pointed out, which in the end is nothing but a disguised form of sacrifice. Still, this Sisyphean attempt defined rather well our notion of democratic progress. Yet, after having more or less tamed private violence, we find ourselves once more drawn into a regression which is more dangerous than it seems, one that is restoring our earlier ingenuous attitude to violence, and a way of persecuting that no longer even feels the need for disguise. No one can deny that a lethargic, or acquiescent, acceptance of "unjust" forms of violence is in the air in our societies.

It's certainly symptomatic. Yet it doesn't represent the whole problem of sacrifice, which is more serious still. Sacrifice is actually not just one among many forms of social violence, the return of which might be viewed as part of a more general process. The opposite is even true, since its very *raison d'etre* is to prevent the contamination of violence from spreading through the group. In fact, sacrifice is not just an aberration in modernity. It is a ritual of exorcism, revived in obedience to an appalling logic. Like the lynchings of former days, today's penal, social and economic exclusion is supposed to help restore social cohesion among those who have not been excluded. Firings in the name of 'competitiveness', by sacrificing the least fit within a company, are supposed to work to the advantage of the remaining employees —though above all to that of shareholders — in the form of a more profitable and harmonious sharing of the benefits. The sacrificial demonizing of some supposedly guilty party affords the group as a whole a greater degree of unanimity and a clearer conscience. Whether in everyday affairs or in politics, the mechanism is the same.

So sacrifice doesn't have much in common with "gratuitous" violence or mere abuses — of which modernity provides innumerable examples. It is central. It pertains to the very concept of "living together". It is, in a form so watered-down that it is no longer so easy to recognize, a throwback to the extremely ancient ritual of the "founding murder". This is what makes the return of the sacrificial mechanism an infinitely more serious matter than a mere increase — even exponential — in anti-social violence or incivility. What is at stake here is the very nucleus of the "Western inheritance", the keystone that still supports — or articulates — the five founding values I have delineated in the preceding chapters. Neither hope for the future, nor equality, nor reason, nor the universalist purpose, nor the autonomy of the self, would have been imaginable unless ritual sacrifice — in other words "magic thinking" — had been given up.

So this covert re-emergence of ritual sacrifice serves to automatically restore the unanimity or unanimism that justify new forms of persecution. Indeed, René Girard has amply demonstrated that the meaning and function of sacrifice depend on just one express condition: every participant in the lynching has to be convinced of the victim's guilt. Unanimism — thinking as one, conformity squared! — is one ingredient of the sacrificial mechanism. To be effective, this requires a demonizing of the victim, who must be held responsible for his own persecution. In other words, it is only the persecutors' sense of their own innocence that gives persecution such lasting appeal. In the same way, holding the poor responsible for their own failure is the best way to provide the wealthy with peace of mind and preserve the harmony of the system.

In this sense, the return of the sacrificial mechanism makes a veritable symbolic disaster possible, one quite capable of ultimately wrecking the very essence of our inheritance. Inviting us to turn back the clock on two thousand years of history, it would mean that once again the victims would be subject to the "point of view" of their persecutors, as they were in the past. Somewhat like a Jurassic Park-style cloning enabling the dinosaurs of a past era to be brought back to life, it would give renewed strength and vitality to an ontological barbarism that seemed gone for ever. Such a prospect lends new urgency to the disquiet so forcefully expressed by René Girard: "For anyone who can see the fearsome relevance of the sacrificial principle to the anthropological understanding of our universe, the direction in which the world is heading with one accord, herd-like, is disturbing to say the least. . . . . It is hard for me not to see the present developments as a regression, as a worrisome return to what we thought we had left behind for ever".[25]

But we still have to understand what this ancient persecution, that we had indeed left behind, consisted in.

A "Thirst For Sacrifice"

Let us start, as usual, with the simplest. Ethnologists and anthropologists, and the Old Testament too, constantly refer to sacrifices, ritual infanticides, the slaughter of the firstborn, and "founding murders". They do so quite openly, and the sacrifices they depict are very real.

The Jewish prophets were not the last to denounce such practices, whose persistence from culture to culture has always troubled ethnologists. European explorers in the New World spoke of their horror on discovering that in the 16th century the Aztecs still practiced human sacrifice on a large scale to honor their gods, whether Huitzilopochtli, the god of night and of war, Quetzalcóatl, the civilizing god, or Tlaloc, the rain god. In 1999, archaeologists found the bodies of three Inca adolescents who had been sacrificed in the 16th century on the slopes of the volcano Llullaillaco in the Andes. Innumerable discoveries of similar kinds had been made during the preceding years, and in other latitudes. Human sacrifice is an enigmatic common denominator of all cultures.

As for our own history, we need to recall the dispute about the central role of human sacrifice during the first centuries of our era — a role that we have minimized for too long. It is a fact that in the various reevaluations of Greek and Roman antiquity carried out by Western thinkers in the 12th century, during the Renaissance, during the Enlightenment, or even in the 19th century, the violent and sacrificial nature of ancient society has often been overlooked. This was a mistake.

Peter Brown is right to point out this neglect, reminding us that violence — and above all the unrestricted violence practiced by those in power — literally inhabited the mental universe of the Greeks and Romans. All the ideas of the Platonists or the Stoics on the necessity of "self-control" have to be interpreted in the light of this incredible brutality.

Violence accompanied the Roman elite throughout every stage of their lives. From the maintenance of slavery by force to violence against

women and children, "a tide of horror lapped close to the feet of all educated persons", and hardly had they set foot outside their doors, young
people "could view the exemplary violence inflicted on their inferiors in
every law court". This violence was an integral part of education. Even a
school textbook for Latin boys learning Greek included scenes of torture as
part of a day in the life of a well-to-do Roman: "The governor's seat is set
up. The judge ascends the tribunal. . . . A guilty brigand is brought in. He is
interrogated according to his deserts. He is put to the torture: the torturer
lays into him, his chest is constricted; he is hung up, racked, beaten with
clubs. He goes through the full cycle of torture. He denies his crime. He is
sure to be punished. . . . He is led out and executed."[26]

As for sacrifices, they were the essential ritual of pagan religions
which, early in our era, merged more and more with the cult of the Emperor, via the cult of Mithra imported from India and Persia.[27] While human sacrifice was no longer practiced (as it was among the Aztecs), the
memory of it was perhaps not as completely buried in the collective memory as one might think. Certain Egyptian religious traditions that were still
observed in Alexandria at the time of the Roman Empire provide an example. When Bishop Theophilus had the army ordered to destroy that city's
pagan temples (most notably the famous *Serapeum*) in 391, certain architec-
tural devices were found that had allowed the priests to practice illusions
that must have made a strong impression on the worshippers. But "other
[discoveries] produced horrified reactions, such as skulls found in the
crypt of the *mithraeum* in Alexandria, where the remains of human sacrifices
were in evidence".[28]

One thing is certain: that the first and perhaps the most serious
"subversion" introduced by Judeo-Christian monotheism into the Roman
Empire was its definitive condemnation of sacrifice. The Jews had already
ceased all sacrifice since the destruction of the temple. One could also invoke the words of certain prophets forbidding sacrifice — for example,
Jeremiah (7: 22): "For in the day that I brought them out of the land of
Egypt, I did not speak to your fathers or command them concerning burnt
offerings and sacrifices".[29]

For the early Christians, in any case, the question was settled on
theological grounds. The sacrifice on the cross was the "last" sacrifice, the
sacrifice that made all others unnecessary. "The Epistle to the Hebrews
squarely tackles the question of the ending of all sacrifices by Christ:

Christ's sacrifice is unique, definitive, carried out for once and for all, and for the benefit of all mankind. It was a blood-sacrifice, like those of the 'first Covenant', but the blood was no longer that of animals, it was His own (see Hebrews 9: 11-14): He brought us 'eternal redemption' (9: 12)".[30]

To remain on historical ground, one of the first decisions taken by Constantine after his conversion to Christianity was, very logically, to forbid sacrifices and the practice of divination. In doing so he denounced, in a revealing choice of words, "the rituals of an outmoded illusion". In a letter to the young king of kings Shapur II, Constantine wrote, around 322: "This (One) God I invoke on bended knee, and recoil with horror from the blood of sacrifice".[31] This prohibition was reformulated and codified on several occasions, by Constantius II (337-361) as well as by Theodosius I (379-395). In 341 an imperial law stipulated: "Let there be an end to superstition, let the folly of sacrifice be abolished".[32]

Hostility towards the early Christians was often related to their rejection of sacrifice, something pagans saw as an intolerable offense against tradition. Most attempts to restore paganism were indeed accompanied by a solemn reaffirmation of the sacred character of ritual sacrifice. Shortly before Constantine's conversion, when the Empire was already leaning towards Christianity, the Emperor Diocletian (284 to 305) took part in sacrificial ceremonies and rituals. In a profoundly unstable empire, pagan society hungered for a return to law and order. *Reparatio* and *renovatio* were the slogans of the moment. "In AD 303, *religio* still meant appearing at a smoking altar, flanked by the ever-present gods and surrounded by the animals deemed, from time immemorial, appropriate for a major sacrifice".[33] Later, the Emperor Julian, called "the Apostate", would also reproach the Christians for no longer making sacrifices, and thus being as bad as atheists in contributing to the decline of Rome. During his brief reign he attempted — with no success — to reestablish the ancient cults and sacrifices.

At the beginning of the fifth century, when Rome was briefly conquered and pillaged by Alaric's Visigoths (410), the pagan philosophers held the Christians responsible, arguing that by abolishing sacrifice they had deprived the Empire of the protection of the gods. These accusations — together with others — would underlie St. Augustine's decision to begin writing *The City of God*, a monumental work intended specifically as a response to the accusations of impiety towards the idols.

For the Romans, this condemnation of sacrifice by the early Christians was the gravest of "scandals", which they saw as a threat to the cohesion of the Empire, destructive of tradition. Why? We have to inquire into the real meaning, and, above all, the extraordinary vigor of the Roman reaction. Above all, of course, it was political in nature. By refusing pagan sacrifice and worship the Christians were simultaneously freeing themselves from any "religious" subjection to the emperor. In denouncing "idolatry" they were also criticizing the cult of the Emperor, which was increasing in importance during the early years of our era, and was making the Emperor more and more into a living God. "Men have given this man the honorary title of Augustus, and are worshipping him in the cities and throughout the nations, raising temples to him and offering him sacrifices", wrote Nicholas of Damascus (a scribe attached to the court of King Herod) about the Emperor in around 23 B.C. As for Virgil (70-19 B.C.), he proclaimed, significantly, in the *Aeneid*: "Caesar Augustus himself, exalted in his line, promised oft, and long foretold, [was] born to restore a better Age of Gold".[34]

So the early Christians were above all questioning the authority of the Emperor when they rejected pagan worship. Insubordinate, refusing to bear arms, they proclaimed that Augustus was not the Savior. Their prayer — "Glory to God in the highest" — had a seditious ring, for it implied a total rejection of any earthly deification of power and might. "A tract dating from around A.D. 120, aimed at worship of the Roman emperor, makes a clear connection between faith in God and the rejection of Rome: 'God alone is worthy to receive the power and the glory, to be magnified, to have victory and dominion'".[35] In this way, New Testament teaching undermined the very principle of temporal power. It also invalidated social morality, whether the practice of taking oaths, the patriarchal conception of marriage, or the arbitrary nature of traditional hierarchies. There is nothing surprising, in the circumstances, in the fact that the Roman authorities considered the early Christians to be dangerous anarchists and amoral people. This is the origin of their persecution.

In most of the great waves of persecution — particularly those carried out under Decius (250-251) and Valerian (257-258) — the question of sacrifice was fundamental. The emperors wanted, at all costs, to impose emperor-worship on the recalcitrant Christians. Some finally gave in to the pressure: they were called the *sacrificati*. Others, the *thurificati*, obstinately refused, thereby risking death. Yet others paid to receive false certificates saying that they had "made sacrifice". They were called the *libellaciti*. On several occasions, in any case, the obligation to sacrifice was enforced by strict imperial edicts. The most severe were doubtless those of the Emperor Diocletian, at the very beginning of the 4th century. Diocletian, it is true, was urged on by the famous Caesar Galerius, a cruel and violent barbarian. Historians estimate that the last wave of anti-Christian persecutions initiated by him alone claimed three thousand five hundred victims. One of Diocletian's edicts, in 304, ordered all living in the Roman world to sacrifice to the gods of the Empire, on pain of severe punishment, death, or deportation to the mines.[36]

But this purely political explanation, showing the Christians to have been a threat to the imperial authority, doesn't go far enough. At this juncture, René Girard's interpretations are of invaluable assistance in helping us reevaluate the real nature of the subversion threatening not only Roman culture but, in addition, all sacrificial cultures and traditions. Girard considers that the cohesiveness of human societies is based, in the final analysis, on the memory of a founding murder, of an original sacrifice. The function of the myths perpetuating its memory, and of the rituals that re-enact it symbolically, is to reactivate its pacifying effect. This calming influence can only be effective, as we have seen, if the victim's guilt has been established. "The myth justifies the violence directed at the scapegoat, with the community never at fault. Thebes bears no guilt towards Oedipus, Oedipus is guilty towards Thebes".[37]

Because they are unanimously convinced of the guilt of the scapegoat the members of a community can recover peace, at the cost of sacrificial violence, which therefore acquires a founding character. The unanimity — one could even say the "perfectly clear conscience" — of the lynch mob is an absolutely essential aspect if the sacrifice is to be effective. So it is that the myths, rituals and religions which are at the root of human cultures (culture, here, meaning "conception of the world") necessarily express what, for the sake of simplicity, we may call the "persecutor's point of view". What is more, this point of view emerges strengthened from each sacrificial rite, since it is indeed successful in containing the violence, and, for a time, in restoring social cohesion and peace. This apparent efficacy makes for increased harmony among the persecutors.

In the traditional symbolic universe — whether that of the Romans or anyone else — the persecutors, and, by extension, those in power, are entirely justified. In all cases they persecute only victims who deserve it. In addition, this "persecution" has only one stated objective: to prevent the contagion of violence. It is motivated by a concern to maintain social order, by a sense of communal responsibility, one could say, whether in the name of the empire, kingdom, clan, or family. Human history, which is written by the victors, ceaselessly repeats and infinitely embellishes its unequivocal words — the words of the sacrificers, which no one is in a position to deconstruct. In the name of what "superior value" or transcendent truth could such a deconstruction be carried out? This is where the entire horror of the sacrificial universe resides: it is a symbolic space, within which any objection to sacrifice — an objection that would destroy the whole coherence of the procedure — is neither thinkable nor even imaginable.

But, on Girard's analysis, the revolutionary character of the New Testament message comes precisely from the fact that it has the capacity to frustrate and breach the unanimity of the persecutors. "Scandalously", it rehabilitates the victims' point of view. It fulfils, and systematizes in different terms, the magnificent, extravagant objection Antigone makes to Creon, in Sophocles' play, in the name of a "higher principle". This is indeed the extraordinary character of the New Testament Revelation: by "revealing" the innocence of the victims it renders the sacrifice invalid, and nullifies all its effects in advance. This revelation threw a wrench into the sacrificial mechanism and, by unmasking the unfounded unanimity of the persecutors, it changed — virtually — the entire course of human history.

But it is even more demanding in that it asks the believer to renounce any thought of participating, in his turn, in the cycle of violence. Its determined rejection of vengeance means no less than this. This is what is truly different about Christianity — something that could not be further from a vague, "forgiving" humanism, and that goes much further than the benevolent attitude advocated by other religious teachings and philosophical traditions. The New Testament idea of "turning the other cheek" after receiving a blow has nothing to do with what was for Nietzsche a "slave morality" leading to "resentment". It expresses an explicit and conscious desire to frustrate the instinct to return violence for violence. "Bless those who persecute you," Paul would write in his Epistle to the Romans, "bless and do not curse them" (*Romans* 12: 14). Love your enemy! This extravagant commandment places its trust in what Dostoyevsky (in *The Idiot*) called the terrible power of gentleness" to avoid the pitfall of sacrifice and the infinite reciprocity of violence.

The symbolism of the cross itself had the same effect, and represented an absolute scandal. To worship a crucified man was, in a Roman's eyes, an obscene, if not repugnant, act. Why was this? Because to someone steeped in sacrificial symbolism it seemed sheer folly to make a victim into a God. The idea of a suffering Messiah condemned to die would be denounced, and even ridiculed, by the anti-Christian polemicists of the first centuries. "You place all your hopes in a man who has been crucified", Trypho remarks with astonishment in the famous *Dialogue with Trypho the Jew* by St. Justin Martyr, the Greek apologist, martyred in 165 under Marcus Aurelius. Celsus, the pagan anti-Christian (and anti-Jewish) philosopher spoke mockingly, long before Nietzsche, about this deification of a crucified man — i.e. of a defeated one — by Christianity. Another pagan writer, Lucian, would mock the man he called "a crucified sophist".

Where the Jews were concerned, it has long been thought that this notion of a suffering Messiah, of God as victim, was as repugnant to them as it was to the pagans. But if we take the teachings revealed by the deciphering of the Dead Sea Scrolls into account, we can no longer be so certain of this. "If, as certain authors think, the Essenes recognized, more or less explicitly, this pontiff of the Messianic era [the Messiah of Israel] as a reincarnation of the Master of Justice, and if moreover it was established that the latter died as a martyr, the conclusion must be drawn that the idea of a suffering Messiah before becoming a triumphant Messiah has not been as totally foreign to Judaism as has generally been thought".[38]

This doesn't change the fact that the initial Christian subversion consisted, above all, in the way it proclaimed the victims' innocence and turned it against the persecutors, in its demonstration of the inanity of sacrifice, and at the same time of the myths, rituals, and cultures or ideologies that derive from it. Speaking of Jesus, the Magnificat is explicit in this respect: "He has scattered the proud in the imagination of their hearts. He has put down the mighty from their thrones, and exalted those of low degree" (Luke 1: 51-52). From their point of view the Roman authorities were perfectly right to see this revelation as a certain danger.

From Subversion To "Official Religion"

Paradoxically, this interpretation is just as awkward for historical Christianity and for the Church itself in the form in which it predominated throughout the centuries. Why? Because, immediately after Constantine's conversion, and as soon as Christianity became an "official religion", it broke almost completely with this subversive dimension of the Christian message. By assuming secular power — which it did for more than 1,500 years (indeed simply substituting itself for the Carolingian regime after it fell) — the Church itself became part of the sacrificial world against which it had revolted when it first grew up. "Beginning with Constantine, Christianity was triumphant on the level of the State and soon began to it put its authority behind persecutions similar to those of which Christians of early times had been the victims. Like so many later religious, ideological and political enterprises, when still weak Christianity suffered persecution, but as soon as it gained strength it became the persecutor".[39]

Thenceforth, this dreadful ambivalence of historical Catholicism — liberating *and* oppressing, subverting *and* repressing, defending victims *but also* conducting inquisitions, anarchist *but also* theocratic — would continue all throughout Western history. It would give rise, for centuries, to an unnatural coexistence between an official Church allied with secular power — in even its worst manifestations — and a New Testament inheritance that, in spite of all, would continue its way from century to century and, deep down, play a major part in the emergence of the Enlightenment and of what today we call modernity.

The worldly inflexibility and even the sacrificial intolerance of Roman Christianity were already evident early in Constantine's reign. The struggle against paganism and the destruction of pagan temples was spread throughout the entire Empire. After freedom of worship was allowed the Christians by the famous Edict of Milan (313), imperial texts intended to eliminate paganism became more and more numerous. In 356, the death sentence was introduced for anyone caught worshipping idols; in 380, the Edict of Thessalonica made Christianity the only state religion; in 392, it became forbidden to honor household gods; in 395, loitering near pagan temples was made a crime; in 435 it was decided to demolish any such temples still standing.[40] The effort to eliminate "superstition" was accompanied by mass violence, the best-known example of which was the lynching, in 415, of the pagan philosopher Hypatia, a prominent figure on the town council of Alexandria.

Simultaneously, the spirit of dissidence was suddenly renounced in favor of obedience to authority. In this respect, the Church invoked the well-known text of Paul's Epistle to the Romans, which it reinterpreted to suit itself: "Let every person be subject to the governing authorities. For there is no authority except from God, and those that exist have been instituted by God" (Romans 13: 1-7). What is more, for more than fifteen centuries, only one sentence from this Epistle would be remembered, *Omnis potestas a Deo* ("All power comes from God"), which would also be regularly trotted out to lend legitimacy to temporal power.[41]

A similar reversal took place in the relationship of Christians to the profession of arms. In 314, in Arles, the Emperor Constantine organized a synod to put an end to what today we would call "conscientious objection" by Christians. The third "canon" of this Council simply excommunicated any soldiers who refused to serve, or took part in mutiny. The seventh canon allowed Christians to serve the State, requiring only that they not engage in any pagan acts (such as emperor-worship).[42]

The New Testament "subversion" was well and truly at an end! However, we shouldn't think that this transformation of the New Testament message into an official religion was carried out without any difficulty or controversy. The establishment of what is called "orthodoxy" — in other words the conformity of the faith to dogmas duly defined and approved by the Roman institution — was actually achieved as a result of a great number of Church councils, in the face of myriad heresies and interminable theological disputes. This turmoil of the first centuries is as troubling as ever for anyone who studies it.

Atheistic Catholicism?

Allied with power and professing an "official doctrine", the Church would manage to eradicate all the threats, protests, heresies, or new varieties of paganism, by calling on an authority that we can only call sacrificial — not to use a stronger word. It is true that the temporal power it acquired enabled Christianity to triumph, and to survive, but at the same time it diverted the Revelation into undertakings (crusades, persecution of the Jews, royal absolutism, etc.) that had little to do with the New Testament rehabilitation of the victim. The Gregorian Reform in the 11th century, in reaffirming the power of the Pope, would help make obedience a virtue, something it had not been previously. "Possibly nothing in Western history had more far-reaching consequences".[43] Historically, there developed in this way an institutional Catholicism with a punitive and authoritarian priesthood, one which certain "dissident" theologians have no hesitation in considering a "religious" form of atheism. It was, in any case, from such a position that Charles Maurras, an agnostic disciple of Auguste Comte and very hostile to what he termed "the Judaic poison of the New Testament", would be able to say: "I am an atheist, but a Catholic one!" It was from a similar standpoint that Napoleon would declare with tranquil cynicism that "the clergy control the people, the bishops the clergy, and I the bishops".

Throughout history there is no shortage of caricatural examples of this sacrificial Catholicism, with its stubborn defense of order and power, an imperious Catholicism that has long been symbolized by the triple tiara worn by the Pope. We only have to think of the theocratic ideal of Popes Gregory VII, Innocent III and Boniface VIII in Rome, or of the Ligue in Henry III's France, the *"parti dévôt"* under Louis XIII, the Compagnie du Saint-Sacrement under Louis XIV, or Pope PiusVI who, in his encyclical *Quod Aliquandum* of 1791 urged "obedience to kings". Closer to us in time, we can cite the famous *Syllabus errorum*, published by Pius IX on December 8 1864, in the appendix to the encyclical *Quanta Cura*. We might also recall the campaigns by Louis Veuillot, for forty years the editor of the daily *L'Univers*, whose dogmatic formula has been handed down to posterity: "The Church is the good, without any admixture of evil; the Revolution is evil, without any admixture of good". Or there was the crisis of 1907, in the course of which Pope Pius X condemned the modernist Biblical exegetes in his encyclical *Pascendi*, to be followed by the decree *Lamentabili*, in which he castigated the "spirit of novelty" within the Church. And let us also recall the condemnation in 1910, by the same Pius X, of the "Sillon", the movement led by Marc Sangnier, accused of "social modernism" and ordered to dissolve.

A theologian like Jacques Ellul minces no words in condemning what he calls the "betrayal of the [historical] Churches". "All the Churches," he writes, have scrupulously respected, and often upheld, State authorities; they have made conformity a major virtue, tolerated social injustices and the exploitation of man by man (explaining to some that it was God's will that there be masters and servants, and to the others that socio-economic success was the outward sign of God's blessing!), and also transformed a free and liberating message into a *moral code*".[44] Numerous would be the uncompromising rebels, from Lamennais to Emmanuel Mounier, Maurice Clavel, Henri Guillemin, and so many others, whom we might call "anticlerical Christians".

It is to the heritage of such — despite of some more questionable extrapolations — that Eugen Drewermann refers today when he exclaims: "Is there a living theologian of whom we can say he is a friend of prostitutes and 'publicans'? Where in contemporary theology are we told to understand others and stand up for them, rather than judge and condemn them? And where, in the contemporary Church, is there any room for the kind of men who destroy themselves by kicking against the laws of bourgeois, ecclesiastical society?"[45]

Yet it must be said that in the West the Catholic tradition has also justified a certain distancing of the Church from the secular powers, some moderating interventions, or protests addressed to the powerful, whether the restrictions placed on private wars in the Middle Ages (the "peace of God" or "God's truce"); or the condemnation or excommunication of certain rulers guilty of immoral deeds. In the East, on the other hand, Orthodox Christianity inherited from Byzantium a tradition of almost seamless loyalty to the secular authorities. The support given by Slav Orthodox patriarchs — the Russians in particular — to the Communist system is the most recent example. This loyalty is a consequence of the mystical, unanimist and fusional character of Orthodoxy. That doesn't mean it should escape criticism, historically. "The historic sin of Orthodoxy has been its frequent failure to protest, in the name of what is essential. For, if it is true that the Empire is 'devoted to the good ordering of human affairs', and that the priesthood is 'devoted to the service of the Divine', the latter cannot remain indifferent, nor confine itself to the service of the Divine, if the Empire neglects its responsibilities".[46]

This loyalty, and this compliant attitude contrast, in any case, with the fractious — and often decisive — resistance to this very same Communism by the Catholic hierarchies of Eastern Europe — the Polish clergy and Father Popielusko murdered by Communist thugs; Cardinal Mindszenty imprisoned for eighteen years in Hungary; Cardinal Tomasek or Father Vàclav Maly, who signed the Charter 77 in Czechoslovakia, and became heroes of the liberation from Communism, etc.

Persecuting Illusions

The most extraordinary thing in the history of Christianity is therefore that, in spite of this weighty Roman, imperial, and sacrificial tradition of the official Church, the original subversive message of the New Testament never ceased to trouble the Western conscience — and not merely the conscience of avowed Christians. Max Weber was referring to this formidable paradox when he pointed out: "However, the demands of the Sermon on the Mount, an acosmic ethic of ultimate ends, implied a natural law of absolute imperatives based upon religion. These absolute imperatives retained their revolutionizing force, and they came upon the scene with elemental vigor during almost all periods of social upheaval".[47]

This same paradox is underlined by René Rémond, who notes the persistence and indefatigable rebirth, throughout more than fifteen centuries, of what he terms a "Christian utopia", acting, to a certain extent, as a corrective to the official Church's inclination to ally itself with secular power. "In the very heart of Catholicism," he writes, "is a current that found its most noble expression in Franciscan spirituality, and which dreams of a world where Isaiah's prophecy would be fulfilled, where wars or conflicts of all kinds would be unknown, and which would be liberated, once and for all, from any relations of inequality or dominion".[48]

How are we to interpret this ambivalence, in the final analysis? By invoking human weakness, as François de Sales, the Bishop of Geneva (1567-1622) did, when he said: "Partout où il y a des hommes, il y aura de l'hommerie (Wherever there man is, there will be man's [mis]conduct)"? Or ascribe it to bitter historical necessity — to ecclesiastical *Realpolitik* and the inevitable snail's pace of moral progress? Aside from the value judgments we could arrive at regarding this form of sacrificial clericalism, the theory proposed by René Girard in answer to these questions is worthy of attention. For him, historical time — the time required for its completion — is inseparable from the Revelation itself. In other words, the anti-sacrificial reversal initiated by the Biblical message is too explosive, too radical, too devastating, to be heard immediately by human societies still immersed in the sacred dimension of the sacrificial universe. To proclaim the innocence of the victim and the persecutors' lack of legitimacy is not merely to breach the unanimity of domination, it means dissolving this sacred dimension, destroying tradition, undermining cultures and launching them on an irresistible path towards the promise of the future.

The fact is that this New Testament ferment, whether secularized or not, will not cease to be active and to achieve results. It makes for what we sometimes call progress, or universality of conscience. Irresistibly, from century to century, the persecutors' point of view will lose its legitimacy. More and more it will be questioned, and questionable. Soon, it will be impossible for anyone to persecute ingenuously. "In this way the credibility of mythological representation will be destroyed".[49] So the illusions underlying persecution will be dispelled, and the endless cycle of violence and the sacred will be virtually broken. Virtually! The adverb is important. The progressive demolition of the sacrificial mechanism will not actually bring all persecution to an end. Far from it! It merely means that, with the occasional exception, no further persecution will be possible unless it is camouflaged in some way.

Persecution has lost the innocent cruelty of pre-Judeo-Christian times; it can no longer be carried out with a clear conscience, in a unanimous quest for vengeance. It is now compelled to take, so to speak, a symbolic detour *via* the victims' point of view. After the Western Enlightenment, it can be said that it is possible to persecute only by hypocritically adopting a victim's point of view. This is, incidentally, a good definition of ideology. The exploited proletariat and the unjustly punished German people were the "victims" pointed to by the two great twentieth-century forms of totalitarianism. Neither was able to simply declare, as it was still possible to do in the ancient world: "I'm persecuting because I'm the strongest", or even: "We're still persecuting, but now we do it shamefacedly".[50] Schumpeter made a similar observation about wars when he commented that "the imperialism which, in ancient times, could dispense with any kind of disguise, and which, in an era of absolute monarchy, could find it sufficient to wear a very transparent veil, must nowadays carefully hide itself behind a whole smokescreen of verbiage — even if this verbiage is not exempt from covert appeals to bellicose instincts".[51]

Alain Besançon's theological reflections on the equivalence of the two forms of totalitarianism — Nazism and Stalinism — fit in exactly with this point of view. Against Raymond Aron, who once thought that in its intentions, at least, Communism was not blameworthy, Besançon maintained that, on the contrary, the misrepresentation of the good, the hijacking of the victim's point of view in the cause of oppression, was the darkest face of Communism. Communism did indeed take over the ideal of humanity in order to subvert it. The faker is at least as immoral as the "ingenuous" barbarian. Besançon is quite right to add that only a theological point of view enables one to account for this unique quality of evil.[52]

On another level — and without at all suggesting they are equivalent — the sacrifice of the least fit and the economic exploitation of the poorest as practiced by unrestrained capitalism in its early years have generally been carried out behind a smokescreen of deliberately reinterpreted

Biblical values. Even today, and particularly in the early '80s, in the context of the "conservative revolution" in America, an abundant literature has attempted to provide unmitigated neoliberals with theological justification. (It is true that these efforts are often rather ridiculous).[53]

Will it be said that such finer points are irrelevant, since persecution still exists? Will the objection be made that it doesn't matter to victims whether they are persecuted in the name of some "point of view" or other? To do so would be to misunderstand the civilizing process and the optimism that are still at work within modernity. No human progress, whether in the legal, ethical or moral spheres, is conceivable unless the sacrificial foundations of persecution are first destroyed. I am even tempted to say that any attempt to define a universal morality, any civilizing ambition, can only begin once this minimal threshold has been crossed. The delegitimization of sacrifice is indeed *the* founding value par excellence. All the others are dependent on it — even if nothing can be taken for granted.

Now we can better understand the extraordinary peril that a predicted return to the ancient practice of sacrifice could represent at the dawn of a new century.

PART III

OUR RENDEZVOUS WITH THE WORLD

THE CASE FOR A PARADOXICAL HUMANISM

Let us pause here, briefly, since we have now come full circle. The six dangers enumerated in the preceding pages are clearly interrelated. It is not too difficult to see how they reinforce — and intensify — one another. Whichever of the founding values we choose to look at first, we can easily see that its particular vulnerability depends on the vulnerability of all the others. Even the implacable coherence of this "negative system" is cause for concern, this system that seems to trap us and threatens to drag us down with the ship. The whole thing combines to compose a new symbolic configuration that we are just beginning to focus on — and with some difficulty, since we are still prisoners of old political and ideological mental categories.

An implacable coherence? The fading of the future, for example, cripples every kind of social or generational foresight. It undermines in advance any kind of reciprocal solidarity, since this is inseparable from a minimal vision of the future: today I give, tomorrow I shall receive, today you receive and in the future you will give. Any kind of social contract has a temporal dimension. The reign of "what's the use?" and of "every man for himself" comes into effect quite naturally when the future is no longer carefully chosen, or has been lost sight of — unless of course we consider the mere accumulation of goods and of technology to be a "purpose". But this acceptance of the immediate present and the eclipse of the future threaten in turn to undermine the political, and with it any minimal aspiration to equality and justice.

Inevitable Oligarchy

"Politics is an appetite for the future", said Max Weber. The weakening of the former is a direct consequence of our fading vision of the latter. No more future means no more politics. But this "dispossession" of the political process immediately clears the way for new forms of domination, and for the thousand and one oligarchic tendencies already beginning to appear in all the advanced democracies. The crisis in democracy is not merely the supremacy of the private domain and of the market but the inexorable return of the rule of a "select few". Every passing day brings fresh signs of this reality. Imperceptibly, people are becoming dangerously re-accustomed to the notion that all the important decisions — political, economic, scientific, and diplomatic — have been taken out of the ordinary citizen's hands, and that that is just the way it has to be. Such a trend is a minor catastrophe. It is the silent victory of the "bronze law" of oligarchy, as shown by so-called "Machiavellian" theoreticians.[1] Its ultimate consequence is the "defeat of justice", as Blandine Kriegel calls it, which imperceptibly gives free rein to the most archaic mechanisms of sacrifice. The "select few", their power no longer restrained by any elected counterbalance, provoke the sporadic fury of the majority. So attempts to "get" the powerful, mostly through judicial channels, occur at regular intervals to halt the drift into oligarchy. The whole thing fits together like those Russian dolls: you open one and the next is revealed. The synergy is striking. And it goes even farther.

The instrumentalization of critical reason and its reduction to the level of a techno-science correspond to an alternate future, to a substitute "design". It is in fact a false one, since it merely launches us on a blind rush forward. Only the Americans, for reasons related to their history, are able to elevate this technological utopia, which continually promotes the *frontier* of possibility and of knowledge to the status of an inspiring myth. For the Americans, technology, as the herald of a "radiant future", has already become the equivalent of the push to the West that held out the promise of adventure and riches to the descendants of the early pioneers. Nothing appeals more to the American collective memory than the remembrance of this frontier that was ceaselessly pushed forward, month by month, by dint of human audacity, to the farthest edge of the California territory. Indeed, what could be more inspiring than the mythology of the covered wagon and the unknown open spaces of the West, gradually conquered and tamed by the settlers as they pushed onward to the Pacific Ocean, their Bible in one hand and their rifle in the other, with pickax and plough carried on the wagon behind?

Today, the technological frontier — computing, cybernetics, and biogenetics — plays exactly the same symbolic role as the plains of the Far West. The same myth is being propagated in a different guise. This explains the indefatigable optimism of the New World, its ability to overcome any disappointment — the optimism Gunnar Myrdal had in mind when he spoke of the "all-conquering charm of the great American auto-suggestion". It also nourishes the spontaneous confidence in technology that we see in North America. It encourages the American preference for a laissez-faire attitude, even in ethical matters. Above and beyond purely commercial competition, the disagreements between the United States and Europe — about genetically modified corn, hormone-fed beef, or the patenting of DNA — provide an almost daily illustration. There is, in America, an irritable impatience with European caution, with the delays and equivocations on such matters.

This grand design symbolized by the frontier is an exception peculiar to the American case and to it alone. There is nothing of the kind here in our old Europe, steeped in skepticism. For the nations of the Old World, whose real milieu is a historical rather than a spatial one, the idea of a frontier as a way of envisaging the future holds little appeal, whether the frontier is geographical or technological. This is why the impatience with Europe, and the occasional criticisms of its lack of zest or so-called "fatigue" are a trifle ridiculous: not all nations share the same founding myths.

Thou Shalt Be King!

Here in Europe, contemporary neo-scientism appears more like an ally of the liberal intoxication that can envisage no other destiny for human societies than getting and spending, the quantitative and the measurable.

For us, techno-science and ultra-liberalism naturally go hand-in-hand; they are the two faces of the same hegemony, one that seems to us both onerous and rudimentary. "The 'econo-reign' is dependent on techno-science, which is assuming a decisive role," as Maurice Bellet aptly remarks. "For the latter lacks any thesis or doctrine: it is an enormous, effectively functioning complex, an inexhaustible reservoir of efficiency — i.e. of expansion — that the 'econo-reign' can draw on".[2]

More precisely still, we Europeans are more conscious of the fact that contemporary techno-science has become the natural ally of the inegalitarian "design" described earlier in this book. It strengthens and justifies the new forms of domination that we find it so difficult to resist. "The complicity between the ideologies of domination — overt or not — and techno-scientism is perhaps the most decisive aspect of present-day global reality. Moribund, or running out of steam, these ideologies have found an unexpected adjunct in techno-scientism".[3]

In the end, the acclamation of the self, the apotheosis of individual freedom — a promise unceasingly held out, broadened in scope, and never satisfied — has become the ultimate stratagem of a modernity that has no clear objective apart from this intoxicated and/or queasy individual-asking, against a backdrop of technological and consumerist plenty. Thou shalt be king! Thou shalt be efficient! Thou shalt be alone! It is a promise that can never be kept, and a fool's paradise. Free, released from all affiliations, the self is near to being swallowed up by its own triumph. Its vocation is indeed to be alone, but ultimately defenseless, deconstructed, and defeated by its own victory.

* *

*

These six interlocking perils thus compose the negative image of the six principles that we have to perpetually re-found and defend, on a daily basis. It isn't difficult to see what principles we mean: they are, simply enough, the renewal of hope in place of desolation or mockery; the defense of equality against domination by the strongest; the restoration of the political process so that it can resist the "fatalities" of the market; critical — and modest — reason, a thousand times preferable to disquieting scientism; social solidarity and common beliefs instead of vindictive individualism; the substitution of justice for sacrificial vengeance.

Is the framework for such a re-foundation clear enough? Indeed it is.

But, in the final analysis, its definition, however obvious it may appear, runs up against a difficulty infinitely more difficult to resolve, namely the question of whether these values — which are our values, and those of Judeo-Christianity — are as obviously universal as we like to think? Can they be extended, just like that, to the rest of the world?

Today, this (age-old) problem is being raised in entirely new terms.

A Rainbow World

The rest of the world, indeed, is no longer "far away" and never will be again. We, the inhabitants of the blessed Euro-American promontory, no longer stand facing out to the wide world the way we did for centuries. The world in question is not just within our reach, it has not only shrunk in size: it is now *with us*, even part of our very selves. Globalization, which is spoken of so indiscriminately, doesn't just mean opening up our borders, our trade, or our curious minds. More essentially, it means the sudden intrusion of the outside world and of otherness into the very core of our societies and our consciousness. Now, internal and external realities have come together: the rest of the world is already there — all of it. Now, different, exotic realities mingle with one another right where we live; the kind of contradictions that we once upon a time confronted on a geopolitical level are emerging within our borders: the contradiction between a center dispensing modernity and a periphery rooted in tradition; between a first-world country promoting Enlightenment values and "exotic" lands still immersed in darkness and superstition; between a central colonial power and its periphery. This is a reinvention of the globe: the end of empires and colonies, of a world centered on the West, and of the white man's privileges. The old bulwarks are gone! Why cry over spilt milk? That is how things are.

Multiculturalism, immigration, the intermingling and interbreeding of cultures and human bodies mean that the old imperial or colonialist confrontations of yesteryear have now become domestic problems. The outside world has moved into our territory. It is hammering on our door and, inexorably, crossing the threshold. No barriers, no customs officers, no police force, can protect us from such insistence, nor will we be able to postpone the encounter for much longer. Whether we want it or not, there will be cultural pluralism and racial mixture. Whatever we may do, we shall have to coexist with people who have come from elsewhere. As for hatred of others, the urge to send them back to where they came from and padlock the gates, or, on the contrary, to force them to assimilate, and all such reactions which are sometimes provokes by our uneasy consciences, are as ineffective as the attitudes of the "civilizers" who formerly attempted to subject whole nations to the authority and rule of the "mother country". That is not how things are done any more, and we are perfectly conscious of the fact.

The questions now being raised are very different. The needed new foundation runs up against an unexpected paradox. Still jealously attached to our essential convictions, we are heading towards an encounter for which history has ill prepared us. The same doubts rise up to meet us on all sides. They take the following form: are all these certitudes — egalitarian, secularist, progressist, individualist, reasonable, critical, etc. — not the latest guise assumed by the same old Western, Judeo-Christian arrogance? In wanting to re-lay the foundations of these principles so as to consolidate them and give them greater universality, aren't we falling back into a kind of neo-colonialism? Aren't the well-meaning initiatives, human rights mantras and justifications of humanitarian interventions not just the same old gunboat diplomacy, beneath an outward air of innocence and irreproachable intentions? Aren't we trying to impose our image of mankind and the universe on others? Within each individual country, is the move towards plurality not just a continuation of the "civilizing mission" of Christopher Columbus, Louis-Hubert Lyautey, Jules Ferry, or Cecil Rhodes, but this time on the home front? In any case, the Afro-Americans of New York, the Sioux of Arizona, the Sonninkes of the Parisian suburbs, the Turks of Bavaria, the Chinese of Chinatowns everywhere, or the Kabyles living in Bordeaux, pose this kind of a question. It is hard to think of a more difficult one. Why? Because it is impossible to give it a simple, direct answer. The bitterness of the debates over multiculturalism or communitarianism underlines the fact that the answers proposed by all sides in such debates mostly simplify the problem too much to be of use.

Is there a simple answer? Are we to say that neither universality nor our constitutions can be put into question, that acculturation and assimilation to "our" values can't tolerate any exceptions? In that case, we shall sooner or later have to accept that if necessary this assimilation will be forced on people who do not want it by the forces of law and order. We will find ourselves involved in an intolerant repression that, to give itself the energy required, will have no alternative but an obsessive evocation of "the way things used to be" — a mostly imaginary state of affairs, merely reconstructed, retrospectively, out of our nostalgia.

What is in tatters today is nostalgia for the united and indivisible Republic, a coherent and homogeneous nation, an organic acceptance of the community, a minimal kind of holism, or a sacred realm. The whole litany is familiar. Whether such nostalgia is morally justified — and even respectable — is not the real problem. The problem is that it becomes less and less meaningful as the community into which outsiders have to be assimilated (the nation, the family, the State, etc.) crumbles away. Losing its meaning and its strength, an excessively rigid republican and integrationist approach is thus turning into a despairing — and frustrating — incantation, if not just a waste of time. We are sensitive to the concern it expresses and the dangers it points to, and to the worthiness of the voluntarism underlying it, though we doubt it can still serve any useful purpose.

But what alternative is there? Are we to say, on the contrary, that plurality and relativity should rule in a society lacking any shared collective representations? Are we to accept the idea that no integration or assimilation of an individual or group can be considered legitimate, or even be countenanced, in societies that have become multicultural? Do we also have to accept that an infinite plurality of principles and convictions, with no limits apart from those imposed by civil and criminal law, is the necessary corollary of this individual diversity in which everyone is different and all equally sovereign? Will it be objected that we have to organize, respect, and accept the infinite variety of the world — including what we might call its moral variety — within each of our societies? We know very well that such absolute relativism leads nowhere either. It means resigning ourselves to the atomization of society and to the kind of individualistic or tribal frenzy in which everybody is ultimately a loser. It implies, rather spinelessly, that the various dislocations that leave the individual to cope with market mechanisms on his own are inevitable. Paradoxically, it is the corrupt and the dishonest that would get the best of the bargain. "In the name of what moral code are we supposed to respect a kind of behavior that is obviously bad, and justify the strongest, or those who act out of self-interest? There is urgent need for a moral Law: if discussions are to be useful, the exchange must produce one well-founded proposition, and only one".[4]

At best, this relativism revives the Byzantine debates in American political philosophy about the neutrality of the State, the rejection of any overarching point of view, the unreality of any kind of "common good" — the threefold profession of faith of North American liberal-libertarians and Utilitarians.

John Rawls's "Intuitions"

This "best case" scenario merits further attention. John Rawls's attempt to confront this contradiction is probably the most significant and one of the most praiseworthy. Rawls's initial undertaking, in opposition to the nihilism of utilitarian philosophies, is an attempt to lay the foundations of a rational theory of justice, one acceptable to all, in spite of the pluralism of values and points of view. How can we define the notion of the Good in a society that specifically rejects any shared "point of view"? Rawls sets out to defend this pluralism of values and opinions (which he considers a fundamental step forward), while at the same time rejecting an absolute social fragmentation dangerous to the cohesiveness of democratic society. He is trying to square the circle. The difficulty of his undertaking is easy to see: it means making one out of many, deriving a norm from the absence of norms, and creating a set of rules by combining freedoms. Such is the audacity of his undertaking. That is also its merit.

Without going into the details of his analysis, we can say that Rawls is induced to put forward the notion of a "thin theory" of the good, or, more precisely, of minimal principles of political justice, considered less constraining than common values in the traditional meaning of the term. The reasoning, understandably, is finely honed. Rawls doggedly tries to trace a narrow path between holism and individualism, between multicultural relativism and the dogmatism of moral law, between political anarchy and official ideology. In the process he uses concepts or metaphors that are at once subtle and questionable: the "veil of ignorance", the "duty of civility", etc. He mostly encounters theoretical difficulties that his adversaries have jumped on. I shall look at two of these.

The first is related to the deep-seated reasons that are supposed to encourage the citizens of a pluralist society to prefer the principle of justice to any other. If there is no strong belief to unite us, in the name of what will we choose justice over injustice? And how will we manage to agree about even the definition of this same justice? Will it be in the name of the best interest of the individual and the expectation of reciprocity? By virtue of a calculation that would impel us in the direction of the good in the expectation of some personal benefit that is merely postponed? Such a motivation seems both too weak and too sophisticated. It is hard to see how it would be enough to convince criminals or profiteers! For Rawls, citizenship properly understood should be enough to bring about the attachment of individuals to the democratic ideal, despite the diversity of their beliefs. He considers pluralism "the long-run result of the powers of human reason within an enduring background of free institutions".[5] From his point of view, such a harmonious attachment implies that certain conditions must be fulfilled: whatever pertains to the private sphere (i.e. the individual's personal beliefs and cultural inheritance) must be kept completely separate from public reason as exercised in the deliberative forum. The problem is that he doesn't manage to combine and articulate these two separate dimensions, or does so only poorly.[6] Could each of us, without any difficulty or absurdity, lead a "double entry" existence, to borrow an accounting term? It's far from certain. Nor does the ongoing debilitation of the democratic process in America contribute anything to the case for such a radical separation between the public and private spheres.

The second criticism has been brought out by communitarians like Charles Taylor or Michael Sandel. It concerns the very deep-rootedness of the notion of justice and, more precisely, the "desire" for justice. John Rawls reasons as if this were a *fait accompli*, as if the desire for a just world was shared, without any problems, by all the men and women on the face of the earth. He takes for granted not so much the definition of justice but at least the desire for justice. His point of departure is the notion that all individuals cherish this desire, whatever their culture, their race, their difference. This covert Rousseauism dispenses him of any need to explain his own basic intuitions — the intuitions of one John Rawls, born in 1921, in Baltimore, Maryland, on the shores of Chesapeake Bay — the intuitions of a white American who, even though unconsciously, has absorbed the double heritage of Christianity and the Anglo-Saxon liberal tradition. However, a multicultural society includes a large number of individuals coming from the four corners of the world, who have very little in common with a worthy, scrupulous WASP from Baltimore.

Going a bit farther, we could say that basically Rawls is taking the very problem he claims to be framing as already solved. Without really saying so, he is postulating that, in spite of everything, the multiple and dissimilar "opinions" he wants to see freely coexist share the same common capital, the same ethical tendencies from the word go. But we know very well that this is not so. We have seen, chapter by chapter, that the founding values comprising this "common capital" have never been anything but the unique, vulnerable, fortuitous product of a specific historical development. They are neither natural, nor necessarily very robust. Yet this criticism takes nothing away from the considerable merit of Rawls's thinking, which has gone as far as possible in its search for a reasonable compromise between an excess of "we" and too much "me".

Our consideration of Rawls takes us back to the initial problem that has been behind this book from the first page, namely the urgent need to redefine, and therefore re-found, the essential principles, the "values", the shared convictions, the symbolic infrastructure, the collective representations (the terminology is unimportant), which make it possible for us to live together. Unlike Rawls, I am actually far from convinced that these principles can be taken for granted to the extent that there is no need to give them new roots.

Self-Acceptance

This necessary re-foundation leads to what we might term a paradoxical humanism. It consists in opening oneself to the other, to the diverse, to the multiple, without yielding any ground on what is essential. It means simultaneously rejecting both an imperious imposition of norms (which leaves only one point of view, take it or leave it) and an excessively accommodating relativism (to each his own rules, his own truth). In other words, it sets out to do battle on two fronts: against intolerance on the one hand and against nihilism on the other, and to do so on behalf of each of the principles reviewed in the preceding pages. Making the case for a modest kind of reason, in opposition to scientism, doesn't mean we have to lower our guard against sectarian illuminism and esoteric mumbo-jumbo. Making the case for a minimum of social cohesion doesn't mean we have to accept all kinds of radicalism. Making the case for political — and democratic — control over the market doesn't mean we have to place our trust in some kind of authoritarian planning. Making a case for secular hope doesn't mean we have to return to a Hegelian fetishization of History. Isn't it characteristic of any reasonable struggle that it does battle on two fronts?

Our rendezvous with the world, the new requirement that we open ourselves to difference, learn to deal with diversity, and accept otherness, nevertheless implies a renewed resolve in respect to the principles we have inherited, and certainly not moving farther away from them. Forgetfulness or self-hatred are not, any more than renouncing the truth, or some kind of demagoguery, the best way to approach otherness. Humanity sings best from its own branch of the genealogical tree. The encounter with the other begins with self-acceptance. The love of what is different also means looking for similarities. There is something alarming about the aberration that allows people to move in the direction of multiplicity and pluralism only after they have weakened or even abandoned any kind of fidelity to what they are.

One more point.

Where we feared cacophony and relativism, the thing that minimizes differences and re-founds a minimal solidarity is above all a lucid awareness of the danger. The doubts we might have entertained regarding the relevance of the Western and Judeo-Christian inheritance are soon dispelled when we witness the assaults presently being made on it. We soon abandon our rather faint-hearted indulgence for what is different and exotic when we catch sight of the direction in which certain paths can lead.

CHAPTER IX

BARBARISM'S NEW CLOTHES

"All that has really been at stake for the past thousand years is
the decision whether we belong, mentally, to the peoples of the
forest, or to the tribe of goatherds who, from its desert, pro-
claimed itself the chosen people of a strange god, a "jealous god".
Pierre Vial,
National Hebdo, March 26, 1998.

Denunciations of "barbarism" come up so often, it is part of the most ordinary political — and electoral — ritual. As thought the adversary will be easier to defeat once he has been labeled, if not as a barbarian strictly speaking, as at least an accomplice of barbarism. Ah yes, the famous "objective" complicity! The word is just as much abused in the realm of ideas. Barbarism, past, present and future, is a dragon everyone is eager to slay, and never tires of calling forth to battle. This valiant combat — in which Good triumphs over Evil — is most rewarding when the barbarism in question is an old one (for instance Hitler, Stalin, or Pol Pot), a distant specter we can keep bringing up, while swearing that we are eager to prevent its re-emergence. Standing watch from the battlements does serve a useful purpose, even if it is sometimes a bit overdone and somewhat gratuitous.

It is not at all evident how we should deal with the real barbarisms of today or tomorrow. The desire to resist them first requires an attempt at definition (not always so simple) and even, sometimes, a minimum of courage (a commodity not in plentiful supply). Most often, then, present or future forms of barbarism meet with resistance only when they do not go against the reassuring unanimity of the herd. The certainty of having identified someone as "evil" makes it so much easier to speak out courageously, when everyone is in agreement and there is little serious likelihood of contradiction. We are familiar with some of these representatives of barbarism: say, Le Pen in France, Jörg Haider in Austria, Zhirinovsky in Russia, and a few other less prominent examples. Their immediate function will turn out to have been to keep the defenders of the good constantly on their toes in combating the evil personified with such dark satisfaction by these barbarians.

No one could question, retrospectively, the merit and the usefulness of these forced marches, mobilizations, denunciations and resistances. It's good that they happen, but it's a shame things aren't taken any farther. It's a pity that, hypnotized by these Mussolinian gesticulations and repugnant rhetoric, people haven't reflected, calmly and resolutely, on the deeper meaning of a vicious trend that has resurfaced in the modern world, at the turn of the century. The lack of consideration given the major ideas for which this trend is the vehicle, and the feebleness of the intellectual investigation in this area are — with a few exceptions[1] — evident. However, no one should underestimate such an adversary. Raymond Aron wrote, in the mid-1980s, that anyone who abominates Alain de Benoist's ideas "should combat them with ideas, not with clubs or vitriol".[2] His daughter, Dominique Schnapper, was quite justified in criticizingthe inadequacy of reflection on the extreme right. "It's high time that the anti-Lepenists stopped underestimating the thinkers of the *Front National*," she wrote. "Contempt for one's adversary is misplaced in a democracy. They're up against an opponent who is far from intellectually insignificant. His arguments have to be dealt with on an intellectual level".[3] But Schnapper was speaking only of the troublesome "planet" of the National Front, and forgetting the rest of the solar system. Perhaps she too was sinning by omission. It seems as though here in France the Lepenist tree (or scarecrow) has prevented us from seeing a whole different forest.

What forest? The great primitive forest, that's what.

The New "Pagans"

Neo-paganism is making a comeback in most of the Western democracies. What does this signify, exactly? In France, it isn't just an innocuous product of the "cocktail-party Nietzscheism" mocked by François Chatelet. It is more combative, and has its source in a much stronger aspiration:

to repudiate twenty centuries of Judeo-Christianity and return to the innocence of our origins; to break once and for all with New Testament "resentment" and social permissiveness and rediscover Dionysian vitality or the enchantments of the forest of Brocéliande; to dump "Americanized" democracy and consumerist materialism; to reject the morality of the weak and the preference for the victim in order to liberate the energy of the strong, etc.. None of the three most common reactions against this protean neo-paganism — viewing it as a harmless eccentricity, as a political fad for some insignificant splinter groups, or as a trend whose subterranean influence can be downplayed to non-existence — is beyond criticism.

The first response is to view of them as eccentricities. They do have picaresque features that lend themselves to this view. Take, for instance, the purely regionalist dimension of the great search for roots (musical and oceanic Celticness, ceremonial Druidism, Wagnerian Germanism, Viking exaltations, etc.) that has given rise to so many festivals and musical trends. We instinctively think of such strange and colorful images when we talk about our pre-Christian roots. Taken as pure folklore, this return to "pagan" roots need give little cause for concern, even when there is a (sometimes unconscious) flirting with dubious mythologies, whether the hammer of Thor, son of Odin and god of thunder, Jul's tower, or the kingdom of Thule. This folkloric, provincialist vision certainly doesn't justify any kind of suspicion — which would only seem ridiculous, considering its target. Peace to the Breton festivals, the *Troménies* of Locronan, in Brittany, the solstice rituals, the celebration of the mistletoe, and the Celtic harp! But is that all there is to it?

There are other kinds of folklore. In a much less pleasant mode, I am thinking of the innumerable manifestations of adolescent and "rock" brands of occultism and Satanism. The symbolic universe inhabited by their practitioners, fascinated by the symbolism of the "living dead", vampires and black masses, almost cries out for a psychiatric approach. Many books have been published on the subject. To cite just one example, the *Black Metal* movement and the group *Cradle of Fields*, which announced in 1998 that it had "declared war on Christianity", are a curiosity that people are mostly overlook, except when a crime (a murder, a desecration, etc.) is committed by one of these unhappy crazies. A few Nazi swastikas spray-painted on a headstone, a collection of Nazi emblems and two or three texts speaking of an (imaginary) black mass: these are the signs reported in the media. There's a flutter of alarm at the appeal this kind of thing seems to have for the young, and then the whole thing is quickly forgotten. Does this kind of news item have any greater importance than that? Surely there's nothing in it, people think; nothing that deserves our ongoing serious attention.

Similarly, there are innumerable factions, groups, secret societies and publications proliferating on the Internet that are viewed as a (sinister) kind of folklore. From "hating Jesus" to praising cannibalism, from esotericism to magic cults, from necrophilia to the occult and the bizarre, from the very superficial reading of Nietzsche's work (his name comes up a lot) to the ecstasies of provocative orgies: almost every nook and cranny of this darker side of European culture is now accessible on the Web. Visiting these extreme sites allows one to put in perspective not so much their quantity or their violence, but rather their theoretical importance. It's true that it doesn't require much effort to analyze them, for they mostly tend toward fatalism. However gloomy and pathological it may be, and however repugnant its verbal or musical expression, this kind of Satanism never amounts to anything but a secondary phenomenon. There are plenty of others, after all, that we manage to tolerate somehow or other, for such is the inevitable price of freedom. The mistake would be to confuse all barbarism with these tiny groups, which are no more than a hallucinating version of it.

Such eccentricities mustn't be allowed to distract our attention from a less picturesque reality. The constellation of parties, groups, magazines and publishing houses belonging to the extreme political right bring us onto much more serious ground. The leaders of these groups give much greater importance than is generally thought to neo-pagan analyses and the struggle against "religious totalitarianism" — what some of them call "Christian prevarication". Take the Nouvelle École or Labyrinthe publishing houses in France, for instance; in addition to the journals *Éléments* or *Krisis* and the better-known authors of similar persuasion (Alain de Benoist, Ernst Jünger, Ortega y Gasset, Carl Schmidt, René Guénon, Louis Rougier, Julius Evola), they also publish polemical monographs on such subjects as *Celsus against the Christians*, pamphlets on *The Religious Question*, essays on the *Pagan Renewal in French Society*, not to mention more conventional studies on Greek religion, the Indo-Europeans, and Darwinism. In all these publications and in these various clubs or movements — of which

254

the Group for Research and Examination of European Civilization (GREECE) is the best known — the struggle against Judeo-Christianity and the values associated with it remains the central preoccupation.

People usually explain that these different pagan movements are merely an offshoot of the extreme right, and a very minor one at that. They are basically seen as no more than a tiny sect, closed and jealously protective of its uniqueness but exerting only negligible influence on the outside world. If people do take up arms against the New Right propagandists, they do so almost reluctantly and only sporadically — as, for example, when there is some new incident involving the National Front (of which this current is, indeed, a part). This was also the case in 1993-1994, when the editor of the journal *Krisis*, Alain de Benoist, in his quest for intellectual respectability, managed to get his hands on some texts emanating from the legalist left. This so-called scandal caused quite an uproar at the time, but was soon forgotten. Otherwise, the very notion of "revolutionary neo-paganism" is mostly considered an intellectual oddity, an obsession of no importance.

This is a mistake. To interpret the movement as a sect or tiny group means confusing the vessel and its contents, putting the emphasis on evaluating it in terms of organizational or electoral strength while neglecting any serious examination of its ideas. To make neo-paganism into a matter of sects or cults, to consider hatred for Judeo-Christianity the obsession of a few harebrained extremists, is to commit a two-fold error.

The influence — by infiltration and contagion — of the authors or texts cited above is infinitely more important than people generally imagine. In choosing, from the outset, a strategy of gradual cultural conquest, inspired by the Italian philosopher Antonio Gramsci (1891-1937), the moving spirits behind the neo-pagan New Right have at the same time failed and partially succeeded. They have failed because they have not been able to capture a real "position" in the intellectual domain or in the media — except, briefly, when Louis Pauwels opened the columns of *Figaro Magazine* to them. Their partial success is due to the fact that a good few of the ideas they put forward are actually omnipresent in the surrounding culture. I think the preceding chapters have shown this clearly enough.

These kinds of ideas are present in a watered-down, disguised, and partial form in numerous areas of thought and of politics. They advance under cloak and mask, so that even those who spread them are unaware of what is really at issue. They take effect by means of a slow, invisible infusion. But even so the paradox is a real one, for everywhere in Europe there is a noisy resistance to the extreme right as a cult or parliamentary movement, while at the same time many of the themes and counter-values of neo-paganism are absorbed without any real resistance by the symbolic environment.

Nothing signifies postmodern imprudence or confusion better than this contradictory relationship with "Nietzschean" anti-values that are, theoretically, at the opposite pole to the dominant beliefs, but which the latter nevertheless welcome with open arms. Is this due to lack of caution? Lack of thoughtfulness? Mere foolishness? It sometimes seems as if a race of ventriloquists is busy attacking a cynicism and barbarism that, at the same time, it accepts deep within itself. So, contemporary discourse ingenuously expresses criticisms, refusals, denunciations, and points of view, of a kind that the Fascist theoreticians of neo-paganism articulate in their naked reality. A taste for mockery, the gospel of inegalitarianism, the cult of the winner, and of winners, emerge like a more deep-seated ideological "stratum" once the top layer — provided by the catechism of human rights — is stripped away. This ideological schizophrenia and outlandishness emerge clearly once we move on from this broader consideration to examine more closely one or the other of these thinkers. It's an understatement to say that the struggle against barbarism doesn't take it seriously enough.

The Case Of Julius Evola

Let us take just one instance. Of all the pagan thinkers whose underground influence is undeniable today, the case of Julius Evola is without any doubt the most interesting. The breadth of his work, the significant ambiguity of certain of his contacts, the durability and strength of his influence, all make Evola an exemplary case.[4] Born in Italy in 1898 (he died in 1974), this Italian philosopher gave merely "critical support" to Mussolini and refused to join the Italian Fascist Party, which he considered "petit-bourgeois". This didn't prevent him, in 1940, from writing a text lacking any reticence whatsoever, *The Aryan Doctrine of Struggle and Victory*. Discovered at the end of the 1920s, in particular by Mircea Eliade, the orientalist René Guénon, and even Marguerite Yourcenar,[5] Evola was initially considered a gifted popularizer of Buddhism, Taoism, and oriental esotericism. However, he had already written the earliest version of his major work, *Revolt against the Modern World*, early in the 1930s, and it was published in Italy in 1934. Revised, added to and re-published in 1951 (i.e. after the war, a significant detail), this text was rediscovered thanks to the "creeping May revolt" of 1968 in Italy, and has been regularly re-printed since then. It wasn't till 1991 that the book was published in France, when it was hotly defended by Alain de Benoist.[6]

This weighty tome is disturbing to the attentive reader on several scores. Why? Because, with great consistency and (unwitting) pedagogical clarity, it denounces one by one each of the six founding principles we have outlined in the preceding pages. Anyone who believes, to whatever degree, in the values in question (hope for the future, equality, reason, justice, etc.) can therefore discover, by reading Evola, the step-by-step development of a world-view exactly contrary to his. In other words, this Italian neo-fascist is proposing a total reconstruction of what we usually call "civilization", but one that is turned on its head in every way. This is why I use the term "barbarism" to describe it.

A first example: referring simultaneously to Nietzsche, Lao Tzu, and Gobineau, Evola condemns outright the "bourgeois" morality and humanist moral code inspired by Judeo-Christianity. "In almost every instance we have to agree with Nietzsche," he writes, "that wherever the preoccupation with 'morals' arises, a process of decadence is already at work; the *mos* of . . . 'heroic ages' never had anything to do with moralistic limitation. The Far Eastern tradition especially has emphasized the idea that morals and laws in general (in a conformist and social sense) arise where 'virtue' and the 'Way' are no longer known".[7] In his eyes, Judeo-Christianity demystified the myth and the sacred, thus interrupting the development of a "traditional" history; to him, it represents what he calls a "weak turn" of the Western tradition (that's the name of one of his chapters). That's an excellent way to describe what we, for our part, have termed, Biblical "subversion" — but seen from the opposite viewpoint. So which is it: "weak turn" or subversion? It's a matter of perspective.

Julius Evola, who is lacking in neither talent nor erudition, is in any case a militant immoralist, quick to celebrate Dionysian hedonism and appeal to that enormous reservoir of amoral energy represented by nature. Evola's polemic against any form of ethical control is strangely close to many contemporary theories, whether those of the liberal-libertarians, the post-Leftists, or the modern Nietzscheans. No doubt the latter would be surprised to find themselves in such embarrassing company. Adulation of solar happiness and the eulogy of vitalism are integral aspects of Evola's form of Fascism. Morality is not always "on the Right". Let us add that Evola is also the author of a work published in 1959, *The Metaphysics of Sex*,[8] which is quite close to the case for permissiveness made by Wilhelm Reich, one of the gurus of May 1968 and a major mythical figure of the "sexual revolution".

The media, in any case, should be infinitely more cautious in dealing with this kind of question. Where permissiveness and prohibitions are concerned, it would be better to remember the warnings of a psychoanalyst like Pierre Legendre instead of prudishly sermonizing from some pulpit or other. Legendre warns, for instance, that "What is important is not that talk of the Good should triumph over talk of Evil, but that some Forbidden thing be kept as a lifebuoy for humanity. But Forbidding raises, hypothetically, the question of limits. We really lack any coherent thinking on this question".[9]

The Rejection Of "Linear Time"

On the crucial theme of hope and of progress, of "linear time", Evola's point of view is even more instructive. He does indeed consider that Jewish propheticism was the origin of the importance given the future and hope, i. e. to the Messianic vision of which Western "progress" is no more than the secularized successor. The only difference is that far from seeing it as a positive factor, he views it as the *onset of decadence*. "For Judaism, as in the case of other civilizations," he writes, "the time frame between the seventh and the sixth centuries B.C. was characterized by upheaval. Once the military fortunes of Israel declined, defeat came to be understood as a punishment for 'sins' committed, and thus an expectation developed that after a dutiful expiation Jehovah would once again assist his people and restore their power. This theme appeared in Jeremiah and in the second Isaiah. But since none of this came about, the prophetic expectations decayed, becoming the apocalyptic, messianic myth, the fantastic vision of a Savior who would redeem Israel. This was the beginning of a process of disintegration".[10]

In opposition to the idea of historical and linear time, Evola naturally adopts the role of an *apologist for cyclical time* and the "eternal return". In the name of this succession of cycles, which he calls a "series of eternities", Evola refers continuously to the traditions prior to Judeo-Christianity: the 'great year' of the Chaldeans and Greeks, the *saeculum* of the Etruscans and Romans, the eons of the Iranians, the "suns" of the Aztecs, the Hindu *kalpas*, etc.. "Time," he writes, "did not flow uniformly and indefinitely, but was broken down into cycles and periods in which every moment had its own meaning and specific value in relation to all others, a lively individuality and functionality of its own".[11]

Where could we find a clearer expression of the rejection of "linear time" and progress that has been the central theme of counter-revolutionary thinking, from Barrès to Drumont, from Hippolyte Taine to Nietzsche, and so on? Moreover, it is with reference to this theme of the eternal return and of decadence that a group of researchers, under the direction of the Israeli historian Zeev Sternhell, attempted a few years ago to show how this counter-revolutionary tradition has been continuously present throughout history.[12]

Evola's position on equality is even more radical. For him, present-day egalitarianism follows in the (disastrous) footsteps of the Enlightenment and of the "unleashing of the European plebs, the French Revolution".[13] He defends the durability of traditional hierarchies and the natural order of society, perceived as an organic entity. He praises leadership, obedience, and social status, if not a system of castes. Christianity seems to him primarily responsible for promoting egalitarianism, "which had already found a way to weasel its way into Roman law during the decline and fall". For him, this Christian egalitarianism — which "is evidence of southern, non-Aryan influences" — is in unhappy contradiction with the Roman virtue of virtues, namely heroism. "It exerted a function antithetic to the heroic ideal of personality, to the value acquired by everything a being wins for himself in a hierarchical order by differentiating himself, by giving himself a form".[14]

But Evola rages most against certain specifically modern forms of equality. This includes equality among men and women — a catastrophic evolution for which he holds men's pusillanimity and lack of virility responsible: "Just as the plebeian masses would never have been able to insinuate themselves into every domain of social life and of civilization if real kings and a real nobility had been in power, in a society governed by real men, woman would never have yearned for, or even been capable of taking, the path she is following today. The ages in which women have attained autonomy and pre-eminence have almost always coincided, in ancient civilizations, with periods of manifest decadence".[15]

The third founding value, the reason introduced by Greek thought, is not granted any greater indulgence, and the same is true of universalism. For Evola it is all obvious. The emergence of humanism and of philosophy in 6th century Greece is the *beginning of a decadence* that he doesn't hesitate to compare to "the spread of a cancer throughout what was still healthy and anti-secular in the body of Greece". In this, he is in the Nietzschean tradition. Indeed, "there is a theme in Nietzsche, running all through his work, namely a critique of rationality, of Reason, as the history of decadence, of a Fall".[16] As a faithful disciple of Nietzsche, Evola also attributes the progressive ruin of the traditional order to the corrosive action of critical thought. "The figures of the philosopher and the 'physicist' were merely products of the already advanced degeneration of the last age, the Iron Age. . . . The emancipation from Tradition of the individual as a 'thinker', and the affirmation of reason as an instrument of unhampered criticism and profane knowledge, came about in parallel to this situation. . . . A way of thinking that tries to account for the universal and for existence in the way that is proper to it — i.e. rationally and philosophically. . . became the most dangerous of seductions and illusions, the instrument of the humanism, and, consequently, of a much more profound and corrupting unrealism, which would later seduce the entire Western world".[17]

To this corrosive triumph of speculative reason of which Greece was the cradle, Evola significantly opposes the counter-example of India at the same period. There, he assures us, Brahmanic thought represented a similar danger. Nevertheless, it was countered by a defensive reaction on the part of Tradition, one that was made possible by the pragmatism and realism of Buddhism. In other words, Indian society was much more able than Greek to defend itself against desiccating philosophical rationality.

It is hardly surprising to discover similar hostility to the European Renaissance. For Evola, viewing the Renaissance as a rediscovery of the luminous civilization of antiquity, as opposed to Medieval Christianity, is a huge mistake. What Christian Europe rediscovers at that time, he explains, is the worst (i.e. rationalist and individualist) side of Antiquity, an ancient tradition already contaminated by philosophy. "The Renaissance took nothing from the Ancient world apart from decadent forms: not the original ones, which were impregnated with sacred and supra-personal elements. . . . Actually, within the Renaissance, 'paganness' was basically used to develop the simple affirmation of humanity, to incite passionate individualism, which became intoxicated with the productions of an art, an erudition, and a speculative thought devoid of any transcendent, metaphysical element".[18]

Where the sovereignty of the individual is concerned, finally, a virulent denunciation of America is at the heart of Julius Evola's argument. For him, American "civilization" is the "exact contradiction" of the European tradition. Giving precedence to "the religion of pragmatism and productivity", it detaches man from the "organic system" to which he belonged, turning him into "a mere instrument of production and material productivity within a conformist social conglomerate".[19] It should be noted however that, contrary to what one might imagine, Evola is hostile to modern nationalism, in which he sees only a decadent, plebeian form of traditional "nationality". The fifteenth chapter of his book, which deals with nationalism, is actually entitled: "Nationalism and Collectivism" — two terms which, for him, are practically synonymous.

* *
*

Rejection of propheticism and disavowal of progress, praise for inequality, criticism of reason, a denunciation of universalism: it would be difficult to find a more coherent and systematic rejection of everything that we hold to be constitutive of the Western inheritance. If it troubles us to find such an accurate negative fit, this is not just because it does in effect provide an outline of the potential face of barbarism, it's also because we recognize in it bits and pieces of ideas or theories that are common currency today. In other words, these "enormities" bother us all the more because we hear them repeated every day, in a barely diluted form, in everyday conversation.

But what are we to think? Has Enlightenment humanism become so debilitated that it can allow itself to be invaded, colonized, and contaminated without being aware of what is going on? Is it so full of self-doubt that it can't even recognize its adversary? What's the use of so ostentatiously keeping watch on the battlements if the enemy is already inside?

Pierre Legendre seems to be echoing the question when he says, bluntly: "A social debacle is above all a debacle of ideas. I think we're living in the trough of the wave".[20]

Tradition vs. Subversion

In any case, we can't just leave the Evola "case" there. There are other even more valuable lessons to be learned from reading him. His interpretation of sacrificial Christianity, for example, helps us understand the historical deviance of an element of European Catholicism and its stupefying readiness to compromise with authoritarian ideologies, despite the very obvious "pagan" inspiration of the latter.

While he rejects Jewish propheticism and, even more strongly, New Testament "subversion", Evola nevertheless remains faithful to all the "Roman" or "traditional" elements that have survived in established Catholicism. For example, he defends feudal society, chivalry, and the temporal theocracy of the Carolingians. Why? Because this combative form of Christianity, one that gives society a rigid structure, seems to him precisely to have turned its back on the promises of the New Testament. For him, this was a Christianity reconciled with power, authority, and tradition, to the extent of identifying itself with them. He rejoices that feudalism was able to reinvent the figures of the hero and the warrior knight (as opposed to the saint), and restore the eminent dignity of military combat (instead of love for one's enemy), never mind the blessing given to "just war", held to be preferable to "spineless" pacifism. "The case of chivalry," he writes, "shows us clearly the extent to which the fundamental themes of Christianity had been left behind, and how the Church was obliged to approve, or at least tolerate, a set of principles, values, and customs that were difficult to reconcile with the spirit of the primitive Church. . . . Chivalry affirmed an Aryan ethic in almost its original form within a world that was Christian in name only".[21]

This passage is of the greatest interest. What it does is trace from the outside, much better than any convinced Christian could do, the outline of that sacrificial and authoritarian Catholicism that, throughout the centuries, was one of the Church's major temptations, attaining its most perfect form in the reign of Louis XIV with the party of "*dévots*" surrounding Madame de Maintenon. It was this basically quite un-Christian form of Catholicism that Maurras and other counter-revolutionary theoreticians revered. Evola himself points out the paradox of an "un-Christian Catholicism" when he writes: "Anything in Catholicism that has a truly traditional character has very little that is Christian about it, and whatever is Christian about it turns out not to be traditional". In saying this, he is speaking in exactly the same terms as progressive theologians, except that he draws the opposite conclusion.

Evola's very political indulgence towards this "un-Christian" Catholicism is only equaled by his visceral hatred for the Christian ferment inspired by New Testament teachings, and for the original Biblical subversion. The rehabilitation of the victim, the refusal to return violence for violence, contrition, and hope for the future, are all superior values that for him seem to proceed from what he calls a "broken human type". He sees them as a symptom of "Semitic influence", and the sign of a "despairing form of spirituality". "In these currents," he writes, " a despairing form of spirituality emerged, in which the type of warrior-Messiah as an emanation of the 'Lord of Hosts' was replaced by the 'Son of Man', predestined to be a sacrificial victim. He is the persecuted one, the hope of the afflicted and the outcast, the object of a confused, ecstatic fervor."

As for the idea of hope and the prophetic dimension of the Revelation, they seem to him to have arisen "in an atmosphere steeped in this Messianic pathos", and he considers them the carriers of an "anti-traditional virus, particularly in its opposition to Roman tradition". He finds Christianity reprehensible precisely because of what we consider its most positive features: the foundational and universal transformation it brought about in the old sacred — and persecuting — order of human societies.

Furthermore, in an even more revealing chapter of *Revolt against the Modern World*, Evola deals with the question of sacrifice properly speaking. It is because of its refusal of sacrifice, he explains, that the Christianity that developed under the Roman Empire was unable to take its place in the religious pantheon of the age, i.e. as the cult of the Savior and a splinter group within Judaism. Evola, for his part, justifies the sacrificial worship of the Emperor, and criticizes the Christians for not accepting it: "It was typical imperial universality," he wrote, "to exercise a superior unifying and organizing function above and beyond any particular cult, which it had no need to deny. But there was a requirement for an act demonstrating a superordained *fides*, related precisely to the principle of a 'higher' authority embodied in the representative of the Empire, the 'Augustus'. But the Christians refused to perform this act — a ritual, sacrificial offering made before the imperial symbol — for they declared it to be incompatible with their faith."

For Evola it was only logical that, having refused to participate in this sacrificial worship, the Christians should be persecuted and an "epidemic of martyrs" take place. For a Roman magistrate, this refusal of emperor-worship could have seemed nothing but "pure folly" — as was the Christian claim to have rejected once and for all the confusion between the functions of priest and king, the traditional union on the *sacerdotium* and of the *regnum*. Reading this, it is easy to guess that Evola's preference goes to the "Roman magistrates".

For him, if Christianity succeeded in imposing itself on the Empire, leading to the "final victory" of Constantine's conversion, this was only because the "vital possibilities of the Roman heroic cycle" had already been exhausted, while "ancient traditions had been dimmed". In describing this decadence, he uses a tone that resonates strangely today: "Amidst ethnic chaos and cosmopolitan disintegration, the imperial symbol had been contaminated, and was merely a surviving relic in a world in ruins".[22]

In his eyes, the initial — and irremediable — fault of Christianity was to have introduced a ferment of "disintegration" into the history of Rome, and then the West as a whole. This reproach is the direct heir of a "pagan" critique as old as Christianity itself: that of Celsus, a 2nd-century philosopher who, as we have seen, inspired Nietzsche, or of the neo-Platonist Porphyrus (234-305), the author of numerous writings against Christianity. But very few modern theoreticians have taken up these themes, and detailed them so clearly. "The lunar-priestly spirit," Evola writes without any hesitation, "its specific dualism, and the attitudes of Hebrew origin that have become an essential part of the Christian spirit, represented a kind of barrier, in Catholicism, to any possibility of giving Europe's body a spirituality conforming to its essence, i.e. a spirituality reflecting what we have called the Northern Light".

The development of Evola's argument, even though such was not his purpose, thus clearly demonstrates the persistence of two versions of Christianity: one of them Constaninian and Roman, the other evangelical and anti-sacrificial. Furthermore, returning to this theological opposition on several occasions, Evola — as a good Italian — doesn't miss the opportunity to bring up the famous quarrel between the Guelphs and the

Ghibellines that was basically a transposition of this antagonism into the political domain. Setting two great families of the Florentine nobility at one another's throats early in the 13th century, this quarrel was between the supporters of Otto of Brunswick (the Guelphs), defenders of the papacy, and those of Frederick II of Sicily (the Ghibellines), resolute partisans of imperial centralism and advocates of strong temporal power. It will come as no surprise to learn that Evola strongly favors the Ghibelline side against the "cosmopolitanism" of the papacy.

On the other hand, the Ultramontanist Catholics of 19th-century France, fearful of the "modernism" of the Enlightenment and the Revolution, revived the Guelphist tradition, relying on the papacy to defend the idea of a hierarchical and traditional society founded on the primacy of a Roman pontiff. This was the whole argument of Joseph de Maistre's famous book, *The Pope*, published in 1819.

Catholic or Christian?

But, one may ask, why am I bothering to give such importance to such a suspect theoretician, so little known to the general public, whose work has received little commentary and who stands outside the narrow circles of militant neo-paganism?[23] I believe it is justified. Apart from the fact that Evola's hatred for Judeo-Christianity represents a sensibility that is more widespread, in a dilute state, than is generally imagined, his analyses are of real help in making sense of certain ideological configurations — for instance the (at first sight) bizarre symbiosis between confirmed pagans and conservative Catholics in much of the European extreme right, especially in the French National Front.

The ongoing presence of a traditionalist Catholic current (led, in France, by men such as Bernard Anthony [Romain Marie] and represented by newspapers and magazines such as *Présent* and *Itinéraires*, whose editor is Jean Madiran), alongside defectors from the pagan New Right, is a phenomenon that we have become accustomed to view as a harmless curiosity. It is sometimes used (unfairly) as an excuse to identify Catholicism with the extreme right. The identification is facilitated by the fact that the Lepenist leaders have been careful to take over a whole range of ostensibly Christian symbols, from Joan of Arc to Clovis, from the "Christian West" to the epic history of the Franks. Actually this paradox is, in almost the same terms, the same as one that existed in France from the 19th century on, and which has dominated the entire history of the Action Française movement.[24]

Charles Maurras, although a militant atheist, represented himself as a defender of the Catholic Church against Revolutionary and Enlightenment "modernism", as we have said. For Maurras, if New Testament Christianity was a Semitic "fable", the Catholic establishment, on the other hand, was deserving of respect and support as the guarantor of social order and steadfast ally of the Throne. It was a classic distinction: he accepted sacrificial Catholicism while at the same time rejecting faith and the New Testament message. So in spite of his ideological atheism he was able to win the support of a large fraction of French Catholicism which was fearful of the Republican anticlericalism of such men as Émile Combes, a former seminarian whose virulent attitude is now long forgotten. Action Française was even able to win the support of prelates like Monsignor de Cabrières, Bishop of Montpellier, and of intellectuals like René de La Tour du Pin, Humbert Clérissac, Ernest Psichari, Jacques Maritain and Georges Bernanos, in the early stages of their careers. Maurois fought in vain against Pope Leo XIII's endorsement of the Republic. It was indeed after an intervention by "supportive" bishops that Pius X decided, by a decree of January 29, 1914, to put Maurras's daily newspaper and certain of his writings on the Index. Towards the end of 1926, his successor, Pius XI, would pronounce a solemn condemnation of Action Française, a doctrinal condemnation that was reinforced in 1927. "Farewell Maurras, may God's sweet mercy be with you", Georges Bernanos would write as he distanced himself from the Action Française movement.

Underlying this long-lived quarrel, we once again discover the same old opposition, so conveniently underlined by Evola, between institutional Catholicism, interpreted and experienced as a "tradition", and New Testament Christianity, more or less faithful to the subversion of the first centuries. If Maurras was condemned in the end, it was for four fundamental reasons: for his atheistic positivism, the autonomy he wanted to allow the political process ("Politics first!"), his unconditional nationalism, and his anti-Semitism. On this last point, it is sometimes forgotten that Leo XIII sided with Captain Dreyfus, or that Pius XI, going even farther, declared that "Spiritually, we are Semites", and forcefully asserted that "hatred of the people once chosen by God, the hatred that is today called anti-

Semitism," was an unjust assault on the rights of the human person.[25] His successor, Pius XII, as we know, was not so unequivocal in dealing with Hitler's Germany.

Basically, the situation has not changed all that much. It is the direct continuation of a history even longer than that of Action Française. As a political force, this unnatural alliance between "pagans" and "Catholic traditionalists" goes back to the French Revolution of 1789. In France, counter-revolutionary thought has, from the beginning, fed on two very different — if not contrary — types of sensibility. One of them is Catholic, with Count Joseph de Maistre, a Savoyard philosopher and minister plenipotentiary, the author of *Considerations on France* (1797), and Viscount Louis de Bonald, a political writer from Millau, the author of a *Theory of Political and Religious Power in Civil Society* (1796). If both men condemned the Revolution and (already!) viewed it as a return to barbarism, this was above all because it desacralized tradition and overturned the natural order. In a phrase that has become famous, Maistre stated that it was not his purpose to carry out "a contrary revolution, but the contrary of a revolution", by giving France back its place in the providential order, of which human pride and Enlightenment philosophy had deprived it.[26]

The other branch of the counter-revolution is doggedly agnostic. It is dominated by the figure of Auguste Comte (1798-1897), the founder of a "social physics", i.e. sociology, a science that does not study the individual, seen as a pure abstraction, but humanity. Comte, the celebrated author of the *Course of Positive Philosophy*, was to have a decisive influence on Maurras. But what happened then? A revealing definition of this counter-revolutionary positivism would be suggested: it was Catholicism minus the Christian belief.

Closer to us, the German philosopher Carl Schmitt, while he called himself a Catholic, also referred to an authoritarian Catholicism (like de Maistre or Bonald), which he saw as the cornerstone of sovereignty and of the social order — so he was a Catholic, then, but not necessarily a Christian. This Catholicism, which has very little of the New Testament about it, is the exact contrary — almost word for word — of Henri Le Saux's, for example. This admirable pioneer of dialogue with Hinduism lived in an *ashram* in India. He claimed to want to pave the way for a "non-mythic Church", using "the Church as myth" as his starting-point. In his personal journal he noted, "What now has to be constructed is a Christianity for the post-religious age. It has to transcend all of twenty-century-old Christianity. It must accept the revolution brought by Jesus — one that immediately lost its power with the first generation of Christians".

In the same spirit, the renowned Pastor Dietrich Bonhoeffer, murdered by the Nazis, called for the creation of a "non-religious Christianity". Humanity, for him, was heading towards "liberation from religion" (i.e. from the sacred, and from sacrifice), but this liberation, as he pointed out, has only been possible because of Christianity itself.[27]

The Temptation Of The East

After this brief journey in time, a short journey in space is called for, because the new "barbarian" sensibility has affinities with the East, just as it has with a sacrificial, authoritarian form of Catholicism. I'm not just thinking here of the way different contemporary varieties of fundamentalism have re-interpreted the Koran, the Torah, the New Testament or the Brahmanas, with an intolerance much in the news at present. I am referring rather to the equally ancient links between the authoritarian European ideologies and Eastern "wisdom".

It is not so easy to determine what is "barbarous" in this temptation of the East. It does indeed lead to both the best and the worst, and the two are interwoven. Of course, it would be nonsensical — even laughable — to condemn the receptiveness to Buddhist, Taoist or Hindu teachings demonstrated by a growing number of Westerners. There are a thousand instances showing the irreproachable authenticity of a spiritual quest that has attracted large numbers of men and women devoid of any ulterior motives. The popularity of Buddhism in the developed world points to a specific spiritual need that neither modernity, nor traditional religions, seem able to satisfy. Buddhism, which is not strictly speaking a religion, with its teachings based on detachment from and the down-playing of belief, on a distancing from the world and its "impermanence", seems to act as an antidote to consumerist frenzy, to the current tension and competitiveness, while at the same time it protects against intolerance.

Furthermore, it is symptomatic of what we could call the "new deal" of our times, under which each faith is showing some readiness to enter into a necessary dialogue with the others. In this respect, the success of Buddhism is neither fortuitous nor something to be criticized. It is evident in Europe and in the United States, and even in the Jewish Diaspora or in Israel. If a believer like Shmuel Trigano deplores it, this is not because of a negative attitude towards Buddhism itself but because of the weakening of Judaism to that it indirectly indicates. "It is pathetic," he writes, "to see Jews looking elsewhere, and far off, for what they already had in abundance at home! No doubt it shows that the spiritual strengths of Judaism are slumbering at present, repressed by institutional Judaism and Jewish modernity".[28]

Let us note in passing that this dialogue with the East in general and with Buddhism in particular has a much longer history than people think. Indeed, as early as the second century B.C., Buddhist missions had spread through Western Asia, even reaching Alexandria. Later, in the Christian era, a Christianized version of the Buddha story resulted in his being canonized. "Under the name Saint Josaphat, he was added to the Greek and Latin list of martyrs in the 13th century, together with his teacher, Saint Baarlam, and his day, November 27, still features on the calendar".[29]

Having paid tribute to this "spiritual Orientalism" which from time to time grips Western intellectuals, let us remind the reader that it has also had negative consequences — namely an uncritical acceptance of "barbarous" mind-sets antagonistic to certain values such as equality. Using Eastern "teachings" and traditions as a justification, legitimacy has often been bestowed on ideologies out of sympathy with our conception of an open society and "human rights". Actually, what the thousands of people going on a pilgrimage to the source were seeking in India was a "re-enchantment" of the world, in the sacrificial sense of the word (a recurrent theme in neo-paganism).

Pursuing their quest for this new "enchantment", the Western devotees of Hinduism or Buddhism didn't pay much attention to the everyday reality of the Eastern societies they were idealizing. Jean Mouttapa, a respected specialist on these forms of Eastern spirituality, and himself of Indian origin, is quite rightly critical of these new Western converts. "It was rare for Western intellectuals who have shown an interest in India," he writes, "to display very much critical awareness of its fundamentally inegalitarian socio-religious structure. They were mostly content to accept the arguments of Hindu defenders of the system. Impressed by the apparent perfection of an order that seemed immutable, and that had governed the lives of hundreds of millions for centuries, they didn't dare question its legitimacy".[30]

It is sometimes alarming to see the ingenuousness with which so many Westerners, using fascination for the East or respect for other cultures or for the "dialogue of different teachings" as an excuse, have given their approval to traditions against which the Indians themselves — or at least a large proportion of them — are in revolt. Such is the perverse effect of the taste for the spiritually exotic which is itself a product of Western spiritual indigence. But it has to be said that most admirers of the Vedic or Tantric mythologies, whether Mircea Eliade or Lanza del Vasto, Jean Hébert or Arnaud Desjardins, René Guénon or Alain Daniélou, did not come from the political left! Not everything is innocent in this temptation — far from it. It was no coincidence that such an emblematic representative of neo-paganism as Julius Evola was also an orientalist, an admirer of Buddhism, with a good knowledge of Tantric yoga, Taoism, and the magic of "Ur" and of "Krur". "Dressed up in anthropological language, there is indeed an orientalist intellectual extreme right".[31]

Such people, clearly, have little interest in knowing that India and Nepal are also flesh and blood societies that are prey to forms of oppression and inequality that no religious teaching could ever justify, societies in which men and women are involved in an inch-by-inch struggle to free themselves from the caste system (abolished in theory only), and are attempting to bring about — against local tradition — the triumph of values of "Western" origin. "The devotees of Indian spirituality, who have often averted their eyes from the abominable injustices resulting from the caste system," continues Jean Mottapa, "will have to swallow their disappointment: 'ancient' India has become part of history".[32]   Indian novelists like Salman Rushdie or V.S. Naipaul are quite right to mock these loving devotees of the East and their pig-headed ignorance of it.

Let us go even further. In present-day India, which is achieving modernity but is torn apart by social struggles comparable to those in other countries of the world, the men and women to be found in the front line, shoulder to shoulder with the poorest, are often... Christians. Against the Hindu fundamentalists who defend inegalitarianism, it is (mostly) they who lend support to the lower castes and play a decisive role, for instance, in the movement fighting for the rights of the Untouchables, "victims" sacrificially excluded by the indigenous religions. It has even been written that a real Indian "liberation theology" has come into existence on the Indian sub-continent.

Exotic or not, there is also, on the other hand, an incoherent, fanciful and superficial form of religiosity. It is disquieting to see this confused mysticism, this irrationalist euphoria, gain ground among us under the guise of accepting "differences". Alas! This is not the way we Westerners should keep our rendezvous with the rest of the world. We should enter into dialogue with the East without any blindness or "guilty conscience". It is only after a careful investigation, eyes wide open, that we should accept these riches and teachings from outside. Paradoxically, certain Eastern spiritual teachers are among the first to warn us. I am thinking in particular of Thich Nhat Hanh, a Vietnamese Buddhist very well known in France, who, in several of his books of wisdom, implores us to beware of certain "misappropriations" or erroneous interpretations of the Buddha's teaching.[33]

Theological Folly?

Underlying a number of temptations of the East there is indeed — but this time in the theological or philosophical domain — a "self-dissatisfaction" comparable in every respect to what Pascal Bruckner once denounced in criticizing the cult of the Third World.[34] The rather uncritical openness to teachings from elsewhere is sometimes a compensation for some kind of doubt, or sense of loss, or despair. Little by little, accepting one thing after another, people end up rejecting universalism itself because it is Christian and Western. In this way, with the best of intentions, a new "differentialism" is invented, which can lead to disastrous compromises of principle.

To cite a single instance, Eugen Drewermann, the German "anti-establishment" theologian who is also a psychotherapist, does not always manage to avoid this pitfall, although his critical contribution is interesting. A good number of Drewermann's analyses proceed from a desire to "de-Westernize" Christianity in order to make it "less aggressive" towards other cultures. He therefore attempts to root Christian "mythology" in the undifferentiated soil of the great traditions of mankind (Buddhism, or the religions of ancient Egypt) — traditions of which Christianity is supposed to be, somehow or other, the continuation, or fulfillment.

"No Christian belief," he writes, "can force us into historical dishonesty. We must therefore admit, with gratitude, that the theology of divine descent is not a uniquely Christian notion, but that Christianity merely borrowed it. So the central concept of the Christian faith is indebted to the three-thousand-year-old religion of the Nile region. . . . Faith in the divine descent of a man is not a sufficient basis, on its own, to differentiate between Christianity and the Pharaonic faith of Egypt".[35]

This discovery of distant connections, of symbolic continuity, of ontological proximity, is perfectly legitimate in itself. Furthermore, it rests on a truth: the fact that the very ancient Egyptian teachings were indeed passed on, in part, through Judaism, and later Christianity. "All one needs to be convinced of this is to compare the very rich wisdom literature of the Biblical proverbs, or the rule of St. Pacôme, in the third century: 'God allows the acquisition of wealth in order to do good. He who feeds the poor is embraced by God in his infinite mercy,' the Insinger papyrus reminds us, summing up the whole Egyptian ethic".[36]

Nevertheless, Drewermann's insistence on establishing what he considers similarities ultimately creates a problem, in the same way as his stubborn rejection of any idea of "revelation" or innovation specific to the Religions of the Book. Drawing on evidence provided by "mythical language" and even psychoanalysis, Drewermann actually considers treating the idea that the Christian faith was *revealed*, unlike pagan representations (seen only as forms of longing, or as yet unfulfilled teachings), as a "thought-taboo" (i.e. imposed by official theology) — a taboo he has every intention of breaking.

So far so good. This kind of assault, out of modesty, on one's own faith, such voluntary distancing of oneself from any set of beliefs, is understandable, and may even elicit a sympathetic response. It is certainly preferable to stubborn intolerance or triumphalist arrogance. But the approach is so systematic and so ostentatious that it leads to the suspicion there is a hidden agenda behind it.

Drewermann's argument is built up in four stages. The first consists in subjecting the historicity of Christianity to radical criticism, even if this means provoking the wrath of the Vatican — a papal "persecution" that can nonetheless be used to provide a kind of legitimacy as a victim. Next, Drewermann sets out to minimize (or even deny) the "originality" of Christianity (and Judaism) compared to the great pagan religions — even though we have seen how the Greek and Roman philosophers of the first centuries were scandalized by its novelty and subversive effect. Then he goes on to make the Biblical stories more poetic by steeping them in the hazy imprecision of some immemorial wisdom. "If it were possible," he writes, "to explain the mysteries of God in the Biblical texts in this manner — the manner of musicians, painters, and poets — their message would touch the heart of *everyone* on earth, and God would be heard in joyful anthems, in visions of beauty and prayerful poetry of worship and love". Who wouldn't be won over by such poetry? But who could be satisfied by it? Finally, Drewermann introduces — sometimes at the cost of considerable contortions — what he calls "depth psychology", which he uses as an explanatory principle.

In its basic principles this attitude is as well intentioned as that of the Third-Worlders of the previous generation, with their eagerness to make up for the crimes of the colonialist West. It shares the same passion, but perhaps it also makes the same error of analysis. Drewermann does indeed refuse to see that the "modernity" that is triumphant all over the world, for the worse but also for the better (bringing human rights, freedom, individualism, equality, etc.), is a secularized and most often perverted product of Judeo-Christianity. The latter, in the form of fidelity to the Bible, therefore involves — among other things — a radical critique of that kind of Westernization. It is at once a poison and an antidote to it, spreading over the face of the earth. The poison is the limitless expansion of market rationality, techno-science, nihilism, avid consumerism, and the Western sub-culture. The antidote, as we have seen, is composed of the "modern" values with their basically three-fold Jewish, Greek and Christian origin. No doubt they are genetically "Western", but they ceased, long ago, to be the exclusive property of the West.

So we can criticize Eugen Drewermann for being sadly wide of the mark when he rejects the specific qualities — and the universalist demands — of the Judeo-Christian inheritance. His arguments make it sound as if he agrees with the "temporal" Westernization of the world (the economy, consumption, the market, etc.) while rejecting its "spiritual" Westernization, i.e. the universalization of certain non-negotiable values such as equality or progress. This amounts to saying "yes" to the poison and "no" to the antidote. The road to hell is paved with good intentions, and anyone who turns his back on universal values runs the risk of being obliged to live with barbarism.

Preferable by far to the excessively "differentialist" theology of Drew-ermann is the much more demanding, but also much more balanced approach of the so-called theology of "enculturation". Developed about thirty years ago, it was a departure from the old missionary doctrine of what was called "adaptation" (a theology that, in its relations with local cultures, left room for influence in only one direction). Enculturation, on the contrary, was an attempt to develop a new kind of dialogue between cultures without leading to a denial of the Christian message properly speaking. The Superior General of the Jesuits, Father Aruppe, defined it in rather attractive terms in the 1970s: "Enculturation," he wrote, "is the incarnation of the life and message of Christ in a concrete cultural domain, in such a way that not only is the Christian experience expressed through elements unique to the culture in question (which would still be nothing more than a superficial adaptation), but that this same experience becomes a principle of inspiration, both a norm and a unifying force, *transforming and re-creating that culture*".[37]

Independently of the religious terminology employed, these few lines basically express a point of view that can be perfectly well expressed in secular terms: absolute respect for the other does not exclude objections on moral grounds, nor even the spiritual "right to intervene".

CHAPTER X:
THE FUTURE OF JUDEO-CHRISTIANITY

"Only someone who cries out in support of the Jews is entitled to
Gregorian chant."

Pastor Dietrich Bonhoeffer

In a short story published in *The New Yorker* in 1998, John Updike describes the heroine, who goes by Robin (though her real name is Rachel Tiergarten), as "post-Jewish". Updike is not the only one to have used this strange expression, which has become common in the United States and in Europe. Already in the 1960s Isaac Deutscher spoke of a "non-Jewish Jew" in speaking of intellectuals emancipated from their religious tradition, such as Marx, Freud, and Kafka. In the same way, people speak today of "post-Christians", or of "cultural Christians" to designate men and women who have definitively abandoned religion but who retain a bond of identity with their original faith, in the form of traces or mental categories. We must admit that this is the case for a growing number of men and women. They have maintained a sort of complicity with their childhood religion — rather vague but still surviving, remote, but still part of them in spite of everything. Generally, Western modernity as a whole is sometimes described as a "post-Judeo-Christian" reality, meaning that it has moved beyond Judeo-Christianity, developing an attitude to the world free of Biblical influences, and even of any religious belief whatsoever.

In the circumstances, do theological problems that may well appear to be obscure deserve so much attention? Is it really necessary to keep returning indefatigably to the different inheritances, contentions, contradictions, and reciprocal influences between the three "Religions of the Book", in their relations with one another and with "paganism" or philosophy? Is it justified to keep referring to a Biblical past that is receding from us at the speed of light? Does it make any sense to keep our eyes glued on the new relationship between Judaism, Christianity, and Islam, as if the future of the entire planet depended on it? These are all good questions, yet they overlook an obvious fact, namely that Judeo-Christianity is, essentially, at the roots of our modernity, and in the final analysis, of worldwide "Westernization". Neither its content nor its history is therefore irrelevant to the way we inhabit the world — and this is true for even the most humble aspects of daily life. We only have to think of the role it still plays in the world-view and political and cultural life of the leading — and also the most religious — world power, the United States. Renouncing religion, which is the fundamental trend of modernity, doesn't imply breaking with it, or forgetting it — quite the opposite in fact. The abandoning of religion is, deep down, a transmutation of the old religious element into something other than religion, in the traditional meaning of the word.

In fact, what we are experiencing in the West is anything but a greater detachment from religion. We are still preoccupied by the question of Judeo-Christianity, with or without the prefix "post" — and perhaps more so today than just a short time ago. There is a considerable contrast between the loss of influence, or the collapse, of Church institutions — whether Christian or Jewish — and the renewed curiosity for the history of religions, Biblical study, and theological debate. Many publications, a multitude of journals, the vitality of inter-faith dialogue, and the revival of late Antiquity as a subject for study and research, all show that the crisis of faith or of religious practice does not imply indifference to the history and content of the religious message.

The New Secular Paradox

There are several reasons for this. The first, and decisive, one is obviously the impact of recent memory. Half a century after the Holocaust, Western modernity is still obsessed by the memory of this indelible crime, a still gaping black hole in our era, which is still facing up to its "invisible remorse for the Holocaust", to borrow Vladimir Jankélévich's expression. We are far from finished with this ordeal. It turned the Jews, and Judaism, not into just a "nation bearing witness", but the incarnation of the "universal oppression"[1] in which, one way or another, the West was involved, and which is still an immense, unresolved question. No reflection on modernity can hope to dismiss this problem, nor avoid it, nor quietly forget it, to make room for some vague "new reality". It is still central, and will be for a long time to come. Rightly so. Not a single inhabitant of the West, however "post-religious" or remote from the Church, can escape the nagging question of the historical responsibility of Christianity in this matter.

The second reason, referred to throughout these pages, is obviously related to our pressing need for a new foundation. The past preoccupies and torments us, even when we no longer learn anything from it. Sometimes it is our inner void that makes us turn to it. The original conjunction of the Bible and Greek reason, the initial intertwining of the two that we have spoken of so frequently, is not just ancient history: it is alive and active today, even if the terminology and semantic references are no longer quite the same. Is the perpetual question of secularism anything but a transposition of the old debate between reason and faith, between philosophy and theology, that took place in the first centuries? When we come back to it today again and again we are, basically, talking about the same things. But what is happening here? Don't we belong to an irreligious society? Haven't be become "absolutely" rationalist and secularist?

In theory, there can be no doubt about it. The separation of church and state in France was even, as we know, the culmination of a long, tumultuous struggle, marked by excesses on both sides, by unrelenting disputes but also by reversals of the trend, such as the period from 1925 to 1955 when the Catholic Church attempted to re-assert its influence over an "apostate society", and partially succeeded in doing so. But now it's settled: the seminaries are empty, the churches are deserted, and it's no longer possible to imagine a Church-dominated society (except, perhaps, for some nostalgic traditionalists). But that doesn't at all mean that the debate has become irrelevant. The question of the separation of church and state has simply taken on a different form since the collapse of institutional Catholicism, starting in the middle of the 1970s.[2] It was indeed in opposition to the latter that secular republicanism developed. Deprived of this close enemy that, by reaction, helped make it what it was, the latter underwent a similar crisis, and with it the republican State itself. "Far removed from fundamentalism of any kind," writes one theologian, "both believers and nonbelievers were happy with this typically French kind of secular society they inherited. Just like religious faith, unbelief lost its arrogance and renounced dogmatism: both inhabit a common space of uncertainty and questioning".[3]

A crisis of meaning, a crisis of content, a moral crisis, or the inadequacy of the political system: the words we use are unimportant. Religious communities are no longer viewed by the secular State as rival powers to be kept in their place. Quite to the contrary, it calls on them, consulting them again and again, in a multitude of ways, as the guardians of meaning, of ethics, values, or morality. One only has to think of the ongoing debates over bioethics, test-tube fertilization, cloning, or the status of the fetus. It is enough to think of the care the government now takes to win the support of the very "faiths" and religious authorities that only yesterday it spent so much energy resisting. "What has brought religions back into the spotlight, strange as it may seem, is nothing but their shrinking power. The disappearance of what used to be the core of their political pretensions is transforming democracy and giving them a new voice in society".[4]

A comment: if this change of perspective is more clear-cut in France than anywhere else, this is hardly surprising. Secularism is a happy French exception, practically without equivalent in the developed countries, except possibly in Kemalist Turkey or Bourguiba's Tunis. Once the "eldest daughter of the Church", France, and France alone, has given herself a second identity, a scrupulously secular one, which is as much complementary to its religious identity as its rival, so that in the French memory there are now two founding traditions, not just one. France is the daughter of the Revolution *and* of the Enlightenment as much she is the daughter of the Church. It is this indissoluble complementarity which, notwithstanding the occasional confrontation, was emphasized by the historian Marc Bloch when he wrote: "There are two kinds of French people who will never be able to understand French history: those who refuse to be thrilled by the memory of the coronation [of Charles VII by Joan of Arc] at Reims, and those who can read about the Fête de la Fédération without feeling a thrill of emotion". For the French, the new order, which altered roles and created a completely new relationship between religion and democracy, was experienced much more intensely than anything in America, Germany, Great Britain, or elsewhere. This is all very logical. And, in France, this intensity lends a new relevance to the great theological debates and, above all, to what can be called the Judeo-Christian question.

A Dialogue, Or "Judeo-Christian" Ideology?

But what exactly is this question? In 1997, an Israeli Jesuit of the Pontifical Institute of Jerusalem, David M. Neuhaus, published a long article in the very scholarly *Revue de science religieuse* with the provocative title: "The Judeo-Christian Ideology and the Jewish-Christian dialogue". An ideology! Well, well! The choice of the word was significant. In the article, the author deliberately questioned the very meaning of the expression "Judeo-Christianity" and the reality for which it stands. For him, such a concept is a kind of ideological reconstruction that seriously confuses "mythical Judaism" with the real thing, and underestimates the fact that Judaism has undergone profound modifications since Old Testament days.

Christianity and Judaism, he assures us, were not engendered by one another, but actually appeared from the outset as the *divergent heirs of a common tradition.* Opposing the Judaism of the Temple to a rabbinical Judaism "based on the study of the Torah, a life of *mizvoth* (obedience to the Commandments) and acts of compassion", he criticizes the appearance, thirty-five years after Vatican II, of a truly "Judeo-Christian ideology", which he views as pernicious. It is this ideology Cardinal Jean Daniélou defended in the 1960s. Such an ideology, adds Neuhaus, by failing to recognize the specific evolution of Judaism, has become an obstacle to genuine dialogue, while claiming to promote it. "Only a recognition of the Talmud," he writes, "can enable us to grasp the difference between real Judaism and a Judaism that exists only in the Christian imagination".

It is true that if we look only at History, and if we take the expression in its literal meaning, "Judeo-Christianity" had no more than a fleeting existence, as a branch of the ancient Church that claimed to combine faith in Jesus as the Messiah with a rigorous observance of Jewish law. "Its adherents were, historically, the descendants of the first Jerusalem community, which had emigrated, at least in part, to the West Bank town of Pella during the events of 66-70. . . . Under the name of Ebionites or Nazarenes they led an obscure existence, until almost the beginning of the 5th century. Then they disappeared, some probably absorbed into the greater Church, others into the Synagogue".[5]

It is also a fact that Christianity was not really the heir of Judaism, but that *both* were the heirs of original Judaism, and of what the Christians call the Old Testament — like two separate boughs springing from the same tree-trunk. "A dialectic of continuity *and* of discontinuity with the Hebrew tradition is at work in *both* traditions".[6]

That is hard to dispute. Still, the objection can be made to Neuhaus that the expression "Judeo-Christianity", which has actually been in use since the Enlightenment, designates something quite different from a purely historical phenomenon. It refers to its *content* rather than to its historicity, to Abrahamic monotheism rather than to later divergences or evolutions. In actual fact, a more fundamental reproach underlies this historical criticism voiced by the Israeli Jesuit. Neuhaus insists that the recent desire for rapprochement between the two traditions — coming mostly from the Catholic side — leads to minimizing the things that, in spite of everything, separate Jews and Christians. Furthermore — and this is the nub of his criticism — a reunion of separated brethren might well encourage a new kind of closure, an exclusive universalism at the expense of other world religions, starting with Islam. "The Judeo-Christian ideology," he writes, "sometimes tries to involve the Church and the Synagogue in a system that can be just as contemptuous of the 'other' [i.e. the Muslim, the Atheist, the Buddhist, etc.] as the anti-Jewish teachings of the past".[7]

This accusation, as we can see, is not fundamentally different from the criticisms made by Eugen Drewermann. In trying to bring about reconciliation, even to the extent of joining forces, Jews and Christians are supposedly running the risk of falling prey — but this time together — to a new form of West-centeredness. This could bring about a rejuvenated version of the proselytizing and even colonialist triumphalism of the past. Neuhaus's analysis thus expresses the same differentialist attitude. The concept of Judeo-Christianity seems to him to derive from a universalist arrogance that implicitly reduces the other world religions to archaic "superstition", to the dead weight of their traditions, and to the inadequacy of their morality. This point of view is partially justified. However, it is still open to the same objections that we made to Drewermann in the preceding chapter.

Common Enemies

To these objections we must add another, which I think is even more decisive: if Jews and Christians, as part of one and the same modernity — the modernity of the Enlightenment — are coming together today, it is above all because of their sense that they are experiencing an identical crisis, and confronting similar difficulties. In any case, it is no coincidence if Judeo-Christianity, as a concept, regained such currency immediately following the war, after the defeat of Nazism and, later, in the thinking of Vatican II. Neither its culpable indulgence nor the silence of the Catholic hierarchy (headed by Pius XII) in relation to Nazism, nor Hitler's maneuvers as he tried to keep the Holy See (with which he signed the famous Concordat of July 1933) temporarily on side, nor the support of a section of the German Evangelical Church after the schism of 1934,[8] are enough to erase the memory of the radical hatred shown by the Nazis for *both* Judaism and Christianity. It was basically Hitler who gave new life to the concept of Judeo-Christianity by including the two monotheistic religions in the same condemnation. But the rabid anti-Semitism of the Nazis and its horrendous consequences have, for a long time — quite appropriately, it must be said, pushed Hitler's hatred for Christianity itself into the background.

Yet this hatred was all too obvious. Walther Darré, the future Agriculture Minister of the Third Reich, was among the principal proponents of the doctrine of "land and blood", and advocated a return to the old Germanic religions. The Nazi newspaper, *Der Stürmer*, under Julius Streicher, the Gauleiter of Franconia, spearheaded violent attacks against Christians as well as Jews. Likewise, Alfred Rosenberg (born in Estonia in 1893 and editor of the newspaper *Völkischer Beobachter*) published in 1930 his celebrated *Myth of the 20th Century*, in which he developed the central ideas of Germanic racism, of anti-Christianity, and of a return to Nordic mythology. As for Hitler himself, the least one can say is that he was explicit on this point: "In the long run," he declared in July 1941, "National-Socialism and religion will no longer be able to coexist. . . . The advent of Christianity was the hardest blow dealt humanity. Bolshevism is the illegitimate child of Christianity. Both of them are Jewish inventions. Through Christianity, conscious untruth in matters of religion was introduced into the world".[9] Do we need to be reminded that when the Allied troops liberated the camp at Dachau in 1945, they found 800 priests among the prisoners?

So, in contrast to Pope Pius XII with his careful silences, history and truth have proven his predecessor Pius XI to have been right. On March 14, 1937, he published the encyclical *Mit brennender Sorge* ("With Burning Concern"). Prepared by the German Cardinal Faulhaber, it stressed the radical incompatibility between Christianity and the ideas of racial superiority, glorification of blood, and idolizing of the nation — all three of them at the core of the Nazi ideology. Smuggled into Germany, it was read from the pulpit of fifteen thousand Catholic parishes. In 1938, speaking to Belgian pilgrims, Pius XI made an even clearer declaration, one that caused quite a stir: "Anti-Semitism is a movement in which we Christians can take no part. Spiritually, we too are Semites".[10] The same Pius XI, finally, that same year, prepared a second encyclical, *Humani Generis Unitas*, an even more violent denunciation of Fascism and Nazism. "The word 'catholic' means universal", he recalled: "There is no other possible translation, whether into Italian or in any other language. . . . There is only one human race." This "secret encyclical" was suppressed, thanks to the very bitter conflict between Mussolini and Pius XI, and remained so until the latter's death in February 1939. Its content would only become known much later.[11]

"Religions? They're all the same! They have no future — certainly not for the Germans. Fascism, if it likes, can make its peace with the Church. So shall I. Why not? That won't stop me from rooting out Christianity from Germany. The Italians, a naïve people, are quite capable of being pagans and Christians at the same time. The Italians and the French are essentially pagans. Their Christianity is superficial, no more than skin deep.

But your German is different. He is serious about everything. He's either a Christian or a pagan, but never both. . . . It all depends whether he will remain faithful to the Judeo-Christian religion and its servile morality of pity, or develop a new, strong, heroic belief in himself, in a God who is part of his destiny, of his blood. . . . Forget the hair-splitting. Whether it's the Old Testament or the New, or simply the sayings of Jesus, as Houston Stewart Chamberlain would have it, it's all the same old Jewish swindle. A German Church! German Christianity! It's a joke. You're either a Christian or a German. You can't be both at the same time. You can throw that epileptic Paul out of Christianity. Others have done it already. You can make Christ into a figure of nobility, and deny his divinity at the same time. People have always been doing it. . . . All this exegesis is no use — that's not the way to get rid of the Christian mentality we want to destroy. We don't want people with one eye always on the afterlife. We need free men, who feel that God is in them.

The peasant has to be told what the Church has deprived him of: the mysterious, direct connection with Nature, the instinctive contact, communion with the Earth-spirit. That's the way he'll learn to hate the Church. Little by little he'll learn what wiles the priests have used to rob the German people of their soul. We'll scratch away at the Christian veneer until the religion peculiar to our race emerges. And it's here we must begin. Not in the great cities, Goebbels!

Yes, we are barbarians! We *want* to be barbarians! It's an honorable title.

We shall rejuvenate the world. The world is near its end. It is our mission to cause unrest."

Words of Adolf Hitler, recorded by Hermann Rauschning, Gespräche mit Hitler, op. cit

Hitler and the hatred of Christianity

Sixty years later, a rather extraordinary resurgence of the fundamental solidarity between Jews and Christians has taken place; they find themselves today confronting a common enemy. Let us say, more specifically, that each has rediscovered the fact that, where essential questions are concerned, they are on the same side. Militant paganism, or the more watered-down version that is in the air at the present time, is actually out to destroy not just Christianity but, implicitly, the Judeo-Christian heritage itself. More serious is the fact that the present-day contempt for Christianity is often nothing more than covert anti-Judaism, if not an embarrassed anti-Semitism. Shmuel Trigano is quite correct to point out this poisonous confusion, and to feel concern for the future because of it: "Critics of Christianity," he writes "who accuse it of having degraded pagan man by its morality of sin and of having imposed a straitjacket of totalitarian monotheism on the pluralism and freedom inherent in paganism," are "taking indirect aim at Judaism, which is the source of Christianity".[12]

In a similar perspective, other Jewish intellectuals such as Alain Finkielkraut sometimes speak of their uneasiness at the cloying ambiguity of the contemporary — and false — philo-Semitism that sometimes serves to disguise unspoken hatred or manipulative posturing.[13] Since the Holocaust, unless one is mad or negationist (which comes to the same thing), it has actually become impossible to openly express the slightest hint of anti-Semitic feelings. Anti-Semitism has quite appropriately become an absolute no-no, the epitome of evil. It is like a magic spell, or total taboo, helping to keep racism and hatred at bay. This new situation is justified, and even encouraging in many ways. But such a demonizing of anti-Semitism is also more ambiguous, and consequently more precarious, than one might think. It does indeed sometimes happen that this kind of exploitation of the Jewish identity, or hijacking of a legitimate status as victim, allows some people to ride on the back of the struggle against anti-Semitism in order to "chalk up symbolic ideological points". It is posturing rather than genuine conviction, a social strategy rather than real commitment. So there is a risk that the fight against anti-Semitism may become imperceptibly "emptied of its content and its dignity", making it useless "when a genuine emergency arises".[14]

This new form of anti-Semitism is in any case learning to make use of various symbolic substitutions, ruses, and linguistic precautions that allow it to survive unnoticed. And a spontaneous anti-Christianity is unquestionably part of these strategies of concealment. The Christian is taken to task when secretly it is the Jew under attack; the New Testament is rejected while the Old is really meant; the Church is criticized in order to indirectly hurt the Synagogue. A media-savvy, gratifying struggle against "religious obscurantism" thus becomes the form assumed by a covert hostility to the Biblical heritage as a whole.

What I am saying here is actually nothing new. It was pointed out long ago by Anatole Leroy Beaulieu, a professor at the Free School for Political Science and the author of an impassioned indictment of anti-Semitism, *Israel among the nations* (1893), in which he remarked that anti-Christianity and anti-Semitism "are merely equivalent and complementary to one another".

The Culture Of Disdain

It is justifiable, however, to recall these truths and denounce such a "ruse" on just one condition: that we first confront squarely, without any deviousness or hypocrisy, the questions of Christian anti-Judaism and Catholic responsibility for the appearance of modern anti-Semitism. It would be dishonest to try to avoid or minimize this aspect of things. Yet it is important, in discussing this crucial question, not to lump things together, or mistake one for another.

The historical responsibility of Catholicism is overwhelming; there can be no question about that. Published in the middle of the 1950s, Jules Isaac's passionate indictment, *Genèse de l'antisémitisme* (The Genesis of Anti-Semitism) remains a classic on the subject today, together with Jean-Paul Sartre's *Reflections on the Jewish Question* (1948), Hannah Arendt's *On Anti-Semitism* (1951), and Marcel Simon's *Verus Israel* (1948). Moreover, it is important to note how close to one another in time these books were published. Each appeared at the end of the 1940s and each provided, in its own way, evidence of the real spiritual upheaval that resulted from the discovery of the camps at the end of the war, the recognition of the enormity of the Nazi crime, and — above all — of the part played by Christianity in allowing this evil to emerge. The theological stupor and retrospective vertigo felt by Christians would culminate in a radical break with the past, and in a progressive rereading of all of Western history — a rereading that is still in progress, and probing ever deeper.

"Spread for hundreds and hundreds of years by thousands and thousands of voices," wrote Jules Isaac, "Christian anti-Semitism [was] the powerful, age-old trunk, with many strong roots, upon which other varieties of anti-Semitism were grafted (in the Christian world) — even the most naturally opposed, and even anti-Christian".[15] Jules Isaac, speaking of Christian anti-Semitism, would popularize two accusatory formulas that would subsequently be heard all the time: "the teaching of scorn", and "the system of degradation". They went hand in hand with the age-old accusation of deicide made against the Jews by the Church fathers.

This Christian anti-Judaism, which was theological in nature, was strengthened by the Jewish refusal to convert — something that seemed incomprehensible to early Christians. In addition, since the Jews refused to join *Verus Israel* (the true Israel, i.e. Christianity), it became "necessary" to pronounce them fundamentally wicked and ungrateful, and heap crimes and opprobrium on them. They had to be exhorted untiringly to convert, and even forced to do so. Let us note that this anti-Judaism arose in troubled times (the 3rd and 4th centuries), was characterized by a proliferation of sects, Aryanism in particular, by intense Christological disputes, by the death-throes of paganism, and by the barbarians' assault on the hastily fortified outposts (the *limes*) of the Roman Empire.

At the time, the early Church was experiencing great difficulty in freeing itself from the Synagogue, and ties were constantly being reforged thanks to the tendency of the Christians to "Judaicize everything, all the time" (Isaac). So this Church was all too ready to see the Jews as accomplices of heresy, and even as sharing the responsibility for the Roman persecutions. (Such, for example, was the thesis put forward by Tertullian, one of the Fathers of the Church.) "This explains the Church's energy in combating what it called the *Jewish sickness*, a sickness of which it felt it had to cure the Christian world at all costs, even by the most draconian means — justifiable self-defense in its eyes, since it considered that what was ultimately at stake was no less than the salvation of souls, their salvation for eternity".[16]

Immediately after Constantine's conversion and the triumph of Christianity, the introduction of anti-Jewish laws began. The first of these, in 315, condemned any Jew to death who dared stone co-religionists who had converted to Christianity, and at the same time outlawed any Jewish attempt to proselytize. In 409, a further law made Jewish propaganda equivalent to the crime of lese-majesty. In 438, a law specified capital punishment for any Jew guilty of converting a Christian, whether slave or free man. A sense of being under threat from Judaism would persist among Christians for longer than is generally thought, and would be used to justify measures directed not only at Jews, but also at Christians tempted to "Judaicize" themselves. "Again, in 691, a Council renewed some of the most typical proscriptions against Christians adopting Jewish practices: eating unleavened bread with Jews, keeping their company, asking their help in case of sickness, accepting their cures, engaging in ritual ablutions in their baths".[17]

A number of other laws and texts would follow, while, from century to century, books denounced the "insolence" of the Jews, their "perfidy" or their "superstitions". This terminology would be incorporated into the Christian canon and liturgy, usually expressed in terms if contempt. This was the case for the famous prayer, *Oremus pro perfidis Judaeis*, which was recited by generations of Christians. It was only after World War II that Catholic authors like Erik Peterson and Father Oesterreicher set out to show that, in Church Latin, *perfidius* means neither "perfidious" nor "disloyal", but "unbeliever" or "infidel". This new, less defamatory, translation was sensibly approved by the Sacred Congregation for Rites in 1948. However, it was not until Vatican II (1962-1965) and the encyclical *Nostra aetate* (1965) that all references to the "perfidious Jews" and "deicidal people" were finally done away with. So, for more than a thousand years the "culture of contempt" spoken of by Jules Isaac prevailed. "Such teaching," adds Jules Isaac, "disseminated from century to century, from generation to generation, by hundreds and thousands of voices, was. . . the primary and permanent source of anti-Semitism in the Christian world, . . . the powerful, age-old trunk on which all the varieties of anti-Semitism were grafted, so to speak".[18]

The "Archivist" People

It is true that this theological anti-Judaism is very different from modern anti-Semitism, founded on the (absurd) concept of "race". The unrelenting exhortations to convert suggested that on converting to Christianity the convert ceased to be a Jew, a view quite contrary to modern anti-Semitism's racist hatred, with its obsession with the "secret Jew" and "tainted blood". "For Nazi anti-Semites, a Jew converted to Christianity is still a Jew, because the Jew is defined by his race, and it is neither desirable nor possible to change his ethnic characteristics: total extermination is the only solution".[19] Such was obviously not the case for anti-Judaism. Indeed it was quite the opposite. Far from calling for, or thinking of, the elimination of Jews who refused to convert, Catholic theology paradoxically never gave up calling for their protection. Why was this? Because, even if not converts, they were still essential witnesses, attesting to the truth of the Old Testament message.

This is what St. Augustine meant when he wrote: "And if it should come about that some pagan raises doubts when we tell him of these prophecies and is tempted to think we have invented them, the books of the Jews are there to provide proof of the ancient predictions. So our enemies serve us to confound our enemies". (Commentary on Psalm 18:22). It was also St. Augustine who invented an idea that would be constantly repeated, seeing the Jew as "a kind of archivist for the Christians" (*Against Faustus*, Book XII, Ch. 23). In another text he used an equally eloquent image: "Like milestones placed along a road, [the Jews] inform the traveler, though they themselves remain fixed and unmoving" (Sermon 199, N 2). Commenting on this attitude of St. Augustine, Marcel Simon writes: "If the Jews remained attached to their law, partially and in a purely fleshly manner, this also had value as a sign and witness. So, not only did Christian apologetics tolerate their continuous presence, they demanded it".[20]

Centuries later, Pascal, to cite only one instance, made his own this paradoxical theology, which condemns the Jews at the same time as it calls for their protection. "Being necessary to prove Jesus Christ, let [the Jewish people] subsist to prove him, and let it know misery since it crucified him".

This Christian anti-Judaism was, moreover, less monolithic and systematic than is generally thought. Jules Isaac was the first to remark that "there is not just *one* tradition in the policies of the Papacy towards Jews, but really *two*".[21] Certain Popes and Catholic monarchs set themselves up as protectors of the Jews. The most widely cited examples are King Theodoric (493-526), who decreed that "no-one should be forced to believe in spite of himself"; Pope Gregory the Great (590-604), who condemned forced baptism; and Rémy of Auxerre, master of the Episcopal School of Reims and close to Clovis, who — already rejecting the notion of a "deicide race" — insisted on the responsibility of "all sinners" in Christ's crucifixion. In the same way, certain long periods of history went more or less without any persecution of the Jews. This was also so under the Carolingians in the 8th and 9th centuries. These periods of relative goodwill towards Jews were moreover, it is hardly necessary to recall, in accordance with certain New Testament texts such as the celebrated Epistle of Saint Paul to the Romans, three chapters of which are devoted to the Jews,[22] or with St. John's famous saying: "Salvation comes from the Jews" — two fundamental texts that were all too often forgotten by the Church.

As we know, indeed, on several occasions throughout the history of Christianity, the "condemnation" of the Jews was to take drastic precedence over their "protection", and to do so to a scandalous degree. The pogroms associated with the First Crusade, in 1096 from which the Jewish communities of the Rhine valley suffered,[23] and the expulsion of the Jews of Castile by Isabella the Catholic (1451-1504) are two appalling examples. But, more fundamentally, this "culture of scorn" was to instill deep within the Catholic consciousness a deep-seated hatred for Jews that would give rise to the hatred and rejection of later times, more than enough to justify the remorse we feel today.

Pagan Anti-Semitism

However, a full recognition of the part played by Christian anti-Judaism, and something approaching a re-foundation of Christianity based on this remorse, are still not enough to protect our societies against a possible reemergence of anti-Semitism. At this juncture we have to dispel a huge, and durable, misunderstanding. When people insist, with the best will in the world, on this Catholic remorse, the most common error is to dangerously minimize the presence, and the age-old virulence, of another kind of anti-Semitism-a steadfastly pagan one. Some people, absurdly, even go so far as to ignore or deny the existence of this pre-Christian anti-Semitism. Its origins date back to before the birth of Christianity, but its historical role and its contemporary influence have been no less disastrous for all that, since it inspired — this time directly — the genocidal racial anti-Semitism of the 19th century, particularly as practiced in Hitler's Germany. To go no further than a reactive denunciation of Christian anti-Judaism and fail to recognize the pagan roots of this older form of anti-Semitism makes it impossible to understand very much about the contemporary situation. Worse still, it means running the risk of being literally helpless in confronting the new forms of barbarism.

The difficulty is to evaluate the importance of this pagan anti-Semitism. Jules Isaac and Marcel Simon disagreed on this matter — courteously, for the two men held one another in high esteem. The latter criticized the former for minimizing the impact of this pagan anti-Semitism in his desire to denounce primarily the "culture of contempt" propagated by the Catholic Church. Jules Isaac, it is true, was afraid that any insistence on recalling the pagan hatred for Jews would make it easier to excuse or minimize Christian anti-Judaism. One thing is certain: the contempt for the Jews, the violence with which they were persecuted, and the rhetoric with which ignominious accusations against them were articulated, were attested long before our times.

The most frequently cited example is that of Apion, the Greco-Egyptian grammarian of the 1st century of our era, whose anti-Semitism is best known to us through its refutation by the Jewish historian Flavius Josephus in his famous treatise *Against Apion*. Vain, irascible, and full of spleen towards the Jews, Apion is the author of a collection of historical essays on ancient Egypt — the *Ægyptiaca* — in which he enumerates, with evident satisfaction, all the supposed vices of the "Judeans". In Book III of this collection, Apion "has collected, meticulously and laboriously, all sorts of accusations previously leveled at Israel, adding some new ones of his own. Possibly he also composed a pamphlet aimed specifically at the Jews of Alexandria".[24] These calumnies would serve as a basis for all subsequent anti-Semitic invective. For Apion, the Hebrews were, originally, impoverished Egyptians, afflicted with every imaginable physical and mental defect; they were lepers, blind people and cripples, who had supposedly been expelled from Egypt in the first year of the 7th Olympiad; they were a sort of rabble thrown out by Pharaoh, the way modern despots drive the homeless out of downtown areas.

He states that the origin of the Sabbath, which is at the core of their religion, is directly connected with this forced Exodus. "After six days on foot," he writes, "they developed tumors in the groin, and this is why they rested on the seventh day, once they had reached their country, which today has been given the name Judea, and they called this day *Shabbat*, keeping the Egyptian word, for among the Egyptians an irritation in the groin is called 'sabbô'".[25]

To these extravagant details, Apion added allegations and accusations that, all throughout History, would foster the most usual anti-Semitic fantasies. The Jews were presented as misanthropic, swearing "to wish no good to any foreigner, and least of all to the Greeks". Apion accused them of practicing a barbarous religion that worshipped an ass's head. More significantly still, he was quite definite that the Jews practiced ritual murder, always choosing a foreigner as victim, preferably a Greek. Now, as we know, this fantastical accusation would be repeated throughout History, most notably in the notorious *Protocol of the Elders of Zion*, the anti-Semitic forgery fabricated by the Tsarist police in the 19th century. In the circumstances, Jules Isaac is quite right to represent the pagan Apion as one of the first theoreticians of anti-Semitism.

But Apion was far from alone. Tacitus, the great Roman historian, proconsul of the Roman provinces in Asia (55-120), repeated and rephrased most of the pagan anti-Semitic calumnies. Whether their shameful origins, their religious abominations, their misanthropy, or the "hostility and hatred they demonstrate towards the rest of mankind", all these slanderous descriptions can be found in Book V of Tacitus's *Histories*. In speaking of Jews in general, Tacitus doesn't hesitate to call them "that repulsive people". He claims to explain their dietary prohibitions concerning pork "by the memory of the leprosy that once defiled them, and to which this animal is subject". He developed the accusations of lewdness and debauchery that would also become part of the modern anti-Semitic armory. "Very inclined to debauchery," he wrote, "they [the Jews] abstain from all intercourse with foreign women; among their own kind anything is permitted".

Analyzing this pagan anti-Semitism, Marcel Simon believes he can discern its causes in monotheist belief itself and in the "insulating properties" of the Law. "Enveloping the daily life of the Jews in a network of observances, the Law placed them on the margin of society, outside the general rule, as a group all of whose scattered members are one, which is totally inflexible, exclusive, an enemy of the human race. And other complaints were born of this fundamental one. By the fact that they live apart . . . they leave themselves open to all the kinds of allegations that the mob in its viciousness can make against closed societies".[26]

All future anti-Jewish sentiments, in any case, were latent in this original hatred. However, not only does it (by definition) have nothing to do with Christianity, but the pagan anti-Semites, from the 1st century on, would heap the same opprobrium on Christians as on Jews. In this respect, they can be seen even more as the precise forerunners of the contemporary hostility towards Judeo-Christianity. In his *Annals*, Tacitus speaks of the first Christians in terms almost identical to those he used in speaking of the Jews: "Men hated for their infamy, whom the common people call Christians. . . . Their execrable superstition reared its head not only in Judea, where this plague was born, but in Rome, where everything the universe has conceived by way of atrocities and abominations flocks and finds disciples".

This pagan anti-Semitism was not merely theoretical. It was accompanied by a violence the extent of which is often seriously underestimated. The earliest anti-Jewish persecution we know of dated from 168 B.C. It was carried out by a Greek king of the Seleucid dynasty, Antiochos IV Epiphanos, who, returning home from a campaign in Egypt, entered Judea as if it was a vanquished country. He attacked the Temple in Jerusalem, razing it, together with the city walls. Outlawing the religion of Israel, he forced the Jews to worship Greek idols, and set up a sacrificial altar to Zeus on the spot where the Temple had stood. This episode, which sparked the first Jewish revolt, is called "the abomination that makes desolate" by the (contemporary) author of the Book of Daniel.

Subsequently, the Roman emperors Vespasian (70), Trajan (117), and Hadrian (135), conducted several anti-Jewish campaigns. It is true that the specifically anti-Jewish inspiration of these wars of pacification carried out against a small, rebellious people is sometimes questioned. Yet there can be little doubt about it. Moreover, these so-called wars of pacification were accompanied by an unbelievably bloody repression. Speaking of the campaign of 70 AD, Flavius Josephus paints a horrifying figure of 1,110,000 dead, and 97,000 prisoners (*The Jewish War*, VI, 9). As for the campaign of 135, the Greek historian Dio Cassius (155-235) the author of a *History of Rome*, speaks of 500,000 dead. These figures — which must however be taken with a pinch of salt — are enormous when compared with the size of the Jewish population, estimated at five or six million, i.e. seven percent of the total population of the Roman Empire.

These pogroms before the fact did not make all their victims in Jerusalem. Speaking of the Jewish War of 117, Marcel Simon, from whom I have borrowed these estimates, notes that the Diaspora was also affected: "The war of extermination carried out by Trajan," he writes, "caused terrible ravages in the Jewish communities of Egypt, Cyprus, and Cyrene".[27] As for Jules Isaac, he writes, "Never, perhaps, before the unspeakable atrocities of the Third Reich, which took place only yesterday, has the Jewish people suffered such blood-letting as it did during the thirty years between the death of Tiberius and that of Hadrian".[28]

Strange Free-Thinkers

What are we trying to demonstrate by recalling these different facts? A fundamental truth, namely that the anti-Semitism which arose in the 19th-century West was, without any doubt, enormously facilitated by the existence of a particularly fertile soil, the "culture of contempt" developed over the centuries by Catholic theology, but that its real roots and themes go even deeper. It was fed by more ancient springs that, even today, have still not run dry. We have no hope of eradicating it if we restrict ourselves to condemning the transgressions of the Catholic Church. Shortly after the Second World War, Hannah Arendt was already warning against confusing "anti-Semitism, a 19th-century secular ideology (which only appeared under this name after 1870), with hatred of the Jews, which is of religious origin, inspired by the mutual hostility of two antagonistic faiths". She also called the widespread notion that modern anti-Semitism is only a secularized version of medieval superstitions a fallacy.[29]

Actually, the secular and sometimes left-wing anti-Semitism of the 19th and early 20th centuries can be traced back to an age-old pagan attitude. Karl Marx's case is the most instructive, but it is far from alone. "What is the profane basis of Judaism?" he asks. "Money. . . . The Jews became emancipated to the precise extent that Christians became Jews. . . . The God of the Jews was secularized and became the God of the whole world. Currency trading, that's your Jew's real god".[30] Beside this anti-Semitism, which sees the Jew, emancipated since the Napoleonic concordat of 1801 as a symbol of capitalist and bourgeois exploitation, historians such as Zeev Sternhel,[31] Léon Poliakov and Pascal Ory have analyzed a whole atheistic anti-Semitic culture that developed on the political left and extreme left. Not only did this owe nothing to Christianity but, most often, was just as anti-Christian as it was anti-Jewish. The anti-Christian writings of Holbach and of Voltaire, let us remember, are not without anti-Semitic traits.

From the middle of the 19th century on, in any case, texts appeared explicitly invoking the pagan tradition, which was opposed to Judeo-Christianity. They basically accused Judaism — as Hitler was to do later — of having given birth to Christianity. There were steadfast, militant atheists on the editorial board of *La Libre pensée*. So what kind of things were some of these people writing? "Jesus was a Jew, a Semite; the Semites are an inferior race, a collection of superstitious peoples who have dreamed up barbarous, bloodthirsty, oppressive religions, while the Aryans, a race truly fitted for civilization, have given us the handsome, smiling creations of Greek genius".[32] An atheist publicist like Eugène Gellion-Danglar, a great admirer of Gambetta — and of Voltaire — published a long written study, in the same tone, entitled *Du sémitisme* (On Semitism). Another advocate of laicism, also a follower of Gambetta, Albert Regnard refused to "couple the Jewish horde and ancient Greece", or to consent to "such an inoculation of monotheism".[33] In September 1889, at the first International Congress of Free Thought, the same Albert Regnard was met with applause when he argued that "the Semitic race culminates in monotheism, and the Aryan race in polytheism". Referring incessantly to Voltaire, whom he fervently admired, he didn't have any hesitation in writing: "[Voltaire], who has demolished the Bible and undermined the New Testament [is] the first coherent anti-Semite".

The same kind of anti-Semitism, allied with aggressive atheism, was found in Jules Soury, one of the most prominent figures in 19th-century secularist circles. "Rome," he wrote, "was swarming with the fantastic Jewish horde," adding: "The old Hebrew book is the most implacable enemy of our race and of our civilization". As for Lucien Pemjean, the author of *La Revanche de la raison* (1880), he would shift between ultra-revolutionary and atheistic Blanquism and obsessive anti-Semitism. Before ending his career in the Vichyist press, Pemjean published, in 1934, a pamphlet the title of which is totally explicit: *Vers l'invasion, la mafia judéo-maçonnique* (The Coming Invasion; the Jewish-Masonic Mafia).

We could cite numerous other examples to illustrate the virulence, of this atheistic anti-Semitism, in the 19th century, which, leapfrogging over nineteen centuries of Christianity, attempted to make a new place in contemporary culture for the old fantasies and calumnies of ancient anti-Semitic paganism. Sometimes this ancestry was explicitly claimed, in retrospective homage to the emperor Julian the Apostate, who attempted to "restore the pagan religion in its ancient splendor", and eulogized Hellenistic inegalitarianism whose "decline dragged down all of civilization with it", etc. "It would have been a most fortunate thing," wrote Eugène Gellion-Danglar, "if the Aryan nations, who are popularly termed the barbarians of the 5th century, had escaped Nazarene Semitism and regenerated the West just by the high virtue of their blood".[34]

It doesn't take exceptional perspicacity to recognize in all this the themes, obsessions, and nostalgia for paganism that the Nazi theoreticians would fan into an exterminating flame, and with which someone like Julius Evola continually compromises himself.[35] The Catholic leadership of today, whether the Episcopacy or the Pope himself, is therefore on the right track when, while asking forgiveness for the historical responsibilities of Christian anti-Judaism, it adds that Hitlerian anti-Semitism arose out of a vision of the world fundamentally alien to Christianity. This was recalled in the long Vatican declaration on the Holocaust made in March 1998: "The Holocaust," it noted, "was the fruit of an utterly neo-pagan modern regime. Its anti-Semitism had its roots outside Christianity, and in pursuing its objectives it had no hesitation in opposing the Church and also persecuting its members".[36]

The reticence or disappointment expressed in some Jewish quarters about this declaration has two basic explanations. On the one hand, the terms in which the Vatican condemned Christian anti-Judaism as a "fertile soil" for anti-Semitism were not felt to go far enough; on the other hand, the Jews would have liked to see an unambiguous indictment of Pius XII's silence in the face of Nazism. Let us comment that historians like Émile Poulat, a professor at the École des hautes études en sciences sociales, show considerable circumspection on this specific point. "This debate is biased on every side because of its passionate nature. Pius XII did much more than is thought, despite his public silence. The debate should continue, but without any hypocrisy, remembering the terrible silence of the whole of the West, Christian or not, towards the extermination of European Jews".[37] This debate will have to take place when all the archives become available.

It remains true that, apart from these isolated criticisms, where the very substance of the Vatican's interpretation of anti-Semitism is concerned it is difficult to argue with the import and significance of the 1998 declaration. A year previously, moreover, Jean-Marie Lustiger, Archbishop of Paris, had spoken some powerful words that deserve to be recalled: "The Holocaust," he declared in 1997, "took aim particularly at the Jewish people, the bearers of the Word of God, of the Law, of the Commandments, with indisputable importance of these for the Jewish and Christian cultures which are duty bound to observe them. Against this cultural background, Nazism appears as a denial, a negation of the Commandments. . . .

The revelation on Mount Sinai illuminates the common ethical treasure of all mankind. That is why the extermination of the witness of the One God, is also, in this respect, a crime against humanity".[38]

Let us add that the Jewish leaders are the first to recognize that, in this domain, the French Episcopacy has already gone much further than the Vatican. "The French Episcopacy, to which I wish to pay tribute," noted Rabbi Josy Eisenberg, "has been completely in the vanguard, and still is today, because of certain declarations it has made concerning the Jews, among other things. . . . On all these points, the French Bishops are an example to the world".[39]

In Crisis

Repentance? Reconciliation? Reunion? The dialogue has unquestionably been recommenced, and some even go as far as to suggest a merger of the two religions! Others would at least like the Church to rediscover its Jewish identity, and the Hebrew language. This was the case for one of the great figures of the Judeo-Christian dialogue, who passed away in Haifa on July 30th, 1998, Father Daniel Oswald Rufeisen, a Polish Jew converted to Christianity who became a Carmelite monk and then emigrated (not without difficulty) to Israel in 1959. "We can still hope for a Christian Judaism or a Jewish Christianity to emerge," he declared. If the concept of Judeo-Christianity is regaining its significance today, and if it is prepared to open itself to the third Abrahamic religion, Islam, this is not just because Jews and Christians have to confront the same "enemies", it is also because they are both traversing the same intense crisis, and are confronting the upheavals of modernity.

Less is said about the crisis in Judaism than about the crisis in Catholicism, although it no less profound. The philosopher Stéphane Moses, the translator of and commentator on Franz Rosenzweig, comments that at the turn of the century Judaism is endangered by three schisms that threaten its identity. "The first schism is one that separates the minority of believing and practicing Jews from the secular, agnostic, or indifferent, majority. The second opposes a hard core that wishes to preserve Jewish identity in one form or another (not necessarily religious) to the great mass of Jews borne along, consciously or not, by the enormous tide of assimilation into the surrounding world. The third is the one that differentiates between the State of Israel and the Diaspora".[40]

Apart from the last — the problem of the State of Israel is indeed a special one — these cracks are quite similar to those in the edifice of Christianity. They confront both religions with the same challenge: how can they accept modernity without being absorbed into it? How can they continue to provide the foundation of modernity, but without complacency or nostalgia? How can they change without renouncing their identity? Judaism, also, is obliged to "reassess its entire historical tradition"[41] by being willing to confront it with what is now a very different world. Pauline Bèbe, the first woman rabbi in France, a member of the liberal Jewish movement, provides an excellent definition of the challenge when she writes: "Judaism must submit to a universal morality, even if this means accepting change. Any religious system that isn't putting the ideas of tolerance or universal morality into practice has to undergo change".[42]

So, a reinterpretation of their own tradition as a means of reinventing it is just as much an imperative for Jews as for Christians. In support of her point of view, Pauline Bèbe cites certain changes in the Jewish ritual that she considers essential. The passages in which God asks the Jews to go and smite Amalek and all his people (I Samuel 15: 3) are for her "unjustifiable". Similarly, a verse quoted each year at Passover has been removed from the liberal ritual: "Pour out thy wrath upon the nations that know thee not" (Jeremiah 10:25). But, for Jews as for Christians, such a reinterpretation is not as easy as reformers sometimes think. Carried out without due consideration, it puts Judaism at risk of losing "its most essential advantages (its historicity, its social ties, the power of revealed truth) as the consequence of a modernist contextualizing of its truths".[43]

This careful, critical review of Judaism is, moreover, not just a recent phenomenon. After the last World War and the horrors of the Holocaust, a loss of confidence in modernity led some Jewish intellectuals to attempt to return to their roots in the Talmudic or Biblical tradition. This was to the credit of what has been called the "School of d'Orsay", founded during the French Resistance under the influence of the Jewish Scouts of France, and which numbered people like Emmanuel Lévinas, André Neher, Léon Askenazi, and Éliane Amado in its ranks. Their purpose was to subject modernity to a critical examination, while re-evaluating the Jewish heritage from the same perspective. It proved to be a fruitful approach. "A Jewish thought was reborn. Faithful to Judaism and conscious of what is at stake today, it made its voice heard in the modern world."[44] It was no accident that these postwar reflections, like those of Hannah Arendt, exerted, and are still exerting today, an influence that extends far beyond Judaism.

On the Christian side, the reinterpretations and expropriations of tradition are as active as they are necessary, as is demonstrated by the constant disputes over new translations of the Bible. It is a fact that no one any longer reads the Bible the way it was often read only a half-century ago. Let us remember, for instance, the re-evaluation of Jesus' words (Matthew 5:17), when he says he did not come to do away with the Torah, but to fulfill it. Let us also mention the re-interpretation of the New Testament passage that speaks of "loving one's enemies" (Matthew 5: 44), a passage that was long used against the supposedly sectarian character of Jewish Law. In general, the rediscovery by Christians of the Jewish component — or Jewish "source" — of their faith opens up new possibilities for dialogue. It gives them access to a wealth of interpretations they had never suspected. Hence the extraordinary increase in interest for Judaism that is now becoming evident in certain Catholic quarters. "A reassessment of the entire history of their tradition: this will ultimately be, for Christians, the reward of their dialogue with Judaism. And it is indeed to avoid the resulting sense of vertigo that they have so long been unconsciously opposed to such a comparison".[45]

This recharging of the batteries, these critical reinterpretations, these renewed contacts, are in any case at the opposite extreme from the voluble, confused, or esoteric religiosity that noisily fills public space, causing a great commotion in the media, and deceiving the masses. They have no similarity to the confused jumble of fashionable forms of spirituality, the infatuation with any kind of spiritual exoticism, which, without realizing it, is re-creating the "sacred" in the archaic meaning of the word. Denouncing this sacrificial circus, one theologian described magnificently the paradoxical solitude and needs of the Christian confronted with this so-called "re-birth of religion": "It is a strange solitude, indeed, that of the Christian at the end of this century, who, because he practices a religion that is principally the New Testament, and that contains a critique of all religion, discovers he is deficient in religion compared to his fellows."[46] Many Jewish or Muslim intellectuals could say the same thing.

A New Enlightenment?

A new, critical, exacting, Judeo-Christian dialogue has again been launched today, out of sight of the media. It is, day by day, becoming more open to Islam. Its relations with modernity have nothing to do with obscurantist rejection, or, least of all, with mystical or esoteric escapism. It is concerned with laying a new foundation. As such, this reconciliation represent the best possible guarantee against a "renewal of the sacred", an emotional and reactive phenomenon, which — for Christians as well as for Jews or Muslims — is always accompanied by intolerance. But there is nothing to say we shouldn't expect further results from a dialogue that has been resumed with such patience.

After all, the previous encounter of Jews and Christians took place between the 18th and 19th centuries, as a result of the European Enlightenment. Enlightenment philosophy, by enabling the emancipation and assimilation of Jews, at the time enabled a re-reading of the Bible that drew Jews and Christians closer by reducing the differences between them. Paradoxically, this divergence from "tradition" in the limited meaning of the term, and initiation of a relative desacralizing of the Biblical text (by Spinoza on the Jewish side), enabled it to be shared. "Between the 18th and 20th centuries, one had the impression that the European Jews and Christians in Western Europe were together creating a common culture — a 'Judeo-Christian' culture".[47] After Spinoza, a number of names represent this early "modernist" undertaking on the Jewish side: Moses Mendelssohn, Zachariah Frankel, Solomon Schechter, Hermann Cohen and, closer to us, Martin Buber, Franz Rosenzweig, Gershom Scholem, and others.

This "dialogic" Judeo-Christianity, born of the Enlightenment, showed itself able to take account of the achievements of modernity. This was not accomplished without encountering difficulties or resistance, on both the Christian and Jewish sides. We have already spoken of the Catholic counter-revolutionary tradition, and there is no need to bring it up once again. But let us remember that Judaism experienced a comparable "reaction" in its own ranks. Some practicing Jews did indeed reject the emancipation of the individual and entry into the modern world. They thought such a development represented a danger to their identity, and in certain respects they weren't mistaken. Indeed, it was not the Jewish community that was emancipated by the Napoleonic concordat, but isolated individuals by whom assimilation may have been experienced as a form of alienation. Moreover, there were numerous assimilated Jews who, at that particular moment, were abandoning their faith, even allying themselves with proponents of the most aggressive kind of rationalism, and placing their desire for definitive integration into the nation above anything else.[48]

The reaction of the remainder — those more attached to their tradition — was similar to that of Catholics faced with the principle of secularism. Many refused to go along with the changes introduced into the synagogues by reformers, or were bothered by the abandonment of certain requirements of the *Halakah*. In Germany, one individual, Rabbi Samson Raphael Hirsch (1808-1888), personified this traditionalist resistance. In his *Nineteen Letters on Judaism* (1836),[49] he declared: "Sorrowfully indeed would I mourn if Israel were so far to forget itself as to deem emancipation not too dearly bought by a capricious curtailment of the Torah, a fickle abandonment of the chief element of our being ". His influence is again becoming quite strong in orthodox Jewish circles today, and there is nothing surprising about this. In fact, the modernist, creative, and productive Judaism of the Enlightenment nevertheless encountered the same difficulties as the liberal Protestantism or republican Catholicism with which it was conducting a dialogue. From reform to reform, it ran the risk of reducing a living religion to no more than an abstract, impoverished, and rootless form of Judaism. So the two sides are re-learning, with additional requirements and prudence, to carry on their dialogue, while remaining open to the world.

* *

*

In many respects, the situation of Judeo-Christianity is strangely reminiscent of what it was at the time of the Enlightenment, while gradually the outlines of a different and unprecedented "modernity" are emerging, involving not only the "West" but also the entire planet. We are still hesitating between the risk of regression into barbarism and the possibility of a new Age of Enlightenment. This indecision of History, the still open possibility of re-founding the world in its *humanity*, is obliging Judeo-Christianity to take a fresh look at itself, and at its history. Can it possibly remain indifferent to a reality that, in the final analysis, it itself produced?

EPILOGUE: THE NEXT PLANET

"What is inept is the attempt to reach a conclusion".
Gustave Flaubert[1]

People used to be able to say: that's *probably* what the next century will be like! But nowadays who would dare utter such an outrageous speculation? The next century! Well, maybe next year, or the next six months. The world is moving faster all the time. Its progress has become more rapid, even crazy at times. The immediate future has come to look like a magical mystery tour. Tomorrow is always an unknown quantity. We're on a forced march, our vision blurring, our hearts thumping in our breasts. Because of such rapid change, our relationship to time has been utterly transformed, and in both backward and forward directions, one could say, for if we can no longer see beyond the very short term into the future, our conception of the past has been similarly foreshortened. Six months ago is already "back then". A year ago is already "once".

These aren't just random impressions. In 1991 the New York cultural magazine *Spy* published a long article on the way we perceive the past. It was attempting to find out what the "good old days" meant for us, and above all to which period in history we would like to return. After much analysis, supplemented with graphs and diagrams, the magazine reached a strange conclusion. Our tendency for nostalgia is becoming stronger all the time, but, statistically, the "good old days" are drawing closer and closer. As the future becomes more uncertain, we are becoming increasingly nostalgic for the past, but for an ever more recent one. At the time of the

Enlightenment people idealized Greek and Roman antiquity. In the 19th century there was more nostalgia for the feudal and chivalrous Middle Ages — but time was still reckoned in centuries. For people between the two wars, it was the "roaring Twenties", only a few decades earlier in the same century. Just the other day it was the 1960s that were the lost paradise of the *baby boomers*, who remembered the Vespa scooters, Brigitte Bardot's Vichy dresses, and Beatles songs. In the 1990s it the preceding decade — the 1980s — was already being viewed with melancholy affection. If we go on like this, it will soon be the six months before last that we'll be seeing as a lost golden age.

This phenomenal foreshortening of the past is folding time back on itself and dividing it up into tiny intervals. The only thing comparable is the unpredictability of the immediate future. So, our lives, our societies, our symbolic representations, are built on tectonic plates that are constantly in motion. It's not just a question of a devaluing of the future and a crisis of progress.[2] Reality is now changing so fast that it seems to be slipping from our grasp. The present trickles through our fingers like water, before we have had any time to explore and to understand it. Knowledge, fragmented and ever more complex, comes and goes without end. Our awareness of reality and of the world is no longer anything more than a sequence of incidental configurations, a succession of ephemeral concretions, an uninterrupted current of hypotheses with their best-after dates coming up soon. Our ideas are outmoded in six months, our computers in three. Our "political" forecasts rarely survive the current session. We no longer have the time to feel the "harmony between earth and foot" cited by Albert Camus. The earth shakes; time flies. Only the fluctuations in the stock market express, in their way, this disquieting fibrillation of time. Isn't the Dow Jones able to change attitudes worldwide in the space of a morning? And the CAC 40 calculates the state of the market minute by minute, claiming to know what is in people's minds from the way trading is going. The speed with which the world is becoming computerized helps us grasp, metaphorically, the real nature of our vertigo.

The Laughter Of The Gods

The famous "Moore's law", the general truth of which has been confirmed again and again during the past quarter-century, predicted for instance that the progress of computer technology would allow the number of transistors on computer chips — i.e. the speed and power of these — to double every year. "From 1956 to 1996, the memory capacity of computer hard disks increased 600-fold, and the density of the recorded information 720,000 times. On the other hand, the cost of a megabyte fell during the same period from 50,000 francs to two". If we are to believe the experts, this phenomenal rate of growth in computing capacity, accompanied by a reduction in cost, will certainly continue well beyond 2010 or 2050, bringing with it a corresponding progress in "communications hardware" — the transportation system of the worldwide cyber-revolution. So, communications and storage capacities advance at the same pace. And that isn't all. The "dark fiber" that is being developed in research laboratories is an optical channel as fine as a hair, but it will soon replace fiber-optics: a single one will be able to transmit all the telephone messages made in the United States on even the busiest day. Minimal use of this fiber would increase our communications capacity a 1000-fold worldwide!

The exponential growth in these two items of hardware is causing considerable upheavals in almost all areas of our existence: the preservation of data and access to information, the manipulation of sounds and images, control over the economy or finances, the use of memory, the increased complexity of all kinds of networks, the progress of artificial intelligence, our relationship to culture, to learning, to knowledge. "When computerization creates a bridge, and a retroactive loop between physical, biological, psychic, economic or industrial processes that were previously sealed off from one another, the cultural and social implications have to be re-evaluated on each occasion".[4] We will never be done with these "re-evaluations". The speed of change thus escapes not only our control but also the mere ability we use to evaluate — however roughly — its consequences. "Things" have run far ahead of us and of our ideas. Sheepishly, in a daze, we try to keep up. Reality is escaping our former ability to *conceive* it. "Any theory," said Sören Kierkegaard, "is exposed to the laughter of the gods". We have already gone far beyond this divine "laughter". We sometimes feel our intelligence is running out of steam in its attempt to understand an uncontrollable reality that constantly evades us. As for the ability of politics to predict and act, the less said the better.

This racing machinery, this cyclone of things, is imperceptibly replacing what was intelligible in human societies and in the world with a new phantasmagoria, a fabulous reality offered our imagination daily. In our inability to conceptualize the immediate future, we dream it — it's a dream or a nightmare, whatever. Fantastic images are born of such uncertainty. The Jules Verne syndrome returns, but now to the power of a thousand, or ten thousand. We are told of a soon-to-be "bionic man", virtual reality, landings on Mars, or the charting of the human genome. We are invited to wait no longer to frolic in cyberspace[5] or sample the benefits of cyberculture. Some of these prospects are exciting. Others fill us with foreboding. "Ever more efficient prostheses replace our sense-organs; technographs invade and colonize the body itself, turning it into a machine. Electronic simulations are substituted for the stimuli of the concrete world, affording the body pleasures more intense than our perceptive faculties, now rendered irrelevant, can provide".[6]

Futurist discourse, more frenzied and lyrical than ever, is flourishing all around us. It is brimming with wild possibilities, vague terrors and extravagant hypotheses. It can never decide whether to promise us paradise on earth or the apocalypse. Technology is its principal source of images. It reinvents scientist propheticism of the 19th century, without always being aware it is doing so. Salvation will come from the Internet! Computerization will save the world — or engulf it. To characterize this stupendous wave of messages, information and "signs" with which we are being swamped every day, an American commentator, Roy Ascott, speaks of a "second Flood". Unlike the first, it will neither stop nor recede. The metaphor is revealing. What we need now is a Noah's ark.

To quote a further example, the "cyborg", or cybernetic man, symbolizes the humanity of tomorrow and has replaced the "new man" of older ideologies in the repertoire of futurist images. A portmanteau word composed of "cybernetic" and "organism", *Cyborg* was first the title of a novel by Martin Caidin, published in 1972, which inspired the American television series, *The Six Million Dollar Man*.[7] Fitted with hearing devices and miniaturized microphones, equipped with eyeglasses incorporating a liquid crystal screen and micro-cameras, permanently linked to the Web and able to access all human knowledge and memory in almost real time, the cyborg existed simultaneously in both virtual and actual realities. His body incorporated extensions that increased his mental and physical capacities tenfold. He was both man and machine. He was equipped simultaneously with the gifts of ubiquity, total knowledge and immense brainpower. He pushed the myth of the new technological frontier to its limit by combining the human and the electronic to create a hybrid creature, endowed with new powers. He revived the will to power, and achieved it in concrete terms. The bionic man, who could be repaired and upgraded indefinitely, with his microprocessors and his modified genes, became a miracle child, a Superman the likes of which even Zarathustra did not dare dream of.

This emergence of a cyberworld, of such fractal complexities and networks of realities, have inspired a rather over-wrought public and journalistic discourse, which easily comes to assign guilt. The computerization of the planet and the digitalization of social reality, have led to pressures that make people feel culpable. We are told to "get connected". The old France of tradition is stigmatized for some tardiness or other. Slowness and caution are viewed as a lack of civic responsibility, if not as criminal. The stick-in-the-mud of the twenty-first century will be anyone who isn't at home on the Web. God help anyone who won't get with it! God help the old fuddy-duddies and dreamers without any gigabytes!

Cyberculture At Your Fingertips

Speaking of the Web — the fantastic and extravagant things said about the Internet provide quite a good illustration of the new cult of scientific progress, which mistakes a tool for a culture, information for knowledge, logorrhea for a message, and a technological device for a destiny. These urgings and these fantasies are all the more revealing in that they are frequently taken up by a number of leaders, public officials and government people, who are only too ready to hold up the Internet as the hope of the future. For years now, without any restraint or critical detachment, the cyberworld has been held out as a substitute Eldorado, a mythical territory over which our 21st-century conquistadors are already quarreling.

Secondarily, there is tremendous reliance on the products created by these technologies (micro-computers, portable telephones, DVDs, etc.) to awaken the consumerist appetite of Western societies, kick-start growth, and absorb European unemployment. Already the mirage of these new "markets" has sent stock markets crazy and brought into existence a new generation of instant millionaires and software virtuosos, the "golden boys" of the Net. Our leaders have become strangely feverish in their impatience to explain to the masses that cybernetics has arrived just in time to save them from the inertia of the old world. Make haste, citizens, reality is behind you, with its cumbersome materiality and old-fashioned life forms! This substitute mythology, this topical giddiness has been creating quite a fuss in the media and in politics for a few years now — and it is far from finished.

People are trying to convince us that the sudden emergence of cyberspace, of virtual reality, and of computers, have made all our conceptions of the world out of date, devalued our beliefs, and undermined all our certitudes. We are told that all humanity is approaching previously uncharted territory, as it prepares to land on the next planet. We are supposed to sweep away the old reality and the past. All around us we find a new form of naïve modernism, of unprecedented ingenuousness.

Genuine scientists are among those who tend to smile at this "cyberbliss". They are critical of the whole phantasmagoria, and of the media's adoption of a kind of techno-scientific religion, or gnosis. They are made uneasy by this cybernetic mysticism, a form of brainwashing nearly as dangerous as any sectarian demagoguery. They call for calm. "The explosion of the Web opens up new perspectives," one of them conceded in 1999, "but it is more and more difficult to tell the difference between bluff, the usual concessions to modernity, and what is going to have a decisive effect, be the start of something new. . . . We need to revive the vision of a physical or virtual community, made up of individuals with a sense of sharing a common destiny".[8] Another expresses a truth so obvious we have to wonder how it has been overlooked for so long: "Individual happiness is no more to be found in front of a keyboard than the society of tomorrow on the Net".[9] In other words, being "connected" does not create, as if by magic, social links or meaning. It's really nothing to get so excited about!

It would be better to begin to confront right now the fact that the next century will no doubt be cybernetic, connected, and digitalized. However, that doesn't mean it won't have to contend with the same contradictions, disputes and shortcomings as the one that has just ended. Not only are our debates and concerns not "outmoded", but also, as the verbal fog begins to lift, we see the basic questions reemerging one by one. They seem to rise up out of the haze of the current brouhaha like familiar characters we had lost from view. No doubt they're expressed differently, and are viewed from a slightly different perspective, but they are indeed the same.

Cyberculture, for example, with its infinite powers of outreach and exchange, raises the question of *universality* in different terms. In appearance, everything has been changed by the triumph of the "Web". "Each additional connection adds a new heterogeneity, new sources of information, new perspectives, so that global meaning is less and less legible, more and more difficult to circumscribe, to limit, to master. This universality provides access to an appreciation of the entire world. It allows us to participate more intensely in the life of humanity, but without this being in any way at odds — far from it, indeed — with a explosion of singularity and an increase in disorder".[10] Actually, the basic question is still exactly the same. It is true that its scope has been virtually extended to the entire planet, and that the number of points of view that have become accessible or expressible has become infinitely expandable. But this doesn't alter the fact that the nature of the problem basically has not changed: namely, how can we reconcile the general and the singular? How can we make room for differences within a totality? How can we create something based on likeness — our common humanity — out of distinctive realities? The problem of the destination is still the same, even if the mode of transport is different. No tool, cybernetic or otherwise, comes complete with a meaning and instructions on how to use it. Neither the Web nor digitization has modified the givens of the human equation. The next planet will actually be rather similar to the old one.

In the same way, the difficult conjunction of "me" and "we" may well be enriched by this principle of universal interconnectedness. But that doesn't mean it has been settled or resolved. It is enriched to the extent that cyberculture puts within reach what its keenest proponents call "collective intelligence", which is to say the possibility of putting an infinite quantity of talents, knowledge, insights, or different sources of creativity, into *immediate* synergy, and to do so without any limits imposed by location, language, or distance, and free from any encumbering materiality. Ideally, indeed, it is possible for innumerable cybernauts to collaborate on the creation of a work without any specific author — like the Bible or the Gothic cathedrals — which would be far beyond the capacity of a single person. It is possible for them — or will shortly be so — to access *all human information*, thanks to the "deterritorializing" of the notion of a library. This would open the way to a new kind of relationship to knowledge, to an unprecedented kind of encyclopedism, one no longer produced by "scholars" in the old meaning of the word, but by "living human collectivities".

In describing such aggregates of spontaneous and evolving types of knowledge, the keenest cybernauts speak of "knowledge trees" that will unite multiple intelligences as a continuously evolving arborescence — trees that, in other terms, go on growing, spreading, and sending out new branches. Also mentioned are the cases of certain cities, such as Amsterdam, which have created a complete digital city on the Web, able to offer — at no charge — all the services of a normal city.

Utopians of the Internet, like Pierre Lévy (to whom I am indebted for these examples), are filled with enthusiasm at such a prospect. "I am deeply convinced," he writes, that allowing human beings to bring together their imagination and intelligence to further people's development and emancipation is the best possible use of digital technology. The idea of a collective intelligence comes, more or less, from the people who first conceived and defended the idea of cyberspace. In a sense, such a project is a continuation of Enlightenment philosophy,[11] though it goes much farther". This collective intelligence has perhaps been made not only desirable but necessary by the new requirements peculiar to our times — the need to master much more complex knowledge, new technological problems, etc. It is a fact that most major contemporary techno-scientific undertakings can no longer be mastered without the help of new cybernetic tools. Whether in particle physics, astrophysics, human genome research, space exploration, nanotechnology, or monitoring the ecology and the climate, all these activities depend on cyberspace and the powerful collective intelligences it has the power to mobilize.

If the enthusiastic proponents of "collective intelligence" are to be believed, absolute individualism, a defining value of Western modernity, will prove to have been only a transitional phase, pending the reconstitution of the "we", of the collective and social reality, by means of cyberculture. Such optimism is admirable and even congenial. And indeed we can say that it is partially justified. Cyberculture does indeed enlarge the range of possibilities. Thanks to it, we have been granted increased analytic and conceptual powers. Yet we have to recognize that this changes absolutely nothing in the substance of the fundamental questions, including those relating to collective reality — questions it is quite easy to formulate. How can we reconstitute a "we" capable of standing together, yet avoid imposing excessive constraints? How can we rediscover the other, and others, without having recourse to the severe mutilations associated with holism?

Gradually awakening from our daydream, we are today rediscovering that combining talents doesn't automatically produce an increase in collective intelligence, any more than a "flood" of information can replace knowledge or culture. The Internet, in other terms, doesn't abolish either the questions or the important part to be played by the people still able to ask them. "The transparency and intelligibility of the world are not the result of a continuous flow of information, nor of its apparent accessibility. The information is too dense, too noisy, too unstable, too rapid, too frivolous, to be enlightening and useful".[12]

To fish a little meaning out of such a flood, we will need some pretty good anglers.

From Social Movement To Virtual Market

The same commentary is valid for the specifically social and political aspects of the cyberculture utopia. Initially, indeed, the Internet came into existence, not as a governmental or technocratic "project", but as a pure explosion of technology, connected with a genuine social movement. The Web is therefore — admirably — anarchist in its genesis. It is true that, technically, the Internet came into being thanks to a decision made by the American armed forces, which wanted to find a way to connect up their various giant computers and laboratories scattered all over the United States. The widely dispersed structure of the network was intended to provide optimum immunity to possible nuclear attacks by the USSR. Very quickly, however, the idea was diverted from its original purpose.

American scientists working for the Pentagon became accustomed to communicating by way of this network. Then, in the very early 90s, an imaginative little group within the European Council for Nuclear Research (CERN), in Geneva, broadened the social use of interconnected computers, and in doing so created a basis for the World Wide Web. The weaving of this immaterial "Web", and its dizzying spread to the entire planet, was a self-regulating movement, without any rules or constraints. Having no particular location, it was uncontrollable. Cyberspace was everywhere and nowhere. It made a mockery of frontiers and bureaucracies. It operated on a virtual landscape as vast as the human imagination, and as rich in promise as a second "New World".

Cyberculture, improvised in this way, and soon becoming very complex, was strongly influenced by the spontaneity and dream-like content it inherited from its origins. It was seen, and rightly so, as the work of a multi-centered and internationalist social movement, as a new voice that would shake up all state institutions and controls. This, then, was the origin of the extraordinary potency of utopian cybernetics. The appearance of the Web, this carnavalesque, untamed novelty, was experienced like the student revolt of May 1968 transposed onto a worldwide scale, with its millions of "sites" speaking every imaginable language taking the place of the graffiti. It was not only "forbidden to forbid", but it became technically impossible even to think of doing so. By its very structure, the Web thumbed its nose at constraints and controls. And it should be added that, with few exceptions, the Web gave new vigor to the most incredible of all subversions: it was free, or at least the exchanges and services provided were virtually cost-free.

In theory, the promise of the Web was even greater. It would bring about a revolution in communications by putting an end to the hegemony of the media. The media, as we know, are handed down from the "one" to the "many", i.e. from an autonomous center (the radio or television station, the newspaper) to a passive consumer fringe of "users". The Internet replaced this pyramidal, elitist transaction with an incredible channel of communication going from everyone to everyone else — in other words a sort of direct democracy of information, without any spatial or temporal limits. In theory, this new way of doing things deconstructed all the centralized forms of control that the traditional media still perpetuate today. The arrogant power of the scribe dispensing knowledge to the common herd was replaced by what a Quebec scientist, Jean Cloutier, has called "self-service media". Permanent and self-regulating forums, the celebrated BBS ("Bulletin Board Systems"), liberated communication, making its directing principle interactive, collective, self-organizing, and fiercely anti-establishment. The Web, it was thought, would enable "the spread of a worldwide language and culture that would be a collective creation, not that of a particular caste".[13]

For all these reasons, the cyberculture of the early 1990s was pregnant with an invigorating social utopia. It seemed about to give birth to a radical revolution, to promise a massively new historical beginning. For the first time the locus of the revolution was not a specific region, country, or given geographical borders, some countryside or *sierra maestra*, but a non-space, with no limits or contours, a cyberspace more magically liberated than was ever the case for a territory of the old real world. Alas, it was only a false pregnancy. Soon, its all too business-like exploitation brought things back to normal. The revolution was a damp squib.

Gradually all the old fatalities, constraints, perils, wickedness, power grabbing, greed and power struggles which always were and always will be characteristic of the real world, re-emerged everywhere on this virtual planet. Cyber-crime affected the Web. The only new thing about it was the form it took, or the means it used. And business was no "nicer" on the Web than anywhere else. Extremely ruthless struggles and strategies for conquest took place. Betrayals of confidence, greed and trickery again reared their heads, and with them came the need for rules, for "cyber-patrols", and policing. In the form of an obsessive and irrepressible competition between "viruses" and "anti-viruses", the struggle between Good and Evil made its symbolic re-appearance in the landscape. The now infinite possibilities for virtual policing and surveillance raised the old problem of order and liberty once again, in almost identical terms. "Traces" that can record all computer connections also created a frightening transparency, capable of annihilating the very notion of private freedom. Existing institutions, whether crime police or human rights commissions, learned — contradictorily — to make the Web part of their field of investigation. The world had changed in scale, but not in nature. The old educational constraints — the organization of knowledge, the necessary mediation between the "flood of information" and those for whom it was intended — became necessary once again.[14] As for the pedophile, Holocaust-denying, or virtually murderous abominations that took up residence in this new space, they would help to transform the Web, *in turn*, into a new world-wide cesspool, which it was impossible to leave unregulated.[15]

Cyberspace became again what it had always really been: an amazing tool, but *no more than a tool*, capable of evil as well as of good. Its use, meaning, and impact were moot, impossible to determine *a priori*, dependent on an unpredictable power struggle, and foolishly bringing political and moral considerations back into play. Like all technological tools, it held out unprecedented promise, but also brought with it new threats, new types of inequality, new kinds of domination, etc. It did not *replace* the real world with a new, enchanted landscape, but simply *expanded* the real world, as an extension of it.

Today, everyone projects his or her own conception of the world, his or her projects and prejudices, into this expanded space. The most powerful and the smartest impose their own vision of things. The way the Web is viewed by Bill Gates[16] gives a glimpse of this new type of imperialism. For him, the Web is — and *should* be — above all an unrestricted worldwide marketplace allowing all the goods and services available on the planet to be available without any intermediaries or constraints. Completely free of government regulation and protectionism, it should enable the creation of ultra-liberalism's "ultimate market" to an extent no economist had ever dared imagine. So it helps the wildest dreams of liberal thought to come true. Everything else, for Gates, is just folklore or romanticism.

It's not hard to measure the gap between this Web supermarket as envisaged by Bill Gates and the libertarian and disinterested "social movement". The first wants to create the most gigantic shopping mall of all times, while the second imagined cyberspace as "a practice of interactive, reciprocal, community and inter-community communication, as a living virtual horizon for our world, heterogeneous, never a finished whole, in which every human being would be able to participate, and to which he or she could contribute".[17] In fact, this is the confrontation of two very classically contradictory interpretations. Two familiar projects and ideologies are facing off on this virtual landscape, just as only a short while ago they did on more concrete terrain. This confrontation is political in nature, in the most basic meaning of the word. It is already giving rise to a number of legal, media, technological, and financial battles, not noticeably different in kind from traditional power-struggles.

For the time being, it looks very much as if the commercialized Web, *à la* Bill Gates, is winning out over the libertarian Web of the cybernauts. Still, for the long term, nothing has been decided. It will all be a matter of priorities, of shared values, of collective choices. The future is still wide open.

Universal Morality And Universal Law

A brief word by way of an ending, in the absence of any conclusion as such. The link between the worldwide interconnection of computers and the development of a "world law" is far from evident. I am convinced, however, that there is such a link, and that it is actually of fundamental importance. In both cases, it is above all a question of the de-territorializing of human activity, a development that is at the same time irreversible and problematic. Since it has no specific location, or territorial base — and thus escapes any kind of control — cyberspace is immune to both the law and to politics. Even more than global finance or globalization in general (of which it is in any case an instrument) it heralds the inevitable demise of a certain notion of "local" sovereignty (whether national, regional or continental) that up to now has determined almost all collective discipline and choice. But, notwithstanding, cyberspace is far from unifying the planet in a single stroke by turning it into a "global village" uniting citizens wishing to live together and ready to accept a globalized "social contract".

On the contrary, it leaves differences, rivalries, conflicts, inequalities, or exploitation of man by man, intact. On the other hand, it puts an increasingly vast domain of human activity out of reach and out of control. In the same way as free trade and globalization allowed the genie of the market to come out of the national bottle within which, previously, it had been possible to contain him, cyberspace dissolves in its uncontrollable void any attempt, however modest, to regulate it. The non-space it establishes is also a space from which law is absent — as is also civilization itself, maybe.

Cyberspace confronts politics and the law with an impossible alternative: to simply throw in the towel (the 'law of the jungle' hypothesis), or to make themselves universal, now. So, the most difficult question of all, that of universality, comes up again, but this time in operational terms.

Universality now becomes not just a civilizing project that can be conceived in the very long term, but an absolute democratic emergency. Most disputes of the moment, which are supposedly between "sovereigntists" and "globalizers", are merely an illustration — on an aggressive level, and, often, on one of deliberate misunderstanding — of this new squaring of the circle. There can indeed be no law without sovereignty. But sovereignty becomes invalid or purely theoretical as soon as it is no longer territory-based. Any future "European sovereignty" itself — if it ever comes about — cannot avoid facing up to this contradiction, which is already eroding the various national sovereignties. In a world where there is no sovereignty because no frontiers or territories are possible, it becomes impossible to resolve a contradiction of this kind by simply altering the scale.

So, we cannot escape the urgent need for a minimal kind of universality endorsed and enforced by world law. The proposal is surprisingly complex. There do not yet exist any genuine international institutions with the capacity to implement such a law, by force if necessary. "In dealing with the globalization of research networks, the powers of the international institutions are still lamentable".[18] None of the United Nations, the Courts of Justice at The Hague or in Luxemburg, the World Trade Organization, or the International Labor Organization, is an institution of sufficient legitimacy and power to exercise genuine worldwide sovereignty. World law can therefore be nothing more than a pragmatic compromise, a modest, aleatory conceptualization. Mireille Delmas-Marty, a jurist specializing in such matters, provides a good description of the need for it, and its limitations.

"The law," she writes, "has no all-powerful magic with which to prevent intolerance and injustice, but it is nevertheless not powerless, as long as it selects the appropriate objective. The purpose of world law is certainly not to lead to the disappearance of States and of their national laws. State institutions remain indispensable to contain the expansion of networks of private interests, and organizing individual and collective rights, as is amply shown by the tragic situation of people without any State to represent them".[19]

It is a matter of instituting a permanent and constantly re-negotiable *transaction* between what has survived of State sovereignty and what is being developed on a worldwide scale. And this will be possible to the extent that some kind of universal awareness takes over — with difficulty, slowly, and through contradictions. The question of the right to intervene and the indictment of dictators guilty of "crimes against humanity", are never anything but the extension of a much more general approach to the criminal domain, one that is still feeling its way. In our urgent situation, to deal with the barbarisms that have been predicted, and without the assistance of any territorial "home" whatsoever, universal law is becoming both necessary and impossible. We are witnessing a revival of the problems once posed by the theories of natural law — theories and utopian visions that the inexpiable ideological wars of the 20th century had made us all but forget.

These problems are not limited to questions of procedure, of sovereignty, and perhaps of force. This is above all a question of substance. Of course, the collapse of Communism — which had denounced the "hypocrisy of bourgeois law" for three-quarters of a century — has permitted some kind of global consensus to develop, as is shown by the various declarations of human rights, and above all by the Universal Declaration of Human Rights of 1948. This consensus, which has been solemnly proclaimed, is nevertheless far from being universal, or real. In other words, the peoples of the world have not yet reached even minimal agreement about the founding values examined in our earlier chapters. The universality of founding values, we have seen, is more conjecture than reality — except, perhaps, within the frontiers of Europe. How then, in the circumstances, can we imagine a way to define a "natural law" that would be something other than the law of the strongest, of the victor, of the richest?

Not only residual tyrannies or totalitarian regimes are at issue here. Nor is the problem restricted only to the traditional societies of the southern hemisphere which still adhere to customs or practices that we consider barbaric such as female "circumcision", the infanticide of girl children, the oppression of women, the continued practice of slavery, etc.. Lawyers are the first to highlight a paradox that is extremely embarrassing for the democratic community. It is the fact that the principal and even unique superpower on earth, America, is also the country that refuses to sign texts or conventions of supposedly universal scope. Think of the international conventions to outlaw anti-personnel mines, for example, which the United States does not support. Think, especially, of the question — the most emblematic of all — of the death penalty. When the United States ratified the International Pact on Civil and Political Rights (IPCPR) in 1992, it expressed precise and detailed reservations, reservations that would have been subjected to much more rigorous criticism if they had been made by a non-democratic government. In reality, the United States affirmed its intent to preserve the right to impose the death penalty on anyone it sees fit, including not only minors — even very young children — but also, for example, the insane or mentally handicapped, with the sole exception of pregnant women.[20]

More embarrassing still, the U.S. Administration has accepted only half-heartedly, and with certain restrictions, the outlawing of torture and of inhumane or degrading punishment or treatment. As for the various "social" declarations cited above,[21] dealing with the right to an adequate standard of living, or the prohibition against considering labor a commodity or object of trade, it is not at all clear that they are compatible with the

Anglo-Saxon model of capitalism and hard-nosed liberalism, as characterized by Michel Albert.[22]

Cyberculture and world law are only two examples. They have the advantage of illustrating a truth that, henceforth, we can no longer allow ourselves to forget. The next planet will not be one we inherit, but one we create. The world that awaits us is not one that we have to conquer, but that we have to found.

Notes

[*Translator's note*: Whenever we have been able to identify an English-language original of sources consulted by the author in French translation, we have referred to the former.]

Introduction

1. I have borrowed this image from Shmuel Trigano, *Un exil sans retour? Lettres à un Juif égaré*, Stock, 1996.

2. *Le Monde*, July 8, 1998.

3. Cioran, *Précis de decomposition*, Gallimard, 1949.

4. Pierre Legendre, *L'Inestimable Objet de la transmission. Études sur le principe généalogique en Occident. Leçons IV*, Fayard, 1985.

5. Cornélius Castoriadis, *La Montée de l'insignifiance*, Seuil, 1996.

6. Karl Marx, Troisième Thèse sur Feuerbach in *L'Idéologie allemande*, Éditions. Sociales, 1968.

7. Maurice Bellet, *La Seconde Humanité. De l'impasse majeure de ce que nous appelons l'économie*, Desclée de Brouwer, 1994.

8. Jacob Taubes, *La Théologie politique de Carl Schmitt, Benjamin, Nietzsche et Freud*, Seuil, 1999.

9. This is a sentence from Rousseau which Schmitt himself quotes, significantly. See Carl Schmitt, Théologie politique (1922). French translation,. Jean-Louis Schlegel, Gallimard, 1988.

10. This expression, "disenchantment *(Entzauberung)* of the world", borrowed first by Max Weber and then by Marcel Gauchet, who used is as the title of his major work, actually comes from Friedrich von Schiller (1759-1805). Originally, it referred to the disappearance of superstitions and "magic" as techniques for salvation.

11. Charles Taylor, *Sources of the Self. The Making of the Modern Identity*. Cambridge, Mass., Harvard University Press, 1989.

12. André Gorz, *Misère du présent. Richesse du possible*, Galilée, 1997.

13. Paul Valadier, *Inévitable Morale*, Esprit-Seuil, 1990.

14. Charles Taylor, *Sources of the self, op. cit.*

15. Antoine Garapon and Denis Salas, *La République pénalisée*, Hachette, 1996. I have dealt at length with this question in *The Tyranny of Pleasure*, NY, Algora, 1999.

16. Maurice Merleau-Ponty, *La Prose du monde*, Gallimard, 1968.

17. Edgar Morin, *Science avec conscience*, Fayard, 1982.

18. Marcel Gauchet, *Le Désenchantement du monde*, Gallimard, 1985.

19. Paul Thibaud, "Voyage dans la maladie française", *Le Débat* , No. 101, September-October 1998.

20. Maurice Bellet, *La Seconde Humanité, op. cit.*

21. Edgar Morin, *Science avec conscience, op. cit.*

22. Quoted by Françoise Dastur, *Hölderlin. Tragédie et modernité*, Encre marine, 1992.

23. Éric Weil, *Philosophie morale*, Vrin, 1992.

Part I

1. *International Herald Tribune*, February 29, 1996; quoted by Anton Brender, *La France face à la mondialisation*, La Découverte, 1996.

Chapter 1

1. Vladimir Jankélévich, *L'Imprescriptible, pardonner? Dans l'honneur et la dignité*, Seuil, coll. "Points", 1996.
2. And which he contrasts with the "responsibility principle". See Hans Jonas, *Le principe responsabilité*, Flammarion-Champs, 1998.
3. Miguel Benasayag and Dardo Scavino, *Pour une nouvelle radicalité, pouvoir et puissance en politique*, La Découverte, 1997. The authors speak of the "massive deceit" of revolutionary passions.
4. Quoted by Christian Delacampagne, *Histoire de la philosophie au XXe siècle*, Seuil, 1995.
5. Though the responsibility for the Great War mostly belongs to empires rather than to nations—i.e. to Kaiser Wilhelm's Reich, the Austro-Hungarian Empire, and Tsarist Russia.
6. Alain Finkielkraut, *L'Humanité perdue. Essai sur le XXe siècle*, Seuil, 1996.
7. Jacob Taubes, *La Théologie politique de Carl Schmitt, Benjamin, Nietzsche et Freud, op. cit.*
8. François Guéry, in *Quelles valeurs pour demain?* Proceedings of a colloquium held at Le Mans in October 1997, Le Monde-Seuil, 1998.
9. Loïc Blondiaux, *La Fabrique de l'opinion. Une histoire sociale des sondages*, Seuil, 1998.
10. Alain Finkielkraut, *L'Humanité perdue, op. cit.*
11. François Furet, *Le Passé d'une illusion. Essai sur l'idée communiste au XXe siècle*, Robert Laffont/Calmann-Lévy, 1995.
12. Philippe Raynaud, *Max Weber et les Dilemmes de la raison moderne*, PUF, 1987 (Quadrige, 1996).
13. Hermann Rauschning, *Hitler m'a dit*, Hachette-Pluriel, 1996 [original German *Gespräche mit Hitler*; English translation: *Hitler speaks*, London, Butterworth, 1939.]
14. Christian Delacampagne, *Histoire de la philosophie au XXe siècle*, Seuil, 1995.
15. Hermann Rauschning, *op. cit.*
16. Quoted by Pierre Ayçoberry, *La Question nazie. Les interprétations du national-socialisme*, Seuil, 1979.
17. See Michel Winock, *Le Siècle des intellectuels*, Seuil, 1998.
18. Emmanuel Lévinas, "De la phénoménologie à l'éthique", inverview with Richard Kearney (1981), *Esprit*, juillet 1997.
19. Aimé Césaire, *Discours sur le colonialisme*, Présence africaine, 1955.
20. One detail among many symbolizes this return of the right to differentialism: the publication, in 1980, of a special issue of the review *Éléments,* (an organ of the French "new right") entitled "For a New Approach to the Third World".
21. Maurice Bellet, *La Seconde humanité, op. cit.*
22. "The notion of 'warring gods'", writes Philippe Raynaud discussing Weber (*Max Weber et les dilemmes de la raison moderne*, PUF, 1987), "simultaneously raises a question of law (is it

possible to make a rational choice between competing value systems?) and a sociological problem (the impact of the "value"-conflicts that divide humanity)".

23. François Furet, preface to the collection by Alphonse Dupront, *Qu'est-ce que les Lumières?*, Gallimard, 1996.

24. See Gianni Vattimo *La Fin de la modernité: nihilisme et herméneutique dans la culture postmoderne*, Seuil, 1987. [Italian original: *Fine della modernità*. It should be noted that in *Espérer croire*, Seuil, 1998 [*Credere di credere*, Milan, Garzante, 1996], Vattimo seems to distance himself somewhat from "weak ontology", claiming to have returned, in some way, to Christianity under the influence of René Girard in particular.

25. Jean-Marie Vincent, *Max Weber ou la démocratie inachevée*, Éditions du Félin, 1998.

26. See, for example, Rorty's *Objectivity, relativism and truth*, Cambridge; New York, Cambridge U.P., 1991

27. Jean-Marie Vincent, *Max Weber ou la démocratie inachevée, op. cit.*

28. Michel Foucault, "La crise dans nos têtes", interview in *L'Arche* No. 70, 1977, quoted by Joël Roman, *Chronique des idées contemporaines. Itinéraire guidé à travers trois cents textes choisis*, Bréal, 1995

29. Here I am using Joël Roman's analyses in *Chronique des idées contemporaines, op. cit.*

30. Jean-François Lyotard, *La Condition postmoderne, rapport sur le savoir*, Minuit, 1979.

31. Gilles Lipovetsky in *L'Ere du vide*, Gallimard, 1983.

32. Alain Touraine, *Critique de la modernité*, Fayard, 1992.

33. Jacques Rancière, *La Leçon d'Althusser*, Gallimard, 1974.

34. Cited by Antoine Compagnon *Les Cinq Paradoxes de la modernité*, Seuil, 1990.

35. Cornélius Castoriadis, *Le Monde morcelé. Les carrefours du labyrinthe, III*, Seuil, 1990.

36. Dominique Lecourt, *Les Piètres penseurs*, Flammarion, 1999.

37. Alain Caillé, *La Démission des clercs, la crise des sciences sociales et l'oubli du politique*, La Découverte, 1994.

Chapter 2

1. In France, this thesis is defended most notably by Jean Baechler (*La Grande Parenthèse*, Calmann-Lévy, 1993.)

2. Letter to Niethammer in *Correspondance*, Vol. 1, trans. J. Carrère, Gallimard, 1962..

3. Alexandre Kojève, *Introduction à la lecture de Hegel*, 1947 reproduced in Joël Roman, *Chronique des idées contemporaines, op. cit* (Note however that in 1960, in a self-critical note, Kojève would partially correct any over-simplification in this position.)

4. Maurice Blanchot, *L'Entretien infini*, Gallimard, 1969.

5. Karl Raimund Popper, the philosopher of German extraction, who died on September 17, 1994, is best known as the author of a book now considered a classic: *The Open Society and its Enemies*, Princeton, Princeton U.P., 1950.

6. See in particular his novel *The Notebooks of Don Rigoberto*, translated by Edith Grossman, New York, Farrar, Straus & Giroux, 1998.

7. Lester Thurow, *The Future of capitalism*, William Morrow & Co., New York, 1996.

8. John Ruskin, *Unto This Last*, University of Nebraska Press, 1967, quoted by Benjamin R. Barber in *Strong democracy: participatory politics for a new age*, Berkeley, California University Press, 1984.

9. See, in particular, the excellent study by Jean-Pierre Dupuy, *Le Sacrifice et l'envie. Le libéralisme aux prises avec la justice sociale*, Calmann-Lévy, 1992.

10. André Gorz, *Misère du présent. Richesse du possible*, Galilée, 1997.

11. As the economist Jean-Paul Fitoussi has shown, this essential difference is quite easy to describe. For the market, a dollar equals a vote; for democracy, a man (or woman) equals a vote — which, as it is easy to see, is not the same thing.

12. Lester Thurow, *The Future of capitalism*, *op. cit.*

13. René Rémond, *Religion et société en Europe*, Seuil, 1998.

14. See Chapter 7, below.

15. John Kenneth Galbraith, *Economics in perspective: a critical history*, Boston, Houghton Mifflin, 1987.

16. Paul A. Samuelson, *Economics*, 11th. Ed., New York, McGraw-Hill, 1980.

17. Georges Bernanos, *La France contre les robots*, republished by Livre de poche, 1999, with a preface by Jacques Julliard.

18. Pierre Rosanvallon, "Culture politique libérale et réformisme", *Esprit*, March-April 1999.

19. Léo Strauss, *Le Testament de Spinoza*, Cerf, 1991

20. Olivier Mongin, *L'Après 1989. Les nouveaux langages du politique*, Hachette Littératures, 1998.

21. Jacques Rancière, *La Mésentente*, Galilée, 1995.

22. Benjamin R. Barber, *Strong democracy*, *op.cit.*

23. Zaki Laïdi, "Les imaginaires de la mondialisation", *Esprit*, October 1998. (Our ideas in the above are considerably indebted to this remarkable article).

24. This concept of "creative destruction", which is peculiar to capitalism, was invented by Joseph Alois Schumpeter, in 1942, in his book *Capitalism, Socialism and Democracy*, New York, London, Harper & Brothers, 1942.

25. Denis MacShane, in *Quelles valeurs pour demain? Op. cit.*

26. André Gorz, *Misère du présent. Richesse du possible*, *op. cit.*

27. Maurice Bellet, *La Seconde humanité. op. cit.*

28. Paul Berman, *A Tale of two Utopias*, Norton, 1996.

29. Mark Lilla, "La double révolution libérale: Sixties et Reaganomics", *Esprit*, octobre 1998.

30. It is worthy of note that in 1998 there were almost 1,800,000 individuals in prison in America, six times as many as in the 1960s! Lester Thurow also points out that in 1995 California spent double the amount on its prisons as on its universities, and four times as much on every delinquant as on every student (Lester Thurow, *op. cit.*).

31. "The Capitalist Threat", *The Atlantic Monthly*; February 1997; Vol. 279, No. 2.

32. Andrey Alexandrovitch Zhdanov (1896-1948), a member of the Politburo in 1939, became an ardent defender of Stalinian orthodoxy, even in the realm of scientific "thought".

33. Gary S. Becker, *The Economic Approach to Human Behavior*, Chicago, University of Chicago Press, 1976. (Quoted by Michel Beaud, *Le Basculement du monde*, La Découverte, 1997.)

34. Expression used by a Quebec journalist, Jean Pichette, *Le Devoir*, October 23, 1996.

35. Jacques T. Gotbout, "Consommateurs de dons et producteurs de causes: la philantropie et le marché", in *La Résistible Emprise de la rationalité instrumentale*, Éditions Eska, 1998.

36. Dominique Janicaud, *La Puissance du rationnel*, Gallimard, 1985.

37. Jacques T. Gotbout, *La Résistible emprise de la rationalité instrumentale*, *op. cit.*

38. Jean-Marie Vincent, *Max Weber ou la démocratie inachevée*, Éditions du Félin, 1998.

39. Max Horkheimer and Theodor W. Adorno, *La Dialectique de la raison*, 1944. French translation, Gallimard, 1974.

40. Marcel Gauchet, *La Religion dans la démocratie. Parcours de la laïcité*, Gallimard, 1998. (Our italics.)

41. Sartre's expressions, as some may recall, were: "Marxism is the ultimate horizon of History", and "All anti-communists are dogs".

42. Michel Aglietta, "Nouveau régime de croissance et progrès social", *Esprit*, November 1998.

43. This is the expression Georges Bernanos used on his return to France after the liberation.

44. John Kenneth Galbraith, *Economics in perspective: a critical history* Boston, Houghton Mifflin, 1987.

45. Michel Beaud, *Le Basculement du monde, op. cit.*

46. Jean-Paul Fitoussi and Pierre Rosanvallon, *Le Nouvel Age des inégalités*, Seuil, 1996.

47. André Gorz, *Misère du présent. Richesse du possible, op. cit.*

48. I have borrowed this idea from the excellent book by Christophe Dejours, *Souffrance en France. La banalisation de l'injustice sociale*, Seuil, 1998.

49. Anthony Giddens, *The Third Way. The Renewal of Social Democracy*, Cambridge, U.K., Polity Press ; Malden, MA, Blackwell, 1998.

50. This is the question explicitly asked by Jean-Marie Guehenno, Professor of Political Science at the University of Paris, in his book *La Fin de la démocratie*, Flammarion, 1993.

Part II

1. I am thinking here of the—courteous—dispute which, significantly, arose between Marcel Gauchet and Paul Valadier, with the latter paradoxically accusing the latter of allowing Christianity too much credit for the formation of modern thought, at the expense of Greek philosophy whose fertilizing presence, in his view, played a more important part. "Christianity," he added, "needed its 'other', and an 'other' that challenged it, if it was to reveal the potentialities inherent in it" (Paul Valadier, *L'Église en procès*, Calmann-Lévy, 1987).

2. Maurice Bellet, *La Seconde Humanité. op. cit.*

Chapter 3

1. *Le Monde*, June 2 1992, quoted by Jean-Claude Eslin, *Dieu et le pouvoir. Théologie et politique en Occident*, Seuil, 1999.

2. Guy Roustang, "Logique tentaculaire du marché et individualisme négatif", in *La Résistible Emprise de la rationalité instrumentale, op. cit.*

3. Frédéric Lordon, *Les Quadratures de la politique économique. Les infortunes de la vertu*, Albin Michel, 1997.

4. This expression designates all those who, while having stable employment, remain below the poverty threshold. They have continued to increase in number since the end of the 1970s.

5. Jean Peyrelevade, "Le *Corporate Governance* ou les fondements incertains d'un nouveau pouvoir", Notes, Saint-Simon Foundation, June 1998.

6. Lester Thurow, *The Future of capitalism, op. cit.*

7. There is an excellent essay demonstrating this: Louis Chauvel, *Le Destin des générations. Structures sociales et cohortes en France au XXe siècle*, PUF, 1999.

8. Paul Krugman, *The Age of Diminishing Expectations*, Cambridge, Mass. MIT Press, 1990.

9. Hugues Lagrange, "La pacification des moeurs et ses limites", *Esprit*, December 1998.

10. Alain Ehrenberg, *Le Culte de la performance*, Calmann-Lévy, 1991.

11. Lester Thurow, *The Future of capitalism, op. cit.*

12. Paul Virilio, *Cybermonde. La politique du pire*, Textuel, 1996.

13. Mireille Delmas-Marty, *Trois Défis pour un droit mondial*, Seuil, 1998.

14. Jean-Marie Vincent, *Max Weber ou la démocratie inachevée, op. cit.*

15. Lester Thurow, *The Future of capitalism, op. cit.*

16. *Ibid.*

17. Anton Brender, *La France face à la mondialisation*, La Découverte, 1996.

18. Here I am thinking in particular of the polemical book by Hervé Le Bras, *Le Démon des origines: démographie et extrême droite*, Éditions de l'Aube, 1998, in which he sets out to denounce statistical and ideological "manipulations" by official French demography.

19. Fernand Braudel, *La Dynamique du capitalisme*, Champs-Flammarion, 1988.

20. Alphonse Dupront, *Qu'est-ce que les Lumières?* Gallimard, 1996.

21. Marcel Gauchet, "Qu'est-ce que l'intégrisme?", *L'Histoire*, No. 224, September 1998.

22. Dominique Janicaud, *La Puissance du rationnel, op. cit.*

23. Karl Jasper, *Origine et sens de l'Histoire*, 1949, French translation, Plon, 1954. I am here using the analysis by Michel Beaud, *Le Basculement du monde, op. cit.*

24. On this specific topic, a useful reference is Marcel Simon et André Benoit, *Le Judaïsme et le christianisme antique. D'Antiochus Épiphane à Constantin*, PUF, 1994 (First published in 1968).

25. Régine Azria, "Être juif sans le Temple", in *Le Monde de la Bible*, September-October 1998.

26. Shmuel Trigano, *Un exil sans retour, op. cit.*

27. *Ibid.*

28. Marc-Alain Ouaknin, *Les Dix commandements*, Seuil, 1999.

29. Stéphane Mosès, *L'Éros et la loi. Lectures bibliques*, Seuil, 1999.

30. See the magnificent book by Ellul, *La Subversion du christianisme*, Seuil, 1984.

31. Jacques Brosse, "L'aventure intérieure", in *L'Occident en quête de sens*, Maisonneuve & Larose, 1996.

32. See Habermas, *Théorie de l'action communicationnelle*, Francfort, 1981. I have borrowed this analysis (extremely simplified here) from Philippe Raynaud, *Max Weber et les dilemmes de la raison moderne, op. cit.*

33. See Epictetus, *Ce qui dépend de nous*. [New French translation by Myrto Gondicas, Arléa, 1988.]

34. Paul Veyne, *Les Grecs ont-ils cru à leurs mythes?* Seuil, 1983 (Point Essais, 1992).

35. Shmuel Trigano, *Un exil sans retour ?, op. cit.*

36. Maurice Bellet, *La Seconde Humanité, op. cit.*

37. Peter Brown, *The rise of Western Christendom: triumph and adversity*, Cambridge, Mass. Blackwell, 1997.

38. See Chapter 4.

39. Emmanuel Kant, *La Religion dans les limites de la simple raison*, Vrin, 1992.

40. For St. Thomas Aquinas and the Thomist tradition, on the other hand, the idea of "nature" was prevalent—at once a reconciliation with reality and implied submission to a natural norm which was not to be transgressed.

41. Marie Balmary, "La psychanalyse est-elle une expérience spirituelle ?", in *L'Occident en quête de sens*, Maisonneuve & Larose, 1996. See also Marie Balmary, *La Divine Origine*, Livre de Poche.

42. François Châtelet, *Une histoire de la raison. Conversations with Émile Noël*. Seuil "Points Sciences", 1992.

43. Charles Taylor, *Sources of the self, op. cit*, and Henri de Lubac, *La Postérité spirituelle de Joachim de Flore. De Joachim de Flore à Shelling*, Le Sycomore, 1987.

44. Charles Taylor, *Sources of the self., op. cit.*

45. *Ibid.*

46. Dominique Janicaud, *La Puissance du rationnel, op. cit.*

47. I have borrowed these comments from René Rémond, *Religion and society in modern Europe*, Seuil, 1998.

48. *Ibid.*

49. Pierre Manent, *Histoire intellectuelle du libéralisme*, Calmann-Lévy, 1987.

50. Pelagius, a 4th-century monk of British origin, claimed that divine grace was not essential for salvation. He was the source of a long-lived heresy (Pelagianism), attacked by St. Augustine, and condemned by several Councils, including that of Ephesus, in 431.

51. Alain Pons, preface to Condorcet, *Esquisse d'un tableau historique des progrès de l'esprit humain*, GF-Flammarion, 1988.

52. Charles Taylor, *op. cit.*

53. Quoted by Philippe Raynaud, *Max Weber et les dilemmes de la raison moderne, op. cit.* See H. R. Trevor-Roper, *Religion, the Reformation and Social Change*, London, Secker and Warburg, 1984.

54. I have taken this quote from Stéphane Mosès, *L'Éros et la loi. Lectures bibliques, op. cit.*

55. In Karl Marx and Frederick Engels, *L'Idéologie allemande*, Éditions sociales, 1968.

56. The son of Japeth (Iapetus), the Titan of Greek mythology stole the sacred fire from the gods to give it to mankind. Zeus condemned Prometheus to remain chained to a rock in the Caucasus Mountains, where an eagle fed on his liver. The chained Prometheus became—most notably for the English and German romantics—the symbol of human pride and of efforts to re-make the world.

57. Hermann Rauschning, *Hitler speaks, op. cit.*

58. François Fejtö, "Réflexions d'un révisionniste", in *Arguments*, No. 14, 1959. Quoted by Joël Roman, *Chronique des idées contemporaines, op. cit.*

59. Karl Marx, *Contribution à la critique de la philosophie du droit de Hegel* (1844).

60. François Châtelet, *Une histoire de la raison, op. cit.*

61. F. Hayek, Lecture delivered at the University of Brasilia in May 1981, quoted by Hugo Assmann et Franz J. Hinkelammert, *L'Idôlatrie de marché. Critique théologique de l'économie de marché*, Cerf, 1993.

62. Jean-Marc Lévy-Leblond, *La Pierre de touche. La science à l'épreuve*, Folio essai, 1996.

63. Zbignew Brzezinski, *Out of Control: Global Turmoil on the Eve of the Twenty-First Century*,

Scribner's, 1993.

64. I am indebted for some of these remarks to Zaki Laïdi, "Les imaginaires de la mondialisation", *op. cit.*

65. Lester Thurow, *The Future of capitalism, op. cit.*

66. Olivier Mongin, *L'Après 1989. Les nouveaux langages du politique*, Hachette Littératures, 1998.

Chapter 4

1. It is interesting to note that immediately after World War I already, in 1919, the Treaty of Versailles, in creating the International Labor Organization (ILO) contained an affirmation that has been thoroughly forgotten today, namely that labor should not be considered merely as a commodity or object of trade.

2. Cornélius Castoriadis, "La 'rationalité' du capitalisme", in *La Résistible Emprise de la rationalité instrumentale, op. cit.*

3. André Gorz, *Misère du présent. Richesse du possible, op. cit.*

4. I am thinking here of the excellent book by Michael Walzer, *Spheres of justice: a defense of pluralism and equity*, NY, Basic Books, 1983.

5. On the the way public opinion has become acclimatized to inequality, see the book by Christophe Dejours, *Souffrances en France. La banalisation de l'injustice sociale, op. cit.*

6. Leo Strauss, *Natural Right and History*, Chicago, University of Chicago Press, 1950.

7. See especially Luc Ferry et Alain Renaut, *Philosophie politique* (Vols. 1 and 2), Flammarion, 1984 et 1987.

8. François Châtelet, *Une histoire de la raison, op. cit.*

9. Peter Brown, *Power and persuasion in late antiquity: towards a Christian empire*, Madison, Wis., University of Wisconsin Press, 1992.]

10. Emmanuel Lévinas, *Difficile liberté*, Albin Michel, 1976.

11. On the subject of Celsus and Nietzsche, let us note the following comment by Jacob Taubes: "I read Nietsche and asked myself: 'Can you find a single argument that wasn't already made by Celsus?' I couldn't find any". Jacob Taubes, *La Théologie politique de Carl Schmitt, Benjamin, Nietzsche et Freud, op. cit.*

12. Pierre Maraval, *Le Christianisme de Constantin à la conquête arabe*, PUF, 1997.

13. Peter Brown, *Power and persuasion in late antiquity, op. cit.*

14. *Ibid.*

15. François Vouga, *Les Premiers Pas du christinianisme*, Labor et Fidès, 1997. François Vouga teaches the New Testament at the Kirchliche Hochschule Bethel, in Bielefeld, Germany.

16. Peter Brown, *The rise of Western Christendom, op. cit.*

17. Peter Brown, *Power and persuasion in late Antiquity*, op. cit.

18. Peter Brown, *The rise of Western Christendom, op. cit.*

19. Jacques Ellul, *Anarchie et christianisme*, Atelier de création libertaire, 1988. Paperback edition, La Table Ronde, 1998.

20. André Vauchez, *La Spiritualité du Moyen Age occidental. VIIIe –XIIIe siècle*, Point-Histoire, Seuil, 1994.

21. Jacques Ellul, *Anarchie et christianisme, op. cit.*

22. Bossuet, *Sermon sur la mort et autres sermons*, G.F. 1970.

23. Charles Taylor, *Sources of the self, op. cit.*

24. Condorcet, *Esquisse d'un tableau historique des progrès de l'esprit hummain*, GF-Flammarion, 1988.

25. Quotations taken from Arlette Fage, *Dire et mal dire. L'opinion publique au XVIIIe siècle*, Seuil, 1992

26. René Rémond, *Religion et Société en Europe*, Seuil, 1998.

27. Fernand Braudel, *La Dynamique du capitalisme, op. cit.*

28. Cornélius Castoriadis, "La 'rationalité' du capitalisme", in *La Résistible emprise de la rationalité instrumentale, op. cit.*

29. I have borrowed these ideas from Paul Thibaud, "Voyage dans la maladie française", *Le Débat* No.101, September-October 1998.

30. See Chapter 7, below.

31. This is the stimulating theory put forward by Emmanuel Todd in *L'Illusion économique*, Gallimard, 1998.

32. Paul Thibaud, "Voyage dans la maladie française", *op. cit.*

33. Pierre-Noël Giraud, *L'Inégalité du monde*, Gallimard, 1996.

34. *Ibid.*

35. Lester Thurow, *The Future of capitalism, op. cit.*

36. John Rawls, *Theory of Justice*, Harvard University Press (Belknap Press), Cambridge, Mass. 1971.

37. Lester Thurow, *The Future of capitalism, op. cit.*

38. *Ibid.*

39. Quoted by *Le Monde*, May 111999.

40. Lester Thurow, *The Future of capitalism, op. cit.*

41. André Gorz, *Misère du présent. Richesse du possible, op. cit.*

42. Theory suggested by Pierre-Noël Giraud in particular.

43. Daniel Cohen, *Richesse du monde, pauvreté des nations*, Flammarion, 1997].

44. On these "revolutions" in management, there is an excellent little book by Jean-Pierre Le Goff, *La Barbarie douce. La modernisation aveugle de l'entreprise et de l'école*, La Découverte, 1999.

45. See in particular: Jonathan, H. Turner, *Herbert Spencer: A Renewed Appréciation*, Beverly Hills, California, Stage Publishers, 1985, or J.D.Y Peel, *Herbert Spencer, The Évolution of a sociologist*, New York, Basic Books, 1971.

46. Dominique Goux, Éric Maurin, "La nouvelle condition ouvrière", *Esprit*, November 1998.

47. Jean-Paul Fitoussi, "Perfection des modèles économiques, exclusions réelles", *Les Temps modernes*, 1998.

48. Namely Jeffrey Coles and Peter J. Hammond, "Walrasian Equilibrium without survival: Existence, Efficiency and Remedial Policy", in *Choice Welfare and Development*, Clarendon Press, Oxford, 1995.

49. Michael Walzer, "Exclusion, justice et État démocratique" in Commissariat général au Plan, *Pluralisme et équité. La justice sociale dans les démocraties*, Éditions Esprit, 1995.

50. Jean-Paul Fitoussi, "Perfection des modèles économiques, exclusions réelles", *op. cit.*

51. Jacques Marseille, *Marianne*, 7-13 December 1998. The same article revealed that a conference on luxury was held on December 9 and 10, 1998, at the Sorbonne.

52. *Courrier International* No. 382, 26 February-4 March 1998.

Chapter 5

1. The inventor of the term "techno-science" seems to be Gilbert Hottois, *Le Signe et la technique*, Aubier, 1984.

2. Jacob Taubes, *La Théologie politique de Carl Schmitt, Benjamin, Nietzsche et Freud*, op. cit.

3. Jean-Pierre Vernant, *Entre mythe et politique*, Seuil, 1996.

4. In *What is called thinking (Was heisst Denken?)*, NY, Harper & Row, 1968.

5. Jean Beaufret, *Leçons de philosophie*, vol. 2, Seuil, 1998.

6. Jean-Pierre Vernant, *Entre mythe et politique*, op. cit.

7. *Ibid.*

8. See Chapter 3.

9. Paul Veyne, *Les Grecs ont-ils cru à leurs mythes?* Seuil, 1983 (Point Essais, 1992).

10. See the two preceding chapters.

11. Marcel Simon, *Verus Israël. Étude sur les relations entre chrétiens et juifs dans l'Empire romain (135-425)*, Éditions E. de Boccard, 1983 (Earlier editions in 1948 and 1964)].

12. Marcel Simon and André Benoit, *Le Judaïsme et le christianisme antique. D'Antiochus épiphane à Constantin*, PUF, 1994 (First published 1968).

13. Pierre Maraval, *Le Christianisme, de Constantin à la conquête arabe*, PUF, 1997.

14. Marcel Simon and André Benoit, *Le Judaïsme et le christianisme antique*, op. cit.

15. Jean Beaufret, *Leçons de philosophie*, vol. 2, Seuil, 1998.

16. Stéphane Mosès, *L'Éros et la loi. Lectures bibliques*, Seuil, 1999.

17. François Vouga, *Les Premiers pas du christianisme*, op. cit.

18. See the monumental three-volume work edited by: Roshdi Rashed, *Histoire des sciences arabes*, Seuil, 1997.

19. Alain de Libera, "Le don de l'islam à l'Occident", in *L'Occident en quête de sens*, op. cit.

20. *Ibid.*

21. I am thinking here in particular of Chapter 12 in Book II, intitled "Apology for Raymond Sebond" (the author of a work entitled *Theologia naturalis sine liber creaturarum magistri Raymondi Sabone* (Natural theology or the book of creatures by Master Raymond Sebon) In it, Montaigne castigates Christians who betray religious values. The chapter ends with a reference to "our Christian faith".

22. François Châtelet, *Une histoire de la raison*, op. cit.

23. I have borrowed these formulations from Jean-Marie Vincent, *Max Weber ou la démocratie inachevée*, op. cit.

24. Charles Taylor, *Sources of the self*, op. cit.

25. Jean-Marc Lévy-Leblond, *La Pierre de touche. La science à l'épreuve*, op. cit.

26. I am indebted for these ideas to Jean-Pierre Lebrun, *Un monde sans limite. Essai pour une clinique psychanalytique du social*, Érès, 1997.

27. Léo Strauss, *Persecution and the art of writing*, Westport, Conn., Greenwood Press, 1952.

28. Alexandre Koyré, *Du monde clos à l'univers infini*, Gallimard, 1973.

29. François Lurçat, *L'Autorité de la science*, Cerf, 1995. It is from this excellent book I have borrowed these observations on closure.

30. Dominique Janicaud, *La Puissance du rationnel*, op. cit.

31. Boris Cyrulnik, *L'Ensorcellement du monde*, Odile Jacob, 1997.

32. Jean-Marc Lévy-Leblond, *La Pierre de touche. La science à l'épreuve*, op. cit

33. Dennis Gabor, *Inventing the Future*, Penguin, 1964.

34. Alain Finkielkraut, *L'Humanité perdue. Essai sur le XXe siècle, op. cit.*

35. Josiane Nathan (sous la direction de), *La Science sous le Troisième Reich*, Seuil, 1993.

36. Dominique Janicaud, *La Puissance du rationnel, op. cit.*

37. Some of these examples are cited by Jean-Marc Lévy-Leblond, *La Pierre de touche. La science à l'épreuve, op. cit.*

38. Émile Poulat, *Liberté, laïcité. La guerre des deux France et le principe de la modernité*, Cerf/Cujas, 1988.

39. Jean-Marc Lévy-Leblond, *La Pierre de touche. La science à l'épreuve, op. cit.*

40. In a work published in 1859 under the title *La Démocratie.* Quoted by Philippe Portier, *Église et politique en France au XXe siècle*, Montchrestien, 1993.

41. Pierre Grelot, *La Science face à la foi. Lettre ouverte à Monsieur Claude Allègre, ministre de l'éducation nationale*, Éditions du Cerf, 1998.

42. François Lurçat, *L'Autorité de la science, op. cit.*

43. In an article intituled "Sur la notion de race" published in the review *Diogène*, July-September 1967. Jeanne Hersch is notably the author of *L'Étonnement philosophique: une histoire de la philosophie*, Gallimard, 1993.

44. Jacques Barzun, *Begin Here*, University of Chicago Press, 1991, quoted by François Lurçat, *L'Autorité de la science, op. cit.*

45. François Lurçat, *L'Autorité de la science, op. cit.*

46. Éditions Odile Jacob, 1983.

47. Jean-Pierre Changeux and Paul Ricoeur, *La Nature et la règle*, Odile Jacob, 1999.

48. I am thinking here, for instance, of the physicist Bernard d'Espagnat, the author of numerous works on what he calls "veiled reality" and the limits of all scientific knowledge.

49. D. Folscheid, "La science et la loi", *Éthique*, No. 1.

50. Jean-William Lapierre, "A Jean-Pierre Changeux et Paul Ricoeur, quelques remarques sur *La Nature et la règle*", *Esprit*, March-April, 1999.

51. Edward O. Wilson, *On Human Nature*, Cambridge, Harvard U.P., 1978. Quoted by Charles Taylor, *Sources of the self, op. cit.*

52. Nietzsche, *La Généalogie de la morale*, Mercure de France, 1964. It should be noted that, elsewhere, Nietzsche on the contrary violently attacks reason, "this criminal power that kills life" (*Ecce homo*).

53. Jean-Pierre Changeux (ed.), *Fondements naturels de l'éthique*, Odile Jacob, 1991.

54. Bernard Brun, "Sur les fondements naturels de l'éthique", *Agone*, No. 11, 1993.

55. James Watson et al. *Molecular Biology of the Gene*, NY, Benjamin, 1965.

56. Quoted by Zeev Sternhell, "Anthropologie et politique: les avatars du darwinisme social au tournant du siècle", in *L'Allemagne nazie et le Génocide juif*, Gallimard-Seuil, 1985.

57. Pierre Legendre, *L'Inestimable Objet de la transmission, op. cit.*

58. M. Horkheimer & T.W. Adorno, *La Dialectique de la raison, op. cit.*.

59. Jean-Philippe Bouilloud, "Une alternative à la rationalité instrumentale en gestion ?", in *La Résistible Emprise de la rationalité instrumentale, op. cit.*

60. Jürgen Habermas, *La Technique et la science comme idéologie*, French translation by Jean-René Ladmiral, Gallimard, 1990.

61. Jean-Marc Lévy-Leblond, *La Pierre de touche. La science à l'épreuve, op. cit*

62. *Ibid.*

63. Mireille Delmas-Marty, *Trois Défis pour un droit mondial*, Seuil, 1998.

64. *Le Monde*, October 13, 1998.

65. Jeremy Rifkin, *Biotech century: harnessing the gene and remaking the world*, NY, Jeremy P. Tarcher/Putnam 1998.

66. Jean-Pierre Lebrun, *Un monde sans limite. Essai pour une clinique psychanalytique du social, op. cit.*

67. Emmanuel Lévinas, *Totalité et infini*, Martinus Nijhoff, La Haye, 1980.

68. Gustave Martelet, *Évolution et création. T. 1: Sens et non-sens de l'homme dans la nature?*, Cerf/Médiaspaul, 1998.

69. Maurice Bellet, *La Seconde Humanité, op. cit.*

70. See Pierre Lévy, *Le Feu libérateur*, Arléa, 1999.

71. We should note that John Paul II equally condemns a faith "deprived of reason" given over to pure subjectivity. He even reproaches certain theologians for their lack of interest in philosophy.

Chapter 6

1. See, in particular, Jules Isaac, *Genèse de l'antisémitisme*, Press Pocket, 1985 (First published by Calmann Lévy in 1956).

2. Cornélius Castoriadis, "De l'utilité de la connaissance", *Revue européenne de science sociale*, No. 79, 1988, p. 121.

3. See Chapter 1.

4. It is to Bardaisan (154-222) that we owe one of the best descriptions of the Empire— and of the neighboring countries—in the 2nd and 3rd centuries, in *The Book of Countries*, written by one of his pupils.

5. See the excellent study by Bertrand Badie, *Un monde sans souveraineté*, Fayard, 1999.

6. Shmuel Trigano, "L'Universel et la difference", Lecture at the Collège des etudes juives, 1998.

7. Quoted by Zaki Laïdi, *Libération*, April 9 1999.

8. See, for instance, François Dubet and Danilo Martuccelli, *Dans quelle société vivons-nous?* Seuil, 1998.

9. Norbert Elias, *La Société des individus*, traduction française, Fayard, 1991.

10. Last book published: *Du nomadisme, vagabondages initiatiques*, Livre de Poche, 1997.

11. Marcel Gauchet, *La Religion dans la démocratie. Parcours de la laïcité, op. cit.*

12. Fernand Braudel, *La Dynamique du capitalisme, op. cit.*

13. Quoted by Armand Mattelard, *Histoire de l'utopie planétaire: de la cité prophétique à la société globale*, La Découverte, 1999.

14. *Ibid.*

15. Philippe Engelhard, *L'Homme mondial*, Arléa, 1996.

16. Zaki Laïdi, "Les imaginaires de la mondialisation", *Esprit*, October 1998. These analyses have been my inspiration here in part.

17. Quoted by Zaki Laidi, *Ibid.*

18. *Ibid.*

19. Jean Baudrillard, "Le mondial et l'universel", *Libération*, 18 March, 1996.

20. André Gorz, *Misère du présent. Richesse du possible, op. cit.*

21. See the analyses by Ignacio Ramonet, *La Tyrannie de la communication*, Galilée, 1999.
22. "The Playboy Interview", in Eric McLuhan and Frank Zingrone (eds), *Essential McLuhan*, New York, Basic Books, 1995. But we should point out that MacLuhan viewed this retribalization in a rather positive light.
23. This expression was invented in the 19th century, by Gustave Le Bon in *Psychologie des foules*, 1895, re-edited PUF, 1991.
24. See Chapter 2.
25. "Was Democracy just a moment?" *The Atlantic Monthly*, December 1997, Vol 280, No. 6, pp. 55-80.
26. René Girard, "France, Amérique: le mythe croisé", conversation with Guitta Pessis-Pasternak, *Dérives savantes ou les paradoxes de la vérité*, Cerf, 1994.
27. Benjamin Barber, *Jihad vs. McWorld*, New York, Time Books, 1995.
28. Marcel Gauchet, "Qu'est-ce que l'intégrisme?", *L'Histoire*, No. 224, September 1998.
29. André Gorz, *Misère du présent. Richesse du possible*, *op. cit.*
30. Benjamin Barber, *Jihad vs. McWorld*, *op. cit.*]
31. Hugo Assmann, "Idolâtrie du marché et sacrifices humains", in Hugo Assmann and Franz J. Hinkelammert, *L'Idôlatrie de marché*, *op. cit.*
32. John Seabrook, "Rocking in Shangri-la", *The New Yorker*, October 10, 1994. (Quoted by Benjamin Barber, *Jihad vs. McWorld*, *op.cit.*)
33. *Ibid.*
34. *Ibid.*
35. Ignacio Ramonet, *La Tyrannie de la communication*, *op. cit.*
36. Alain Badiou, *Saint Paul. La fondation de l'universalisme*, PUF, 1997.
37. A philosopher such as Shmuel Trigano is quite right to reproach most specialists on the ancient world (the essentially agnostic "French school") for having turned the "miracle that was Greece" into an "ideological construction" which made it possible to minimize the importance of the "Hebrew miracle".
38. Jules Isaac, *Has Antisemitism roots in Christianity? Op. cit.*.
39. Marcel Simon and André Benoit, *Le Judaïsme et le Christianisme antique*, *op. cit.*
40. Marcel Simon, *Verus Israël*, *op. cit.* It is from this masterly study I have borrowed most of the analyses offered here.
41. Philo of Alexandria, *De opificio mundi*, trad. Roger Arnaldez, Le Cerf, 1961. The complete works of Philo are available in English, and also—significantly—are now also available in Hebrew.
42. Isidore Lévy, *Recherches esséniennes et pythagoriciennes*, Droz, 1964. (Here quoted by Marcel Simon).
43. Marcel Simon, *Verus Israël. Étude sur les relations entre chrétiens et juifs dans l'Empire romain (135-425)*, *op. cit.*
44. Marcel Simon, *Verus Israël. Étude sur les relations entre chrétiens et juifs dans l'Empire romain (135-425)*, *op. cit.*
45. It is true that on the Christian side, someone like Origen was ostracized in the same way and for the same reasons, i.e. for an excessive indulgence towards Hellenism. Origen is still not considered one of the Fathers of the Church.
46. Marcel Simon et André Benoit, *Le Judaïsme et le christianisme antique. D'Antiochus Épiphane `a*

Constantin, op. cit..

47. Geneviève Comeau, *Catholicisme et judaïsme dans la modernité*, Le Cerf, 1998.

48. Marcel Simon and André Benoit, *Le Judaïsme et le christianisme antique, op. cit.*

49. Marcel Simon, *Verus Israël. Étude sur les relations entre chrétiens et juifs dans l'Empire romain* (135-425), *op. cit.*

50. See Chapter 11.

51. Peter Brown, *The rise of Western Christendom: triumph and adversity*, *op, cit.*

52. Shmuel Trigano, *Un exil sans retour? Lettres à un juif égaré, op. cit.*

53. Mireille Delmas-Marty, *Trois Défis pour un droit mondial*, Seuil, 1998.

54. Shmuel Trigano, *Philosophie de la Loi. L'origine de la politique dans la Tora*, Cerf, 1991.

55. This lecture has been published in book form: Miguel Torga, *L'Universel, c'est le local moins les murs*, translated from the Portuguese by Claire Cayron, William Blake, 1994.

56. Pierre-Henri Imbert, *Revue universelle des droits de l'homme*, 1989, quoted by Mireille Delmas-Marty, *Trois Défis pour un droit mondial, op. cit*

57. Claude Sahel, in the preface to *La Tolérance. Pour un humanisme hérétique*, Points Seuil, 1998.

Chapter 7

1. Louis Dumont, *Essais sur l'individualisme, Une perspective anthropologique sur l'idéologie moderne*, Seuil, 1983.

2. Charles Taylor, *Sources of the self. op. cit.*

3. Aaron J. Gurevich, *La Naissance de l'individu dans l'Europe médiévale*, translated from the Russian by Jean-Jacques Marie, with a preface by Jacques Le Goff, Seuil, 1997.

4. See espectially Norbert Elias, *La Société des individus*, Fayard, 1991.

5. Fernand Braudel, *La Dynamique du capitalisme, op. cit.*

6. Charles Taylor, *Sources of the self, op. cit.*

7. In a conversation with Stéphane Paoli , France Inter, October 23 1998. See also François Cheng, *Le Dit de Tiany*, Albin Michel, 1998.

8. Jacques Monod, *Le Hasard et la nécessité*, Seuil, 1970.

9. Louis Dumont, *Homo aequalis*, Gallimard, 1977.

10. Hermann Rauschning, *op cit.*

11. Here I am paraphrasing the title of Henri Atlan's *Entre le cristal et la fumée* (Between crystal and smoke), Seuil, 1986.

12. Émile Poulat, *Liberté, laïcité. La guerre des deux France et le principe de la modernité, op. cit.*

13. Tocqueville, *Oeuvres, papiers et correspondances, Démocratie en Amérique*, tome 1, Gallimard, 1951.

14. Gödel is also the inventor of what are called "undecidable propositions". His masterwork on this topic, *Principia Mathematica*, dates from 1931.

15. Quoted by Marcel Gauchet, *La Religion dans la démocratie, op. cit.*

16. I am of course referring to the famous, and very controversial article by Samuel Huntington, published in 1994 in the review *Foreign Affairs* and published in French in *Commentaire* No. 66, Summer 1994.

17. François Vouga, *Les Premiers pas du christianisme, op.cit.*

18. Charles Taylor, *Sources of the self, op. cit.*

19. Gospel of St. Thomas, 75.

20. François Vouga, *Les Premiers pas du christinianisme, op. cit.* (Our italics).

21. I have borrowed this comment and the quotation from Mark from Geneviève Comeau, *Catholicisme et judaïsme dans la modernité, op. cit.*

22. Aron J. Gourevitch, *La Naissance de l'individu dans l'Europe médiévale, op. cit.*

23. See the excellent monograph by Monsignor Claude Dagens, "L'intériorité de l'homme selon saint Augustin", in *Bulletin de littérature ecclésiastique*, Institut catholique de Toulouse, July-December 1987.

24. Étienne Gilson, *Introduction à l'étude de saint Augustin*, Vrin, 1943. Quoted by Charles Taylor, *Sources of the self, op. cit.*

25. Saint Augustine, *De vera religione*, XXXIX, 72, in *La Foi chrétienne*, Desclée de Brouwer, 1982.

26. Eugen Drewermann, "L'Europe chrétienne et l'illusion de Maastricht", in *Cahiers d'Europe*, No.1, Fall-Winter 1996.

27. Charles Taylor, *Sources of the self, op. cit.*

28. *Ibid.*

29. *Ibid.*

30. Serge Latouche, *L'Occidentalisation du monde*, La Découverte, 1992..

31. Marcel Gauchet, *La Révolution des droits de l'homme*, Gallimard, 1992.

32. Charles Taylor, *Sources of the self.op. cit.*

33. Alphonse Dupront, *Qu'est-ce que les Lumières?* Gallimard, 1996.

34. Joseph Alois Schumpeter, *Impérialisme et classes sociales*, (1919), French translation, Flammarion, 1983.

35. Louis Dumont, *Homo aequalis. Genèse et épanouissement de l'idéologie économique*, 1985. (This book was never republished, and is no longer available.)

36. Alphonse Dupront, *Qu'est-ce que les Lumières? op. cit.*

37. *Sturm und Drang*, literally "Storm and Stress", from the title of a tragedy by Klinger. An eighteenth-century German literary movement that set out to react against classicism and Enlightenment rationalism.

38. Dominique Goux and Éric Maurin, "La nouvelle condition ouvrière", Notes from the Saint-Simon Foundation, October 1998.

39. Jean-Marie Vincent, *Max Weber ou la démocratie inachevée, op. cit.*

40. Karl Marx, *La Question juive*, 10/18 , quoted by François Dagognet, *Une Nouvelle morale*, Les Empêcheurs de penser en rond, 1998.

41. Émile Durkheim, *Le Suicide: étude de sociologie*, PUF, 1991.

42. Mary Douglas, "Justice sociale et sentiment de justice. Une anthropologie de l'inégalité", in Commissariat général au Plan, *Pluralisme et équité. La justice sociale dans les démocraties*, Éditions Esprit, 1995.

43. See the monumental work by Georg Simmel, *Philosophie de l'argent* (1900), French translation, PUF, 1987.

44. Christopher Lasch, *The Culture of Narcissism*, New York, Norton, 1978; Richard Sennet, *The Fall of Public Man*, New York, Knopf, 1977.

45. Marcel Gauchet, *La Religion dans la démocratie, op. cit.*

46. Cf. the significant title of a recent book by Jean-Marc Salmon, *Le Désir de société: des restos du coeur au mouvement des chômeurs*, La Découverte, 1998.

47. Jacques Donzelot, *Face à l'exclusion. Le modèle français*, Édition Esprit, 1991.

48. Lucien Karpik, *Le Débat*, November-December 1997.

49. Marcel Gauchet, *La Religion dans la démocratie, op. cit.*

50. André Gorz, *Misère du présent. Richesse du possible, op. cit.*

51. Robert Castel, *Libération*, December 14, 1998.

52. Anton Brender, *La France face à la mondialisation, op. cit.*

53. Jean-Pierre Lebrun, *Un monde sans limite, op. cit*

54. Michel Pinçon and Monique Pinçon-Charlot, *Grandes Fortunes*, Payot, 1998. In English from Algora Publishing, NY, 1999.

55. Jean-Marc Salmon, *Politis*, No. 528, December 24, 1998. See also *Le Désir de société, op. cit.*, by the same author.

56. Alain Touraine, *Critique de la modernité, op. cit*

57. Jean-Marc Salmon, *Politis, op. cit.*

58. François Dubet and Danilo Martuccelli, *Dans quelle société vivons-nous?* Seuil, 1998.

59. See the remarkable article by Paolo Flores d'Arcais (Director of the Italian review *Micromega*), "L'individu libertaire", *Esprit*, August-September 1998.

60. Boris Cyrulnik, *L'Ensorcellement du monde, op. cit.*

61. I have borrowed this comment from an article on anonymous sperm donors, by Geneviève Delaisi de Parseval, *Libération*, November 12 1998.

62. Charles Taylor, *Sources of the self.op, cit.*

63. Michel Meyer, *De la problématologie: philosophie, science et langage*, LGF, 1994.

64. This comment on Aron comes from the excellent study by Lucien Jaume, *L'Individu effacé ou le paradoxe du libéralisme français*, Fayard, 1997.

65. Boris Cyrulnik, *L'Ensorcellement du monde, op. cit.*

Chapter 8

1. I am thinking, in particular, of the reform of the French criminal code, put into effect in 1993, and substantially dominated by the ideas of *violence* and *security.*.

2. From an article in the British Sunday newspaper *The Independent on Sunday*, June 1994.

3. See in particular René Girard, *La Violence et le sacré*, Grasset, 1972; *Des Choses cachées depuis la fondation du monde*, Grasset, 1978; *Le Bouc émissaire*, Grasset, 1982.

4. *Œuvres complètes XIV*, Fragments posthumes 88-89, Gallimard 1977. I am indebted to René Girard for this illuminating quotation (*Quand ces choses commenceront... Entretiens avec Michel Treguer*, Arléa, 1994.)

5. *Le Monde*, February 6 1999.

6. Jean-Pierre Lebrun, *Un monde sans limite. Essai pour une clinique psychanalytique du social, op. cit.*

7. Irène Théry, "Vie privée et monde commun, réflexion sur l'enlisement gestionnaire du droit", *Le Débat*, May-August 1995

8. Bertrand Lemmenicier, *Justices*, No. 1, 1995, Quoted by Mireille Delmas-Marty, *Trois Défis pour un droit mondial, op. cit*

9. *Le Monde*, February 6 1999.

10. *Ibid.*

11. On this topic Pascal Bruckner's *La Tentation de l'innocence*, Grasset, 1995, in English (The Temptation of Innocence) from Algora Publishing, NY, 2000 (in which Girard's influ-

ence is evident), is very useful.

12. Charles Taylor, *Sources of the self, op. cit.*

13. Frédéric Zenati, "Le citoyen plaideur", in *La Justice. L'obligation impossible*, Seuil, 1999

14. Blandine Kriegel, "La défaite de la justice", in *La Justice. L'obligation impossible, op. cit.*

15. I am referring here to the title of the book by Pierre Rosanvallon and Jean-Paul Fitoussi, *Le Nouvel Age des inégalités*, Seuil, 1996.

16. Hugo Assmann, "Idolâtrie du marché et sacrifices humains", in Hugo Assmann et Franz J. Hinkelammert, *L'Idôlatrie de marché, op. cit.*

17. *Ibid.*

18. *Ibid.*

19. Jean-Pierre Dupuy, *Le Sacrifice et l'envie. Le libéralisme aux prises avec la justice sociale*, Calmann-Lévy, 1992.

20. *Ibid.*

21. John Rawls, *Theory of Justice, op. cit.*

22. Quoted by Jean-Pierre Dupuy, *Le Sacrifice et l'envie. op. cit.*

23. Norbert Élias, *La Civilisation des moeurs*, Calmann-Lévy, 1973.

24. Norbert Elias, *La Dynamique de l'Occident*, Calmann-Lévy, 1975.

25. René Girard, *Quand ces choses commenceront..., op. cit.*

26. Peter Brown, *Power and persuasiion in late antiquity, op. cit.*

27. The early spread of the cult of Mithra followed closely on the heels of the Roman campaigns agaist Mithridates VI and against the Cilician pirates (*c.* 67 BC). In St. Clement's Basilica, in Rome, an altar dedicated to the Persian Mithra has been found. The archeological museum in Metz possesses an magnificent altar to Mithra dating from the Roman period.

28. Pierre Maraval, *Le Christianisme de Constantin à la conquête arabe, op. cit.*

29. Quoted by Marcel Simon, *Verus Israël, op. cit.*

30. Geneviève Comeau, *Catholicisme et judaïsme dans la modernité, op. cit.*

31. Quoted by Peter Brown, *The rise of Western Christendom, op, cit.*

32. Quoted by Pierre Maraval, *Le Christianisme, de Constantin à la conquête arabe, op. cit*

33. Peter Brown, *The rise of Western Christendom, op, cit.*

34. Quoted by Eugen Drewermann, *De la naissance des dieux à la naissance du Christ*, Seuil, 1992. (German original: *Dein Name ist wie der Geschmack des Lebens*, 1986)

35. *Ibid.*

36. I have borrowed these examples from Marcel Simon et André Benoit, *Le Judaïsme et le Christianisme antique. D'Antiochus Epiphane à Constantin, op. cit.*

37. René Girard, *Quand ces choses commenceront..., op. cit.*

38. Marcel Simon and André Benoit, *Le Judaïsme et le christianisme antique, op. cit.*

39. René Girard, *Le Bouc émissaire, op. cit..*

40. I have borrowed these remarks from Émile Poulat, *Liberté, laïcité, op. cit.*

41. Actually, here Paul is expressing himself in the context of a first-century Christian Church united in its hostility to Imperial power. In this text he is attempting to moderate this hostility.

42. Quoted by Jacques Ellul, *Anarchie et christianisme, op. cit.*

43. See the remarkable study by Jean-Claude Eslin, *Dieu et le pouvoir. Théologie et politique en*

Occident, op. cit.

44. Jacques Ellul, *Anarchie et christianisme, op. cit.*

45. Eugen Drewermann, *De la naissance des dieux à la naissance du Christ*, Seuil, 1992.

46. Vladimir Grigorieff, *Religions du monde entier. Principe, enjeux, repère historiques*, Marabout, 1996.

47. Max Weber, *Économie et société*, Press Pocket, 1995 (2 Vols).

48. René Rémond, *Religion et société en Europe, op. cit.*

49. René Girard, *Le Bouc émissaire, op. cit.*

50. *Ibid.*

51. Joseph Alois Schumpeter, *Impérialisme et classes sociales, op. cit.*

52. Alain Besançon, *Le Malheur du siècle*, Fayard, 1998.

53. Among these "Christian" protagonists of ultraliberalism, let us mention George Gilder, *Wealth and Poverty*, New York, Basic Books, 1981 and *The Spirit of Enterprise*, New York, Simon and Schuster, 1984 and Michael Novak, *The Spirit of Democratic Capitalism*, New York, Simon and Schuster, 1982—in which the author actually goes to the extent of quoting St. John of the Cross!

Part III

1. I am thinking in particular of the Italian sociologist Vilfredo Pareto (1848-1923)

2. Maurice Bellet, *La Seconde Humanité, op. cit.*

3. Dominique Janicaud, *La Puissance du rationnel, op. cit.* [OK]

4. Claude Sahel, preface to *La Tolérance. Pour un humanisme hérétique, op. cit.*

5. John Rawls, *Political liberalism*, New York, Columbia University Press, 1993.

6. Here I am using the analyses by Rawls's French translator, Catherine Audart, "Justice et démocratie", in *Quelles valeurs pour demain?* Colloque *Le Monde*-Le Mans, Seuil, 1997.

Chapter 9

1. It would be unfair not to pay tribute here to the patient labors carried on for years by Pierre-André Taguieff. I would particularly mention, among others, a major work which has been very useful in writing this: Pierre-André Taguieff, *Sur la nouvelle droite*, Descartes et Cie, 1994.

2. Raymond Aron, *Mémoires*, tome 2, Julliard, 1983

3. Dominique Schnapper, "Le discours du Front national", *Commentaire* No. 75, Fall 1996.

4. In addition to *Revolt against the Modern World* (tr. Guido Stucco, Rochester VT, Inner Traditions International, 1995, with a "Short introduction to Julius Evola" by H.T.Hansen and a "Translator's Preface"), the following titles have been published in English: *Eros and the Mysteries of Love* (1983); *The Yoga of Power* (1992); *The Hermetic Tradition* (1995); *The Doctrine of Awakening* (1995).]

5. Marguerite Yourcenar wrote a long and very complimentary article on Evola in the newspaper *Le Monde* of July 21 1972, on the occasion of the publication of a book of his on the subjec of "tantric Yoga". She paid tribute to him as a "scholar of genius+."

6. Julius Évola, *Révolte contre le monde moderne*, translated from the Italian and with an introduction by Philippe Baillet, followed by a detailed bibliography of books by and on Evola prepared by Alain de Benoist. L'Age d'Homme, 1991. [Original Italian title: *Rivolta*

contro il mondo moderno (1934, with later editions in 1951 and 1970)].

7. Julius Evola, *Révolte contre le monde moderne, op. cit.*

8. Julius Evola, *Métaphysique du sexe*, (First publication in French: Payot, 1959), L'Age d'Homme, 1989.

9. Pierre Legendre, "L'impardonnable" in *Le Pardon. Briser la dette de l'oubli*, Point-Seuil, 1998.

10. Julius Evola, *Révolte contre le monde moderne, op. cit..*

11. *Ibid.*

12. Zeev Sternhell (ed.), *L'Éternel Retour. Contre la démocratie, l'idéologie de la décadence*, Presses de la fondation des sciences politiques, 1994.

13. Julius Evola, *Révolte contre le monde moderne, op. cit.*

14. *Ibid.*

15. *Ibid.*

16. Jacob Taubes, *La Théologie politique de Carl Schmitt, Benjamin, Nietzsche et Freud, op. cit.*

17. Julius Evola, *Révolte contre le monde moderne, op. cit.*

18. *Ibid.*

19. *Ibid.*

20. Pierre Legendre, *Sur la question dogmatique en Occident*, Fayard, 1999.

21. Julius Evola, *Révolte contre le monde moderne, op. cit.*

22. *Ibid.*

23. However, let us mention an important colloquium on Evola, held at the Sorbonne on October 25, 1986, with, in particular, the participation of Pierre-André Taguieff, Émile Poulat et Jean-Pierre Brach: "Métaphysique et politique. René Guénon, Julius Évola", special issue of *Revue Politica Hermetica* No. 1, L'Age d'homme, 1987.

24. This condemnation would be withdrawn by Pius XII in 1939.

25. Quotation taken from Philippe Portier, *Église et politique en France au XXe siècle, op. cit.*

26. See Jean-Clément Martin, *Contre-Révolution, Révolution et nation en France, 1789-1799*, Point-Seuil, 1998.

27. I have borrowed these quotes from Jean Mouttapa, *Dieu et la révolution du dialogue. L'ère des échanges entre les religions*, Albin Michel, 1996.

28. Shmuel Trigano, *Un exil sans retour? Op. cit.*

29. Jacques Brosse, "Le voyage de Bouddha", in *L'Occident en quête de sens*, Maisonneuve & Larose, 1996.

30. Jean Mouttapa, *Dieu et la révolution du dialogue, op. cit.*

31. *Ibid.*

32. *Ibid.*

33. Twenty works by this author are available in French. See in particular Thich Nhat Hanh, *Le Silence foudroyant*, Albin Michel, 1997.

34. Pascal Bruckner, *Le Sanglot de l'homme blanc, op. cit.*

35. Eugen Drewermann, *De la naissance des dieux à la naissance du Christ, op. cit.*

36. Florence Quentin, "La source égyptienne", in *L'Occident en quête de sens, op. cit.*

37. P. Aruppe, "Lettre de 1978 sur l'inculturation" in *Écrits pour évangéliser*, DDB, 1985; quoted by Geneviève Comeau, *Catholicisme et judaïsme dans la modernité, op. cit.*

Chapter 10

1.   I am indebted for this expression to Léo Baeck (*L'Essence du judaïsme*, PUF, 1992).

2.   See Chapter 7

3.   Robert Scholtus, "D'une curieuse solitude des chrétiens", in *Christus*, No. 180, October 1998.

4.   Marcel Gauchet, *La Religion dans la démocratie*, *op. cit*

5.   Marcel Simon and André Benoit, *Le Judaïsme et le christianisme antique*, *op. cit.*

6.   Geneviève Comeau, *Catholicisme et judaïsme dans la modernité*, *op. cit.*

7.   David M. Neuhaus, "L'idéologie judéo-chrétienne et le dialogue juifs-chrétiens", *Revue de Science Religieuse* No. 85/2 (1997).

8.   Another group within this same Lutheran Church, called the "Confessional Church", denounced the National-Socialist ideology in unambigouous terms.

9.   Martin Bormann, *Libres Propos sur la guerre et la paix recueillis sur l'ordre de Martin Bormann*, Flammarion, 1952.

10. *La Croix*, September 16 1938, quoted by Jean-Claude Eslin in *Dieu et le pouvoir. Théologie et politique en Occident*, *op. cit.*

11. On this historical point, see Georges Passelecq et Bernard Suchecky, *L'Encyclique cachée de Pie XI*, La Découverte, 1995.

12. Shmuel Trigano, *Un exil sans retour? Op. cit.*

13. I am thinking in particular of the courageous lines written by Alain Finkielkraut in response to the hate-filled reactions provoked by the beatification of Cardinal Stepinac of Croatia: "Ah, how sweet it is to be Jewish here at the end of the twentieth century! We no longer stand accused by History, we are History's darlings. [...] Am I just a trouble-maker? Despite the emotion I can't help feeling at certain authentic and courageous acts of contrition, I cannot derive an unmixed pleasure from being so courted on all sides. I wish, for instance, that these new, so effusive, friends, were all equally friends of the truth". *Le Monde*, October 7 1998.

14. I owe these analyses and the passages in quotes to Shmuel Trigano, *Un exil sans retour? Op. cit.*

15. Jules Isaac, *La Genèse de l' anti-Semitism*, *op. cit*

16. *Ibid.*

17. Marcel Simon, *Verus Israël. op. cit.*

18. Jules Isaac, *L'Antisémitisme a-t-il des raciness chrétiennes?* [*Has Antisemitism roots in Christianity?* trans. Dorothy and James Parkes, New York, National Council of Christians and Jews, 1961]

19. Marcel Simon, *Verus Israël. op. cit.*

20. *Ibid.*

21. Jules Isaac, *La Genèse de l'antisémitisme*, *op. cit.*

22. See the passionate case made by Jacques Ellul for this Epistle of St. Paul, *Ce Dieu injuste? Théologie chrétienne pour le peuple d'Israël*, Arléa, 1991.

23. See Jean-Claude Guillebaud, *Sur la route des croisades*, Arléa, 1993, Point-Seuil, 1995.

24. Jules Isaac, *Genèse de l'antisémitisme*, *op. cit*

25. Flavius Josèphe, *Against Apio* (II, 2, 21), quoted by Jules Isaac, *Genèse de l'antisémitime*, *op. cit.*

26. Marcel Simon, *Verus Israël*, *op. cit.*

27. *Ibid.*

28. Jules Isaac, *Genèse de l' antisémitisme op. cit.*

29. Hannah Arendt, *The origins of totalitarianism*, NY, Meridian Books, 1958.

30. Karl Marx, *La Question juive*, translated by Jean-Michel Palmier, UGE 10/18, 1975.

31. Zeev Sternhell, *La Droite révolutionnaire*, Gallimard, 1997 (first publication: Seuil, 1978).

32. An article in *La Libre pensée*, dating from 1866, quoted by Marc Crapez, *La Gauche réaction-naire. Mythe de la plèbe et de la race*, with a preface by Pierre-André Taguieff, Berg International, 1996.

33. *Ibid.*

34. Eugène Gellion-Danglar, *Les Sémites*, quoted by Marc Crapez, *La Gauche réactionnaire, op. cit.*

35. See above, Chapter 9.

36. Document of the Roman Commission for Jewish Affairs. Unofficial translation (into French) by the secretariat of the French Episcopacy for relations with Judaism. Translation published in *Le Monde* of March 18 1998.

37. Interview published in *Libération*, March 18 1998.

38. Jean-Marie Lustiger, eulogy for Saul Friedländer, awarded an honorary doctorate by the University of Wittenberg (Germany), on July 8 1997. Text published in *Études*, January 1998.

39. Josy Eisenberg, *Bulletin de l'association Fraternité d'Abraham*, No. 98, April 1998.

40. Stéphane Moses, "Le judaïsme est-il menacé?" in *L'Occident en quête de sens, op. cit.*

41. I am indebted for this formulation to Jean Mouttapa, *Dieu et la révolution du dialogue, op. cit.*

42. Pauline Bèbe, "Sous la coupole des cieux", in *La Tolérance. Pour un humanisme hérétique, op. cit.*

43. Shmuel Trigano, *Un exil sans retour? op. cit.*

44. *Ibid.*

45. Jean Mouttapa, *Dieu et la révolution du dialogue. op. cit.*

46. Robert Scholtus, "D'une curieuse solitude des chrétiens", in *Christus, op. cit.*

47. David M. Neuhaus, "L'idéologie judéo-chrétienne et le dialogue juifs-chrétiens", *op. cit.*

48. I have borrowed this observation from Philippe Portier, *Église et politique en France au XXe siècle, op. cit.*

49. S. R. Hirsch, *Dix-Neuf Épîtres sur le judaïsme*, Le Cerf, 1987.

Epilogue

1. In a letter to Louis Bouilhet dated September 4, 1850.

2. See above, Chapter 3.

3. Pierre Lévy, *La Cyberculture*, Odile Jacob-Éditions du Conseil de l'Europe, 1997.

4. *Ibid.*

5. The word "cyberspace" was invented in 1984 by the novelist William Gibson, the author of a science-fiction story, *Neuromancer*, New York, Ace Books, 1984. It refers to the communication space created by the worldwide interconnection of computer memories and the computers giving access to them.

6. André Gorz, *Misère du présent. Richesse du possible, op. cit.*.

7. Martin Caidin, *Cyborg, a novel* New York, Arbor House, 1972.

8. Pierre Bongiovani, joint director of the CICV Pierre Shaeffer, *Libération*, April 22 1999.

9. Dominique Wolton, head of the "communications" lab of the Conseil national de recher-

ché scientifique (CNRS), *Libération*, April 2 1999.

10. Pierre Lévy, *La Cyberculture*, op. cit.

11. *Ibid.*

12. Pierre Bongiovani, *op. cit.*

13. Patrick Thomas, a professor of Computer Science at the University Paul Valéry in Montpellier, *Libération*, April 2 1999.

14. On this question, see the little book by Dominique Wolton, *L'Internet et après ?*, Flammarion, 1999.

15. I have borrowed this expression, which is certainly intended polemically, from Alain Finkielkraut.

16. See Bill Gates, *The Road Ahead*, Penguin, 1996..

17. Pierre Lévy, *La Cyberculture*, op. cit.

18. Mireille Delmas-Marty, *Trois Défis pour un droit mondial*, op. cit.

19. *Ibid.*

20. *Ibid.*

21. See Chapter 4.

22. Michel Albert, *Capitalisme contre capitalisme*, Seuil, 1991.

Also from Algora Publishing:

CLAUDIU A. SECARA
THE NEW COMMONWEALTH:
FROM BUREAUCRATIC CORPORATISM TO SOCIALIST CAPITALISM

The notion of an elite-driven worldwide perestroika has gained some credibility lately. The book examines in a historical perspective the most intriguing dialectic in the Soviet Union's "collapse" — from socialism to capitalism and back to socialist capitalism — and speculates on the global implications.

DOMINIQUE FERNANDEZ
PHOTOGRAPHER: FERRANTE FERRANTI
ROMANIAN RHAPSODY — An Overlooked Corner of Europe

"Romania doesn't get very good press." And so, renowned French travel writer Dominique Fernandez and top photographer Ferrante Ferranti head out to form their own images. In four long journeys over a 6-year span, they uncover a tantalizing blend of German efficiency and Latin nonchalance, French literature and Gypsy music, Western rationalism and Oriental mysteries. Fernandez reveals the rich Romanian essence. Attentive and precise, he digs beneath the somber heritage of communism to reach the deep roots of a European country that is so little-known.

IGNACIO RAMONET
THE GEOPOLITICS OF CHAOS

The author, Director of Le Monde Diplomatique, presents an original, discriminating and lucid political matrix for understanding what he calls the "current disorder of the world" in terms of Internationalization, Cyberculture and Political Chaos.

TZVETAN TODOROV
A PASSION FOR DEMOCRACY – BENJAMIN CONSTANT

The French Revolution rang the death knell not only for a form of society, but also for a way of feeling and of living; and it is still not clear what we have gained from the changes. Todorov examines the life of Constant, one of the original thinkers who conceptualized modern democracy, and in the process gives us a richly textured portrait of a man who was fully engaged in life, both public and private.

MICHEL PINÇON & MONIQUE PINÇON-CHARLOT
GRAND FORTUNES – DYNASTIES OF WEALTH IN FRANCE

Going back for generations, the fortunes of great families consist of far more than money—they are also symbols of culture and social interaction. In a nation known for democracy and meritocracy, piercing the secrets of the grand fortunes verges on a crime of lèse-majesté . . . Grand Fortunes succeeds at that.

JEAN-MARIE ABGRALL
SOUL SNATCHERS: THE MECHANICS OF CULTS

Jean-Marie Abgrall, psychiatrist, criminologist, expert witness to the French Court of Appeals, and member of the Inter-Ministry Committee on Cults, is one of the experts most frequently consulted by the European judicial and legislative processes. The fruit of fifteen years of research, his book delivers the first methodical analysis of the sectarian phenomenon, decoding the mental manipulation on behalf of mystified observers as well as victims.

JEAN-CLAUDE GUILLEBAUD
THE TYRANNY OF PLEASURE

A Sixties' radical re-thinks liberation, taking a hard look at the question of sexual morals in a modern society. For almost a whole generation, we have lived in the illusion that this question had ceased to exist. Today the illusion is faded, but a strange and tumultuous distress replaces it. Our societies painfully seek a "third way", between unacceptable alternatives: bold-faced permissiveness or nostalgic moralism.

SOPHIE COIGNARD AND MARIE-THÉRÈSE GUICHARD
FRENCH CONNECTIONS –
The Secret History of Networks of Influence

They were born in the same region, went to the same schools, fought the same fights and made the same mistakes in youth. They share the same morals, the same fantasies of success and the same taste for money. They act behind the scenes to help each other, boosting careers, monopolizing business and information, making money, conspiring and, why not, becoming Presidents!

VLADIMIR PLOUGIN
RUSSIAN INTELLIGENCE SERVICES. Vol. I. Early Years

Mysterious episodes from Russia's past – alliances and betrayals, espionage and military feats – are unearthed and examined in this study, which is drawn from ancient chronicles and preserved documents from Russia, Greece, Byzantium and the Vatican Library. Scholarly analysis and narrative flair combine to give both the facts and the flavor of the battle scenes and the espionage milieu, including the establishment of secret services in Kievan rus, the heroes and the techniques of intelligence and counter-intelligence in the 10th-12th centuries, and the times of Vladimir.

JEAN-JACQUES ROSA
EURO ERROR

The European Superstate makes Jean-Jacques Rosa mad, for two reasons. First, actions taken to relieve unemployment have created inflation, but have not reduced unemployment. His second argument is even more intriguing: the 21st century will see the fragmentation of the U. S., not the unification of Europe.

ANDRÉ GAURON
EUROPEAN MISUNDERSTANDING

Few of the books decrying the European Monetary Union raise the level of the discussion to a higher plane. European Misunderstanding is one of these. Gauron gets it right, observing that the real problem facing Europe is its political future, not its economic future.

CLAUDIU A. SECARA
TIME & EGO – Judeo-Christian Egotheism and the Anglo-Saxon Industrial Revolution

The first question of abstract reflection that arouses controversy is the problem of Becoming. Being persists, beings constantly change; they are born and they pass away. How can Being change and yet be eternal? The quest for the logical and experimental answer has just taken off.

PHILIPPE TRÉTIACK
ARE YOU AGITÉ? Treatise on Everyday Agitation

The 'Agité,' that human species that lives in international airports, jumps into taxis while dialing the cell phone, eats while clearing the table, reads the paper while watching TV and works during vacation – has just been given a new title. "A book filled with the exuberance of a new millennium, full of humor and relevance. Philippe Trétiack, a leading reporter for Elle, takes us around the world and back at light speed." — Aujourd'hui le Parisien

PAUL LOMBARD
VICE & VIRTUE — Men of History, Great Crooks for the Greater Good

Personal passion has often guided powerful people more than the public interest. With what result? From the courtiers of Versailles to the back halls of Mitterand's government, from Danton — revealed to have been a paid agent for England — to the shady bankers of Mitterand's era, from the buddies of Mazarin to the builders of the Panama Canal, Paul Lombard unearths the secrets of the corridors of power. He reveals the vanity and the corruption, but also the grandeur and panache that characterize the great. This cavalcade over many centuries can be read as a subversive tract on how to lead.

RICHARD LABÉVIÈRE
DOLLARS FOR TERROR — The U.S. and Islam

"In this riveting, often shocking analysis, the U.S. is an accessory in the rise of Islam, because it manipulates and aids radical Moslem groups in its shortsighted pursuit of its economic interests, especially the energy resources of the Middle East and the oil- and mineral-rich former Soviet republics of Central Asia. Labévière shows how radical Islamic fundamentalism spreads its influence on two levels, above board, through investment firms, banks and shell companies, and clandestinely, though a network of drug dealing, weapons smuggling and money laundering. This important book sounds a wake-up call to U.S. policy-makers." — Publishers Weekly

JEANNINE VERDÈS-LEROUX
DECONSTRUCTING PIERRE BOURDIEU — Against Sociological Terrorism From the Left

Sociologist Pierre Bourdieu went from widely-criticized to widely-acclaimed, without adjusting his hastily constructed theories. Turning the guns of critical analysis on his own critics, he was happier jousting in the ring of (often quite undemocratic) political debate than reflecting and expanding upon his own propositions. Verdès-Leroux suggests that Bourdieu arrogated for himself the role of "total intellectual" and proved that a good offense is the best defense. A pessimistic Leninist bolstered by a ponderous scientific construct, Bourdieu stands out as the ultimate doctrinaire more concerned with self-promotion than with democratic intellectual engagements.

HENRI TROYAT
TERRIBLE TZARINAS

Who should succeed Peter the Great? Upon the death of this visionary and despotic reformer, the great families plotted to come up with a successor who would surpass everyone else — or at least, offend none. But there were only women — Catherine I, Anna Ivanovna, Anna Leopoldovna, Elizabeth I. These autocrats imposed their violent and dissolute natures upon the empire, along with their loves, their feuds, their cruelties. Born in 1911 in Moscow, Troyat is a member of the Académie française, recipient of Prix Goncourt.

JEAN-MARIE ABGRALL
HEALING OR STEALING — *Medical Charlatans in the New Age*

Jean-Marie Abgrall is Europe's foremost expert on cults and forensic medicine. He asks, are fear of illness and death the only reasons why people trust their fates to the wizards of the pseudo-revolutionary and the practitioners of pseudo-magic? We live in a bazaar of the bizarre, where everyday denial of rationality has turned many patients into ecstatic fools. While not all systems of nontraditional medicine are linked to cults, this is one of the surest avenues of recruitment, and the crisis of the modern world may be leading to a new mystique of medicine where patients check their powers of judgment at the door.

DEBORAH SCHURMAN-KAUFLIN
THE NEW PREDATOR: WOMEN WHO KILL — *Profiles of Female Serial Killers*

This is the first book ever based on face-to-face interviews with women serial killers. Dr. Schurman-Kauflin analyzes the similarities and differences between male and female serial killers and mass murderers.

RÉMI KAUFFER
DISINFORMATION — *US Multinationals at War with Europe*

"Spreading rumors to damage a competitor, using 'tourists' for industrial espionage. . . Kauffer shows how the economic war is waged." — Le Monde
"A specialist in the secret services, Kauffer notes that, 'In the CNN era, with our skies full of satellites and the Internet expanding every nano-second, the techniques of mass persuasion that were developed during the Cold War are still very much in use – only their field of application has changed.' His analysis is shocking, and well-documented." — La Tribune

CARL A. DAVIS
PLANE TRUTH — *A PRIVATE INVESTIGATOR'S STORY*

"Raises new questions about corporate and tribal loyalties, structural engineering, and money and politics, in a credible scenario that makes my flesh creep. . . I think I'll take a train, next time. Or walk." — Western Review
"Takes us around the world and finds treasure under stones that had been left unturned After reading these 'travels with Carl,' (or is he Sherlock Holmes?), my own life seems very flat." — Book Addicts

JENNIFER FURIO
LETTERS FROM PRISON — *VOICES OF WOMEN MURDERERS*

Written by incarcerated women, these incredibly personal, surprisingly honest letters shed light on their lives, their crimes and the mitigating circumstances. Author Jennifer Furio, a prison reform activist, subtly reveals the biases if the criminal justice system and the media. The words of these women haunt and transfix even the most skeptical reader.

CHANTAL THOMAS
COPING WITH FREEDOM

40 million American women of marriageable age are single. This approachable essay addresses many of their concerns in a profound and delightful way. Inspired by the author's own experiences as well as by the 18th century philosophers, and literary and historical references, it offers insights and the courage to help us revel in the game of life, the delight of reading, the art of the journey, and the right to say "no" to chains of obligations and family.